作者简介

王方路 重庆师范大学外国语学院副教授，硕士，硕士生导师，中华诗词家联谊会会员，重庆翻译学会理事，重庆市翻译家协会副会长。研究领域：翻译学，典籍翻译。出版著作十余部，发表学术论文20余篇。

本书系2018年度重庆师范大学学术专著出版基金资助立项项目

四书白话
英语新译

（上）

王方路 著

图书在版编目（CIP）数据

四书白话英语新译/王方路著. —北京：中国书籍出版社，2019. 5

ISBN 978-7-5068-7011-5

Ⅰ. ①四… Ⅱ. ①王… Ⅲ. ①儒家—著作—英语—翻译—研究 Ⅳ. ①B222②H315. 9

中国版本图书馆 CIP 数据核字（2018）第 221297 号

四书白话英语新译

王方路 著

责任编辑	朱 琳
责任印制	孙马飞 马 芝
封面设计	中联华文
出版发行	中国书籍出版社
地 址	北京市丰台区三路居路 97 号（邮编：100073）
电 话	（010）52257143（总编室） （010）52257140（发行部）
电子邮箱	eo@ chinabp. com. cn
经 销	全国新华书店
印 刷	三河市华东印刷有限公司
开 本	710 毫米 ×1000 毫米 1/16
字 数	758 千字
印 张	42. 5
版 次	2019 年 5 月第 1 版 2019 年 5 月第 1 次印刷
书 号	ISBN 978-7-5068-7011-5
定 价	168. 00 元（上下册）

版权所有 翻印必究

前　言

《大学》《中庸》《论语》《孟子》合称为"四书",为儒家传道、授业的基本教材。几百年来,"四书"在我国广泛流传,其中许多语句已成为脍炙人口的格言警句。其中,《论语》《孟子》分别是孔子、孟子及其学生的言论集,《大学》《中庸》则是《礼记》中的两篇。首次把它们编在一起的是南宋著名学者朱熹。

翻译"四书"既有历史意义,又有现实意义。历史意义体现在,通过翻译和学习,我们可以更进一步地了解儒家代表人物及其思想,了解其所处时代的特点,了解其思想的独特之处及其广泛影响力。现实意义体现在,首先,可以进行文化传承,将翻译成果用于本科生、研究生的教学实践,让学生们了解儒家代表人物的思想,同时学会向外国传播儒家思想。其次,在全面建成小康社会,构建人类命运共同体的时代背景下,儒家思想的深远影响力会焕发出其新的活力,推动我们搞好各方面工作。

本书依据朱熹《四书章句集注》,按原文、白话译文、英语译文、注释之序编排每一部分内容。两种译文力求忠实,译语力求通顺流畅。如:

【原文】3.6 孟子曰:人皆有不忍人之心。[1]先王有不忍人之心 ,斯有不忍人之政矣。[2]以不忍人之心,行不忍人之政,治天下,可运之掌上。谓人皆有不忍人之心者,[3]今人乍见孺子将入于井,[4]皆有怵惕恻隐之心[5]——非所以内交于孺子之父母也,[6]非所以要誉于乡党朋友也,[7]非恶其声而然也。[8]由是观之,无恻隐之心,非人也;无羞恶之心,[9]非人也;无辞让之心,非人也;无是非之心,非人也;恻隐之心,仁之端也;羞恶之心,义之端也;辞让之心,礼之端也;[10]是非之心,智之端也。人之有是四端也,犹其有四体也。有是四端而自谓不能者,自贼者也;[11]谓其君不能者,贼其君者也。凡有四端于我者,[12]知皆扩而充之矣,[13]若火之始然,[14]泉之始达。苟能充之,足以保四海;[15]苟不充之,不足以事父母。"

【白话译文】

孟子说:"人人都有怜悯心,先王有怜悯心,于是有怜悯别人的政治了。用怜悯心实行怜悯别人的政治来治理天下，不难，能够运用在手掌之中。我说人人都有怜悯心，原因在于：假如忽然看见一个小孩就要掉进井里了，是人都会产生惊惧怜悯的同情心。这种心情的产生，不是为了要和小孩的父母攀交情，不是为了要在乡亲、朋友间讨声誉，也不是被那小孩的哭声惊动而产生的。从这里来看，没有怜悯心，不算是人；没有羞恶心，不算是人；没有推让心，不算是人；没有是非心，不算是人。怜悯心是仁的萌芽，羞恶心是义的萌芽，推让心是礼的萌芽，是非心是智的萌芽。人有这四种萌芽，好比有手足四肢一样，运用自如。有这四种萌芽，自己却说这也不行那也不行的人，是自暴自弃。认为他的君主不行的人，是残害他君主的人。凡是自己拥有这四种萌芽的人都把它们扩大充实了，那就像火开始燃烧，像泉水开始涌出。如果能继续扩充，能够安定天下；如果不继续扩充，连赡养爹妈都办不到。”

【英语译文】

Mencius said, “Everyone has feeling of compassion. The deceased king had feeling of compassion and sympathized with other's governance. It's not difficult and it's just like playing game in one's palm to sympathize with other's governance and rule the land under the heaven with feeling of compassion. I say everyone has feeling of compassion for the reason that anyone will have feeling of surprise and compassion at a kid who is falling down into a well. This kind of feeling isn't aroused by the desire for friendship with his parents, or the honor got among friends and neighbors, or the bitter cry of the kid. From this point, one is not a man who lacks feeling of compassion; one is not a man who lacks feeling of shame; one is not a man who lacks feeling of modesty; one is not a man who lacks feeling of the distinction between the right and the wrong. The feeling of compassion is the beginning of humanity; the feeling of shame is the beginning of righteousness; the feeling of modesty is the beginning of rites, and the feeling of the distinction between the right and the wrong is the beginning of wisdom. These four beginnings are like the four limbs which can move flexibly. A person with the four beginnings claiming that he cannot do this or that abandons himself. Those who think their monarch cannot do things do harms to him. All those who have the four beginnings want to expand them just like fire flaming and water swelling. If he continues expanding he can rule the land under the heaven; but if he doesn't do so, then he cannot support his parents.”

【注释】(1)不忍人之心:不狠心对人的心。即同情心。(2)斯:承接连词。可译作"便""就"。(3)所以:原因,情由。(4)今:连词。表假设关系。相当于"若""假如"。乍:zhà,突然;忽然。孺子:rú ~,幼儿、儿童。将入于井:就要沉落于井中。(5)怵惕恻隐:chù tì cè yǐn,惊惧怜悯;戒惧同情。(6)内交:nà ~,内:纳的古字。内交,即"纳交"。义同"结交"。谓与人交往,建立情谊。(7)要誉于乡党:要誉,读 yāo yù,求取声誉;讨好。乡党:同乡;乡亲。(8)恶:恶 wù,畏惧。其声:指啼哭声。文中但就"乍见"这一瞬间视觉反应,绝无其他因素,就能窥见人的固有怜悯心。所以把听觉反应也除开;当然听觉同样能触动人的固有怜悯心。(9)羞恶:xiū wù,对自己或别人的坏处感到羞耻厌恶。(10)端:开始,开始之点。(11)贼:杀害,毁坏,伤害。(12)我:自己。(13)知:助词,犹"夫"。表议论的开始。(14)然:"燃"的本字。(15)保四海:安定天下。保:安定。四海:犹言天下,全国各处。

愿本书成为文化百花园中的一朵小花,为花园馨香,也为观赏者而奋力绽放。

王方路
丁酉年冬初稿,己亥年春修订稿
于重庆师范大学

目　录
CONTENTS

第一部分 《大学》*The Great Learning*

【原文】1《大学》之道，在明明德，在亲民，在止于至善[1]。知止而后有定，定而后能静，静而后能安，安而后能虑，虑而后能得[2]。物有本末，事有终始，知所先后，则近道矣。[3]古之欲明明德于天下者[4]，先治其国；欲治其国者，先齐其家；欲齐其家者，先修其身；欲修其身者，先正其心；欲正其心者，先诚其意；欲诚其意者，先致其知；致知在格物。物格而后知至，知至而后意诚，意诚而后心正，心正而后身修，身修而后家齐，家齐而后国治，国治而后天下平[5]。自天子以至于庶人，壹是皆以修身为本[6]。其本乱而末治者否矣，其所厚者薄，而其所薄者厚。未之有也[7]！

【白话译文】

《大学》的道理宗旨在于彰明光明之美德，在于使民众革旧换新，在于达到善的最高境界。知识到了所应达到的境界，然后才有确定不易的志向。志向定了然后才能静下心来不妄动。静下心来不妄动然后才能安处。所处而安然后才能思虑精详。思虑精详然后才能举措得当。世上万物都有本有末，万事都有终有始；本末、终始是事物的基本特征，掌握了基本特征并知道本始为先，终末为后，也就接近正道了。古代，要彰明光明之美德于天下的人，先治理好自己的国家。要治理好自己的国家的人，先整治好自己的家庭。要整治好自己的家庭的人，先自我陶冶身心涵养德行。要自我陶冶身心涵养德行的人，先端正自己的心。要端正自己的心的人，先使自己的志意真诚。要使自己的志意真诚的人，先使自己的知识不断推进到相应的最高境界。不断推进知识在于推究事物的道理。事物的道理推究通了，知识也就随即达到相应的高度。知识达到相应的高度了，然后志意诚实。志意诚实了，然后心才能端正。心端正了然后才能陶冶身心涵养德行。做到了陶冶身心涵养德行，家庭才能整治。家庭整治好了，然后国家才能治理好。国家治理好了，才能平定天下。从天子一直到普通百姓都要以自身修养为根本。自身修养这个根本已经乱了，家齐、国治、天下平这些后续之事都没有了。根本不好，枝干会好，从未有过！

【英语译文】

The purpose of *The Great Learning* lies in clarifying virtue, making people's innovation, and reaching the utmost kindness. Only if one's knowledge reaches a certain state can he cherish unchangeable ambition. Only if one cherishes unchangeable ambition can he settle down. Only if one settles down can he stay peacefully. Only if one stays peacefully can he think complicatedly. Only if one thinks complicatedly can he act appropriately. All things in the world have the fundamental and the incidental, and all events have the beginning and the end. Things' basic features consist in the fundamental, the incidental, the beginning, and the end. One approaches the right way when he knows things' basic features and that the fundamental and the beginning are followed by the incidental and the end. In ancient time, one could clarify virtue only if he administrated his state well. He could administrate his state well only if he managed his family well. He could manage his family well only if he nurtured himself well. He could nurture himself well only if he corrected his heart. He could correct his heart only if he had honest will. He could have honest will only if he made his knowledge approach the utmost state. Knowledge approaching the utmost state lies in reasoning things. When things are reasoned thoroughly knowledge can approach the utmost state. When one's knowledge approaches the utmost state, he has honest will. When one has honest will, he can correct his heart. When one corrects his heart, he can nurture his virtue. When one nurtures his virtue, he can manage his family well. When one manages his family well, he can administrate his state well. When one administrates his state well, he can pacify the whole world. Men, from the Son of the Heaven to the common people, should regard self-nurturing as the fundamental. When self-nurturing goes wrongly, family management, and state administration, world pacification will lose completely. There never existed the situation where the branches are good but the fundamental has rotted

【注释】(1)《大学》:大人(小人除外)之学。《大学》之道,犹言大学的道路。明明德:彰明与生俱来的光明之美德。在:犹“在乎”。指出事物的目的、本质所在。下同。亲民:亲,通“新”。朱熹集注:“程子曰:‘亲当作新。’……新者,革其旧之谓也。”止于至善:至于最高境界。止:犹至,到。(2)知止而后有定:知识到了应到的境界然后才有确定不易的志向。定而后能静:志向定了然后才能静。静,指心不妄动。静而后能安:谓心不妄动然后才能安处。安而后能虑:所处而安,然后才能思虑精详。虑而后能得:谓思虑精详然后才能举措得当。(3)物有本末,事有终始:本末、终始是事物的基本特征,掌握了基本特征并知道本始为先终末为后也就接近正道了。(4)古之欲明明德于天下者:指彰明光明之美德于天下的古人。先齐其家:先整治自己的家庭。先修其身:先自我陶冶身心、涵养、德行。先正其心:先使自己的心归向于正。先诚其意:先使自己的心志真诚。先致其知:先使自己的知识不断推进到相应的最高境界。致知在格物:不断推进知识在于推究事物的道理。(5)物格而后知至:事物的道理推究通了,知识也就随即达到相应的高度。知至而后意诚:知识达到相应的高度,然后志意诚实。(6)壹是:一概,一律,一切。(7)本:朱熹注:"本,谓身也。所厚,谓家也。"否:无。

【原文】2《康诰》曰:"克明德。"[1]《大甲》曰:"顾諟天之明命。"[2]《帝典》曰:"克明峻德。[3]"皆自明也。

【白话译文】

《尚书·康诰》说:"能够彰明美德。"《尚书·太甲》说:"重视英明的天命。"《尚书·尧典》说:"能够彰明大德。"这些都是说自己彰明己德。

【英语译文】

Kang Gao in *The Book of History* reads "Good virtue can be upheld". *Tai Jia* in *The Book of History* reads "Mandate of the Heaven should be stressed." *Yao Dian* in *The Book of History* reads "Great virtue can be upheld." All of these show that we ourselves should uphold virtue.

【注释】(1)"《康诰》曰:'克明德。'":《康诰》,《周书》篇名。克明德,谓能崇尚德教。(2)"《大甲》曰:'顾諟天之明命。'":《大甲》,《商书》篇名。顾諟天之明命,谓(先王成汤)重视英明的天命。大甲,读 tàijiǎ。顾,注重。諟(shì),指示代词,这。(3)"《帝典》曰:'克明峻德'":《帝典》,《尚书》篇名,包括《尧典》和《舜典》。克明峻德,《尧典》中作"克明"。峻德一般解作大德,俊德一般解作美德;大德,美德意义可通。或云峻与俊相通。克明峻德,谓能够彰明大德。(4)皆自明也:谓所引《书》上之言皆言自明己德之意。

【原文】3 汤之《盘铭》曰:"苟日新,日日新,又日新。"[1]《康诰》曰:"作新民。"[2]

《诗》曰:“周虽旧邦,其命维新。”[3]是故君子无所不用其极[4]。

【白话译文】

商汤的盥洗盘器上刻的劝诫文辞说:“洗心去恶如沐浴身躯去垢,只要一天洗去了旧染之污而自新爽,就当天天做到新爽,又更新爽,不可略有间断。”《尚书·康诰》说:“鼓舞振作自新向上的民众。”《诗·大雅·文王》说:“周邦虽是古老国,今已受命为新邦。”所以君子没有什么理由不要求最高境界。

【英语译文】

The admonishment words carved in washing basin of Shang Tang read, “Purifying one’s heart is just like bathing and ridding of dust. Only if one feels new and fresh after washing off stain one day, then he should make himself new and fresh each day, and even newer and fresher without any intermittent.” *Kang Gao* in *The Book of History* reads, “Pluck the courage of the ambitious people.” *King Wen* in *Greater Odes* in *The Book of Songs* reads “Though Zhou Kingdom is old state, Nowadays it’s empowered a new one.” Therefore moral man and the rulers all claim for the utmost state.

【注释】(1)汤之《盘铭》:汤,指商汤。盘铭,古代刻在盥洗盘器上的劝诫文辞。苟日新:如果有一天除旧更新了。(2)作新民:朱熹注:“鼓之舞之谓之作,振起其自新之民也。”(3)其命维新:朱熹注“《诗·大雅·文王》之篇,言周国虽旧,至于文王能新其德以及于民,而始受天命也。”(4)无所不用其极:谓自新与新民都要求达到最高境界。

【原文】4《诗》云:“邦畿千里,维民所止。”[1]《诗》云:“缗蛮黄鸟,止于丘隅。”子曰:“于止,知其所止,可以人而不如鸟乎!”[2]《诗》云:“穆穆文王,于缉熙敬止!”为人君,止于仁;为人臣,止于敬;为人子,止于孝;为人父,止于慈;与国人交止于信[3]。《诗》云:“瞻彼淇澳,菉竹猗猗。有斐君子,如切如磋,如琢如磨。瑟兮僩兮,赫兮喧兮。有斐君子,终不可喧兮!”如切如磋者,道学也;如琢如磨者,自修也;瑟兮僩兮者,恂栗也;赫兮喧兮者,威仪也;有斐君子,终不可喧兮者,道盛德至善,民不能忘也[4]。《诗》云:“於戏前王不忘!”君子贤其贤而亲其亲,小人乐其乐而利其利,此以没世不忘也[5]。

【白话译文】

《诗·商颂·玄鸟》说:“领土辽阔过千里,人民定居享安康。”《诗·小雅·绵蛮》说:“羽毛细密小黄鸟,落在路旁的山坳。”孔子说:“对于居住什么地方,人可以不如小鸟么?”《诗·大雅·文王》说:“端庄和美周文王,啊,光明正大最善良!”为人君的,居于仁;为人臣的,居于敬;为人子的,居于孝;为人父的,居于慈;同国人相交的,居于信。《诗·卫风·淇澳》说:“看那静静淇水湾,绿荫一片竹翩翻。文采风流美君子,学问造诣很深渊,道德修养也高尚。庄严然更威武然,光明然更坦荡然。文采风流美君子,永远不可能遗忘然。”如切如磋,就是共同讨论学问;如琢如磨,就是自修学行;瑟兮僩兮,就是恐惧战栗;赫兮喧兮,就是庄重的仪容举止;文明有素的君子,终究不能忘记呀!是说盛美的德和最高境界的善,人民不能忘记。《诗·周颂·烈文》说:“啊,心潮涌动,先王典范刻胸中。”后世君子贤其贤而亲其亲,小人乐其乐而利其利,所以终身不忘。

【英语译文】

Black Bird in *Shang Hymns* in *The Book of Songs* reads, “Territory is so spacious to spread ten thousand *li*. People share prosperity by living peacefully.” *Lovely Oriole* in *Lesser Odes* in *The Book of Songs* reads, “Alovely oriole has densely thin feathers. It has fallen down beside path in valley.” Confucius said, “As for a living place, is a man not equally smart as a little bird?” *King Wen* in *Greater Odes* in *The Book of Songs* reads “Upright and easygoing is King Wen. Oh! He does things so openly and kindly.” The king should observe humanity; the courtier should observe respectfulness; the son should observe filial piety; the father should observe kindness; the men befriending others should observe faithfulness. *Deep Water* in *Ballads of Wei State* in *The Book of Songs* reads, “Look, around the peaceful and deep Qi Shui Bay. Bamboos grow waving all the way. A man is gentle and of unusual literary talent. His knowledge is far from ordinary man. His morality is also above that of anyone. Brilliant is he and downright is he. Gentle and of unusual literary talent is he. A man is gentle and of unusual literary talent. People can never forget that he is competent.” He discussed learning with others, he nurtured himself concerning learning and virtue. He was lofty and dignified and he had modest appearance. That people never forgot his competence meant that his utmost virtue and kindness cannot be forgot. *Moral Achievement* in *Zhou Hymns* in *The Book of Songs* reads, “Oh! I' m so excited. The passed king's model has been in my mind.” The moral men valued virtuous men and intimate, but mean men were glad at benefit. Therefore, people never forget it.

【注释】(1)“《诗》云:‘邦畿千里……’”:《诗·商颂·玄鸟》之篇。邦畿:王城及其周围千里的地区。止:居也。意谓物各有所当居之处。(2)“缗蛮黄鸟……”:缗,《诗》作绵,《诗·小雅·绵蛮》之篇。绵蛮:鸟声。丘隅:犹丘阿。山丘的曲深僻静处。子曰:孔子说。于止:对于居处。(3)“《诗》云:‘穆穆文王……’”:《诗·大雅·文王》之篇。穆穆,谓思虑、计谋等深刻而长远。于 wū,叹美词。缉:继续。熙:光明。敬止:朱熹注:“言其无不敬而安所止也。”(4)“《诗》云:‘瞻彼淇澳,菉竹猗猗’”:《诗·卫风·淇澳》之篇。淇,水名。澳 yù,水边弯曲处。今本《诗经》作“奥”。菉竹:lù ~,荩草的别名。亦作“绿竹”。唐陆德明释文:“《草木疏》云:‘有草似竹,高五六尺,淇水侧人,谓之菉竹也。’”猗猗 yī yī,美盛的样子。有斐君子:斐 fěi,有文采的样子。如切如磋,如琢如磨:切以刀锯,琢以椎凿,都是裁物使成形质。磋以炉锡(炉通“垆”,黑钢土。锡通“緆”,细布。)磨以沙石,皆治物使其滑泽也。治骨角者,既切而复磋之。治玉石者,既琢而复磨之,皆言其治之有绪而益致其精也。瑟兮僩兮:瑟 sè,严密的样子。僩兮:僩 xiàn,勇猛的样子。一说宽大的样子。赫兮喧兮:表露盛大的样子。喧:xuān,忘记。(5)《诗》云:《诗·周颂·烈文》之篇。於戏:wūhū,亦作“于熙”犹于乎。感叹词。前王:谓文王、武王。没世:mò ~,终身,永远。此以:是以,所以,因此。

【原文】5 子曰:“听讼,吾犹人也,[1]必也使无讼乎![2]”无情者不得尽其辞,[3]大畏民志,[4]此谓知本。

【白话译文】

孔子说:“审理诉讼,我和别人差不多。我以为做官一定要使诉讼事件逐渐减少,直到没有才好!”使没有真实情况的得不到狡辩机会;为官正大能使民心敬畏。这叫作知本。

【英语译文】

Confucius said, “I have no difference from others while scrutinizing lawsuit cases. I think an official should make effort to reduce cases until none.” Those who don't know actualities wont be given any chance to argue. An upright official makes common people respect him. This is called knowing the essentials.

【注释】(1)听讼:听理诉讼;审案。犹人:不异于人。(2)必也使无颂乎:一定要使讼案减少到为零吧。(3)无情者不得尽其辞:使没有真实情况的得不到狡辩机会。(4)大畏民志:为官正大能使民心敬畏。

【原文】6 此谓知本,[1]此谓知之至也[2](此节宜在经文之末,是其结语。)

【白话译文】

这叫知道事物之本。这叫知识的最高境界。

【英语译文】

This is called knowing the essentials. This is the utmost state of knowledge.

【注释】(1)此谓知本:这叫知道事物之本。(2)知之至也:知识的最高境界。

【原文】7 所谓诚其意者:毋自欺也,如恶恶臭,如好好色,此之谓自谦,[1]故君子必慎其独也![2]小人闲居为不善,无所不至,见君子而后厌然,掩其不善,而着其善。人之视己如见其肺肝然,则何益矣。此谓诚于中,形于外,故君子必慎其独也。[3]曾子曰[4]:“十目所视十手所指其严乎!”富润屋德润身,心广体胖,故君子必诚其意[5]。

【白话译文】

说使自己志意真诚的原因:就是不要自我欺骗,像憎恨污秽恶臭,像爱好美色,志意十足不虚。所以君子在只有自己才知道的时空中最要谨慎不乱!小人在独处时干坏事,什么事都干得出来。见到君子后遮遮掩掩,遮其不善,亮其善。其实人看自己最清楚,内心世界全明白,掩饰无益。这是说内心诚实,自然见于外表。所以君子必定慎重自己的任何独处时刻。曾子说:“十目所视十手所指,众人监视,严正么!”富实了打整住房,德进了修养身心。心中坦然身体舒泰。所以君子必定使自己志意真诚。

【英语译文】

The reason for making one's will honest lies in that one shouldn't cheat himself, that one's will is honest and and not superficial just like disgusting foul smell and loving beauty. Therefore a moral man should be cautious and careful when he stays alone in his own place and time. On the contrary, a mean man can do anything while he stays alone in his own place and time. As he meets a moral man he will hide his actual mean aspect but show off his kindness. As a matter of fact a man sees himself clearly and he is aware of his inner heart completely. It's no use to hide anything. That is to say one's inner heart will show in his appearance. Therefore a moral man should be cautious when he stays alone at any moment. Zeng Zi said, "It is so lofty that ten eyes are put on you and ten fingers are pointed to you." One should manage his house while being rich and he should nurture himself while being virtuous. When his heart is calm; his body is at ease. Consequently a moral man makes his will honest.

【注释】(1)恶恶臭:wù è chòu,憎恨难受的污秽臭气。好好色:hào hǎosè,喜爱美色。自谦:自足,心安理得。朱熹注"谦读为慊(qiè)。慊,快也,足也……以自快足于己也。"(2)慎其独:在只有自己才知道的时空中最要谨慎不乱。(3)无所不至:犹言无所不为,什么事都干得出来。闲居:犹独处。厌然:yǎn~,闭藏的样子。闭藏其不善之事。见其肺肝然:比喻瞧见内心世界。(4)曾子曰:曾参说。(5)富润屋德润身:富实了打整住房,德进了修养身心。心广体胖:胖 pán,心中坦然,身体舒泰。

【原文】8 所谓修身在正其心者,身有所忿懥,[1]则不得其正;有所恐惧,则不得其正;有所好乐,[2]则不得其正;有所忧患,则不得其正。心不在焉,[3]视而不见,听而不闻,食而不知其味。此谓修身在正其心。

【白话译文】

说修身在于端正自己的心,因为自己有愤怒,就得不到端正;有恐惧,就得不到端正;有嗜好,就得不到端正;有忧患,就得不到端正。心思不在这里,看不清楚,听不明白,吃不出味道。这是说修身在于端正自己的心。

【英语译文】

When one corrects his heart; he can nurture his virtue. This is because that one cannot correct his heart if he is agonized, frightened, and has addict and worries. He cannot see and hear things clearly and cannot taste food if he is absent-minded. That is to say nurturing one's virtue lies in correcting his heart.

【注释】(1)忿懥:fènzhì,愤怒。(2)好乐:hàoyào,喜好;嗜好。(3)心不在焉:心思不在这里。形容思想不集中。

【原文】9 所谓齐其家在修其身者:人之其所亲爱而辟焉,[1]之其所贱恶而辟焉,之其所畏敬而辟焉,之其所哀矜而辟焉,[2]之其所敖惰而辟焉。故好而知其恶,恶而知其美者,天下鲜矣!故谚有之曰:[3]"人莫知其子之恶,莫知其苗之硕。"此谓身不修不可以齐其家。

【白话译文】

说整治自己的家庭在于修养自身的原因:人们对于自己亲爱的就偏爱之,对于自己贱恶的就偏恶之,对于自己敬畏的就偏敬之,对于自己哀怜的就偏怜之,对于自己傲慢怠惰的就老是傲慢怠惰之。所以对于好的而知道其不好处,对于丑恶的而知道其美好点,这样的人,天下很少啊!所以,有这样的谚语说:"溺爱的人不知子之恶,贪得无厌的人不知禾苗肥硕。"这是说本身没修养好就不可能治理好家。

【英语译文】

When one nurtures his virtue he can manage his family well. This is because that one has partiality for his intimate ones; he excessively hates those disgusting ones; he excessively respects those respectable ones, he excessively pities those pitiable ones; and he always neglects those neglected ones. Therefore few people know the shortcomings of good ones and brilliant points of bad ones. The sayings goes like this, "One who spoils his child doesn't know his child's evil; greedy man doesn't know seedlings are fat." That means if one doesn't nurture his virtue, he cannot manage his family well.

【注释】(1)之:于。辟:朱熹注:"辟,读为僻。"谓偏向一方,不正。焉,代词。相当于"之"。(2)哀矜:~jīn,哀怜;怜悯。(3)敖惰:àoduò,傲慢怠惰。谚:yàn,谚语。即长期流传下来的寓意丰富、文辞固定、简练的古训、俗语。

【原文】10 所谓治国必先齐其家者,其家不可教而能教人者,无之。[1]故君子不出家而成教于国:[2]孝者,所以事君也;弟者,所以事长也;慈者,所以使众也。《康诰》曰:"如保赤子"[3],心诚求之,虽不中不远矣。未有学养子而后嫁者也!一家仁,一国兴仁;一家让,一国兴让;一人贪戾[4],一国作乱;其机如此。此谓一言偾事,一人定国[5]。尧舜帅天下以仁,而民从之;桀纣帅天下以暴而民从之;其所令反其所好,而民不从。是故君子有诸己而后求诸人,无诸己而后非诸人。所藏乎身不恕[6],而能喻诸人者,未之有也。故治国在齐其家。《诗》云:“桃之夭夭,其叶蓁蓁;之子于归,宜其家人。”宜其家人,而后可以教国人[7]。《诗》云:“宜兄宜弟。”宜兄宜弟,而后可以教国人[8]。《诗》云:“其仪不忒,正是四国。”其为父子兄弟足法,而后民法之也[9]。此谓治国在齐其家[10]。

【白话译文】

说治国必须先治家的原因:自己家教不行而能教别人的,没有过。所以君子不出家门而实现教育于国内:孝,用来侍奉君主;弟,用来事奉长上;慈,用来使用众人。《尚书·康诰》说:“像保护婴儿一样保护百姓。”心里诚实地这么干,即使做不到恰好,也不会差得很远。从未有过学了养儿然后才出嫁的。一家行仁,一国兴仁;一家行让,一国兴让;一人贪利,一国作乱;事物变化之由就是这样。这叫一句话毁掉事业,一个人安定国家。尧舜用仁统帅天下,于是民众顺从之;桀纣用暴力统帅天下,于是民众顺从之;他们的命令和他们的爱好相反时,于是民众就不顺从。所以君子必须自己有德行才可以要求别人有德行,必须自己没有过失才可以责备别人。自身没有仁爱待物的胸怀而能晓喻别人践行宽恕的,未曾有过。所以治国在于整治自己的家。《诗·周南·桃夭》说:“桃树少壮出彩霞,浓密叶片青日深。这位姑娘将出阁,和悦善处福满门。”结新家庭,以后可以教国人。《诗·小雅·蓼萧》说:“弟兄和睦相互帮。”当哥哥当弟弟都和睦,以后可以教国人。《诗·曹风·鸤鸠》说:“言行如一不绕弯,带领各国安人环。”这足够为父子兄弟的人们效法。以后民众都要效法。这叫治国在于整治家庭。

【英语译文】

When one manages his family well, he can administrate his state well. This is because that there never existed the situation where one can teach others but he cannot teach his family members. A moral man realizes education in his state without going out. The main points are that being filial to one's monarch, being fraternal to one's elder and superordinates, being kind to common people. *Kang Gao* in *The Book of History* reads "We should protect common people like babies." If one does things honestly he will nearly reach the aim even if he hasn't done well. There never existed the situation where a woman got married after she had learned how to raise a baby. One's state carries out humanity if one's family does so. One's state carries out modesty if one's family does so. One's state riots if one person is greedy. The change of things lies in that. This is called that one words destroys a mission and one person settles down a state. Sage Yao and Great Shun govern the land under the Heaven by means of humanity, consequently all people were obedient to them. Jie in Xia Dynasty and Zhou in Shang Dynasty governed the land under the Heaven by means of violence, consequently all people were obedient to them. When their order and preference went oppositely people weren't obedient to them. Therefore a moral man can ask others to be virtuous on condition that he is virtuous. He can scold others on condition that he has no fault. There never existed the situation where one isn't humanistic but he can make others practice forgiveness. Therefore, when one manages his family well he can administrate his state well. *Gorgeous Peaches* in *Zhounan Ballad* in *The Book of Songs* reads, "Gorgeous peach trees grow under twilight. /Dense peach leaves shadow sunlight. /This young girl is bound to marry. /Being kind, she'll bring happiness alright." One establishes his new family and then he can educate his fellows. *Tall Wormwood* in *Lesser Odes* in *The Book of Songs* reads, "Kind brothers help each other." When elder and younger brothers live harmoniously then one can educate his fellows. *Cuckoos* in *Ballads of Cao State* in *The Book of Songs* reads, "They do as what they say. /And they lead the state peacefully." It's enough to serve a model for fathers and brothers. And later on common people should follow. That means if one manages his family well he can administrate his state well.

【注释】(1)其家:指自己的家人、家族、其他成员。(2)成教于国:在国内实现教育。(3)"《康诰》曰:'如保赤子'。":《尚书·康诰》说,"像保护婴儿一样保护百姓。"(4)贪戾:犹贪利。(5)偾事:fèn shì,败事。(6)非:责备,反对。所藏乎身不恕:自身没有仁爱待物的胸怀而能晓喻别人践行宽恕的。(7)《诗》:《诗·周南·桃夭》。(8)《诗》:《诗·小雅·蓼萧》。(9)《诗》:《诗·曹风·鸤鸠》。(10)此谓治国在齐其家:这叫治国在于整治家庭。

【原文】11 所谓平天下在治其国者:上老老而民兴孝,上长长而民兴弟,上恤孤而民不倍,是以君子有絜矩之道也[1]。所恶于上,毋以使下;所恶于下,毋以事上;所恶于前,毋以先后;所恶于后,毋以从前;所恶于右,毋以交于左;所恶于左,毋以交于右;此之谓絜矩之道。[2]《诗》云:"乐只君子,民之父母。"民之所好好之,民之所恶恶之,此之谓民之父母。[3]《诗》云:“节彼南山,维石岩岩,赫赫师尹,民具尔瞻。”有国者不可以不慎,辟则为天下僇矣。[4]《诗》云:“殷之未丧师,克配上帝;仪监于殷,峻命不易。”道得众则得国,失众则失国。[5]是故君子先慎乎德。有德此有人,有人此有土,有土此有财,有财此有用。[6]德者本也,财者末也,[7]外本内末,争民施夺。[8]是故材聚则民散,财散则民聚。[9]是故言悖而出者,亦悖而入;货悖而入者,亦悖而出。[10]《康诰》曰:“惟命不于常!”道善则得之,不善则失之矣。[11]《楚书》曰:“楚国无以为宝,惟善以为宝。[12]”舅犯曰:“亡人无以为宝,仁亲以为宝。[13]”。《秦誓》曰:“若有一臣,断断兮无他技,其心休休焉,其如有容焉。人之有技,若己有之,人之彦圣,其心好之,不啻若自其口出,寔能容之,以能保我子孙黎民 ,尚亦有利哉。人之有技,媢疾以恶之,人之彦圣,而违之俾不通,寔不能容,以不能保我子孙黎民,亦曰殆哉。[14]”唯仁人放流之,迸诸四夷,不与同中国。此谓唯仁人为能爱人,能恶人。[15]见贤而不能举,举而不能先,命也;见不善而不能退,退而不能远,过也。[16]好人之所恶,恶人之所好,是谓拂人之性,菑必逮夫身。[17]是故君子有大道,必忠信以得之,骄泰以失之。[18]生财有大道,生之者众,食之者寡,为之者疾,用之者舒,则财恒足矣。[19]仁者以财发身,不仁者以身发财。[20]未有上好仁而下不好义者也,未有好义其事不终者也,未有府库财非其财者也。[21]孟献子曰:“畜马乘不察于鸡豚,伐冰之家不畜牛羊,百乘之家不畜聚敛之臣,与其有聚敛之臣,宁有盗臣。”此谓国不以利为利,以义为利也。[22]长国家而务财用者,必自小人矣。彼为善之,小人之使为国家,菑害并至。虽有善者,亦无如之何矣!此谓国不以利为利,以义为利也。[23]

【白话译文】

说平天下在于治理本国的原因:君主用敬老之道侍奉老人,老百姓就崇尚孝道。君主敬重长上,老百姓就崇尚顺从和敬爱兄长,君主救济年幼无父的孤儿,老百姓就不会欺凌弱小,所以君子有道德规范之道。厌恶上位的缺失,不可凭那种缺失使唤下位;厌恶下位的缺失不可凭那种缺失服事上位;厌恶前面的缺失不可拿那种缺失引领后面;厌恶后面的缺失不可凭那种缺失跟从前面;厌恶右面的缺失不可把那种缺失传给左面;厌恶左面的缺失不可把那种缺失传给右面;这个叫道德规范之道。《诗·小雅·南山有台》说:“和乐坦荡的君子,为民筹划不迟疑。”民众喜爱什么,他喜爱什么,民众厌恶什么,他厌恶什么,他就叫民之父母。《诗·小雅·节南山》说:“高峻宽广终南山,岩石磊磊百重巅。赫赫长官师和尹,民众眼里怒火燃。”治理国家的人,不可以不慎重,偏离了正道,就会被天下人所杀戮。《诗·大雅·文王》说:“殷商未丢民心时,能顺天命保国疆。应把殷商作鉴戒,保国永昌不寻常。”所行之道能够得到民众赞成,就能得到国家,得不到民众赞成就失掉国家。所以君子首先要慎重道德,有明德就有众人,有众人就有土地,有土地就有财货,有财货就有用。德是本,财是末。疏远本,亲近末,弃德取财,争利的人都施行夺取。所以财聚就民散,财散就民聚。所以胡言乱语的人,也听别人胡言乱语。货物胡乱而入也胡乱而出。《尚书·康诰》说:"天命不至于固定不变!"行道好,可以得到它,不好就要失掉它。《楚书》说:"楚国没有什么作为宝物,只有善用作宝物。"这是说不以金玉为宝以人为宝。晋文公的舅舅子犯说:"逃命的人没有什么宝物,只有把爱父母作为宝物。"《尚书·秦誓》曰:"如果有一个小臣,专诚守一,没有别的技能而心胸宽大,好像很能包容。人家有什么技能就像自己所有一样,人家的善美明达,他心中喜爱,不只是像口中说的那样,实际行为的确能包容。因为这样的人能保我子孙和百姓,还大有利用价值呀。人家有什么技能,嫉妒而厌恶,人家的善美明达,他心中反对,想方设法使人家受阻不顺,实际行为没有一点包容表现;因为这样的人不能保我子孙和百姓,真是危险呀。"只有仁人能放逐危险的人,把他们赶到四周荒远之地不许聚集在中国。这是说只有仁人是既能爱人又能厌恶人。发现贤人而不能举,举而不能先,这是怠慢;发现不好的人而不能斥退,斥退又不能远,这是过错。喜爱人家的厌恶,厌恶人家的喜爱,这是违背人的本性,是不仁,灾祸必至己身。所以在高位的君子有正大之道,一定是忠诚信实而取得,骄恣放纵而失掉。开发财源,管理财政有正大之道,生产的人多,吃白饭的人少,制作者急速,使用者舒缓,那么财富经常充足。仁德的人,散财而得民;不仁的人,亡身来发财。没有君主好仁而臣下不好义的,没有好义的事无下场的,没有府库中的财物因贪腐偷盗而流失的。孟献子说:"士初试为大夫的人不应该过问鸡猪小事,卿大夫以上丧祭用冰的人不应该养牛羊,有采地的人不应该养聚敛财物之臣,与其有聚敛财物之臣,宁可有偷盗之臣。"这是说国家不应该以各级官吏的私利为利,要以正义为利。管理国家却竭力于追求财用不讲平衡,一定是从小人开始。他认为是干好事。让小人治国家,天灾人祸相继。虽有贤者也无可如何了!这是说国家不应该以各级官吏的私利为利,要以正义为利。

【英语译文】

When one administrates his state well; he can pacify the whole world. This is because that if the monarch attends the elder in the way of respecting them then common people worship filial piety, that if the monarch respects the elder then common people worship obedience and respect the elder brother, that if the monarch helps orphans then common people won't bully weak and minor persons. Therefore a moral man has moral integrity. When one disgusts the emptiness of superordinate post; he cannot summon his subordinate due to the emptiness. When one disgusts the emptiness of subordinate post;he cannot attend his superordinate due to the emptiness. When one disgusts the emptiness of fore post; he cannot lead the hind one due to the emptiness. When one disgusts the emptiness of hind post;he cannot follow the fore one due to the emptiness. When one disgusts the emptiness of left post;he cannot pass to the right due to the emptiness. This is called moral integrity. *Trailing Grasses* in *Lesser Odes* in *The Book of Songs* reads, "The gentlemen are honest and upright. /They help people of the state alright." He loves what his people love and he hates what his people hate. He is called people's parent. *Steep South Mountain* in *Lesser Odes* in *The Book of Songs* reads, "Steep is the south mountain. /Rocks pile upon rocks on top. /Famous officers Shi and Yin. /All people were angry at them." A man who governs a state should be cautious and people will kill him if he diverts from the right way. *King Wen* in *Greater Odes* in *The Book of Songs* reads, "When Shang Dynasty still held people's heart. /If obeying heaven's order they'll not perish. /We should regard Shang Dynasty as a mirror. /It's unusually to keep kingdom prosperous." He can obtain the state if what he carries is supported by his people. On the contrary, he will lose his state if what he carries isn't supported by his people. Therefore a moral man should first be cautious at his way and virtue. If he is virtuous then he has his people; if he has his people he has his land; if he has his land he has his wealth; if he has his wealth he has its utility. Virtue is the essential and wealth is the end. If one becomes estranged oneself from the essential and keeps close with the end, i. e. ridding off virtue and getting wealth, then benefit-striving men will strive for benefit. Therefore people will disperse while wealth accumulates and people will accumulate while wealth disperses. People who blather love to hear other's blathering. Goods come in and go out in riot way. *Kang Gao* in *the Book of History* reads, "The mandate of the Heaven won't stay unchanged." One will get it if he carries out right way and one will lose it if he carries out wrong way. *The Book of Chu State* reads, "No treasure exists in Chu State and kindness is regarded as its treasure." This means that gold and jade are not considered as treasure but man is treasure. The uncle of Duke Wen of Jin State said, "A fleeing man has no treasure but treats his parents as treasure." *Tai Shi* in *the Book of History* reads, "A minor courtier is very honest and considerate but hasn't any specific skill. He seems so considerate that other's skill is just like his own; other's virtue and liking are just like his own. His actual actions show that he is really considerate not just in his words. Such kind of man can protect our offspring and common people and he is valuable. On the contrary a person hates and is disgnsted at other's skill, apposes other's virtue, and tries his best to hinder other people. His actual actions don't show that he is not at all considerate. Such kind of man cannot protect our offspring and common people and he is really dangerous." Only a humanistic man can exile dangerous persons and demote them to the remote and barren region not allowing them stay in mid-region. That means only humanistic man can both love person and be disgusted. It is negligence not to recommend virtuous man while noticing him, and not to recommend virtuous man in first order even doing so. It is fault not to dismiss one from his post while finding out the man isn't upright, and not to make him go far away even dismissing him. It isn't humanity and violence of human nature to like the others, disgust and to be disgusted at what others like. Scourge will befall. Therefore a moral man in high post has right and great way. He surely obtain things due to faithfulness and lose things due to arrogance. There is right ways to develop wealth resources and administrate finance. More people produce and less consume, makers haste and users relax. In that case there is always sufficient wealth. A virtuous and humanistic man disperse wealth and obtain people but an inhumane man loses himself to make fortune. There never existed the situation where a monarch was humanistic but his courtiers weren't righteous. No righteous things didn't produce a good result. Goods in warehouse surely reduce due to theft and corruption. Meng Xian Zi said, "A scholar shouldn't care about affairs of raising pigs and chicken when he first came to the post of minister. Officials above minister shouldn't raise ox and sheep when they use ice in sacrificial ceremony. A man owning feoff land shouldn't keep ministers who gathered wealth. We would keep ministers who steal things rather than keeping wealth-gathering ones." That means a state shouldn't benefit from the interest of officials at all levels but from their righteousness. Governing a state but trying hard to search for unbalanced wealth is surely started from mean men. The mean men think they did good things. Scourges and man-caused calamity befell successively if mean men govern a state. No methods could save it even if virtuous men existed. It means that a state shouldn't benefit from the interest of officials at all levels but from their righteousness.

【注释】(1)上老老而民兴孝:上,指君主,皇帝。老老,以敬老之道侍奉老人。民兴孝,老百姓崇尚孝道。上长长而民兴弟:长长 zhǎng ~,敬重长上。兴弟 ~ tì,

崇尚顺从和敬爱兄长。弟,通“悌”。恤孤:存恤(慰抚;救济)孤(无父的幼儿)。倍:通“背”,违背。絜矩:xié ~ 絜,度量。矩,画方形的工具。引申为法度。这里象征道德上的规范。(2)毋以:不可以。(3)《诗》云:“乐只君子,民之父母。”《诗·小雅·南山有台》说:“和乐坦荡的君子,为民筹划不迟疑。”(4)有国者:治理国家的人。辟则为天下僇矣:辟,读作“僻”。邪僻,偏离正道 。僇:同“戮”。(5)仪监于殷,峻命不易:仪,《诗》作“宜”。峻,《诗》作“骏”。(6)有德此有人:有德就有人。此,则,就。(7)德者本也,财者末也:者,语气助词。表提顿语气,提请读者注意,可以去掉不译。(8)外本内末:谓疏远本亲近末。争民施夺:争利之人施行夺取。(9)是故财聚则民散,财散则民聚:财聚,即天下之财被为政者搜刮了。财散,即天下之财分散给天下人了。(10)悖:bèi,违逆;违背。(11)道善:指治国治民所行之道好。(12)《楚书》:不详,朱熹集注以《楚语》列于其次,下注:“言不宝金玉而宝善人也。”(13)舅犯:晋文公舅狐偃,字子犯。亡人:晋文公时为公子,出亡在外故称。仁,爱也。事见《檀弓》。(14)媢疾:màojí,嫉妒。(15)迸:通“屏bìng”,斥逐,排除。(16)命:怠慢。君子而未仁者之缺失。(17)菑:古“灾”字。拂:fú,逆,违背。(18)君子:朱熹注:“以位言之。”道,谓居其位而修己治人之术。(19)恒足:经常足够。(20)发身,发财:郑玄注:“发,起也。言仁人有财则务于施与以起身成其令名,不仁之人有身贪于聚敛以起财务成富。”(21)未有府库财非其财者:谓府库中的财物都是合乎正义的,没有违逆出入的。(22)孟宪子:鲁之贤大夫仲孙蔑。畜马乘:士初试为大夫的人。伐冰之家:卿大夫以上丧祭用冰者。百乘之家:有采地者。(23)长:zhǎng,治理,管理。

第二部分 《中庸》*The Doctrine of Mean*

【原文】1 天命之谓性,率性之谓道,修道之谓教[1]。道也者,不可须臾离也,可离非道也。是故君子戒慎乎其所不睹,恐惧乎其所不闻[2]。莫见乎隐,莫显乎微,故君子慎其独也[3]。喜怒哀乐之未发,谓之中;发而皆中节,谓之和。中也者,天下之大本也;和也者,天下之达道也[4]。致中和,天地位焉万物育焉[5]。

【白话译文】

与生俱来的本质叫作性,遵循本性而行叫作道,遵行正道称作教。道是人生行为的路,再短的时间也不能离开;能离开的就不是道路而是别的什么了。所以君子警惕谨慎自己没见过的,敬畏自己没听过的,避免离开道路。没有人显露隐秘处,没有人显露低贱事,所以君子在独处中谨慎不苟。喜怒哀乐是人的性情感动,在没有任何一种性情感动时,就是没有任何偏倚的本性,这种状况叫作“中”;性情感动适度,无过不及,这种状况叫作“和”。中是天下的根本,是要害处;和是天下公认的准则,不可违背。致中和,就是达到平静不偏向、平衡而和谐的最高境界。这样,天地各居正位,万物各自生长。

【英语译文】

The inborn essence is called nature; observing nature is called way, and observing right way is called education. Way is the road of man's life and conducts and people can't divert from it even if he has a short lifetime. What can be diverted from isn't the way but other thing. Therefore a moral man is alert and cautious at what he hasn't seen, and he reverses what he hasn't heard so that he can avoid diverting from the road. No one exposes privacy and no one exposes humbleness; consequently a moral man behaves cautiously when he stays alone. Pleasure, anger, sorrow and joy are all moved by man's nature. If none of them is moved then there isn't any sided nature. This situation is called “middleness”. If any of them is moved appropriately then there isn't excess or less. This situation is called "harmony". Middleness is the essential in the world, and the vitality and harmony is the commonly recognized standard, which cannot be violated. Approaching middleness and harmony is to reach the utmost state of tranquility, balance and harmonization. Thus heaven and earth are in their right places and things grow.

【注释】(1)天命:上天(的)命令;上天(的)给予;与生俱来(的)。性:指人的本性,即天赋之德,与生俱来的本质。率性:遵循本性为人处世。率 shuài,遵行,遵循。修道:遵行正道。教:引导,教化。道:犹"路"。也者:语气助词,在这里表示提示。此外还可表示疑问或拟度。须臾:~yú,片刻。(2)道也者:指日常生活所涉及的各方面必经之路。戒慎:警惕谨慎。乎:语气助词,用在句中舒缓语气。下同。其所不睹、其所不闻:自己没看见的、自己没听到的。(3)莫见乎隐:没有人显露隐秘事。见,读 xiàn,显现,显露。莫显乎微:没有人显露低贱事。慎其独:在独处中谨慎不苟。(4)谓之中:叫作平静没偏向。中节:zhòng~,适度,刚好,无过不及。谓之和:叫谐和不别扭。大本:事物的根本,要害之所在。达道:天下公认的准则。(5)致中和:达到平静不偏向、平衡而和谐的最高境界。致,谓推而极之,达到顶点(至善处)。位焉:安其所。育焉:遂其生。

【原文】2 仲尼曰:"君子中庸,小人反中庸[1]。君子之中庸也。君子而时中;小人之中庸也,小人而无忌惮也[2]。"

【白话译文】

孔子说:"君子为人处世,行中庸之道,不偏不倚,无过不及,小人却与君子相反。君子的中庸之道,无时不中、时时皆中。小人反中庸之道,任意横行,不顾一切。"

【英语译文】

Confucius said, "A moral man conducts himself in society adopting middle course without sidedness, excess or less. A mean man conducts himself oppositely. The middle course of a moral man is appropriate at anytime. A mean man opposes the middle course and conducts at will caring about nothing."

【注释】(1)仲尼:孔子名丘,字仲尼。中庸:不偏不倚,无过不及,而平常之理乃天命所当然精微极致。唯君子为能体之,小人反是。(2)时中:中无定体,随时而在,是平常道理,君子知其在我,能戒慎不睹,恐惧不闻,而无时不中。小人不知有此,肆欲妄行,而无所忌惮。

【原文】3 子曰:“中庸其至矣乎[1]! 民鲜能久矣[2]!”

【白话译文】

孔子说:“中庸之道太高超了吗? 民众很少能达到已经很久了。”

【英语译文】

Confucius said, “The middle course has reached the utmost state! It has been a long time that people cannot reach it.”

【注释】(1)至:最高超;达到极点。朱熹四书集注:“过则失之,不及则未,故惟中庸之德为至。然亦人所同得初无难事,但世教衰,民不兴行,故鲜能之,今已久矣。”(2)鲜能:xiǎn ~,少能,论语无能“字”。

【原文】4 子曰:“道之不行也,我知之矣,知者过之,愚者不及也;道之不明也,我知之矣,贤者过之,不肖者不及也[1]。人莫不饮食也,鲜能知味也[2]。”

【白话译文】

孔子说:“正道为什么不能通行,我知道了,有智慧的人以为没什么了不起,不足行,智慧差的人不知道怎样行;正道为什么不明显,我知道了,有才能的人不重视,不成材的人或不正派的人不知道怎样行,又不要求行,所以看不见多少正道。人没有不吃不喝的,却没有多少人能知吃喝的味道。”

【英语译文】

Confucius said, “I' ve known the reason why the right way hasn't prevailed. The wise man thinks it's unnecessary to conduct in right way and the unwise man dosen't know how to do it. I' ve known the reason why the right way isn't prevalent. The talented man dosen't pay attention to conducting in right way, and the untalented and indecent man dosen't know how to do it and dosen't want to do so. Therefore they can't see the right way. No one dosen't eat or drink but few can know the real taste of eating and drinking."

【注释】(1)知者:即"智者"。有智慧的人。不肖者:不成材的人或不正派的人。(2)莫不:无不;没有一个不。知味:饮食是人的寻常事,对于酸、甜、苦、麻、辣等味道一尝便知,然而不经过考察和操作实践,又有多少人能知道味的所以然和必然呢,又有多少人能控制味呢。

【原文】5 子曰:"道其不行矣夫[1]!"

【白话译文】

孔子说:"正道就这样不能通行啊!"

【英语译文】

Confucius said, "O, the right way dosen't prevail like this!"

【注释】(1)夫:句末语气助词。表疑问,译为"吗""么",表委婉推测或商榷性询问译为"吧",表感叹译为"啊""呀"。

【原文】6 子曰:"舜其大知也与[1]! 舜而好察迩言[2],隐恶而扬善,执其两端用其中于民[3],其斯以为舜乎[4]!"

【白话译文】

孔子说:"舜是有大智慧的人啊! 舜勤学好问,而且好考察平常人浅近的话。对那些未善的言语,都隐藏起来不宣传,凡是良言善语都宣传,不隐藏。并从各类善言的两端极致,度量出适中点,用来对待民众。大概这么便成就了舜啊!"

【英语译文】

Confucius said, "Great Shun was the utmost wise man! He was so learned that he could scrutinize common persons' shallow speech. He hid those unkind words and those beneficiary ones. He treated masses with appropriate words which he considered proper from extremities of different words. In this way Great Shun established himself!"

【注释】(1)其:副词,表判断,相当于"乃"。大知:大智;有大智慧的人。知,同“智”。也与:亦作“也欤”,语气助词。可表感叹语气或疑问语气。(2)迩言:ěr ~,浅近之言,常人之语。(3)隐恶扬善:对未善之言隐而不宣,对善言播而不匿。执其两端用其中:掌握群众的各类不同善言的两端极致,度量出适中点而用之于民。(4)其斯以为舜乎:其,副词。表推测估计。大概;也许。斯:近指代词。此,这。以为:而为;而成。而,连词。

【原文】7 子曰:“人皆曰予知[1],驱而纳诸罟擭陷阱之中,而莫之知辟也[2]。人皆曰予知,择乎中庸而不能期月守也[3]。”

【白话译文】

孔子说:“人都自认为聪明,可是当把他赶进罟擭陷阱一样的绝境时,他不知道避开。人都自认为聪明,可是选择了中庸之道,他不能保持到一个整月。”

【英语译文】

Confucius said, “Everyone thinks he himself is wise but when he is cornered into a trap he doesn’t know how to dodge. Everyone thinks he himself is wise but when he has chosen the middle course, he can’t stick to it for one month.”

【注释】(1)曰:以为。予知:yúzhì,即“予智”。自谓聪明。(2)而:代词,他。纳诸:入于;进入到。纳,入;使进入。诸,介词。相当于“于”。罟擭:gǔhuò,捕取鸟兽的工具。罟,网的总称。擭,装有机关的捕兽木笼。陷阱:xiànjǐng,捕捉野兽或敌人的陷坑。莫之知:即不知。莫,副词。表否定。不,不能。之,语气助词。用在句中补凑音节。辟:同“避”。(3)期月:jī ~,一整月。

【原文】8 子曰:“回之为人也[1],择乎中庸,得一善[2],则拳拳服膺而弗失之矣[3]。”

【白话译文】

孔子说:“颜回的做人、处事、接物不错,他选择了中庸,他一得了善言善道,就诚恳信奉,衷心信服,绝不丢失。”

【英语译文】

Confucius said, “Yan Hui conducts himself in society well and he chooses the middle course. When he acquires good words or right way he honestly believes in them and never gets them lost."

【注释】(1)回:孔子弟子颜渊名。(2)一善:"善道"或"善言"。(3)拳拳服膺:quán quán fúyīng,诚恳信奉;衷心信服。拳拳:诚挚的样子。服膺:朱熹四书集注:"服,犹着也;膺,胸也。奉持而着之心胸之间,言能守也。"

【原文】9 子曰:"天下国家可均也,爵禄可辞也,白刃可蹈也,中庸不可能也[1]。"

【白话译文】

孔子说:"天下可以平定,国家可以治好,官位和俸禄可以辞去,流血牺牲可以践行,不偏不倚,无过不及,平平常常不可能做到。"

【英语译文】

Confucius said, "The world can be pacified; one state can be administrated; post and salary can be dismissed, and bleeding or sacrifice can be practiced. However we can't manage to be impartial, in. excessive, unapproached, or ordinary."

【注释】(1)均:本指古代制造陶器的转轮。引申用以比喻平天下治国家可以如运均制陶器一样进行。故训均为"平治"。(2)白刃:锋利闪亮的刀。(3)不可能:均天下国家,辞爵禄,蹈白刃,这些事业行为显露于外有目共睹,终始明显,可以量化考察。中庸是道德修养蕴含于内,是一生不可须臾离开的功夫,不是义精仁熟、没有一毫人欲之私的人不能做到。

【原文】10 子路问强[1]。子曰:"南方之强与?北方之强与?抑而强与[2]?宽柔以教,不报无道,南方之强也,君子居之[3]。衽金革,死而不厌,北方之强也,而强者居之[4]。故君子和而不流,强哉矫!中立而不倚,强哉矫!国有道,不变塞焉,强哉矫!国无道,至死不变,强哉矫[5]!"

【白话译文】

子路问怎样才叫坚强。孔子说:"你问南方的坚强呢?北方的坚强呢?还是你的坚强呢?用宽容顺从的方法教诲缺德的人,对强暴的行为不报复,这是南方人的坚强,君子安居于这种坚强。全副军装,刀光剑影,至死不厌,这是北方人的坚强,强壮的人操持这种坚强。所以君子和衷相济而不变自己所见,坚强啊,真雄健!顶天立地不偏倚,坚强啊,真雄健!国家政治通畅,仍然困窘,不变操守,坚强啊,真雄健!国家混乱,到死不变,坚强啊,真雄健!"

【英语译文】

Zi Lu asked what can be called fortitude. Confucius said, "Do you ask Southerners' fortitude or that of the northerners or that of yourself? It is southerners' fortitude to educate men without virtue by means of forgiveness and obedience and not to revenge on violent actions. A moral man feels ease at such kind of fortitude. It is northerners' fortitude to fight with weapon never yielding. A strong man sticks to such kind of fortitude. It's so firm and strong that moral men work together with one heart but doesn't change his philosophy. It's so firm and strong that moral men stand upright of indomitable spirit. It's so firm and strong that moral men never change moral integrity even if they don't do things smoothly when the administration of state is smooth. It's so firm and strong that moral men never change moral integrity till death when the state is in riot."

【注释】(1)子路:孔子弟子。姓仲,名由,字子路。(2)抑:yì,连词,还是。而:代词,你,你的。(3)宽柔以教:以宽容顺从的方法教诲不及的人。宽柔,谓宽缓和柔。不报无道:谓横逆者击来,只承受住,不予反击。(4)衽:卧席。金:刀剑等武器。革:革制造的甲、胄、盾之类。(5)和而不流:和衷相济,不变自己所见。流,据古文尚书和广雅,流有"变""演""化"的意义。矫:jiǎo,雄健的样子。塞:sāi,或读sè,不通显,困窘。

【原文】11 子曰:"素隐行怪,后世有述焉,吾弗为之矣[1]。君子遵道而行,半途而废,吾弗能已矣[2]。君子依乎中庸,遁世不见知而不悔,唯圣者能之[3]。"

【白话译文】

孔子说:"寻找、搜索被掩盖了的事,行动又怪异少见,后代可能有人称述他,我不做这样的事。君子遵循正道走自己的路,如果在半路上停止,我停不住。君子托身于中庸,避开世俗,不被人知而不悔,只有圣人能做到。"

【英语译文】

Confucius said, "A man may be praised by people in future if he searches for hidden things and his activities are also odd. I won't do such kind of things. A Moral man walk on his road by observing the right way, I can't stop in the midcllelray. Moral man find a place to live in doctrine of mean, dodge common customs, and don't regret for being unknown. Only the sages could do so."

【注释】(1)素隐行怪:通"索隐行怪"。谓探索隐晦之事而行怪僻诡异之道。有述焉:有人称述他。(2)半途而废:中途而止。废,中止,停止。已:yǐ,停止。(3)依乎:依附于;托身于。乎,介词,同"于"。遁世:逃避世俗,避世隐居。不见知:不被人知。

【原文】12 君子之道费而隐[1]。夫妇之愚,可以与知焉,及其至也,虽圣人亦有所不知焉;夫妇之不肖,可以能行焉,及其至也,虽圣人亦有所不能焉。天地之大也,人犹有所憾。故君子语大,天下莫能载焉;语小,天下莫能破焉[2]。诗云:"鸢飞戾天,鱼跃于渊。"言其上下察也[3]。君子之道,造端于夫妇;及其至也,察乎天地[4]。

【白话译文】

君子之道作用广大,本体精微。愚昧的平民男女,可以使他们知道君子之道。至于君子之道的极致,即使是圣人也有所不知;不贤的平民男女,能够行君子之道。天地之恩德如此宏大,人还有不少灾害和布施欠均的遗憾,所以君子说大的方面,大得天下承载不起;说小的方面,小得天下不能破开它。诗经上说:"'老鹰展翅飞上天,鲤鱼跳跃在深渊。'这是说他们在上下观察。君子之道,从平民男女开始;至于它的极致,是透视天地。"

【英语译文】

The way of moral men is of utmost usage and complicated essence. We can make foolish common people know about the way of moral men. As for it's extremity, even sages don't know. Wicked common people may carry it out. Mercy of the heaven and the earth is so great but catastrophes still befall and philanthropic actions are not in balance. Therefore moral men discuss the big points which can't be held on the land. Moral men also discuss the small points which can't be broken on the land. *At the Foot of Mountain Han* in *Greater Odes* in *The Book of Songs* reads, "Hawks flutter wings flying in sky, Fish jumps into the deep bliss." That means they are observing different places. The way of moral men starts with common people and its extremity is to grasp the essence of the heaven and the earth.

【注释】(1)费:用多,用广。隐:体微。(2)夫妇:犹言匹夫匹妇,指平民男女。与知:使知道。及其:及,转折连词,至于。其,代词,指君子之道。不肖:不贤能,不成材。(3)诗云两句:见《诗·大雅·旱麓》。鸢:yuān,鸷鸟,属猛禽类;俗称鹞鹰,老鹰。戾:lì,至,到达,指大鱼跃于渊。(4)及其至也:指君子的道的极致。(5)察乎天地:上连天下接地。王引之经义述闻:"此引诗以明君子之道大,上至于天,下至于地也。"

【原文】13 子曰:"道不远人,人之为道而远人,不可以为道[1]。诗云:'伐柯伐柯,其则不远。',执柯以伐柯,睨而视之,犹以为远。故君子以人治人,改而止[2]。忠恕违道不远,施诸己而不愿,亦勿施于人[3]。君子之道四,丘未能一焉;所求乎子,以事父未能也;所求乎臣以事君未能也;所求乎弟以事兄未能也;所求乎朋友,先施之未能也。庸德之行,庸言之谨,有所不足,不敢不勉,有余不敢尽;言顾行,行顾言,君子胡不慥慥尔[4]!"

【白话译文】

孔子说:"循本性而行叫道,道与别人的距离不远。有人违反天生的本性为高远难行的事而远离于人,这不是道。《诗经》上说:'砍斧柄呀砍斧柄,样子就在你眼前。'拿着斧柄来砍个斧柄,斜着眼睛看,还觉得不合标准很远。所以君子用人的准则治人,改正了为止,忠恕距道不远,加在自己头上不愿,也不加在别人头上。君子之道有四条,我没能做到一条,儿子的责任是服侍父母,我没做到;臣子的责任是服侍君主,我没做到;弟弟的礼节是服侍兄长,我没做到;朋友的礼节是先拜访有礼,我没做到。一般道德规范的践行和平常语言的谨慎有不足的地方不敢不努力弥补,有多余的话,不敢出口;言顾及行,行顾及言,君子岂不忠诚老实啊!"

【英语译文】

Confucius said, "It is called the Way to conduct according to the inborn nature and it's not far from others. Someone violates the inborn nature and leaves far away from others in order to reach great ambition. It isn't the Way. *Axe Handle* in *Ballads of Bin State* in *The Book of Songs* reads, 'How could you do just having axe-handle? / You could do nothing not having axe.' When one cuts an axe handle by another ax handle, he squints at it but feels it quite unstandardized. Therefore, moral men govern people by means of man's standard till correction. Loyalty and forgiveness aren't far from Way so that they aren't required for oneself or other people. Moral men's way concerns four aspects but I haven't reached anyone of them. A son's responsibility is to attend his parents, which I haven't shouldered. A courtier's responsibility is to serve his monarch, which I haven't shouldered. A younger brother's etiquette is to attend his elder brother, which I haven't observed. A friend's etiquette is to present gift before visiting, which I haven't observed. I dare not to make up the shortage of practicing moral norms and caution about speaking, and I fear to utter redundant words. I care about action while speaking and care about speech while acting. How couldn't moral men be loyal?"

【注释】(1)远:空间或时间的距离长;不接近。为道:矫性而为高远难行之事。(2)诗云两句:见《诗·豳风·伐柯》。柯:斧柄。则:法则。睨:nì,斜着眼(看),斜视。(3)忠恕:尽己之心为忠,推己及人为恕。违:相距,距离。(4)能:胜任,能做到。所求乎子:责成儿子的事。求,犹"责"。凡所以责人之事都属道义所当然。以:副词,乃(是)。先施:指先行拜访或馈赠礼物。庸德之行:常德(一般的道德规范)的践行。庸言之谨:常言(平常言语)的谨慎,有所不足,不敢不勉,有余不敢尽。言顾行:谨言顾及行。行顾言:力行顾及言。胡不:怎么不,岂不。慥慥:zàozào,笃实的样子。

【原文】14 君子素其位而行,不愿乎其外[1]。素富贵,行乎富贵;素贫贱,行乎贫贱;素夷狄,行乎夷狄;素患难,行乎患难;君子无入而不自得焉[2]。在上位不陵下,在下位不援上,正己而不求于人则无怨。上不怨天,下不尤人[3]。故君子居易以俟命,小人行险以徼幸[4]。子曰:"射有似乎君子;失诸正鹄;反求诸其身[5]。"

【白话译文】

君子是在现在的位置上干所当干的事,不羡慕别的什么。在富贵中,就干富贵所当干的事;在贫贱中,就干贫贱所当干的事;在少数民族中,就干少数民族所当干的事;在患难中,就干患难所当干的事;君子无论到哪里都能自我适应。在上头不欺侮下头的人,在下头不巴结上头的人;端正自己而不央求别人,就没有怨恨。上不怨恨天,下不怪罪人。所以君子处于平地等候天命,小人闯荡险阻窃夺不当得的东西。孔子说:"射箭有点像君子,没射中箭靶中心,就回头检查自身的问题。"

【英语译文】

A moral man does things that he should do in his present post but he doesn't admire other things. He does what he should do while being rich and noble. He does what he should do while being poor and humble. He does what he should do while being among ethnic minority. He does what he should do while being in adversity. A moral man can adjust himself wherever he goes. He doesn't bully his subordinate while he is in high post. He dosen't flatter his superordinate while he is in low post. He has no complaint when he corrects himself and dosen't beg others. He doesn't complain about the heaven and he doesn't blame other people. Therefore a moral man equally awaits the mandate of the Heaven. However, a mean man strives for unjustifiable gains. Confucius said, "Archery game is somewhat like a moral man. If one fails the bull's eye, he checks himself."

【注释】(1)素:犹见在(即"现在")朱熹四书集注:"素,犹见在也。言君子但因见在所居之位而为其所当为,无慕乎其外之心也。"愿:羡慕。(2)患难:huàn nàn,困难和危险的处境。无入:相当于"无往"。后与"不""非"连用,表示肯定。译作"无论到哪里都"。入,泛指往,至。(3)陵:侵犯,欺侮。援:攀援,依附权势往上爬。(4)居易:朱熹四书集注:"易,平地也。居易,素位而行也。"郑玄注:"易,犹平安也。"俟命:等候天命不羡慕其外。徼幸:jiǎoxìng,作非分企求。徼,求,幸,谓不当得而得者。(5)正鹄:zhēnggǔ,箭靶的中心。诸:介词,和"于"相同。

【原文】15 君子之道,辟如行远必自迩,辟如登高必自卑[1]。诗曰:"妻子好合,如鼓瑟琴;兄弟既翕,和乐且耽;宜尔室家,乐尔妻帑[2]。"子曰:"父母其顺矣乎[3]!"

【白话译文】

君子之道,譬如走远路,必须从近处开始,譬如登高,必须从低处起步[1]。诗经上说:"情投意合妻是宝,弹琴瑟和谐到老。兄弟情谊既融洽,和睦欢乐又安好。把你家庭安排好,妻子儿女常欢笑。"孔子说:"父母安乐阿!"

【英语译文】

The way of being a moral man is like walking on a long trip where he should sets off in near place and is like ascending a height where he should starts out at low place.

Chinese Bush Berry in *Lesser Odes* in *The Book of Songs* reads, "Having same ideal wife is so dear. Playing harmonious harp we live. We brothers feel glad and lucky. Passionate feelings go on peacefully. Please do your households orderly. Your wife and kids often wear smile." Confucius said, "The parents live happily and harmoniously."

【注释】(1)辟:同"譬"。迩:ěr,近。(2)诗曰六句:见《诗·小雅·常棣》。翕:xī,和合,聚合。耽:dān,诗作"湛",乐;沉湎。帑:nú,通"孥",儿女的通称。(3)顺:安乐。

【原文】16 子曰:"鬼神之为德,其盛矣乎[1]?视之而弗见,听之而弗闻,体物而不可遗[2]。使天下之人齐明盛服,以承祭祀。洋洋乎!如在其上,如在其左右[3]。诗曰:'神之格思,不可度思!矧可射思[4]!'夫微之显诚之不可掩如此夫[5]。"

【白话译文】

孔子说:"鬼神的性情功效,是很大的么?看,却看不见,听,也听不见,鬼神之道,生成万物无不周遍,无所缺失。使天下的人感恩不尽,都斋戒沐浴,静心洁身,盛饰衣服按时祭祀。小心翼翼呀!好像就在头上,好像就在左右前后。诗经上说:'神灵何时将来到,不可猜测起坏心,何况一直胡乱行。'隐微的暴露,真实无妄就是像这样不可掩盖。"

【英语译文】

Confucius said, "Do gods and ghosts have great influence? We can't see them. We can't hear them, either. The way of gods and ghosts considerately produce all things without any defects. What they do makes people be grateful and calm, take shower, fast and hold sacrificial ceremony in beautiful gown periodically. People are so cautious that gods and ghosts seem to stay above or around." *Dignified Appearance* in *Greater Odes* in *The Book of Songs* reads, 'When the gods will come to you? /Do not make plots by your guess. /Let alone you are doing wrong things.' Once the hidden part is exposed then the actuality can not be covered."

【注释】(1)鬼神:古代指天地间一种精气的聚散变化。朱熹四书集注:"愚谓以二气(阴阳二气)言,则鬼者阴之灵也,神者阳之灵也。以一气(混沌之气)言则至而伸者为神,反而归者为鬼,其实一物而已。"为德:犹言性情功效。(2)体物:生成万物;体现于万事万物中。不可遗:郑玄注:"体,犹生也;可,犹所也。"孔颖达疏:"言鬼神之道生养万物无不周遍,而不有所遗;言万物无不以鬼神之气生也。"(3)齐明盛服:zhāi ~ ~ ~,谓在祭祀前斋戒沐浴,静心洁身,盛饰衣服。洋洋:yǎng yǎng,同"养养"。忧思不安的样子。(4)诗曰三句:见诗·大雅·抑。格:来。思:语气词,用于句末相当"啊"。度:duó,揣测。矧:shěn,况且,而况。射:yì,"斁"的古字。厌弃。(5)诚:真实无妄。

【原文】17 子曰:"舜其大孝也与!德为圣人,尊为天子,富有四海之内。宗庙飨之,子孙保之[1]。故大德必得其位,必得其禄,必得其名,必得其寿[2]。故天之生物,必因其材而笃焉。故栽者培之,倾者覆之[3]。诗曰:'嘉乐君子,宪宪令德!宜民宜人,受禄于天;保佑命之,自天申之[4]!'故大德者必受命[5]。"

【白话译文】

孔子说:"舜算得上大孝了吧!讲品德成了圣人,讲尊贵做了天子,讲财富拥有四海之内。有宗庙祭享他,有后代子孙保护他。所以有大德的人必然得到他应有的地位,必然得到他应有的爵禄,必然得到他应有的名声,必然得到他应有的寿命。所以上天对他所生的万物必定针对其资质加厚,种植的东西培养它成长,倾倒的东西挽救它复起。《诗经》上说:'可敬可爱周成王,美德鲜明如日光!善于安民善用人,受天赐禄万事昌;保佑臣民合理用,全本天意作主张!'所以有大德的人一定受天命为天子。"

【英语译文】

Confucius said, "Great Shun could be the most filial one. He became sage due to virtue, and he became the son of the heaven due to nobility, and he possessed all land due to wealth. There were temples to sacrifice him and there were his offspring who protect him. Therefore a most virtuous man surely obtains a post which he should get, and he surely gets his nobility title and rewards, and he surely becomes famous, and also he surely lives long. Therefore the heaven certainly bestows talent to things that it produces, and the heaven certainly saves those from falling down." *Praise* in *Greater Odes* in *The Book of Songs* reads, "Admirable and respectable is the king. /His morality shines like sun lighting. /He is good at using, calming persons. /Things go on well for heaven blesses. /Ministers and people are protected. /He acts according to heaven's will." Therefore the most virtuous man surely becomes the son of the heaven.

【注释】(1)其:副词,表论断,犹"乃"。子孙:谓虞思、陈胡公之属。(2)寿:舜年一百一十岁。(3)材:资质,本能。笃:加厚,深厚。栽:种植。培:孳息,培养。倾:倾倒。覆:庇护,挽救。(4)诗曰:见《诗·大雅·假乐》。嘉乐:诗作"假乐"。嘉,赞美。乐,喜爱。君子:指周成王。宪宪:诗作"显显",光明的样子。令德:美德。宜民宜人:能安民能用人。宜:适宜。民:庶民。人:指在位的贵族。保佑:诗作"保右"。命:差遣。(5)受命:受天命为天子。

【原文】18 子曰:"无忧者其惟文王乎!以王季为父,以武王为子,父作之,子述之[1]。武王纘大王王季文王之绪。壹戎衣而有天下,身不失天下之显名。尊为天子,富有四海之内。宗庙飨之,子孙保之[2]。武王末受命,周公成文武之德,追王大王,王季,上祀先公以天子之礼。斯礼也,达乎诸侯大夫,及士庶人。父为大夫,子为士;葬以大夫,祭以士。父为士,子为大夫;葬以士,祭以大夫。期之丧达乎大夫,三年之丧达乎天子,父母之丧,无贵贱一也[3]。"

【白话译文】

孔子说:"没有忧虑的人也许只有文王啊!由于王季是他父亲,又因为武王是他儿子,父亲为他做了积功累仁的事,儿子继承了他的事业。武王继承了古公亶父、王季和文王遗留下来没有完毕的事业。一振军威灭了殷纣。自己没失掉天下显耀的名声。做了尊贵的天子,财富拥有四海之内。宗庙祭享他,子孙保护他。武王年老受命为天子,周公成就了文王和武王的仁政。还追尊太王和王季为王,还以天子之礼祭祀组绀以上至后稷诸位先公。这种礼推行到了诸侯大夫,及士庶人。父亲是大夫,儿子是士,用大夫的礼数安葬父亲,用士的礼数祭祀父亲。父亲是士,儿子是大夫,用士的礼数安葬父亲,用大夫的礼数祭祀父亲。"

【英语译文】

Confucius said, "Only King Wen of Zhou Dynasty never worried about anything. Wang Ji was his father who accumulated virtue and humanity for him, and King Wu was his son who inherited his cause. King Wu inherited the great cause that hadn't been completed by Dan Fu, Wang Ji and King Wen. He led his troops to wipe out Shang Dynasty and he didn't lose his brilliant fame. He became the Son of the Heaven and he possessed the wealth among the whole land and seas. There were temples to sacrifice him and there were his offspring who protect him. King Wu became the Son of the Heaven when he was old and Duke Zhou helped King Wen and King Wu to carry out government of humanity. Tai Wang and Wang Ji were given posthumous title as ‘King’, and great grandfathers from Hou Ji to Zu Gan were also sacrificed as ‘King’. Such kind of ritual was spread to princes, ministers, scholars, and common men. When father was a minister and son was a scholar, father was buried as ‘minister’ and sacrificed by rites of scholar. When father was a scholar and son was a minister, father was buried as ‘scholar’ and sacrificed by rites of minister.”

【注释】(1)其:副词,表推测估计。以:连词,表原因或理由。相当于“因为”“由于”。(2)纘:zuǎn,继承。大王:tài ~,太王。王季之父,文王之祖古公亶父的尊号。绪:前人未竟的功业。壹戎衣:戎衣即军服,战衣。意谓一穿上军服而灭纣。末:老,老年。成德:成就仁政。德,善行,仁爱,仁政。追王:谓在某人身后追尊为王。先公:朱熹四书集注:“先公,组绀以上至后稷也。”斯礼:这种礼法。礼法之一,使葬用死者之爵,祭用生者之禄。(3)期:jī,一周年。期服的省称。期服,服丧一年。

【原文】19 子曰:“武王、周公,其達孝矣乎[1]!夫孝者:善继人之志,善述人之事者也[2]。春秋修其祖庙,陈其宗器,设其裳衣,荐其时食[3]。宗庙之礼,所以序昭穆也;序爵,所以辨贵贱也;序事,所以辨贤也;旅酬下为上,所以逮贱也;燕毛,所以序齿也[4]。践其位,行其礼,奏其乐,敬其所尊,爱其所亲,事死如事生,事亡如事存,孝之至也[5]。郊社之礼,所以事上帝也,宗庙之礼,所以祀乎其先也。明乎郊社之礼、禘尝之义,治国其如示诸掌乎[6]。”

【白话译文】

孔子说:“武王和周公,他们的孝道和通常讲的孝道是一样的呀!尽孝的人,善于继承前人的遗志,善于继续前人的事业。春秋两季整修其祖庙,陈列保藏下来的重器,陈设留下的先祖衣裳,奉献应时的食品。宗庙的礼制,用来排列神主;排列子孙在祭祀活动中的站位;排列公、侯、卿、大夫的爵位,用来分辨贵贱;排列宗伯、太祝各官吏的职事,用来分辨贤良;祭礼完毕后下辈和上辈一起相互敬酒这叫旅酬之礼,用来把恩惠施展到地位低下的人;祭毕宴席依毛发的颜色分长幼定席位,用来排列年龄尊敬老人。登先王的位,行先王的礼,奏先王的乐,敬先王尊敬的人,爱先王亲近的人,侍奉死了的人像侍奉在生的人一样,侍奉不在世的祖宗像侍奉在世的祖宗一样，这是最大的孝道了。郊社的祭礼，用来服侍上帝，宗庙的祭礼，用来敬奉祖先。明白郊社和禘尝的礼义，治国就像看自己的手掌一样容易。”

【英语译文】

Confucius said, “The filial piety of King Wu and Duke Zhou was the same as that of ordinary people. A filial man is adept at inheriting the will and cause of his predecessor. In spring and autumn people rebuild their ancestors’ temple, display treasure and clothes left by their ancestors, and devote seasonal food. The ritual rule is used to arrange spirit tablet and the standing post of offspring, to arrange the hierarchy of duke, marquis, earl, and minister, to distinguish nobility from humbleness, to arrange the responsibilities of officials belonging to *zongbo* and *taizhu*, to differentiate the virtuous and talented, to show mercy to people in low position after toast between superiors and inferiors, to show respect fer the elders after sacrificial ceremony since people’s place at table is set according to their hair’s color. It is the utmost way of filial piety to ascend throne of passed king, to conduct rites of passed king, to play music of passed king, to respect those whom passed king respected, to love those whom passed king loved, to serve the dead in the same way serving the alive, to serve the dead forefathers in the same way serving the living ones. The heaven and earth sacrificial ceremony is to serve the god, and the temple sacrificial ceremony is to serve forefathers. If one understands the heaven and earth and the temple sacrificial ceremonies, he will administrates his state as easily as turning his palms.”

【注释】(1)達孝：天下人通常所说的孝。与孟子说的達尊的“达”同义。一说达通“大”，達孝即大孝。(2)述人之事：继续前人事业。(3)祖庙：天子七，诸侯五，大夫三，适士二，官师一。适，读 dí。宗器：宗庙祭器。朱熹四书集注：“宗器，先世所藏的重器；若周之赤刀、大训、天球、河图之属也。”裳衣：先祖之遗衣服，祭祀时授尸着以受祭。时食：四季应时的食品。(4)所以：用以，用来。序：同“叙”，次序，按次序区分、排列。昭穆：古代宗法制度，宗庙或宗庙中神主的排列次序，始祖居中，以下父子(祖、父)迭为昭穆，左为昭右为穆。事：指宗伯、太祝各官吏的职事。旅酬：祭礼完毕后，众亲宾一起宴饮，相互敬酒。下为上：下辈与上辈。为，连词，与、和。逮贱：dài～，义同“逮下”。谓恩惠及于下贱的人。燕毛：祭毕而宴，以毛发的颜色别长幼定座次 。燕，通“宴”。齿：年龄。(5)践其位：践，履。其，指先王。位,特指天子或王侯之位。践位(践其位),犹言登基,即位。所尊所亲:指先王的祖考、子孙、臣庶。(6)郊:祀天。社:祭地。禘:dì,天子宗庙的大祭。尝:秋祭。四时皆祭,举一为例。示:通“视”。视诸掌,谓易见。

【原文】20 哀公问政[1]。子曰:“文武之政,布在方策。其人存,则其政举;其人亡,则其政息[2]。人道敏政,地道敏树。夫政也者,蒲卢也[3]。故为政在人,取人以身,修身以道,修道以仁[4]。仁者人也,亲亲为大;义者宜也,尊贤为大;亲亲之杀,尊贤之等,礼所生也[5]。在下位不获乎上,民不可得而治矣[6]!故君子不可以不修身;思修身,不可以不事亲;思事亲,不可以不知人;思知人,不可以不知天[7]。”天下之达道五,所以行之者三:曰君臣也,父子也,夫妇也,昆弟也,朋友之交也;五者天下之达道也。知、仁、勇三者,天下之达德也,所以行之者一也[8]。或生而知之,或学而知之,或困而知之,及其知之一也;或安而行之,或利而行之,或勉强而行之,及其成功一也[9]。子曰:“好学近乎知,力行近乎仁,知耻近乎勇[10]。知斯三者,则知所以修身,知所以修身,则知所以治人;知所以治人,则知所以治天下国家矣[11]。”凡为天下国家有九经,曰:修身也,尊贤也,亲亲也,敬大臣也,体群臣也,子庶民也,来百工也,柔远人也,怀诸侯也[12]。修身则道立,尊贤则不惑,亲亲则诸父昆弟不怨,敬大臣则不眩,体群臣则士之报礼重,子庶民则百姓劝,来百工则财用足,柔远人则四方归之,怀诸侯则天下畏之[13]。齐明盛服非礼不动,所以修身也;去谗远色,贱货而贵德,所以劝贤也;尊其位,重其禄,同其好恶所以劝亲亲也;官盛任使,所以劝大臣也;忠信重禄,所以劝士也;时使薄敛,所以劝百姓也;日省月试,既禀称事,所以劝百工也;送往迎来,嘉善而矜不能,所以柔远人也;继绝世举废国,治乱持危,朝聘以时厚往而薄来,所以怀诸侯也[14]。凡为天下国家有九经,所以行之者一也[15]。凡事豫则立,不豫则废。言前定则不跲,事前定则不困,行前定则不疚,道前定则不穷[16]。在下位而不获乎上,民不可得而治矣;获乎上有道:不信乎朋友,不获乎上矣;信乎朋友有道:不顺乎亲,不信乎朋友矣;顺乎亲有道:反诸身不诚,不顺乎亲矣;诚身有道:不明乎善,不诚乎身矣[17]。诚者天之道也;诚之者,人之道也。诚者,不勉而中,不思而得,从容中道,圣人也。诚之者,择善而固执之者也[18]。博学之,审问之,慎思之,明辨之,笃行之[19]。有弗学,学之弗能弗措也;有弗问,问之弗知弗措也;有弗思,思之弗得弗措也;有弗辨,辨之弗明弗措也;有弗行,行之弗笃弗措也;人一能之己百之,人十能之己千之[20]。果能此道矣,虽愚必明,虽柔必强[21]。”

【白话译文】

鲁哀公问政事。孔子说:“文王和武王的政事,都公开记在典册上。他们在世时政事相当兴旺;他们去世了,政事就停息了。人的生活道路对于政事勤勉快速,地的运载道路对于生长草木勤勉快速。政事嘛,就像蒲苇一样,易于生长,易于更新。所以治理政事在于得到贤人,要得贤人就靠自身的感召力,就得修身,修身就用天下通常的达道,修道就用仁。仁就是人品和才学,亲爱亲人为第一;义就是适宜,尊敬贤人为第一;亲爱亲人的疏密和尊敬贤人的等差,如何算适宜,礼就因此而产生。在下位得不到上面的信任,就不可能治理民众了。所以君子不可以不修身;想修身,不可以不侍奉父母;想侍奉父母,不可以不知人伦;想知人伦,不可以不知道天。"天下通行的常道有五条,用来实行这五条常道的德性有三种。五条常道是:君臣道、父子道、夫妇道、昆弟道、朋友的交道,这五条道路是天下通行的常道。智慧、仁爱、勇敢这三种德性是天下通行的常德,支撑这三种德性的根本是诚实无欺,有些人不经过学习就知道,有些人学习了才知道,有些人克服了困难后才知道,只要知道了结果都一样。有些人出于自愿安心实行。有些人知其有利而实行,有些人尽力实行,只要成功,结果都一样 。孔子又说:"喜欢学习接近于智能,努力实行,接近于仁爱,知耻接近于勇敢。知道了这三个接近的意义和作用,便知道用来修身;知道用来修身,便知道用来治理人民;知道用来治理人民,便知道用来治理天下国家了。"大概治理天下国家有九条常道,它们是:修养心身、尊敬贤人、亲爱亲人、尊敬大臣、体念群臣、爱民如子、劝勉各种工匠、安抚远方的人、安抚诸侯。修养心身,就能稳定道路不致失足,尊敬贤人就能避免迷惑慌神,亲爱亲人、叔叔、兄弟、姊妹不怀怨恨,尊敬大臣就能避免临事动摇花眼神,体念群臣就能让小臣士人落实责任,爱民如子就能让百姓勤勉各自的事,劝勉各种工匠就能使农业副业互相资助,财用充足,安抚远方的人就能使四方来归,安抚诸侯就能广施德威,让他人不得轻举妄动。端庄严明,衣冠不苟,不合礼制,绝不行动,用以修身;摒弃谗佞和女色,不重财货重德行,用以鼓励贤人。尊重地位,尊重俸禄,认同爱好,用以鼓励亲爱亲人;设置足够令使的官吏,细事不烦大臣,用以鼓励大臣;忠厚信实的人,提高薪俸,用以鼓励士人;使民不误农时,赋税从轻,用以鼓励百姓;天天考察省视,月月考核成绩,发给的月俸粮食同事功相称,用以鼓励各种工匠;送走离境的客人,迎接来访的客人,称赞那些善良的客人,同情那些缺才少能的客人,用以安抚远方的人;恢复绝灭的宗祀,承续断绝的后代,让灭掉的国家复兴起来,治理乱世扶持危局,坚持诸侯定时正常朝聘,宴会赏赐从厚,接受贡礼从薄,用以安抚诸侯。大概治理天下国家有九条常道,用来践行这九条常道的原动力是诚实无欺。不论什么事,事先预备就能办成,事先不预备就办不成。说话前有准备,就不会凝滞不通,做事前有准备,就不会困惑,行路前有准备就不会困苦,选择道路前有准备,就不会没有前途。在下位得不到上面的信任,就不可能治理民众了。

取得上面的信任有办法:得不到朋友的信任,就得不到上面的信任;取得朋友的信任有办法:不顺父母的心,就得不到朋友的信任;取得父母顺心有办法:反求自身不诚实,就得不到父母顺心;使自身诚实有办法:不明白什么是善,自身就不诚实了。诚实,是天的常道;使自己诚实是人的常道。诚实的人,不努力就符合诚实,不须思考就得到诚实,举动符合常道,这是圣人。使自己诚实的人,是向善而且坚持不变的人。广泛地学习,深入地探讨,谨慎地思考,明确地分辨,切实地履行。或许没学,学了没通,不要搁置;或许没问,问了没懂,不要搁置;或许没思考,思考了无所得,不要搁置;或许没分辨,分辨了不明确,不要搁置;或许没履行,履行不切实,不要搁置;人家一次能办到的,自己就百次去办;人家十次能办到的,自己就千次去办,真能这样做,即使愚昧,必然聪明,即使柔弱,必然刚强。"

【英语译文】

Duke Ai of Lu State asked about administrative affairs. Confucius said, "The administrative affairs of King Wen and King Wu were all recorded. When they were alive, administrative affairs went very smoothly; after they died, administrative affairs went to a stop. A man's life journey goes fast concerning diligent administrative affairs, and the earth's carrying journey goes fast concerning trees and grasses' growing. Administrative affairs is easy to grow and renew just as reeds do. Therefore administration lies in obtaining virtuous men; obtaining virtuous men lies in one's own emotional appeal. One should nurture himself. While nurturing himself, one uses the Way, and while cultivating the Way one uses humanity. Humanity consists of moral quality and talent and learning and loving kinsfolk goes first. Righteousness means appropriateness and respecting virtuous men goes first. Rites come into being to decide to what extent can people love kinsfolk and respect virtuous men. When the inferiors cannot be trusted by their superiors, then common people cannot be governed. Therefore a moral man must nurturing himself. When he wants to nurture himself, he must attend his parents. When he wants to attend his parents, he must comprehend human relations. When he wants to comprehend human relations, he must know about the Heaven." There are five constant Ways and there are three virtues being used to conduct the Ways. The five constant Ways are way of king-courtier, way of father-son, way of husband-wife, way of elder-younger brothers, way of making friends. These are the prevalently constant ways. Wisdom, humanity and courage are three prevalently constant virtues. What supports the virtues is honesty. Some people know it without learning. Other people know it after learning. Others know it after overcoming difficulties. The result is the same only if they know it. Some people carry it out willingly. Other people carry it out since they know they can benefit from it. Others try their best to carry it out. The result is the same only if they carry it out. Confucius said again, "Loving to learn approaches wisdom, carrying it out approaches humanity, and knowing shame approaches courage. If one knows their meaning and usage, then he will use them to nurture himself. If one uses them to nurture himself then he will use them to govern common people. If one uses them to govern common people, then he will use them to administrate his state. There are nine constant ways to administrate state and they are nurturing oneself physically and mentally, respecting virtuous and talented men, loving one's parents and kinsfolk, respecting the courtiers, considering all ministers, loving people as one's kids, admonishing various craftsmen, consoling people in remote, and consoling all feudal princes. Nurturing oneself physically and mentally can make one walk on the right road. Respecting virtuous and talented men can avoid confusion. Loving one's parents and kinsfolk can make one's uncles, brothers, and sisters have no complaint. Respecting the courtiers can avoid waving and faltering at big affairs. Considering all ministers can make lower officials shoulder their responsibilities. Loving people as one's kids can make common people work diligently. Admonishing various craftsmen can make all business help each other so as to accumulate wealth. Consoling people in remote can make others in all places submit to your authority. Consoling all feudal princes can spread one's power and benevolence and make them stay in his own posts and places. When one nurtures himself, he conducts modestly and never acts out of rites. When one encourages virtuous men, he rids of slander and sex and doesn't pay attention to wealth. When one encourages loving relatives, he respect other's post and salary and recognizes other's preference. When one encourages the courtiers, he arranges enough officials to deal with trivial affairs. When one encourages scholars, he raises loyal and honest men's pay. When one encourages common people he dosen't hold up farming and levy less while using people. When one encourages various craftsmen, he inspects each day and examines each month and he makes craftsmen's pay meet their achievements. When one consoles people in remote, he sees off the guests who depart, welcomes the guests who arrive, praises the kind guests, and sympathizes the in – talented guests. When one consoles feudal princes, he recovers the demolished temples, connects the broken offspring, revives the extinguished states, makes chaotic situation go in order, insists that princes hold official intercourse periodically, rewards people much in feast, receives less tribute. There are nine constant ways to administrate state and the motivation to carry out them is honesty. Whatever can be done if we prepare beforehandedly and it cannot be done if we don't. Before speaking if we make preparation then we don't hesitate. Before doing if we make preparation then we don't get confused. Before walking if we make preparation we don't get hindered. Before choosing road if we make preparation we don't have no future. If subordinates can't be trusted by superordinates, then common people cannot be governed. There is the method to get trusted by superordinates, i. e. if one can't be trusted by his friends then he can't be trusted by his superordinates. There is the method to get trusted by friends, i. e. if one can't follow his parents' will, then he can't be trusted by friends. There is method to follow one's parents' will, i. e. if one isn't honest, then he can't follow his parents' will. There is the method to be honest, i. e. if one doesn't know what is philanthropic, then he can't be honest. Being honest is the constant way of the Heaven. Making oneself honest is the constant way of human being. An honest man accords to the constant way without trying hard and he gets honesty without thinking over. It's sage whose actions accord to the constant way. A man who makes himself honest is one who intends to be kind and never changes. He learns knowledge widely, explores issues deeply, thinks about questions cautiously, distinguishes things clearly, and carries out task conscientiously. Perhaps one doesn't learn or doesn't comprehend even if he has done. But don't put it aside. Perhaps one doesn't consult or doesn't comprehend even if he has done. But don't put it aside. Perhaps one doesn't think it over or doesn't get anything even if he has done. But don't put it aside. Perhaps one doesn't distinguish things or doesn't do it clearly even if he has done. But don't put it aside. Perhaps one doesn't carry out his task or doesn't do it conscientiously even if he has done. But don't put it aside. If others manage to do anything in one time, he does it in one hundred times. If others manage to do anything in ten times, he does it in one thousand times. If one really does so he will surely be clever even if he is foolish, and he will surely be strong even if he is weak."

【注释】(1)哀公:鲁君,名蒋。(2)布:陈述,抒写。方:版。策:简。息:犹灭。朱熹四书集注:"有是君,有是臣,则有是政矣。"(3)人道:为人的途径。地道:大地的特征与规律。敏:快速。蒲卢:朱熹四书集注:"蒲卢,沈括以为蒲苇是也。以人立政犹以地种树,其成速矣,而蒲苇又易生之物,其成尤速也。言人存政举,其易如此。"(4)在人:家语作"在于得人"。意思更明豁。意谓在于得贤臣。身:指君身。道:天下之达道,公认的准则。仁:天地万物相生之德。(5)杀:shài,减少,降等。等:等级,等列。人:指人身而言。谓人品才学。(6)获:得到信任。郑玄曰:"此句在下误重在此。"(7)知天:为政在人,取人以身,故不可以不修身。修身以道,修道以仁,故思修身不可以不事亲。欲尽亲亲之仁必由尊贤之义故又当知人。亲亲之杀,尊贤之等,都是天理,故又当知天。(8)达道:天下古今所共由之路。即书所谓五典,孟子所谓"父子有亲、君臣有义、夫妇有别、长幼有序、朋友有信"。知:同"智"。智者理解达道,仁者效法达道,勇者强行达道。达德:天下古今所同得的理;通行不变的德。(9)安行:谓发于本愿从容不迫地实行。利行:知道有利而行。勉强:尽力而为。(10)好学近乎知,力行近乎仁,知耻近乎勇:接近于智慧可以破愚,接近仁,可以忘私,接近勇敢,可以起懦。(11)斯三者:指三接近而言。(12)凡:大略,大要,大概。为:治理。经:常。体:体念,体贴。子:如父母之爱其子。来:lài,劝勉。柔:安,安抚。远人:远方的人。指外国人或外族人。怀:与"柔"同义。(13)不惑:谓不疑于理。不眩:谓不迷于事。报礼:报答之礼。(14)齐明盛服:zhāi ~ ~ ~,谓在祭祀前斋戒沐浴,静心洁身,盛饰衣服,亦承祭祀。明,犹洁,洁净。官盛任使:谓官属众盛,足任使令。日省月试:~ xǐng ~ ~,每天考察或省视和每月考核。既禀:xìlǐn,同"饩廪",古代官府按月发给的作为月薪的粮食。亦泛称薪俸。薪俸事:与事功相称(事功大,粮食多;反之则少。)送往迎来:指应酬外国人或外族人。嘉善而矜不能:赞美善人,同情没有才能的人。矜,读 jīn,怜悯,同情。继绝世:谓恢复已灭绝的宗祀,承续已断绝的后代。举废国:犹兴灭国。谓让被灭掉的国家复兴起来。治乱持危:治乱世和扶持危局。朝聘以时:按规定的时间朝聘。朝,谓诸侯见于天子。聘,谓诸侯使大夫来献。《礼记·王制》:"诸侯之于天子也,比年一小聘,三年一大聘,五年一朝。"厚往而薄来:谓燕赐厚而纳贡薄。(15)所以行之者一也:一,专一,纯一。训"诚"。(16)凡事:不论什么事。豫:yù,预备,在事前作准备。前定:预先确定;事先准备。跲:jiá,窒碍不顺。困:困惑。疚:jiù,困苦,劳苦。(17)乎:介词,相当于"于"。(18)而中、中道:而zhòng,zhōng 道。中,符合的意思。从容中道:举动合道。(19)博学之,审问之,慎思之,明辨之,笃行之:广泛地学习,深入地探讨,谨慎地思考,明确地分辨,切实地履行,是君子完整的学行过程,缺一不可。(20)有:用同"或"。1)代词,有人,有的。2)或许。弗:副词。不。不能。表示否定。"弗"与"不"都表示否定,"不"的范围较广,"弗"后面的动词不跟宾语。措:cuò,弃置;搁置。(21)人的气质略有差异,君子之学可以转化其间差异。

【原文】21 自诚明[1],谓之性[2];自明诚,谓之教[3]。诚则明矣。明则诚矣。

【白话译文】

由诚实而明白,是本性的作用;由明白而诚实,是教化的作用。诚实就明白了。明白就诚实了。

【英语译文】

It's the function of human nature for someone to understand something if he is honest. It's the function of education for someone to be honest if he understands something. If one is honest then he understands things. If one understands things, he is honest.

【注释】(1)自:介词。由;从。明:明了,明白。(2)谓:通"为"。是,因为。(3)教:教化。之:助词,用以调整音节。

【原文】22 唯天下至诚[1],为能尽其性[2];能尽其性,则能尽人之性[3],则能尽物之性;能尽物之性,则可以赞天地之化育;可以赞天地之化育[4],则可以与天地参矣[5]。

【白话译文】

只有天下圣人才能发挥自己的本性;能发挥自己的本性,就能发挥别人的本性;能发挥别人的本性,就能发挥物的本性;能发挥物的本性,就可以帮助天地的生化长育;可以帮助天地的生化长育,就可以与天地并立而三:天、地、圣人。

【英语译文】

Only the sages can develop their inborn nature. If one can develop his inborn nature, then he can develop others' inborn nature. If one can develop man's inborn nature, he can develop things' inborn nature. If one can develop things' inborn nature, he can help heaven and earth to produce and raise things. If one can help heaven and earth to produce and raise things, then he can stand together with heaven and earth, i. e. heaven, earth and sage.

【注释】(1)至诚:谓圣人诚实之德已到顶点不能再加,因以至诚指圣人。(2)为:副词,乃,才。尽其性:全部使出自己的本性。人和物的性都包含天理,只有至诚的人,才能发挥人和物的本性使各得其所。(3)人:旁人,别人。(4)赞:辅佐,帮助。化育:生化长育。(5)与天地参:谓与天地并立而三。

【原文】23 其次致曲[1],曲能有诚,诚则形,形则着,着则明,明则动,动则变,变则化,[2]唯天下至诚为能化。

【白话译文】

不及圣人的人,从大贤以下,能把局部的诚实推求到最高程度。局部能诚实,诚实就积聚成形,形就露于外,形露于外就光辉动人,动人就起变,变就自然而化。只有天下圣人能化,由积聚诚实而至于能化,也不异于圣人了。

【英语译文】

A man who can't match sage can enlarge limited honesty to the utmost degree. A limited honesty accumulates to certain form, which is displayed outwards. When form is displayed outwards, it becomes shining and moving, which in turn enhances change. And change naturally transforms. Only sages can produce. If one can accumulate honesty and produce, he equalizes sages.

【注释】(1)其次:次第较后,第二。指整个大贤以下所有未到至诚境界的人而言。致:推化致,谓推求到最高程度。曲:一偏,犹局部,片面。(2)化:化育。

【原文】24 至诚之道,可以前知[1]。国家将兴,必有祯祥[2];国家将亡,必有妖孽[3]。见乎蓍龟[4],动乎四体[5]。祸福将至:善,必先知之;不善,必先知之。故至诚如神[6]。

【白话译文】

最高诚实的方法,可以事先知道事物发展的倾向。国家将会兴盛,必定会出现一些好苗头;国家将会灭亡,必定会出现一些物类反常的现象。好苗头或反常现象,有的或出现在占卜中,有的或直接触动人身。祸福将要来临时:好,必定先知道;不好,也必定先知道。所以最高诚实就像神灵一样。

【英语译文】

The method of utmost honesty can predict the tendency of thing's developing process. If a state will prosper there surely appears some good symptoms; and if a state will perish, there surely appears some extraordinary phenomena. Good symptoms or extraordinary phenomena sometimes appear in divination, and sometimes touch people. When happiness or disasters approach, we should know either good or bad. Therefore utmost honesty is like soul and spirit.

【注释】(1)前知:事先知道,有预见。(2)祯祥:吉祥的先兆。(3)妖孽:yāoniè,物类反常的现象。(4)见:同“现”。蓍:shī,多年生草本植物。古代用以筮卜。龟:guī,爬行动物的一科,生命力强。古代用其甲占卜。(5)动:震动,触动。四体:四肢。引申指整个身体。(6)神:神灵。

【原文】25 诚者自成也,而道自道也[1]。诚者物之终始,不诚无物[2]。是故君子诚之为贵[3]。诚者非自成己而已也,所以成物也[4]。成己,仁也;成物,知也[5]。性之德也,合外内之道也,故时措之宜也[6]。

【白话译文】

诚实不欺是自我成就,而道路是自我开发。诚实不欺始终同人物并存,没有诚实不欺就没有人物。因此君子贵重诚实不欺。诚实不欺,不是只成就自己而已,而是要使身外的一切有所成就。成就自己是仁德,成就外物是智慧。本性的道德,是外表与内心合一的道德。所以适时使用因时制宜。

【英语译文】

Being honest and not cheating is self accomplishment and path is self development. Being honest and not cheating coexists with man from beginning to the end. When there isn't honesty but is cheating, there isn't man. Therefore moral men cherish being honest and not cheating. Being honest and not cheating not only accomplishes oneself but also makes all things accomplished outside oneself. Accomplishing onself is virtue and humanity and accomplishing things is wisdom. The virtue of inborn nature is that appearance is identical with heart. Therefore appropriate use is adopting measures according to time.

【注释】(1)自成:成就自我。自道:~dǎo,同“自导”。谓自我开发。(2)诚者物之终始:谓诚实与物并存。不诚无物:没有这诚实便没有这物。(3)是故:连词,因此,所以。(4)成己:成就自己。成物:使身外的一切有所成就。(5)知也:智也。(6)性之德也:合外内之道也。时措:“郑玄注:‘时措,言得其时而用也。’”谓适时使用。

【原文】26 故至诚无息,[1]不息则久,久则征[2],征则悠远,悠远则博厚,博厚则高明[3]。博厚,所以载物也;高明,所以覆物也;悠久,所以成物也[4]。博厚配地,高明配天,悠久无疆[5]。如此者,不见而章,不动而变,无为而成[6]。天地之道,可一言而尽也;其为物不贰,则其生物不测[7]。天地之道:博也,厚也,高也,明也,悠也,久也[8]。今夫天,斯昭昭之多,及其无穷也,日月星辰系焉,万物覆焉。今夫地,一撮土之多,及其广厚,载华岳而不重,振河海而不泄,万物载焉。今夫山,一卷石之多,及其广大,草木生之,禽兽居之,宝藏兴焉。今夫水,一勺之多,及其不测,鼋鼍、蛟龙、鱼鳖生焉,货财殖焉[9]。诗云:“维天之命,于穆不已!”盖曰天之所以为天也。于乎不显!文王之德之纯!盖曰文王之所以为文王也,纯亦不已[10]。

【白话译文】

所以最高的诚实不欺没有间断的时候。不间断就长久存于内心中,长久存于内心中就必然验证于外,验证于外就悠远了,悠远了就宽广厚实起来,宽广厚实了就高大光明起来。宽广厚实,能够承载万物,高大光明,能够覆盖万物;悠远长久,能够成就万物,宽广厚实与地并列,高大光明与天并列,悠远长久就无时空限制。像这样的人,不显示就鲜明,不行动就变化身外物,不作为就成就身外物。天地的规律,可以概括为:它们对于人物诚实不欺又神秘地生出无数不同的物事。天地的规律有六个要点:宽广、厚实、高大、光明、悠远、长久。说到天,似乎就是眼前一片明亮的范围那么大,到后来找不到它的边,才知道空旷无底,日月星辰都在天上,天覆盖着万物。说到地,似乎就是眼前一片土地,到后来才知道它宽广厚实没边际,承载华山一类山岳如羽毛,收取黄河沧海而不泄漏。说到山,似乎就是眼前一些岩石,到后来才知道它也宽广高大,草木丛生,鸟兽聚居,宝藏丰富。说到水,似乎就像一勺水那么不起好多作用一样,到后来才知道水早就多到没法实测,鼋鼍、蛟龙、鱼鳖在其中滋生,货物财物不断增加。《诗经》上说:“常想天道在运行,肃静善美永不停。!”这是说天之所以为天,至诚不息。啊多么辉煌光明,文王的品德高尚纯真!这是说文王之所以为文王,循天道,无二无杂无停。

【英语译文】

Therefore there isn't pause for the utmost honest. When there isn't pause, it will store in heart permanently. When it stores in heart permanently, it must be verified outside. When it is verified outside, it will become quiet and remote. When it become quiet and remote, it will be spacious and thick. When it is spacious and thick, it becomes tall and brilliant. Being spacious and thick, the earth can hold all things, and being tall and brilliant, the heaven can cover all things. Being quiet, remote and permanent one can accomplish all things. Spaciousness and thickness coexist with the earth; tallness and brilliance coexist with the heaven, and there isn't limit for being quiet, remote and forever. A person like this will be bright without show, and will change things without action, and will accomplish things outside him by doing nothing. The law of the earth and the heaven can be generalized as that it produces various things honestly and secretly towards human beings. There are six key points concerning the law of the earth and the heaven, i. e. spaciousness, thickness, tallness, brilliance, remoteness and permanence. As for heaven, it seems to be a limited bright space in front of us, but later on we can't find it's boundary but find that it is spacious and endless. The sun ,the moon and the stars hang in the heaven, which covers all things. As for earth, it seems to be a piece of land in front of us, but later on, we find that it is spacious and endless. It holds mountains such as Huashan Mount just like a piece of feather, and it keeps Yellow River without leaking. As for mountains, they seem to be piles of rocks in front of us, but later on we find that they are high and spacious where trees and grasses grow, birds and beasts gather, and treasures abound. As for water, it seems to be as useless as a spoonful of it, but later on we find that it is unfathomable at the very beginning. It produces turtles, alligators, dragons, and fish. Consequently, goods and wealth accumulate continuously. *Divine Way* in *Zhou Hymns* in *The Book of Songs* reads, "I always think of Divine Way going. Dignified kind it has no stopping." That means the heaven is utmost honest, never stopping. O, how bright and brilliant, King Wen's virtue is so noble and so pure! That means KingWen followed the Divine Way without diverting, confusing or stopping.

【注释】(1)息:间断。(2)征:验证。(3)悠远:长久,久远。指空间距离的辽远。(4)所以:可以,能够。(5)配地、配天:谓与地(天)比并,与地(天)并列。(6)见:同"现"。(7)不贰:谓诚实不欺。不测:谓不知其所以然,神秘。(8)薄厚、高明、悠久:是天地六大不灭的规律。(9)今夫:俞樾解作发语词。见其古书疑义举例·古书发端之词例。斯:指示代词。此:这。以下地山水后省略了"斯"。昭昭:明亮。之:代词,这样,那样。多:数量大。振:收取,约束。卷:quán,通"圈"。郑玄注:"卷,犹区也。"朱熹四书集注:"卷,平声,区也。"区和圈都有"一定的范围内"的意义。(10)诗云:诗,指《诗·周颂·维天之命》。维:同"惟",想。于:wū,叹词。穆:深远。不显:pī~,同"丕显",大显。不通丕。盖:gài,语气助词。表议论的开始,常用在句首或段落的前面,甚至用在篇章的开头。现代汉语没有这种用法,可以去掉不译。

【原文】27 大哉圣人之道[1]!洋洋乎!发育万物,峻极于天[2]。优优大哉!礼仪三百,威仪三千[3]。待其人而后行[4]。故曰苟不至德,至道不凝焉[5]。故君子尊德性而道问学,致广大而尽精微,极高明而道中庸。温故而知新,敦厚以崇礼[6]。是故居上不骄,为下不倍,国有道其言足以兴,国无道其默足以容。诗曰:"既明且哲,以保其身。"其此之谓与[7]!

【白话译文】

伟大呀!圣人之道,与天道、地道并称;是人事、人伦、处世的法则。它既充足又扎实呀!萌发万物,生长万物,大体大用,如山触天。宽裕充足,美不胜收呀!礼仪的纲领八百条,礼仪的具体项目三千条。等待着贤人来实行。所以说只要没有大德,大道就不成立。所以君子恭敬地奉持天赋的善性,而且通过博学审问来培养本性以求达到博大渊深又极细微,达到崇高明睿又遵行中庸之道。温习学过的知识得到新的理解和体会,保持宽厚诚朴,尊崇礼仪。因此居上位不骄傲,做下属不背离,国家政治清明,君子的言论,足够兴起在位的人,国家政治混乱,君子的沉默,足够容身。《诗经》上说"知识渊博明大理,立身正派挡恶浪。"就是说的这个意思吧!

【英语译文】

O, great! The way of sage coexists with the way of heaven and the way of earth. It is the law of human relations, human affairs, and conducting oneself in society. It's full and solid. It produces and raises all things. Its essence and uses touch the heaven. It's so wide and pleatifol, and it's too beautiful to be absorbed all at once. There are eight hundred guides and three thousand specific items concerning etiquette, which await virtuous man to implement. Therefore great way cannot be established if great virtue doesn't exist. Therefore moral men modestly stick to kindness bestowed by heaven. Furthermore they cultivate their nature by means of learning broadly and inquiring thoroughly so that they can reach breadth and depth of knowledge; they can approach wisdom and nobility and observe the doctrine of mean. They review what they have learnt and get to know new understanding so that they can be considerate and unsophisticated and respect etiquette. Consequently a moral man isn't arrogant when he is in superior post and he doesn't betray when he is in inferior post. His words can enlighten those who are in power while state politics is in order, and his silence can keep himself safe while state politics is chaotic. *Common People* in *Greater Odes* in *The Book of Songs* reads, "He's been logically knowledgable. And he behaves uprightly and drives away evils." It means exactly in that way.

【注释】(1)圣人之道:包括28、29两节而言。(2)洋洋:充足扎实的样子。发育:萌发,生长。峻极于天:郑玄注:"峻,高也。"孔颖达疏:"言圣人之道高大,与山相似,上极于天。"朱熹四书集注:"此言道之极于至大而无外也。"(3)优优:充足有余之意;宽裕的样子;美盛的样子。礼仪三百,威仪三千:朱熹四书集注:"礼仪,经礼也,仪礼,曲礼也。"经礼,谓礼的纲领,曲礼,谓礼的具体仪节。(4)其人:指能践行礼仪的贤人。其,代词,表特指。(5)凝:níng,凝聚,形成。(6)尊德性:谓恭敬奉持天赋的善性。道问学:谓通过博学审问而培养本性。道,由,经过。致广大而尽精微:致,使达到。广大,指内容博大渊深。而,进层连词。尽,达到极限。精微,细微(如毫毛)。极,达到。高明:崇高明睿。道,遵行。温故而知新:温习学过的知识得到新的理解和体会;温习历史经验认识现在。敦厚:dūn~,诚朴宽厚。崇礼:尊崇礼仪。(7)倍:同"背"。兴:谓兴起在位。诗曰:见《诗·大雅·烝民》。既明且哲:又心明眼亮又有智慧。以:用。

【原文】28 子曰:"愚而好自用,贱而好自专,生乎今之世,反古之道。如此者,灾及其身者也[1]。"非天子,不议礼,不制度,不考文[2]。今天下车同轨,书同文,行同伦[3]。虽有其位,苟无其德,不敢作礼乐焉;虽有其德,苟无其位,亦不敢作礼乐焉[4]。子曰:"吾学夏礼,杞不足征也;吾学殷礼,有宋存焉;吾学周礼,今用之,吾从周[5]。"

【白话译文】

孔子说:"愚蠢又好自行其是,不接受别人的意见,低贱又好逞己意,独断独行,生在今天这个时代,走复古的道路。像这样的人,灾难会落到他头上。"不是天子不议论礼制，不制定法规，不考正人的字或别名。现在天下统一，车轨相同，文字相同，行为的道德标准相同。即使有天子之位，假如没有天子之德，也不敢制作礼乐；即使有天子之德，假如没有天子之位，也不敢制作礼乐；制作礼乐的，必是圣人在天子之位。孔子说："我谈夏朝的礼，他的后代杞国不够验证；我学殷朝的礼，宋国有文献保存；我学周朝的礼，现在正使用，我遵从周朝的礼。"

【英语译文】

Confucius said, "Disasters will befall those who are foolish but do things at will, refusing others' advice, who are humble but show themselves off, who live in the present time but take the path to return to the ancients." If one isn't the son of the heaven, he shouldn't discuss rites and rituals; he shouldn't stipulate rules and regulations, and he shouldn't test other's name or nickname. Nowadays the land under the heaven is unified, carts run on the same track, characters are in the same format, and moral standards are also the same. One dares not stipulate rites and music even if he is in the post of the son of the heaven but isn't virtuous. One dares not stipulate rites and music even if he is virtuous but isn't in the post of the son of the heaven. He who stipulates rites and music must be a sage in the post of the son of the heaven. Confucius said, "I mention rites of Xia Dynasty but in offspring Qi State there isn't enough to be tested. I learn rites of Yin Dynasty and it was recorded in literature. I learn rites of Zhou Dynasty which are conducted nowadays, therefore I observe them."

【注释】(1)好:hào，爱好。自用:自行其是，不接受别人的意见。自专:一任己意，独断独行。反:复。(2)议礼:议论礼制。不制度:不制定法规。不考文:不考正书名。后泛指考订文辞。按:这里的书名不是书籍的名，是人的字，别名。(3)车同轨:各种车辆的车轨大小相同。书同文:文字相同。行同伦:行为同一道德标准。(4)这一段是说作礼乐者必是圣人在天子之位。(5)杞:qǐ，古国名。周武王克殷纣，求夏禹之后，得东楼公，封之于杞。杞是夏的后代。征:证明，证验。

【原文】29 王天下有三重焉，其寡过矣乎[1]！上焉者虽善无征，无征不信，不信民弗从；下焉者虽善不尊，不尊不信，不信民弗从[2]。故君子之道:本诸身，征诸庶民，考诸三王而不缪，建诸天地而不悖，质诸鬼神而无疑，百世以俟圣人而不惑[3]。质诸鬼神而无疑，知天也；百世以俟圣人而不惑，知人也。是故君子动而世为天下道，行而世为天下法，言而世为天下则。远之则有望，近之则不厌。诗曰："在彼无恶，在此无射；庶几夙夜，以永终誉！”[4]君子未有不如此而早有誉于天下者也。

【白话译文】

称王天下，在治理议礼、制度、考文三个重任中过失很少吧！从前称王的，如夏朝、商朝，虽然很好，却没有实据验证，没有实据验证的事，不敢轻信。不敢轻信的事，老百姓不听从。在当代君王之下的圣人，虽然很好却没在尊位上，没在尊位上的人，不敢轻信，不敢轻信的人，老百姓不听从。因此君子欲王天下，议礼、制度、考文的根本在自身，验证在平民百姓，参考夏、商、周三代圣王，自己没有错误，立于天地间没有哪里不适宜，询问鬼神，没有疑虑，等到百代以后圣人复起，也无怀疑。询问鬼神没有疑虑，是知道天；等到百代以后圣人复起也无怀疑，是知道人。所以君子的举动世世代代为天下的先导，行为世世代代为天下的楷模，言语世世代代为天下的准则。离开君子时指望靠近，靠近君子时没有厌倦。《诗经》上说：“在他国内没怨言，很受欢迎来我帮。但愿日夜多勤勉，永久保持美名扬。!”君子没有不这样自强不息就早有名誉于天下的。

【英语译文】

A man who became a king seldom made mistaks in important tasks concerning rites discussion, rules stipulation, and name test. In old days those who became kings, for example, in Xia Dynasty and Shang Dynasty, had no proof to test even though they were very good. We dare not believe things which have no proof to test. And common people never follow them. At present time sages under king aren't in respectable post even if they are very good. We dare not believe men who aren't in respectable post and common people never follow them. Therefore, if a moral man wants to become a king, he should basically rely on himself concerning rites discussion, rules stipulation, and name test. Common people are obliged to prove him. Referring sage kings of Xia, Shang, and Zhou dynasties he hasn't made any mistakes, and conducts appropriately in the world; he has no doubts while consulting ghosts and spirits, and he has no doubts while awaiting sages' appearance one hundred generations later. If one has no doubts while consulting ghosts and spirits, he does know the heaven; if one has no doubts while awaiting sages' appearance one hundred generations later, he does know human being. Therefore a moral man's action is a model for generations and his behavior is an example for generations, and his words is the law for generations. While leaving a moral man one wishes to approach him and while approaching him one doesn't feel bored.

Egret Fluttering in *Zhou Hymns* in *The Book of Songs* reads, "In his country no one complains him. And he's very popular in my country. I hope he will be diligent through time, And his reputation will last forever." No moral man became famous in the world who didn't renew and restrengthen himself.

【注释】(1)王:wàng,统治,称王。有:治理。三重:~ zhòng,三个重任,即议礼、制度、考文。其:承接连词,和则差不多。寡过:少犯错误。(2)上焉者:前于此的,谓当代的君王以前。上,前面。焉,近指代词。无征不信:没有验证的事不敢轻信。下焉者:低于此的,谓在当代君王下的圣人。不尊:不在尊位。不尊不信:不在尊位的人不敢轻信。(3)君子之道:指王天下者而言。其道即议礼、制度、考文的事。(4)诗:《诗经·周颂·振鹭》。

【原文】30 仲尼祖述尧舜,宪章文武;上律天时,下袭水土[1]。辟如天地之无不持载,无不覆帱,辟如四时之错行,如日月之代明[2]。万物并育而不相害,道并行而不相悖,小德川流,大德敦化,此天地之所以为大也[3]。

【白话译文】

孔子效法尧舜的大道,主张仿效文王、武王的法度;上遵循天道运行的规律,下适应山川自然环境的演化。如同天地承载万物,没有什么不支持,覆盖万物,没有什么不爱护,如同四季的交替运行,日月的轮流照耀。各种各样、不计其数的东西,同在天地间发育,生长,繁衍,不互相侵害,各种不同的规律在天地间运行不相违乱,德行小的,像河流灌溉,滋润万物;德行大的,仁爱敦厚,化生万物,没有穷尽,这就是天地为什么为大。

【英语译文】

Confucius followed the example of the Great Way of sages Yao and Shun, and he proposed to imitate the rules and regulations of King Wen and King Wu, i. e. to observe the law of the heaven and to get adjusted to the transformation of nature. Nothing won't be held just as heaven and earth support all things. Nothing won't be protected just as the alternation of four seasons and the alternatively shining of the sun and the moon. Various uncountable things produce, grow, reproduce at the same time in the world and they don't harm each other. Various laws function in the world and don't violate each other. Those of lesser virtue nourish all things just like river water irrigation.

Those of greater virtue produce and raise all things kindly without limit. That's why the heaven and earth are great.

【注释】(1)仲尼:孔子字。祖述:效法,仿效。宪章:朱熹四书集注:"祖述者,远宗其道。宪章者,近守其法。"律:遵循,取法。天时:天道运行的规律。袭:通"习",习惯,适应。水土:山川,国土。(2)辟如:同"譬如",如同,好像。持载:承载,谓地能承载万物。覆帱:fùdào,覆盖,谓加恩施惠。四时:四季。错行:交替运行。代明:轮流照耀。(3)小德川流,大德敦化:小德,德行、节操之小者。大德,德行、节操之大者。郑玄注:"小德川流,侵润萌芽,喻诸侯也;大德敦化,厚生万物,喻天子也。"朱熹四书集注:"小德者全体之分,大德者万殊之本。川流者,如川之流,脉络分明而往不息也。敦化者,敦厚其化,根本盛大而出无穷也。"

【原文】31 唯天下至圣,为能聪明睿知,足以有临也,宽裕温柔,足以有容也;发强刚毅,足以有执也;齐庄中正,足以有敬也;文理密察,足以有别也[1]。溥博渊泉,而时出之。溥博如天,渊泉如渊。见而民莫不敬,言而民莫不信,行而民莫不说[3]。是以声名洋溢乎中国,施及蛮貊;舟车所至,人力所通天之所覆地之所载日月所照霜露所队;凡有血气者莫不尊亲,故曰配天[4]。

【白话译文】

只有天下最高尚的圣人才能达到聪明智慧,够得上治理天下,宽大温和,够得上包容万物;坚强果决,够得上判断取舍;严肃诚敬不偏不倚,够得上人人敬仰;条理缜密明晰,够得上区分是非。胸怀广阔深远,随时随事真诚出现。思虑如渊泉。胸怀广阔周遍如天,思虑静深如渊泉。来到民众中间,没有人不敬礼,说话没有人不相信,行动举止,没有人不喜悦。因此声名不只是充满中国,还传扬到了四方的边远部族;车船所到的地方,人力所去的地方,上天所覆盖的地方,大地所承载的地方,太阳月亮所照耀的地方,霜露所坠落的地方,凡是活着的人没有不尊敬亲爱圣人的,所以说,圣人与天比并。

【英语译文】

Only the noblest sage can be clever and wise enough to govern the world under the heaven, be mild and considerate enough to embrace things, be firm and decisive enough to make judgement, serious and honest and impartial enough to be respected, be logical enough to distinguish the right from the wrong. He is broadminded and farsighted to show honestly in any time at any place. His thinking is like deep spring. His broad mind is as wide as the heaven and his deep thinking is like spring. While he is among masses no one doesn't salute to him. While he is speaking no one doesn't believe him. While he is acting no one doesn't like him. Therefore his fame not only fills in mid state but also spreads around ethnic tribes nearby. Where carts and boats reach, where human beings go, where the heaven covers, where the earth supports, where the sun and the moon shine, and where frost and dew fall down, whoever alive all respect and love sage. Therefore, a sage coexists with the heaven.

【注释】(1)唯:只有。为能:才能。为,副词,乃,才。睿知:ruì zhì 同“睿智”,智慧。足以:完全可以,够得上。有:词头。下文四个“有”同此。临:统治,治理。宽裕温柔:宽大温和。容:包容。发强刚毅:奋发坚强果决。执:判断。齐庄中正:zhāi ~ ~ ~,严肃诚敬不偏不倚。敬:敬仰。文理密察:犹条理缜密明晰。别:区分,辨别。(2)溥博:pǔ ~,周遍广远。渊泉:深泉。时出:适时出现。(3)溥博如天,渊泉如渊:喻智慧广大如天,思虑深邃如渊。见:同“现”,显现,显露。谓出现在群众面前。(4)洋溢:充满,广泛传播。施及蛮貊:~ ~ mǎn mò,散布到四方落后部族。蛮貊,古代指南方和北方的落后部族。也泛指四方的落后部族。队:同“坠”,落。有血气者:指“活人”。血液和气息,是人和动物体内维持生命活动的两种要素。

【原文】32 唯天下至诚,为能经纶天下之大经,立天下之大本,知天地之化育。夫焉有所倚[1]?肫肫其仁!渊渊其渊!浩浩其天[2]!苟不固聪明圣知达天德者,其孰能知之[3]?

【白话译文】

天下只有最诚实的人才能筹划治理天下大事的常道常规,建立天下根本事业的基础,知道天地的生物化物长物育物。哪里有依靠?诚实无欺,静深如潭,广大如天!如果不是本来聪明智慧无所不通德性及天的人有谁能知道?

【英语译文】

Only the utmost honest man can stipulate the constant rules and ways to administrate great affairs in this world, and lay foundation for the basic cause, and know how the heaven and the earth produce and raise all things. What does he rely on? He relies on honesty, tranquility, and broad-mindedness! Who knows this if he isn't inborn wise and knowledgeable and utmost virtuous?

【注释】(1)经纶:整理丝缕、理出丝绪和编丝成绳统称经纶。引申为筹划治理国家大事。大经:常道,常规。大本:根本,事物的基础。化育:生化长育。夫焉:夫,语首助词。现代汉语没有这种用法去掉不译。焉,疑问代词。(2)肫肫:zhūnzhūn,诚恳。渊渊:深广深邃。渊:深潭。浩浩:广大无际的样子。(3)圣知:同“圣智”,谓聪明睿智,无所不通。天德:天的德性。汉董仲舒《春秋繁露·人副天数》:“天德施,地德化,人德义。”

【原文】33 诗曰:“衣锦尚絅。”恶其文之着也。故君子之道,暗然而日章;小人之道,的然而日亡。君子之道,淡而不厌,简而文,温而理,知远之近,知风之自,知微之显,可与入德矣[1]。诗云:“潜虽伏矣,亦孔之昭!”故君子内省不疚,无恶于志。君子之所不可及者,其唯人之所不见乎[2]。诗云:“相在尔室,尚不愧于屋漏。”故君子不动而敬,不言而信[3]。诗曰:“奏假无言,时靡有争。”是故君子不赏而民劝,不怒而民威于鈇钺[4]。诗曰:“不显惟德!百辟其刑之。”是故君子笃恭而天下平[5]。诗云:“予怀明德,不大声以色。”子曰:“声色之于以化民,末也。”诗曰:“德輶如毛”,毛犹有伦。“上天之载,无声无臭”至矣[6]!

【白话译文】

《诗经》上说:“穿着锦服单罩衣。”嫌文采太显眼了。所以君子的人生道路平平淡淡,越走越宽广;小人的人生道路红红火火,越走越熄灭。君子的人生道路:平常而不厌倦,简朴而有条理,温和而有理智,知道远和近,知道风向和源头,知道幽微和显著,可算进入圣人品德修养的境界了。《诗经》上说:“虽能潜入深水里,水清日照难脱逃。”所以君子自我反省不会痛苦,问心无愧。君子之所以不被一般人赶得上,只是独居时和平时没有两样。《诗经》上说:“看你独自处室内,还没有隐恶,愧对神明。”所以君子在闲静时也是恭敬不苟的,没有说什么话时也是诚实不欺的。诗上说:“诚心默祷没言语,一片敬慕起和风。”所以君子不颁奖,民众自觉努力,不发怒,民众畏惧刑法。《诗经》上说:“光明最是先王德,诸侯应当永敬宗。”所以君子纯厚恭敬,天下就会治平 。《诗经》上说:“正大光明我表扬,不须厉声又厉色。”孔子说:“拿声色教化民众是最差的办法。”《诗经》上说:“德轻如毛。”可是还有比毛轻的东西,《诗经》上说:“上天的事最神秘,无声无息无迹象”,最好了!

【英语译文】

The Tall Beauty in *Ballads of Wei State* in *The Book of Songs* reads, "She wears silk clothes, thin cover." It seems conspicuously ornamental. Therefore a moral man's life journey is simple and plain and it becomes wider and wider. On the contrary, a mean man's life journey is flourishing but it gradually perishes. On his life journey a moral man behaves ordinarily and tirelessly, simply and orderly, mildly and rationally; he knows far and near places, and he knows the direction of wind blowing, and he knows depth, tranquility and conspicousness. He has reached the state of a sage concerning virtuous cultivation. *Summer Day* in *Lesser Odes* in *The Book of Songs* reads, "Though they duck in deep water. They cannot escape the sunshine as the riwer is clear." Therefore a moral man reflects himself and feels no pity. The reason why an ordinary man cannot catch up with a moral man is that a moral man behaves all the same even if he stays alone. *Dignified Appearance* in *Greater Odes* in *The Book of Songs* reads, "I see when you stay alone in your room. You do not hide your evils to the gods." Therefore a moral man in casualty is also modest and conscientious, and he is honest while keeping silence. *Ancestors* in *Shang Hymns* in *The Book of Songs* reads, "Honest pray is for ancestors. Admiration leads to harmony." Therefore when moral monarch doesn't give award the common people still work hard. When moral monarch doesn't issue punishment the common people still fear criminal law. *Moral Achievement* in *Zhou Hymns* in *The Book of Songs* reads, "It's brightest the passed king's morality. All ministers should keep it in mind." Therefore the world will be governed when moral monarch is honest and modest. *The Great God* in *Greater Odes* in *The Book of Songs* reads, "You being upright I will praise you. Do not need to be serious and cruel." Confucius said, "It's the worst method to educate people by means of being serious and cruel." Common People in *Greater Odes* in *The Book of Songs* reads, "One's virtue is featherlike light." However there's something which is lighter than feather. King Wen in *Greater Odes* in *The Book of Songs* reads, "Things in the heaven are the most mysterious. There're no sound, no signs and no traces." That is the best.

【注释】(1)诗曰句:《诗·卫风·硕人》和《诗·郑风·丰》皆作“衣锦褧衣”。衣:yì,动词,穿(衣服)。衣锦:穿锦绣衣裳。尚絅:~jiǒng,加上麻纱单罩衣。“絅”同“褧”。“尚絅”与“褧衣”义同句法不同。谓锦衣外面再加上麻纱单罩衣以掩盖其华丽。比喻不炫耀于人。暗然:淡淡无色的样子。日章:一天天发展成章。章,指事物发展的阶段。的然:dì ~,明显刺眼的样子。知远之近:知道远和近。之,连词。和,与。下文三个之同此。自:由来,缘由。可与:可谓,可以叫作。入德:进入圣人品德修养的境界。(2)诗云:见《诗·小雅·正月》。潜虽伏矣:在水下算是躲藏了。亦孔之昭:还是明显。亦,副词。尚;犹。孔,副词。甚,很。之,助词。补凑音节。昭,明显。诗作"照",义同。故君子内省:~ xǐng,内心自我反省。不疚:~jiù,内心不惭愧痛苦。疚,因有过失内心感到惭愧痛苦。无恶于志:朱熹四书集注:"无恶于志,犹言无愧于心"。其唯:也许只有。其 ,副词,表推测或论断。(3)诗云:见《诗·大雅·抑》。相:xiàng,看,观察。屋漏:古代室内西北隅为安藏神主所设的小账。后亦泛指屋的深暗处。(4)诗曰:见《诗·商颂·烈祖》。奏假:~gé,诗作"鬷假",祭祷,鬷同奏。时:连词,相当于"而"。靡有:没有。争:对抗,争辩。劝:quàn,勤勉,努力。威:畏惧。鈇钺:fū yuè,斫刀和大斧。腰斩和砍头的刑具。(5)诗曰:见《诗·周颂·列文》。不显:bù ~,谓幽深玄远。与26章的"不显"用意不同。不显,pǐ ~,同"丕显",大显。不通丕。惟德:其德。惟,代词。和"其" 差不多。译作他(它)的。百辟:诸侯,百官。其:语气助词。刑:效法。笃恭:纯厚恭敬。(6)诗云:见《诗·大雅·皇矣》。以:连词。和,与。色:脸色。于以化民: 被用来教化百姓。诗曰:见《诗·大雅·烝民》。輶:yóu,轻。有伦:有伦比者,有可比者。上天之载,无声无臭:见《诗·大雅·文王》。载:事,事业。臭:xìu,气味。

第三部分 《论语》(*The Analects*)

学而篇第一(共十六章)

《学而》,《论语》第一篇。《论语》各篇均以第一章前二三个字命名。《学而》包括十六章,内容涉及诸多方面。

【原文】1 子曰[1]:"学而时习之[2],不亦说乎[3]?有朋自远方来[4],不亦乐乎?人不知而不愠[5],不亦君子乎[6]?"

【白话译文】

孔子说:"进德修业并且按时实习它,不也高兴吗?有志同道合的人从远处到来,不也快乐吗?人家不了解我,我不怨恨,不也是君子吗?"

【英语译文】

Confucius said, "Isn't it a happy thing to cultivate and practice moral integrity? Isn't it a happy thing that a friend with common ideal has come from afar? Isn't he a moral man that he doesn't get enraged when he's unknown?

【注释】(1)子:论语"子曰"的"子"都是指孔子。(2)学:受教与仿效。而:进层连词。并且。时:副词。按时,及时,适时。习:温习,实习,演习。之:代词。指所所受教、仿效的内容项目。(3)不亦:不也。说:音读和意义跟"悦"相同。高兴、愉快。乎:语气助词。表反问。(4)有朋:古本有作"友朋"的。这里的"朋"有"朋友""弟子"。"志同道合的人"等含义。远方:距离很远的地方,远处。(5)人不知:谓别人不了解我。愠:yùn,怨恨。(6)君子:论语的君子,有时指"有位者",

有时指“有德者”,这里是指“有德者”。

【原文】2 有子曰[1]:“其为人也孝弟[2],而好犯上者[3],鲜矣[4];不好犯上,而好作乱者[5],未之有也[6]。君子务本[7],本立而道生[8]。孝弟也者[9],其为仁之本与[10]!”

【白话译文】

有子说:“有种人,做人、处事、接物啊,孝顺爹娘,敬爱兄长;却喜欢冒犯长上。这种人实在不多。不喜欢冒犯长上,却喜欢捣乱造反;这种人,从来没有。君子致力于根本,根本确立了,行大道从此起步。孝悌这种行为,是行仁道的根本吧!”

【英语译文】

You Zi said, “There are few people who are filial to their parents and respect brothers but are inclined to violate superiorities. There are no people who don't violate their superiorities but always disturb things. A moral man commits himself to his fundamentals on which he could follow up Great Way. Filial and fraternal actions should be the fundamental for humanity!”

【注释】(1)有子:孔子的学生,姓有,名若。比孔子小十三岁。一说小三十三岁。以小三十三岁较可信。(2)其:代词,这里表远指。那;那些。为人:做人处事接物。也:语气助词,表停顿,可译作啊、呀或去掉不译。孝弟:孝,子女对父母的尊敬。弟,tì,同“悌”。弟弟敬爱兄长。亦泛指尊重长上。(3)而:转折连词,然而,却。好:hào,喜爱。犯上:冒犯或违抗尊长。者:用在形容词、动词、动词词组、数词或主谓词组之后组成“者”字结构,指代人、事、物。这里指代人。(4)鲜(xiǎn):少。《论语》的“鲜”都是这样用。(5)作乱者:制造叛乱的人;暴乱的人。(6)未之有也:“未有之也”的倒装。古代汉语否定句中的宾语若是指示代词,都是放在动词前的。(7)君子:指有德者,包含有位而非小人者。务本:致力于根本。(8)本立而道生:本,草木的根;事物的根基或主体。道:指宇宙万物的本源、本体,即宇宙万物的根本。本立,谓君子致力于根本就不会背离或丢失根本。从而永恒践行不停并发扬开去。这就是君子之道自此而生。君子之道是天下的大道。道生:君子行道起步。(9)孝弟也者:这是动词词组“孝弟也”与“者”字构成的“者”字结构。(“也”是语气助词,不改变搭配词的词义。)意谓孝弟这件事(或这种行为)。(10)其:近指代词。指代“孝弟也者”在句子中作主语。为仁之本:其(孝弟这件事)的表语。为仁,行仁。为,于此是“作为”“施行”的意思。不是“是”的意思。与:yú,同“欤”。语气词。这里表感叹。

【原文】3 子曰:“巧言令色[1],鲜矣仁[2]!”

【白话译文】

孔子说:“言语好听脸色谄媚,仁德很少啊!”

【英语译文】

Confucius said, “A man who speaks superficially and unreasonably shows flattery is seldom a moral one.”

【注释】(1)巧言:表面上好听而实际上虚伪的话。令色:伪善、谄媚的脸色。(2)矣:语气助词,表感叹,犹“啊”。鲜矣仁:犹“仁鲜矣”。

【原文】4 曾子曰[1]:“吾日三省吾身[2]:为人谋而不忠乎[3]?与朋友交而不信乎[4]?传不习乎[5]?”

【白话译文】

曾子说:“我每天都从三个方面反省自己:为别人谋事是否尽心竭力了呢?与朋友交往是否有虚假呢?老师传授的道德学业是否复习了呢?”

【英语译文】

Zeng Zi said, “Each day I reflect myself from three aspects: Have I done things wholeheartedly for others? Have I shown pretense while befriending others? Have I reviewed what the master ever taught?”

【注释】(1)曾子:孔子的学生。名参(shēn),字子舆,南武城(故城在今山东省 平邑县附近)人,比孔子小四十六岁(公元前505—公元前435年)。(2)日:每天。三省(sānxǐng):省察三事。或解作“多次省察”亦通。吾身:我自己。身,谓自身,自己。(3)为人谋:特指为求助的人指点方向、提建议等。谋:谋虑;谋划。忠:忠诚无私,尽心竭力,厚道。(4)交:交往,相处。信:诚实不欺,无虚假。传(chuán):名词,指老师(孔子)传授的道、业。习:同学而时习之的习一样包括温习、实习、演习、可译作复习。

【原文】5 子曰:“道千乘之国[1],敬事而信[2],节用而爱人[3],使民以时[4]。”

【白话译文】

孔子说:“治理有一千辆兵车的国家,专一政事去掉杂念,取信于民;节约政事费用,爱护人民;征用民工不违农时。”

【英语译文】

Confucius said, “Governing a state with one thousand warrior carts, one focal administrative affair should be emphasized, expenditure reduced, its subjects protected and farming schedule not violated while recruiting peasant labors.”

【注释】(1)道:治理。千乘之国:乘,shèng,古代用四匹马拉的兵车。千乘之国,拥有一千辆兵车的国家。春秋时代,打仗用兵车,国家的强弱也用兵车的数目来衡定。春秋初期,大国都没有千辆兵车,但是那个时代战争频繁,各国都必须扩充军备;侵略者因为兼并的结果,兵车发展的速度更快。譬如晋国到平丘之会,据叔向的话,已有四千乘了(见左传昭公十三年)。千之乘国,到孔子之时已经不是大国了。所以子路说“千乘之国摄乎大国之间”(见11.26)。(2)敬事:专一政事而无杂念。信:不虚假,取信于民。(3)节用:节约政事费用。爱人:爱护人民。(4)使民以时:征用民工,不违农时。

【原文】6 子曰:“弟子[1],入则孝[2],出则弟[3],谨而信[4],泛爱众[5],而亲仁[6]。行有余力[7],则以学文[8]。”

【白话译文】

孔子说:“年轻小子,在家孝顺父母,出门尊敬长上,语言谨慎不虚假,博爱大众,亲近仁人。”

【英语译文】

Confucius said, “Youths should be filial to their parents at home, respect their superiorities in society, talk about things cautiously and authentically, love masses of common people, and make intimate friends with humanistic men.”

【注释】(1)弟子:年纪幼小的人,学生。就本章全文看,它是指年纪幼小的命士(受命于朝廷的士)。《礼记·内则》:"由命士以上,父子皆异宫(分宅而居)。昧爽而朝,慈以旨甘(黎明前儿子前往父母住所请安,并用美食孝敬父母)。日出而退,各从其事。"(2)入则孝:进入父母住宅尽孝。(3)出则弟悌:弟同"悌",这里泛指尊重长上。(4)谨而信:谨慎言语而不虚假。(5)泛爱众:广泛地施爱于大众。(6)而:进层连词。并且。亲仁:亲近仁人。古汉语词汇常用某一具体的人或事物的性质、特征甚至原料来代表那一具体的人或事物。如:善恶,指善人和恶人;医卜,指医生和卜人;丝竹,指弦乐器和竹管乐器。(7)行:躬行,实践。"入则孝"至"而亲仁"都是行的宾语。这里在句法上视为宾语提前或宾语承前省都可以。余力:余裕的力量。(8)以:介词,表示对事物的处置,相当于"用""拿"。学文:学习文化知识。

【原文】7 子夏[1]曰:"贤贤易色[2];事父母[3],能竭其力[4];事君,能致其身[5];与朋友交,言而有信[6]。虽曰未学[7],吾必谓之学矣[8]。"

【白话译文】

子夏说:"无论对谁,尊重贤德,不以貌取人;侍奉爹娘,能尽心竭力;服侍君主,能献出身躯;和朋友交往,说话算数。这种人,即使没学习过,我一定说他已经学习过了。"

【英语译文】

Zi Xia said, "A man worships morals and never judges a person from appearance; he tries his best to attend his parents; he even loses his life while serving monarch; he keeps his promise while making friends. From perspective of my thinking such kind of person has learned even though he did not."

【注释】(1)子夏(公元前507年—?):孔子的学生,姓卜名商字子夏比孔子小四十四岁。(2)贤贤:动词+名词。崇重贤德。易色:轻视美容。贤贤易色,谓对待包括妻子在内的任何人,崇重贤德,不以貌取人。(3)事:事奉,侍奉。(4)竭其力:用尽自己的力量。(5)事君:侍奉君主。致其身:奉献自己的身躯。(6)有信:有信用;算数;说一不二。(7)虽曰:假设连词。犹"纵然""即使"。(8)必谓之:一定说他,一定认为他。

【原文】8 子曰:“君子不重[1]则不威[2],学则不固[3]。主忠信[4]。无友不如己者[5]。过则勿惮改[6]。”

【白话译文】

孔子说:“君子不庄重就没有威严,所学德行也就不坚固。君子崇尚忠诚信实。君子不要结交不像君子的人。君子有了过错就不要怕难改正。”

【英语译文】

Confucius said, “A moral man can't be dignified if he behoues casually, thus his learning is not solid. A moral man should worship loyalty and honesty and not befriend immoral one. A moral man should be brave to correct his faults.”

【注释】(1)君子:指有德的人。君子,是本章的唯一主语。后跟四个并列谓语。后三个谓语也可看成承前省略了主语。重(zhòng):厚重,庄重。(2)则:承接连词,表示上文引起的发展或结果。下同。威:威严。(3)学:所学。特指德行方面所学。固:坚固。(4)主:崇尚,注重。忠信:忠诚信实。(5)无(wú):通“毋wú”。副词。表示禁止。犹“不可”“不要”。友:结交。不如己者:如,像。己,因主语是君子,“己”即是君子,所以“不如己者”即“不像君子的人”。(6)过:错误;过失。勿(wù):副词,表示禁止。犹“不可”“不要”。惮(dàn):畏惧,畏难。

【原文】9 曾子曰:“慎终追远,[1]民德归厚矣[2]。”

【白话译文】

曾子说:“居父母丧遵守礼制,祭祀远祖恭敬虔诚,上行下效,社会风气就会归向淳厚了。”

【英语译文】

Zeng Zi said, “One should observe rites and rituals while being in mourning one's parent; he should show humble piety while sacrificing far ancestors. If ruling class do so and common people follow suit, social customs will tend towards honesty.”

【注释】(1)慎终追远:谓居父母丧,祭祀祖先,要依礼尽哀;要恭敬虔诚。终,指父母丧。远,指祖先。(2)民德:民众的道德。民众道德的具体表现,为社会风气。归厚:归向淳厚。矣:语气助词。表将然之事,与“了”相当。

【原文】10 子禽问于子贡曰[1]:“夫子至于是邦也[2],必闻其政[3],求之与[4]? 抑与之与[5]?”子贡曰:“夫子温、良、恭、俭、让以得之[6]。夫子之求之也[7],其诸异乎人之求之与[8]?”

【白话译文】

子禽问到子贡说:“孔夫子到一个国家,就能听说这个国家的政事。是求来的呢? 还是人家主动说的呢?”子贡说:“他老人家温和、善良、恭敬、节制、谦逊,因而能得人家主动讲述,或者他老人家的所求啊,不同于一般人吧?”

【英语译文】

Zi Qin asked Zi Gong, “The master, Confucius can know of the administrative affairs when he arrives at any state. Has he requested for it or others tell him initially?” Zi Gong answered, “He is moderate, benevolent, humble, restrained and modest, therefore, he can get voluntarily-told message. Otherwise his request differs greatly from others'.”

【注释】(1)子禽:姓陈,名亢,生卒年不详。《论语》中此人出现三次,每一次都在打听孔子的为人,应是对孔子感兴趣的人,是否是孔子的学生历来有争论。或曰:“亢,子贡弟子。”问于:向……提问,相当方言中的“问到”。多用于质疑,质询。子贡:姓端木,名赐,是孔子最得意的学生之一。(2)夫子:古代对男子的敬称;孔门尊称孔子为夫子。后因以特指孔子,后世亦沿称老师为夫子。至于:到达。是邦:任何国家。是,概括之词。凡是,任何。邦,古代诸侯的封国;后泛指国家。也:语气助词。这里用在复句的前一分句末,表提顿语气,可译作“啊”。(3)闻:听说,知道。(4)之:代词。代“闻其政”。与(yú):同“欤”。语气词。表疑问语气。(5)抑:连词。还是。表选择。与(yǔ):给予。之、与:同注释4。(6)温、良、恭、俭、让:温和、善良、恭敬、节制、谦逊。以:连词,表承接,相当于“而”。(7)之:结构助词。用在主语和谓语间,取消句子的独立性,形同偏正结构。(8)其诸:犹“或者”。表测度语气。异乎:乎,相当介词“于”。异乎,即异于(异于)。

【原文】11 子曰:“父在[1],观其志[2];父没[3],观其行[4];三年无改于父之道[5],可谓孝矣[6]。”

【白话译文】

孔子说:“父亲活着,看儿子的志向;父亲死了,看儿子的行为,三年不改变父亲的某些陈法,可称为孝了。”

【英语译文】

Confucius said, “Son’s ambition is considered when his father is alive; his action will be considered after his fatheris dead. If he hasn’t changed his father is way of life for three years, then he will be called a filial son.”

【注释】(1)父在:父亲活着。(2)其:代词。这里表第三人称领属关系。他(们)的。这里即儿子的。(3)父没:父亲死了。(4)行:行为。(5)三年:古代丧礼,臣为君、子为父、妻为夫等要守丧三年。意在巩固至爱,慢慢平静哀痛。父之道:父亲在生时为人处世的行径。父道若有误或者已不合时宜,应当改变。三年不改,孝子他有所不忍。(6)可谓:可以称为,可以说是。

【原文】12 有子曰:“礼之用[1],和为贵[2]。先王之道[3],斯为美[4];小大由之[5]。有所不行[6],知和而和[7],不以礼节之[8],亦不可行也。”

【白话译文】

有子说:“礼的作用,以行为适中恰到好处最贵重。过去圣明君王治国美好处就在这里;小事大事都奉行适中,恰到好处。如果行不通,想行为适中而行为适中,不用礼来调节,也是行不通的。”

【英语译文】

You Zi said, “The role of rites is to make sure one’s actions are appropriate and that’s most important. In the past the key for monarchy to govern states lies in here; all affairs went on their exact and appropriate way. If things don’t go smoothly and there’s no rites to regulate, then things also go astray even if you want to do so.”

【注释】(1)礼:社会生活中由于风俗习惯而形成的行为准则、道德规范和各种礼节。用:使用,运用,作用。(2)和:适中,恰到好处。由中和、中道、中庸而和谐安泰。为贵:最贵重,最重要。为,在比较句中作谓语动词,含有"最""更"的意思。(3)先王之道:指上古贤明君王之治道。(4)斯:近指代词。此、这。指代"和"。(5)小大由之:小事大事奉行"和"。由:奉行,遵从。(6)有所不行:有,连词,表假设。犹如果,即使。所:结构助词。所不行:谓不行,行不通。知和而和:想适中而适中。知,望,欲。

【原文】13 有子曰:"信近于义[1],言可复也[2]。恭近于礼[3],远耻辱也[4]。因不失其亲[5],亦可宗也[6]。"

【白话译文】

有子说:"约定之言不违背道德规范,才可以兑现。容态恭敬合于礼节,就能避免侮辱。亲近依托关系深的人,也能不失自主地位。"

【英语译文】

You Zi said, "If one's promised words concord with morals then they can be realized. If one's appearance and behaviors observe rites, then one can be free from insult. Even if he relies on intimate persons, he can also keep his own identity."

【注释】(1)信:约定之言。近:靠近,不离,不违背。义:符合正义或道德规范。(2)言:即约定之言。复:实践;履行。(3)恭:恭敬,谦恭。礼:礼节、规矩。(4)远(yuàn):离开,避免。(5)因:亲近,依托。亲:关系深的人。(6)宗:宗主(一姓的继承人;众所景仰归依者;某一方面的代表与权威)。这里用作动词。作宗主;宗主之。训为"不失自主地位"。

【原文】14 子曰:"君子食无求饱[1],居无求安[2],敏于事而慎于言[3],就有道而正焉[4],可谓好学也已[5]。"

【白话译文】

孔子说:"君子饮食不寻求饱足,居住不寻求安逸,敏捷做事却谨慎言语,拜访有道德、有学问的人匡正自己,这样可以说是好学了。"

【英语译文】

Confucius said, "A moral man could be regarded as dedication to learning if he doesn't eat too full and live indulgently, but does things nimbly and drops in learned men and corrects his faults."

【注释】(1)君子:这里应是兼指有德的人和有位的人。求饱:寻求饱足。(2)求安:寻求安逸。(3)事:做事,工作。(4)就:主动造访。有道:有才艺或有道德的人。正焉:匡正之。焉,代词。犹"之""此"。(5)也已:语气助词。这表肯定,可译作"了"。表感叹可译作"啊""了""啊"。

【原文】15 子贡曰:"贫而无谄[1],富而无骄[2],何如[3]?"子曰:"可也;未若贫而乐[4],富而好礼者也[5]。"子贡曰:"诗云:'如切如磋,如琢如磨[6],'其斯之谓与[7]?"子曰:"赐也[8],始可与言 诗已矣[9],告诸往而知来者[10]。

【白话译文】

子贡说:"贫穷却不巴结奉承,富实却不怠慢自大,怎么样?"孔子说:"可以了;但还比不上贫穷而乐于走自己的路,富实而谦虚有礼的人。"子贡说:"诗经上说:'要像切治兽骨,磨治象牙,雕刻玉石,打磨玉石一样,相互勉励。'那就是这样的意思吧!"孔子说:"赐呀,你正可参与谈论《诗》经了,告诉你已往的,你就知道未来的。"

【英语译文】

Zi Gong asked, "How about a person who never flatters anyone when he's poor and never be conceited when he's rich?" Confucius answered, "It's all right. But he cannot be compared with a man who observes his own way while being poor and always be modest while being rich." Zi Gong asked, "As *Book of Songs* tells us, 'we should encourage each other just as cutting beast bones, grinding ivories, carving and polishing jade stones,' Does it means so?" Confucius said, "Ci, my boy, you can participate in discussing *Book of Songs* and after I tell you past things you could know future things."

【注释】(1)贫:缺少财务,贫困。与富相对。谄:奉承;献媚。(2)富:财物多(古跟"贫"今跟"穷")。骄:怠慢:轻视。(3)何如:怎么样。(4)未若:不如,比不上。乐:皇侃本"乐",下有"道"字,郑玄注:"乐谓志于道,不以贫为忧苦。"(5)好礼:爱好礼节。(6)如切如磋,如琢如磨:像切治兽骨、磨治象牙一样,像雕刻玉石、打磨玉石一样。比喻道德学问方面互相研讨勉励。语出《诗·卫风·淇奥》:"瞻彼淇奥,绿竹猗猗。有匪君子,如切如磋,如琢如磨。"(7)其:远指代词,代指所引诗经语。斯:近指代词,代指当前孔子的话。之谓:的意思。与:语气词,表疑问。(8)赐:子贡名。孔子对学生都称名。子贡(公元前520—公元前456)姓端木,名赐,字子贡,也作子赣,亦称卫赐,春秋末卫国人,少孔子三十一岁。也:语气词,这里表呼唤语气,相当于啊、呀。(9)始可:正可。始,副词。正,正在。与(yù):参与。言(yán):说,谈论。诗:指《诗经》。已矣:语气词。用于句末,与"矣"同义。(10)告诸:告诉你。诸,在这里相当于"之",代词,第二人称,你。往:往者。"往"字后,省略了"者"字,过去的。来者:未来的。

【原文】16 子曰:"不患人之不己知[1],患不知人也[2]。"

【白话译文】

孔子说:"不要担心别人不了解自己,担心自己不了解别人呀。"

【英语译文】

Confucius said, "Don't worry about that others know nothing of you. Do worry about that you know nothing of others."

【注释】(1)不:勿,不要。患:忧虑,担心。人:别人,旁人。之:结构助词。使句子失去独立性。不己知:不知己的倒装。(2)也:语气助词。用在感叹句、祈使句或呼语后,可译为"啊""呀""哪"。

为政篇第二(共二十四章)

本篇篇名,取自第一章的开头是"子曰:'为政以德,譬如北辰,居其所而众星共之。'"

【原文】1 子曰:"为政以德[1],譬如北辰[2],居其所而众星共之[3]。"

【白话译文】

孔子说:"用美德来治理国政,好像北极星一样,处在自己的位置上,别的星体都环绕着它。"

【英语译文】

Confucius said, "Government by virtue is just like North Star which locates in its own place while other stars support it."

【注释】(1)德:一般解作道德。可是各种学派对"道德"都有各自不同的解说与体认,为了避免含糊,笔者以粗浅的话解作:指人的善良品行有同天地化育万物一样的精神,是"美德",绝非"恶德"。(2)北辰:北极星。古人以为北极星是天上最高贵的星体。(3)居其所:处在自己的位置上。共,通拱(gǒng):环绕;环卫。

【原文】2 子曰:"诗三百[1],一言以蔽之[2],曰[3]:'思无邪[4]。'"

【白话译文】

孔子说:"《诗经》三百篇,用一句话概括它,就是'思想纯正'。"

【英语译文】

Confucius said, "*The Book of Songs* consists of three hundred poems and in one word, the significance of it lies in 'pure thought'"

【注释】(1)诗三百:《诗经》实有三百零五篇,"三百"只是举其整数。已成惯例。(2)一言以之:"以一言之"的倒装。即"用一句话来概括它。"一言,一句话。以:用。蔽:涵盖,概括。(3)曰:是,为。(4)思无邪:思想纯正,无邪念。

【原文】3 子曰:"道之以政[1],齐之以刑[2],民免而无耻[3];道之以德[4],齐之以礼[5],有耻且格[6]。"

【白话译文】

孔子说:"用政法来诱导,使刑罚来惩治,民众避开罪过,而无知耻心。用美德来引导,使礼节来规范,民众不但有知耻心,而且迁善归服。"

【英语译文】

Confucius said, "If people are directed by governing approach and punished by penalty, then they can just avoid crime but have no feelings of shame. If people are led by virtue and regulated by rites, then they not only have feelings of shame but also yield wholeheartedly.

【注释】(1)道:引导,诱导。政:政法。(2)齐:整治,整理。刑:刑罚。(3)民:民众。免:避开罪过。无耻:不顾羞耻,不知羞耻。(4)德:美德(特指儒家道德)。(5)礼:礼制,礼节。(6)有耻:谓人有知耻之心。且格:且,而且;格,迁善归服。

【原文】4 子曰:"吾十有五而志于学[1],三十而立[2],四十而不惑[3],五十而知天命[4],六十而耳顺[5],七十而从心所欲[6],不踰矩[7]。"

【白话译文】

孔子说:"我十五岁立志做学问,三十岁学有所成,立于礼不动摇,四十岁于事物当然之理不再困惑,五十岁知道天下事物之所以然,六十岁能听明人家讲话、知其言外之意,七十岁不加约束、随心所想都不越出规矩。"

【英语译文】

Confucius said, "I determined to pursue learning at the age of fifteen and accomplished a little bit on rites at age thirty. I was not confused at natural way at age forty and got to know the reasons for natural things at age fifty. I could absorb what others said and implied and do things according to my thinking without breaking rules.

【注释】(1)有(yòu):同"又"。用于整数与零数之间。《易·系辞》(上):"干之策,二百一十有六;坤之策,百四十有四,凡三百有六十。"《后汉书东夷传序》:"百有余岁,武帝灭之。"志于学:立志做学问。(2)立:学有所成不动摇。(3)不惑:于事物当然之理不再困惑。(4)知天命:知道事物之所以然(即自然的规律与法则)。(5)耳顺:听人讲话知道其言外之意。(6)从心所欲:随心所想,自由自在地想。(7)不踰矩:不越出规矩,合乎规矩。

【原文】5 孟懿子问孝[1]。子曰:"无违[2]。"樊迟御[3],子告之曰:"孟孙问孝于我[4],我对曰,无违。"樊迟曰:"何谓也[5]?"子曰:"生,事之以礼[6];死,葬之以礼,祭之以礼。"

【白话译文】

孟懿子问怎样做才是孝。孔子说:“不要违背礼节。”樊迟为孔子赶车时,孔子告诉他说:“孟孙问我怎样做才是孝,我告诉他,不要违背礼节。”樊迟说:“这是什么意思?”孔子说:“父母活着,依规定的礼节侍奉他们;死了,依规定的礼节埋葬他们,祭祀他们。”

【英语译文】

Zhongsun Heji asked how to be filial. Confucius answered, “Not violating rites.” Fan Chi drove cart for Confucius and the Master told him, “Zhongsun asked me how to be filial. And I told him not to violate rites.” Fan Chi asked, “What does it mean by not to violate rites?” Confucius answered, “According to rites, you should attend them while your parents are alive and bury them, sacrifice them while they are dead.”

【注释】(1)孟懿子:鲁国的大夫,三家之一,姓仲孙,名何忌,“懿”是谥号。他的父亲是孟僖子,仲孙貜(jué)。左传昭公七年说,孟僖子将死,遗嘱要儿子说(yuè)与何忌(孟懿子)向孔子学礼。问孝:问行孝之道。(2)无违:黄式三论语后案说:“左传桓公二年云:‘昭德塞违’,‘灭德立违’,‘君违,不忘谏之以德’;六年传云:‘有佳德而无违心’。襄公二十六年传云‘正其违而治其烦’……古人凡背礼者谓之违。”东汉王充论衡问孔篇曾经质问孔子,为什么不讲“无违礼”而故意省略“礼”讲成“无违”,难道不怕人误会为“无违志”吗?足见东汉时“违”字的“背礼”含义已不被人所了解了。(4)樊迟御:樊迟(为孔子)驾车。樊迟,孔子的学生,名须,字子迟。比孔子小四十六岁。御,驾车,赶车。孟孙:即仲孙。问孝余我。(5)何谓也:这是什么意思?(6)生:活着。事:侍奉。

【原文】6 孟武伯问孝[1]。子曰:“父母唯其疾之忧[2]。”

【白话译文】

孟武伯问怎样做才是孝。孔子说:“父母只有孝子的疾病的忧愁。”

【英语译文】

Zhongsun Zhi asked how to be filial. Confucius answered, “Parents only worry about their filial kids’ diseases.”

【注释】(1)孟武伯:仲孙彘,孟懿子的儿子。(2)唯其疾之忧:唯,只有。其,这里是表领属关系的第三人称代词,指代孝子(子女)。疾,疾病。之,结构助词,相当于"的"。忧,名词,忧愁。这句话的意思是,除了疾病这个人皆不愿的情况外,孝子不可妄自为非。也许孔子认为孟武伯有点逞强吧。

【原文】7 子游问孝[1]。子曰:"今之孝者[2],是谓能养[3]。至于犬马[4],皆能有养[5];不敬[6],何以别乎?"

【白话译文】

子游问怎样做才是孝。孔子说:"现在的孝道,是所说能养活父母。说到养活,即使是狗马都能得到养活;若不尊敬父母,养活父母与养活狗马怎样分别呢?"

【英语译文】

Zi You asked how to be filial. Confucius answered, "Nowadays to be filial means just to support parents. Even dogs and horses can be kept alive; therefore, if you don't respect your parents, what's the difference between keeping parents alive and keeping dogs and horses alive?

【注释】(1)子游:孔子学生。姓言,名偃,字子游,吴人。比孔子小四十五岁。(2)孝者:孝道,孝的内涵。(3)养:供给食物及生活所必需,使生活下去。(4)至于:连词。犹即使是,即便是。(5)有养:得到饲养。有,得到。(6)不敬:不尊敬。

【原文】8 子夏问孝。子曰:"色难[1]。有事,弟子服其劳[2];有酒食,先生馔[3]。曾是以为孝乎[5]?"

【白话译文】

子夏问怎样做才是孝。孔子说:"在父母面前保持和颜悦色很难。遇到事情由年轻人操劳;有好吃好喝的让长辈享受,就这样可认为是孝吗?"

【英语译文】

Zi Xia asked how to be filial. Confucius answered: "It's quite difficult to keep calmness and tranquility in the presence of one's parents. The youths make their efforts to do things and the elder enjoy delicious foods and drinks. Can this be regarded as being filial?"

【注释】(1)色难:有两种解释,一说孝子侍奉父母,以做到和颜悦色为难;一说难在承望理解父母的脸色。今取前一说。(2)弟子:年轻的子弟。服其劳:执行劳务;效力。(3)先生:长辈。馔(zhuàn):吃喝。(4)曾(zéng)副词,乃,竟。是:这,这样。以为:认为。

【原文】9 子曰:"吾与回言终日[1],不违[2],如愚。退而省其私[3],亦足以发[4],回也不愚[5]。"

【白话译文】

"我曾整天给颜回讲学,他没提出过疑问和反对意见,像个蠢人。讲学完毕,各自回到住所,我查看他的闲居独处,在日用动静、语默之间,都能够蕴含我讲之道,回啊,哪里蠢呢?"

【英语译文】

Confucius said, "I elaborated learnings for a whole day to Yan Hui but he didn't raise any question or refute me. He just acted as a fool. After schooling and returning to our dwellings, I checked his own living and behaviors, he could imply ways taught by me. How could we call him a fool?"

【注释】(1)回:颜回,字渊,亦作子渊,鲁国人,是孔子最得意的学生,《史记》说他比孔子小三十岁。但毛奇龄和崔适的考证则说《史记》的三十岁应为四十岁之误,颜渊(公元前511—公元前480)实比孔子小四十岁。言:谈论;讲学。终日:整日。(2)不违:朱熹集注:"意不相背,有听受而无问难也。"(3)退而省其私:退,指讲学完毕师生各自退堂回住所。省(xǐng):视察,察看。其私,指颜回的燕居独处,非进见请问时。(4)亦足以发:亦,语气助词。用在句首或句中补凑音节,有时兼有语意强调作用。现代汉语没有这种用法,可以去掉不译。足以发,谓颜回在日用动静、语默之间,都能够蕴含老师之道,坦然由之而无疑。(5)也:语气助词,相当于"啊"。

【原文】10 子曰:"视其所以[1],观其所由[2],察其所安[3]。人焉廋哉[4]?人焉廋哉?"

【白话译文】

孔子说:“对于一个人,看他的所作所为,观察他的来历和动机,明辨他的所喜所乐,他的真面目能藏在哪里呢?他的真面目能藏在哪里呢?

【英语译文】

Confucius said, “As for judging a man, we observe his doings, scrutinize his experiences and motivations, and differentiate his loving and preferences. Where could he hide his reality? Where could he hide his reality?”

【注释】(1)视:看。所以:所作所为。(2)观:观察。所由:所经历的道路,所作所为的动机。(3)察:明辨。所安:所乐。(4)焉:疑问代词,哪里,何处。廋(sōu):隐藏,藏匿。哉:呢。

【原文】11 子曰:“温故而知新[1],可以为师矣[2]。”

【白话译文】

孔子说:“复习学过的知识,能有新的收获,就可以做老师了。”

【英语译文】

Confucius said, “Reviewing what we've learned, we can obtain new knowledge and then we can act as a teacher.”

【注释】(1)温故:复习已学过的知识。而(néng):通“能”。“而”若读本音 ér 的话,意即“温故就知新”。温故就知新,理应人人都做得到,可事实上总有些人做不到。正因为这样,孔子的话是指能做到温故知新的人可以为师。所以笔者认为“而”读“能”最贴切。知新:懂得、参悟到新的知识技能。(2)可以为师:可把“温故而知新”作为自己的师法,自己也就可做别人的老师。

【原文】12 子曰:“君子不器[1]。”

【白话译文】

孔子说:“君子不是一个有限的器皿或工具。”

【英语译文】

Confucius said, "A moral man is not a limited utensil or tool."

【注释】(1)器:器皿,用具。君子和器不同类。用异模拟君子,足见孔子对君子的殷切警戒。器不能自主,其作用也是人所赋予,而且非常有限。如果君子像器,任人摆布利用,则是孔子所不愿看到的现象。

【原文】13 子贡问君子[1]。子曰:"先行其言而后从之[2]。"

【白话译文】

子贡问怎样才能做一个君子。孔子说:"你要说的话先实行了,才说出来。"

【英语译文】

Zi Gong asked how to be a moral man. Confucius answered, "Practice what you want to say first, and then speak it out."

【注释】(1)问君子:探问君子之道。(2)行:实践。从之:从,跟从。之,指代"行"。"从"字前省略了"言"字。

【原文】14 子曰:"君子周而不比[1],小人比而不周[2]。"

【白话译文】

孔子说:"君子忠信亲密而不勾结营私;小人勾结营私而不忠信亲密。"

【英语译文】

Confucius said, "A moral man is loyally intimate but not benifiting himself. A mean man benifiting himself but not being loyally intimate."

【注释】(1)周:忠信亲密。比:勾结营私。(2)小人:为人处世,与君子相反。

【原文】15 子曰:"学而不思则罔[1],思而不学则殆[2]。"

【白话译文】

孔子说："只学习但不思索考虑,就会困惑迷乱;只思索考虑但不学习,就会危险不安。"

【英语译文】

Confucius said, "Learning without thinking leads to confusion. And thinking without learning leads to perils."

【注释】(1)学而不思:学,是指效仿,受教。思,是指思索,考虑。只学不思,犹如囫囵吞枣,不能正常消化,难以吸收营养并排除糟粕。学习时不思则不能深入所学的境界,更不能与当今的现实境界正确连接。罔:困惑,迷乱。(2)思而不学:只思不学,犹如如坐井观天,见识狭窄,难以做出正确判断而做出错误选择。殆:危险;不安。

【原文】16 子曰:"攻乎异端[1],斯害也已[2]。"

【白话译文】

孔子说:"如果专心致志于不正确的议论、主张,那就是祸害呀!"

【英语译文】

Confucius said, "It is scourge if one is absorbed in wrong arguments and statements."

【注释】(1)攻:专治,治学。杨伯峻说:《论语》共享四次"攻"字,像《先进篇》的'小子鸣鼓而攻之',《颜渊篇》的'攻其恶,无攻人之恶'的三个'攻'字,都当'攻击'讲,这里也不例外。"笔者认为这里就是例外。看作'攻击'讲的三个'攻'字都是直连宾语(之、其恶、人之恶),中间没加别的字;因为"攻击"是及物动词,用不着衬字、助词、介词什么的。这里却加了个"乎"字,乎,在这里只能解作介词,与介词"于"同义。"乎异端"即"于异端"也就是说异端不是杨先生所说的攻击的宾语而是介词"乎"的宾语。所以,笔者以为这里就是例外。这是从语法上说,再就历史经验看,异端邪说,不是你一攻击、批判,其"祸害就可以消灭了"。我想孔子不会说出这样不更事的话。他的意思想必是在告诫弟子们,如果往异端研习,那就是祸害了。乎:介词。同"于(于)"。异端:指不同于孔子自己的言论、主张。

(2)斯:连词。这就,那就。害:祸害。也已:语气助词。

【原文】17 子曰:"由[1]! 诲女知之乎[2]? 知之为知之,不知为不知,是知也。"

【白话译文】

孔子说:"由啊! 我的教诲你了解了吗? 了解了就是了解了,不了解就是不了解,这是真正的了解啊!"

【英语译文】

Confucius asked, "You, have you understood my teaching? If you do, you say you understand it; if you don't, you say not understand it. This is real understanding."

【注释】(1)由:孔子的高才生,姓仲,名由,字子路(公元前 542 年—公元前 480 年),卞(故城在今山东平邑县东北仲村)人。小孔子九岁。(2)诲:教诲,名词。女:汝。知:了解,知道。之:本章的三个"之"字作代词解或作助词解都通。

【原文】18 子张学干禄[1]。子曰:"多闻阙疑[2],慎言其余[3],则寡尤[4]。多见阙殆[5],慎行其余[6],则寡悔[7],言寡尤,行寡悔,禄在其中矣[8]。"

【白话译文】

子张请教如何求得俸禄。孔子说:"多多听听,不明白的,暂时空缺,只慎重地讲那些真正明白的。这样就少犯错误;多多看看,危险的事,就不去做,只慎重地做那些真正不危险的事。这样就少有懊悔。说话少犯错误,做事少有懊悔,俸禄就在这里面了。"

【英语译文】

Zi Zhang asked how to get more salary. Confucius answered, "Listen more and talk cautiously about those you've really understood; let it be those you have not knew. Thus you can make less mistakes. Observe more and do cautiously things which are really safe, don't do dangerous ones. Thus you can regret less. While speaking, you make less mistakes, and while doing things you regret less, in which your salary lies."

【注释】(1)子张(公元前 503 年—?):孔子的学生,姓颛(zhuān)孙,名师,字子张,陈人。比孔子小四十八岁。干禄:干,求;禄,旧时官吏的俸给。(2)阙疑(quēyí):遇有疑惑,暂时缺着,不主观推测。(3)其余:指没有疑惑的那些听闻。(4)寡尤:少错误。(5)多见:多看多观察。阕殆:不做危险的事。(6)其余:指不危险、有把握的事。(7)寡悔:少懊悔。(8)其:近指代词。这。指代"言寡尤,行寡悔"。

【原文】19 哀公问曰[1]:"何为则民服[2]?"孔子对曰[3]:"举直错诸枉[4],则民服;举枉错诸直,则民不服。"

【白话译文】

鲁哀公问孔子:"要干些啥事百姓才会服从呢?"孔子回答道:"提拔正直人,不任用邪曲人,百姓就会服从;提拔邪曲人,不任用正直人,百姓就不会服从。"

【英语译文】

Duke Ai of Lu State asked Confucius, "How can I make my subjects obedient?" Confucius answered, "Promote upright men and reject immoral men, and then your subjects will be obedient; on the contrary, promote immoral men and reject upright men, and then your subjects won't be obedient."

【注释】(1)哀公:鲁哀公(公元前 494 年—公元前 466 年),鲁国国君,姓姬名蒋。定公之子,继定公而即位,在位二十七年。"哀"是谥号。(2)服:服从,顺从。(3)对曰:回答道。(4)举:提拔。直:指正直人。错(cù):同"措",指舍弃,置而不用。诸:语气助词,用在句中舒缓语气。枉:指邪曲人。

【原文】20 季康子问[1]:"使民敬、忠以劝[2],如之何[3]?"子曰:"临之以庄[4],则敬;孝慈,则忠[5];举善而教不能,则劝○[6]。"

【白话译文】

季康子问:"要使人民恭敬、忠诚和互相勉励,应该怎么办?"孔子说:"你用庄重不苟的态度治理人民,他们就会恭敬;你孝顺父母长辈,慈爱下属或晚辈,他们就会忠诚;你提拔好人,教育能力弱的人,他们就会互相勉励。"

【英语译文】

Ji Kang asked, "What should I do to make the subjects humble, loyal and encourage each other?" Confucius answered, "If you govern your subjects with modesty, they will be humble; if you are filial to your parents and elder people and be kind to minors or younger people, they will be loyal; if you promote moral men and educate weak men, they will encourage each other."

【注释】(1)季康子:鲁大夫季孙桓子的儿子,名肥,鲁国正卿,"康"是谥号。(2)敬:恭敬。忠:忠诚。以:连词,同"和"。劝:勉励 (3)如之何:怎么办。(4)临之:临民,治理人民。之,代指"使民"的"民"。庄:庄重不苟。(5)孝慈:对尊长孝敬,对下属或晚辈慈爱。(6)举善:提拔好人。不能:指能力弱的人。

【原文】21 或谓孔子曰[1]:" 子奚不为政[2]?"子曰:"书云[3]:'孝乎惟孝[4],友于兄弟[5],施于有政[6]。'是亦为政[7],奚其为为政[8]?"

【白话译文】

有人问孔子:"先圣您怎么不当官参与政治呢?"孔子说:"《尚书》中说'孝呀只有孝顺父母 ,友爱兄弟,这种风气能引导善政。'这也就是参与政治了啊,为何定要做官才算参与政治呢?"

【英语译文】

Somebody asked Confucius, "Why didn't you participate in politics as an official?" Confucius answered, "*The Book of History* says 'Filial piety means to be filial to one's parents and befriend brothers, which can lead to philanthropic government.' Doing so means participating in politics. Why does becoming an official necessarily mean participating in politics?

【注释】(1)或:有人。(2)奚(xī):疑问词。何,怎么,为什么。为政:从政。(3)书:指尚书。书云以下三句见伪古文《尚书》君陈,略有出入,可能是《尚书》逸文。孝乎惟孝:乎,表提顿,犹"呀"。(4) 惟,只有。(5)友:亲近相爱。(6)施(yì):延伸到,影响到。有政:有,在这里是名词词头,无实义。有政,即"政"。(7)是亦:是,代指此。是亦,指这也是。(8)奚其:奚,义见注2。其,远指代词,指当官从政。为:是。

【原文】22 子曰:“人而无信[1],不知其可也[2]。大车无輗[3],小车无軏[4],其何以行之哉[5]?”

【白话译文】

孔子说:“人不讲信誉,那怎么可以。譬如大车没有安鬲的关键,小车没有安衡的关键,那怎么能驾行呢?”

【英语译文】

Confucius said, “How could it be if a person has no credibility. For example, how could it be if a carriage or a cart has no jointing key on its yoke?”

【注释】(1)而:结构助词。与“之”同,用在主语和谓语间,使句子在形式上转化为偏正词组,失去独立性,从而成为句子成分。人而无信,这个偏正词组是句子的宾语,由于强调而提前。其在句中的本位由代词“其”代占。(2)不知其可也:这个句子省略了主语“我”。谓语动词“知”后的“其”代替“人而无信”作宾语。可,补语。(3)大车:用牛拉的车。輗(ní):大车辕端与横木(鬲 gé)相接处的关键(活销)。小车:用马拉的车。軏(yuè):小车辕端与横木(衡)相接处的关键(活销)。辕端的横木(鬲、衡)就是驾牲口(牛、马)之处。(5)其:指代大车和小车。

【原文】23 子张问:“十世可知也[1]?”子曰:“殷因于夏礼[2],所损益可知也[3];周因于殷礼,所损益可知也。其或继周者[4],虽百世可知也[5]。

【白话译文】

子张问:“今后时代的礼仪制度可以预先知道吗?”孔子说:“殷代沿袭夏代的礼仪制度,所减去的、所增加的、是可以知道的;周代沿袭殷代的礼仪制度,所减去的、所增加的、也是可以知道的。将来有继周代而当政者,即使一百代,其礼仪制度的兴废,也是可以推知的。”

【英语译文】

Zi Zhang asked, “Could we know beforehand the rite system of next generations?” Confucius said, “Yin Dynasty followed the rite system of Xia Dynasty, and we know what were added and were what deleted; Zhou Dynasty followed the rite system of Yin

Dynasty, and we know what were added and were what deleted; in the future, when those become governers replacing Zhou Dynasty even for hundred generations, we can also infer their addition and deletion of rite system."

【注释】(1)世:根据孔子的答语举夏、殷、周三世(代)为例,这里的世,应作易姓为王的"朝代"解,不宜以"古时称三十年为一世"作解。也:语气助词。这里用于疑问句,表疑问语气,相当于"耶"。(2)因:沿袭,承袭。礼:礼仪制度。(3)损益:减去与增加。(4)其:副词。这里表时间的未来,犹将来,以后。或:有。(5)虽:连词。这里表假设关系,犹纵然,即使。

【原文】24 子曰:"非其鬼而祭之[1],谄也[2]。见义不为无勇也[3]。"

【白话译文】

孔子说:"祭祀别人的祖先,是献媚。眼见符合道义的事不做,是没有勇气。"

【英语译文】

Confucius said, "It's flattery to sacrifice other's ancestor. It's cowardly to do nothing upon moral things."

【注释】(1)非其鬼:不是所当祭之鬼。鬼:古代人死都叫"鬼",一般指已死的祖先而言,也偶有泛指的。(2)谄(chǎn):求媚,阿谀。(3)见义不为无勇也:眼见符合道义的事不做,是没有勇气。

八佾篇第三(共二十六章)

本篇主要涉及"礼"的问题,主张维护礼在制度上、礼节上的种种规定,重点讨论如何维护"礼"的问题。

【原文】1 孔子谓季氏[1]:"八佾舞于庭[2],是可忍也[3],孰不可忍也[4]?"

【白话译文】

孔子谈论季氏说:"他用天子才能使用的六十四人的阵容,在家庙中伴随音乐献舞，这样的事都可以容忍，别的什么事不可以容忍？”

【英语译文】

While talking about Jisun people, Confucius said, “He ranked Monarch's level to summon sixty four persons to dance with music in his yard. If we can stand this, then what cannot be stood?”

【注释】(1)谓：评论。季氏：鲁大夫季孙氏。其人是谁，韩诗外传似以为季康子，马融注则以为季桓子；杨伯峻根据左传昭公二十五年的记载和《汉书·刘向传》断定为季平子(季孙如意)(2)八佾：佾(yì)，古代奏乐舞蹈，八个人一行，这样一行叫一佾；八佾(8×8)共六十四人。这样的舞蹈阵容，只有天子才能使用。诸侯用六佾(8×6)共四十八人。大夫用四佾(8×4)共三十二人。士用二佾(8×2)共一十六人。四佾才是季氏所应该使用的。庭：指季氏家庙。(3)忍：容忍。一解作“忍心(干)”也通。(4)孰：谁，什么。

【原文】2 三家者以雍彻[1]。子曰：“‘相维辟公[2]，天子穆穆[3]，’奚取于三家之堂[4]？”

【白话译文】

孟孙、叔孙、季孙三家祭祖时，也唱着《周颂雍篇》来撤除祭品。孔子说：“雍诗有‘助祭的人是诸侯，天子主祭庄严肃穆’两句，怎么能拿到三家的堂上去唱？”

【英语译文】

When the three ministers Mengsun, Shussun and Jisun sacrificed their ancestors, they sang the song of *Yong* in *Hymns of Zhou* to retreat sacrificial objects. Confucius said, “Poetic lines in *Yong* says, ‘Lords from each state aid sacrificing and King Wu perform modestly leading.’ How could they sing in their own halls?”

【注释】(1)三家：鲁国当政大夫孟孙、叔孙、季孙三家。者：语气助词，表停顿。以雍：以，用。训“歌唱。”雍，亦作“雝”，《诗经·周颂》中的一篇。彻，同“撤”，古代祭礼完毕后，撤祭品祭器时，乐人唱诗以娱神。(2)相(xiàng)：助祭的人。维：是。辟公(bìgōng)：诸侯。(3)穆穆：庄严肃穆。(4)取于：拿到。

【原文】3 孔子曰:“人而不仁,如礼何[1]? 人而不仁,如乐何[2]?”

【白话译文】

孔子说:“一个不爱人的人,怎样对付礼仪制度? 一个不爱人的人,怎样对付音乐感化?”

【英语译文】

Confucius said, “If a person doesn't love others, how could he treat rites and rituals? If a person doesn't love others, how could he be moved music?”

【注释】(1)不仁:没有仁心,不爱人。如:对付,处置。何:怎么样。礼:礼仪制度。(2)乐:音乐,乐章。

【原文】4 林放问礼之本[1]。子曰:“大哉问[2]! 礼[3],与其奢也[4],宁俭[5];丧[6],与其易也[7],宁戚[8]。”

【白话译文】

林放问礼仪的根本是什么。孔子说:“你问得对,这个问题的意义很大呀! 礼仪,与其奢侈浪费,宁可朴素俭约;丧事,与其尽力置办,宁可内心悲伤。”

【英语译文】

Lin Fang required the root of rites and rituals. Confucius said, “A good question and it has great significance! Rites and rituals should be simple rather than extravagant; funeral ceremony should be inner sad rather than superficial shows.”

【注释】(1)林放:鲁人。本:根本。(2)大哉问:感叹句。赞叹所问得体,意义很大。(3)礼:礼仪。(4)与其:连词。同“宁”“孰若”“不如”等配合,表示选择。“与其”后跟舍项,“宁”“孰若”“不如”等后跟取项。奢:奢侈,浪费。(5)宁:宁可,宁愿。俭:节省。(6)丧:丧事,丧礼。(7)易:治理。戚:悲伤。

【原文】5 子曰:“夷狄之有君[1],不如诸夏之亡也[2]。

【白话译文】

孔子说:四方蛮邦虽然各有君主,但还不如中国在没有君主时。

【英语译文】

Confucius said, "Although there're monarchs in states of minority ethnic regions, these states still cannot be compared with Mid-Chinese Kingdom without a monarch."

【注释】(1)夷狄:古称东方部族为夷,北方部族为狄。常用以称除华夏族以外的各族。(2)诸夏:周代分封的中原各个诸侯国。泛指中原地区。亡(wù):无,没有。《论语》中"亡"后不用宾语,"无"后都有宾语。

【原文】6 季氏旅于泰山[1]。子谓冉有曰[2]:"女弗能救与[3]?"对曰:"不能。"子曰:"呜呼!曾谓泰山不如林放乎[4]?"

【白话译文】

季氏祭祀泰山。孔子对冉有说:"你不能阻止吗?"冉有回答道:"不能。"孔子说:"哎呀!怎么说泰山神还不如林放懂得不接受无礼的朝拜吗?"

【英语译文】

Ji Shi sacrificed Mountain Tai. Confucius asked Ran You, "Couldn't you prevent him?" Ran You answered, "I couldn't." Confucius said, "Alas, how could they know less than Lin Fang does that mountainous spirit never accepts sacrifice without rite?"

【注释】(1)季氏:鲁国大夫。旅:祭山。泰山:五岳之首。天子登位或国有大故,天子可祭泰山。(2)冉有:名求,字子有,孔子的学生。比孔子小二十三岁。冉有当时在季氏门下做事。(3)女:汝。救:制止,阻止。与:语气助词汝弗能救与。(4)曾(zēng):代词,表示疑问。相当于"何""怎"。

【原文】7 子曰:"君子无所争[1]。必也射乎[2]!揖让而升[3],下而饮[4]。其争也君子[5]。"

【白话译文】

孔子说:"君子没有什么可争,如果必须争,就是在射礼中射箭了!拱手行礼,相互谦让登场,力争中的(箭靶中心)。射完后,再行礼,退场,饮酒,负者要按规定加饮罚酒。这么争嘛不失为君子。"

【英语译文】

Confucius said, "A moral man has nothing to strive for. If there is any, that's archery! They are modest and humble toward each other to stage on and try to succeed in shooting. After that, they retreat to have a drink and the loser should be fined to drink more. They strive in such way to be still a moral man."

【注释】(1)无所争:争权夺利、争夺财物、争斗事理、争强好胜等都是为一己之私而争。君子对于此无所争。(2)必:指一定要争。射:射礼,比射箭。大射礼规定两人一组,相互作揖谦让,然后登场;射完再相互作揖退下。按中靶多寡分胜负。各组射完后再作揖登堂饮酒。胜者罚负者饮酒。(3)揖让:拱手行礼,相互谦让。升:登场。(4)下:下场。(5)其争也君子:这是一个判断句,其争,即"这么争",是主语。也,是语气助词,表停顿。君子,是表语,前面省略了"是"或"为"。揣摩孔子之意,大约是通过射礼之争,不仅不是小人那种一己之争,而是正好体现"君子求诸己"和"天行健,君子以自强不息"的精神。

【原文】8 子夏问曰:"'巧笑倩兮[1]。美目盼兮[2],素以为绚兮[3]。'何谓也?"子曰:"绘事后素[4]。"曰:"礼后乎?"子曰:"起予者商也[5]!始可与言诗已矣[6]。"

【白话译文】

子夏问道:"'美好的笑容酒窝靓丽啊,秀美的眼睛黑白闪烁啊,使用白绢好做彩色绘画啊。'这几句诗是什么意思?"孔子道:"先有白色粉底,然后绘画。"子夏道:"这么说礼仪是在仁德之后产生的了?"孔子道:"真能启发我的是卜商呀!你正可参与谈论《诗经》了。"

【英语译文】

Zi Xia asked, "'While she is smiling sweetly, all men are so attracted by her brightly shining eyes. Colorful drawings can be drawn on white silk.' What does it mean?" Confucius said, "When you have white silk, you begin to draw picture." Zi Xia said, "Does it mean that humanity leads to morality?" Confucius said, "It's you who enlightened me, and you can discuss *Book of Songs* with me."

【注释】(1)巧笑:美好的笑。倩(qiàn):笑靥美好的样子。靥(yè):面颊上的微窝,俗称酒窝。(2)美目:秀美的眼睛。盼:眼睛黑白分明的样子。(3)素:指素质,即白色质地。以:用,使用。为:绘画,撰写。绚(xuàn):有文采,多彩。素以为绚兮:犹言用白色质地(如白绢)来作彩色绘画啊。这三句诗,第一、二句见于《诗经·卫风·硕人》。第三句可能是逸句。王先谦三家诗义集疏以为鲁诗有此一句。(4)绘事后素:先以粉底为质而后施五彩,比喻有良好的质地,才能进行锦上添花的加工。(5)起:启发。商:子夏,姓卜,名商,字子夏。(6)始可:正可。与言:参与谈论。已矣:语气词。用于句末与"矣"同义。

【原文】9 子曰:"夏礼吾能言之,杞不足征也[1];殷礼吾能言之。宋不足征也[2]。文献不足故也[3]。足则吾能征之矣。"

【白话译文】

孔子说:"夏代的礼,我能讲述,它的后代杞国的礼尚不足以证明;殷代的礼,我能讲述,它的后代宋国的礼尚不足以证明。这是他们的历史文件和贤者不够多的缘故。若有够多的档案和贤者,我就可以引来证明了。"

【英语译文】

Confucius said, "I could elaborate rites in Xia Dynasty but I couldn't prove those in its descendant , Qi State; I could elaborate rites in Yin Dynasty but I couldn't prove those in its descendant , Song State. This is because there were little historic profiles and sages. If there were enough historic profiles and sages, then I could quote them to prove their rites."

【注释】(1)杞:古国名。公元前十一世纪周封诸侯国。公元前445年灭于楚。起初的故城在今河南杞县,后迁至今山东安丘东北。《史记·陈玘世家》:"周武王克殷纣求禹之后,得东楼公,封之于杞。"故知杞君是夏禹的后代。征:证明;证验。(2)宋:周代诸侯国名。子姓,周武王灭商后,封商纣子武庚于商旧都(今河南商丘)。成王时,武庚叛乱被杀,又以其地封与纣的庶兄微子启,号宋公,为宋国。战国初年曾迁都彭城(今江苏徐州)公元前286年为齐所灭。其辖地在今河南东部及山东、江苏、安徽之间。(3)文献:有关典章制度的文字数据和多闻熟悉掌故的人。

【原文】10 子曰:"禘自既灌而往者[1],吾不欲观之矣[2]。"

【白话译文】

孔子说:"现代的禘祭,从把香酒浇在地上求神降临起,往后的程序,我都不想看了。"

【英语译文】

Confucius said, "Nowadays the king's sacrificial procedures after wine has been splashed on ground cannot arouse my interest."

【注释】(1)禘(dì):古代帝王者的大祭。王者立始祖之庙,又推始祖所自出之帝祀之于始祖庙内,而以始祖配之。成王以周公有大勋劳,赐鲁重祭。故得禘于周公之庙。以文王为所出之帝,而周公配之,这是非礼的。灌:古代祭祀的一种仪式。祭祀开始时把香酒浇在地上,求神降临。而往者:指灌祭后接下去的祭祀仪式。(2)之:远指代词,那个,那些。

【原文】11 或问禘之说[1]。子曰:"不知也;知其说者之于天下也[2],其如示诸斯乎[3]!"指其掌[4]。

【白话译文】

有人问天子举行祭祖大典的意义。孔子说:"不知道啊,知道的人治理天下,好比瞧这里一样清楚明白吧!"一边说一边指指自己的手掌。

【英语译文】

Somebody wondered the significance of king's sacrificial ceremony. Confucius answered, "I don't know. Those who know it govern this world. They are quite clear about it just as we see our palms." He pointed to his palm as he was saying so.

【注释】(1)或问:有人问。说:意思,意义。(2)之:结构助词。于:为,治。作"对,对于"解,亦通。天下:古时多指中国范围内的全部土地;全国。后来增加"全世界"一义。(3)示:同"视"。示诸斯:指示代词,这里代指"掌"。犹言"如瞧自己的手掌一样,了如指掌"。又解:示(zhì),通"置"。犹言"如像置于掌中,很有把握”。(4)指其掌:孔子自指其掌。

【原文】12 祭如在[1],祭神如神在[2]。子曰:“吾不与祭[3],如不祭[4]。”

【白话译文】

祭祀祖先就像祖先真在那里,祭鬼神就像鬼神真在那里。孔子说:“我没有参与祭祀,就像没有举行祭祀。”

【英语译文】

It seems that ancestors were there while we sacrifice them; it seems spirits were there while we sacrifice them. Confucius said, “ It seems that there were no sacrificial ceremony while I didn’t participate in it. ”

【注释】(1)祭:指祭祖先神。如在:如真在那神位上。(2)祭神:指祭百神。(3)不:没有。与(yù):参与。不与祭,即没有参与。(4)如不祭:像没有举行祭祀。

【原文】13 王孙贾问曰[1]:“与其媚于奥[2],宁媚于灶[3],何谓也?”子曰:“不然[4];获罪于天无所祷也[5]。”

【白话译文】

王孙贾问:“‘与其向房屋里西南角求福,宁可向灶台求福,’这话是什么意思?”孔子说:“这话不对。得罪了上天,没有地方祈祷。”

【英语译文】

Wang Sunjia asked, “ ‘You would pray for the place of cooker rather than south-west corner in the room. ’ What does it mean?” Confucius answered, “It’s wrong. There were no place to pray if you offended the heaven. ”

【注释】(1)王孙贾:卫灵公的大臣。(2)与其:选择连词。这里与“宁”配合使用。媚:逢迎取悦。于:介词,向。奥(ào):室内西南隅,古时祭祀设神主或尊长居坐的地方。(3)灶:弄饭的设备,古人认为灶有灶神。(4)不然:不合理,不对。(5)获罪:得罪。无所祷:没有地方祈祷。

【原文】14 子曰:“周监于二代[1],郁郁乎文哉[2]! 吾从周[3]。”

【白话译文】

孔子说:“周代借鉴夏代和商代,礼乐制度是多么丰富多彩呀! 我采取周代的。”

【英语译文】

Confucius said, “Zhou Dynasty learned from Xia and Shang Dynasties and it had rich and colorful rules and regulations! I'll adopt those of Zhou Dynasty.”

【注释】(1)周:周代。监(jiàn):通“鉴”,指借鉴,参考。二代:指夏代和商代。(2)郁郁:文采盛美的样子。文:指礼乐制度。(3)从:谓采取某种方针方法。从周,谓采取周代的礼乐制度。

【原文】15 子入太庙[1],每事问[2]。或曰:“孰谓鄹人之子知礼乎[3]? 入太庙,每事问。”子闻之,曰:“是礼也[4]。”

【白话译文】

孔子进入周公庙,每件事情都发问。有人便说:“谁说叔梁纥的这个儿子懂礼呀? 他到了太庙,每件事都要向别人请教。”孔子听到了这话,便说:“这正是礼呀!”

【英语译文】

Confucius asked about everything while he entered Zhou Gong's Temple. Somebody then said, “Who said that Shuliang He's son understood rites? He asked about everything while in the Temple.” Hearing this, Confucius said, “It is just rite!”

【注释】(1)太庙:古代开国之君叫太祖。太祖之庙叫太庙。周公旦是鲁国最初受封之君。因此这太庙就是周公旦的庙。(2)每事问:每件事(遇事)都发问。(3)鄹(zōu):又作“郰”,地名。史记孔子世家:“孔子生鲁昌平乡郰邑。”有人说,这就是今山东省曲阜市东南的西邹集。鄹人:指孔子父亲叔梁纥。叔梁纥曾经作过鄹大夫。古代通常把某地的大夫称为“某人”,因之这里也把鄹大夫叔梁纥,称为“鄹人”。(4)是礼也:犹言“每事问是礼也。”

【原文】16 子曰:“射不主皮[1],为力不同科[2],古之道也[3]。”

【白话译文】

孔子说:“射箭比赛不以射穿靶子为主,射中了就可以,因为人的力量各自不同;古代就是这么主张的。”

【英语译文】

Confucius said, “Archery contest doesn't emphasize breaking target skin. It's alright if one gets a shot because each person has different strength. In ancient time, it was like this.”

【注释】(1)射:指古人习礼的射箭比赛,不是军事中的射敌。不主皮:“皮”指兽皮做的箭靶子。古代箭靶子总名叫“侯”,用布制的叫“布侯”,用兽皮制的叫“皮侯”。“不主皮”意谓习礼的射箭比赛,以射中箭靶为主而不以贯穿箭靶(皮侯)为主。(2)为(wèi):因为。科:等级。(3)道:政治主张,思想体系。

【原文】17 子贡欲去告朔之饩羊[1]。子曰:“赐也[2]!尔爱其羊,我爱其礼。”

【白话译文】

子贡想把鲁国每月初一例行虚假祭祖庙的那只活羊取消不用。孔子说:“赐呀!你可惜那只活羊,我可惜那项礼制。”

【英语译文】

Zi Gong didn't want to use the alive sheep as a sacrificial symbol in ancestral temple on the first of every month. Confucius told him, “Oh! Ci, you cherish the sheep but I cherish the ritual.”

【注释】(1)去:去掉,除去。告朔饩羊:“告”,古读gù,今读gào。“朔”(shuò):旧历每月初一。“饩羊”:用为祭品的羊。“饩”(xì):活牲,亦指生肉。“告朔饩羊”,周制,每年季冬,周天子把第二年的历书颁给诸侯。这历书中包括那年有无闰月,每月初一是哪一天,因之叫“颁告朔”。诸侯接受了这一历书,藏于祖庙。每逢初一,便杀一只活羊祭于庙,然后回到朝廷听政。这祭庙叫“告朔”,听政叫“视朔”或“听朔”。鲁国从文公开始不视朔,而有司仍然供给饩羊,所以子贡认为不必虚应故事,干脆连羊也不杀。孔子认为尽管这是残存的形式总比什么也不留好。(2)赐:子贡名。

【原文】18 子曰:“事君尽礼[1],人以为谄也[2]。”

【白话译文】

孔子说:“为君主做事,全依君臣之礼去做,别人认为是谄媚。”

【英语译文】

Confucius said, “If you do things for your king based on king-official rite, others will regard it as flattery.”

【注释】(1)事君:为君主做事。尽礼:全依君臣之礼。(2)人:旁人,别人。以为:认为。谄:谄媚。

【原文】19 定公问[1]:“君使臣,臣事君,如之何[2]?”孔子对曰:“君使臣以礼,臣事君以忠。”

【白话译文】

鲁定公问:“君主使用臣下,臣下服侍君主,各自应该怎么样?”孔子答道:“君主使用臣下,应该依礼;臣下服侍君主,应该没有二心。”

【英语译文】

Duke Ding of Lu State asked, “When a king employed his officials and his officials serve the king, what should they do?” Confucius answered, “A king should employ his officials according to rites and officials should serve their king without loyalty.”

【注释】(1)定公:鲁君,名宋,“定”是谥号。昭公之弟,继昭公而立,在位十五年(公元前 509 年—公元前 495 年)。(2)如之何:“之”,代词。指代“使”与“事”。

【原文】20 子曰:“关雎[1],乐而不淫[2],哀而不伤[3]。”

【白话译文】

孔子说:“关雎这诗好哇,快乐而不放荡,哀愁而不痛苦。”

【英语译文】

Confucius said, “The poem *Guan Ju* is very good. It expresses unwanton happiness and unbitter sympathy.”

【注释】(1)关雎:在《诗经》的编排上是《国风周南》的第一首诗,即是整部《诗经》的第一首诗。这首诗是歌咏男性追求女性的诗。描写真实、朴素、生动、形象,情感纯洁、雅致,有爱慕、向往,有担忧不安,有欣喜快乐。(2)乐:满足心愿时的心情和举动。淫:古人凡过分以至于失当的地步叫“淫”。(3)哀:怜悯,怜爱,同情,担心得失等都是“哀”,不是“乐”。“哀”而过分,有毁身心健康便是“伤”。

【原文】21 哀公问社于宰我[1]。宰我对曰[2]:“夏后氏以松[3],殷人以柏,周人以栗[4],曰,使民战栗。”子闻之,曰:“成事不说[5],遂事不谏[6],既往不咎[7]。”

【白话译文】

鲁哀公问宰我,作土地神木主用什么树木。宰我答道:“夏代用松木,殷代用柏木,周代用栗木:意在使民战战栗栗。”孔子听到了这话,〔责备宰我〕说:“对做过的事不要再提它了,往事或已经完成的事不要再挽救了,对过去的过错不要再责难追究了。”

【英语译文】

Duke Ai of Lu State asked Zai Wo what kind of tree can be used for wood-made memorial tablet of Earth. Zai Wo answered, “ Pine was used in Xia Dynasty, and cypress was used in Yin Dynasty. Chestnut was used in Zhou Dynasty in order to make common people tremble.” Confucius reproached him after he heard this, “Don’t mention what has been done. Don’t remonstrate things in the past or completed. Don’t reproach what have been wrongly done.”

【注释】(1)哀公:鲁国君,名蒋,鲁定公之子,继定公即位在位二十七年,谥号“哀”。社:古代谓土地神。从宰我的答话可知哀公所问的社是指社主。古代祭土地神要替他立一个木制的牌位,这牌位叫主,也叫木主。它是神灵的凭依。如果国家有对外战争还必须载这木主而行。(2)宰我:孔子学生,名予,字子我。(3)夏后氏:指禹受舜禅而建立的夏王朝。氏,在此指"朝代"。以松:用松木作土地神木主。下以柏、以栗同此。(4)殷人,周人:殷代,周代。"人"在此指特定的人。君:最高统治者。(5)成事不说:对做过的事不再提它。(6)遂事不谏:往事或已经完成的事不再挽救了。"谏":匡正,挽回。(7)既往不咎:对过去的过错不再责难追究。

【原文】22 子曰:"管仲之器小哉[1]!"或曰:"管仲俭乎[2]?""管氏有三归[3],官事不摄[4],焉得俭[5]?""然则管仲知礼乎[6]?"曰:"邦君树塞门[7],管氏亦树塞门。邦君为两君之好[8],有反坫[9],管氏亦有反坫。管氏而知礼[10],孰不知礼[11]?"

【白话译文】

孔子说:"管仲的度量很小呀!"有人问:"管仲是不是很节俭呢?"孔子说:"管子用价格规律、借贷手段,在重敛下又巧取百姓粮食,他手下的人员,从不兼差,怎么能够节俭呢?"那人又问:"那么,管仲知礼吗?"孔子又说:"国君宫殿门前立照壁,管子门前也立照壁,国君招待外国君主,堂上有放酒杯的土台,管子也有这样的土台。管子假若懂礼,还有谁不懂礼?"

【英语译文】

Confucius said, "Guan Zhong was very narrow-minded!" Somebody then asked, "Was he very frugal?" Confucius said, "He collected common people's grains by price law and method of loan. His subordinates never took two posts. How could he be frugal?" The man asked again, "Then, did he know rites?" Confucius answered, "A screen wall was set facing the gate of king's palace. Guan Zi also set a screen wall. There was earth terrace for placing wine cup in the hall when his king diverted foreign king visitor. Guan zi also had such kind of terrace. If Guan Zi knew rites, whoever didn't?"

【注释】(1)管仲:春秋时齐国人,名夷吾,做了齐桓公的宰相,使桓公称霸诸侯。器:度量;胸怀。(2)俭:节俭。(3)管氏:氏系于姓或姓名字号后以为敬称。可不译或译作管子。三归:管仲为相时,每年在重敛下,百姓手里只得到十分之三的谷物,管仲用价格规律、借贷手段再将百姓手中十分之三的余粮收走。三归,犹言“重敛巧取”。(4)官事:官府的事,公事。不摄:不代理,不兼职。(5)焉:疑问代词,作状语,指怎么,哪里。得:能够。俭:节俭,俭约。(6)然则:连词,连接句子。犹“如此,那么”“那么”。(7)邦君:国君。树塞门:树,动词,立。塞门:塞读 sāi 或读 sè。所谓“塞门”,包括屏和影壁。门外的叫屏,包括照壁(大门外正对面筑的屏风状的墙)和小墙(对着一般门筑的墙);门内的叫影壁(大门内或屏门内做屏蔽的、有浮雕的墙壁)。屏门,指分隔内院和外院的门。(8)邦君:国君。为两君之好:国君与外君友好会见。(9)反坫:坫(diàn),古代筑在殿下屋和太庙内两柱间的土台。饮宴礼毕,将空酒杯放回坫上。(10)而:假设连词,指假如,假若。

【原文】23 子语鲁大师乐[1],曰:“乐其可知也[2]:始作[3],翕如也[4];从之[5],纯如也[6],皦如也[7],绎如也[8],以成[9]。”

【白话译文】

孔子告诉鲁国太师音乐的演奏道德,说:“音乐是可以感知的,不可胡来呀。开始弹奏,应当和合盛美,接下来展开演奏,应当纯净如丝,孱杂不得;清晰分明,含糊不得;相续不绝,打断不得;从而演奏一个完整的乐曲。”

【英语译文】

Confucius told the great music master of Lu State the way of playing music. He said, “Music can be recognized and you cannot play casually. At the beginning, it should be harmonious and then it should become pure without noise, clear without confusion, continuous without interruption. Thus you can make a whole musical melody.”

【注释】(1)语(yù):告诉。鲁大师乐:“大”(tài),太的古字。鲁大师,鲁国乐官之长。乐,音乐。(3)其:结构助词,和之的作用相同,用在句子的主语、谓语间,取消其独立性,使句子词组化,从而作为句子成份。这里是用在复合句的前一分句里的,取消了分句的独立性,读听起来觉得语意未完,急欲知道下文。译时去掉不要。(3)始作:开始演奏。(4)翕(xì)如:和合盛美的样子。(5)从(zòng):展开演奏,继续演奏。(6)纯如:纯净如丝。(7)皦(jiǎo)如:清晰分明的样子。(8)绎如:相续不绝的样子。(9)以成:而奏完一曲。有人认为本章有疑点,看不出孔子对一个掌管音乐的太师讲这些演奏常识的旨归所在(太师不懂这个程序吗?)。孔子此论仿佛俗言所说关公面前耍大刀,圣人面前诵三字经。怀疑本章文字可能有错误。或者孔子讲这些话时另有当下情境,更有可能是孔子“问乐”,后文为鲁太师答语。如此,“子语鲁大师乐”改一字,为“子问鲁大师乐”则全章皆通。笔者以为正是因为当时礼崩乐坏这个大情境,乐师也已有慑于权势而媚俗迎合,胡乱演奏之弊(如八佾等)。孔子以温和的态势历数演奏程序以警示太师,音乐是人们能够感知的,不可胡来。所谓“改一字”也应属不可胡来之列。

【原文】24 仪封人请见[1],曰:“君子之至于斯也,吾未尝不得见也[2]。”从者见之[3]。出曰[4]:“二三子何患于丧乎[5]?天下之无道也久矣[6],天将以夫子为木铎[7]。”

【白话译文】

仪地的长官要求谒见孔子,他说:“凡是君子、贤人到了这里,我从来没有不求见的。”孔子的追随者引他拜见了孔子。他出来说:“诸位,你们何必担忧夫子失位离国呢?天下纷乱已经很久了,上天要夫子成为指引天下的圣人。”

【英语译文】

An official in Yi requested to visit Confucius, he said, “Whenever moral man or virtuous man come here, I never miss visiting them.” The adherent of Confucius led him to visit Confucius. After that he came out saying, “All of you, don't worry about that Confucius will lose his post and leave his country. The Heaven ordered Confucius to be sage, leading the common people since disorder has lost for a very long time.”

【注释】(1)仪:地名。卫邑(见《朱熹集注》)。封人:掌管守护边疆的官员。请见:见,古读 xiàn,胡三省注:“凡下见上之见,音贤遍翻。”。请见,犹言仪封人,向孔子的学生请求谒见孔子。(2)未尝不得见:未尝,即未曾,不曾。不得见,即得不到谒见,没有谒见。这里是两个否定词连用构成双重否定,比肯定句委婉。(3)从者:从,zòng,通“踪”。从者,即追随者。指孔子的学生。见之:见(xiàn)指介绍,荐举。见之是指介绍仪封人谒见孔子。(4)出曰:仪封人谒见孔子后退出来说。(5)二三子:犹诸君,几个人。何患:为什么忧虑。丧(sàng):指失位离国。(6)无道:指社会政治纷乱、腐败。(7)木铎:以木为舌的大铃,铜质。古代宣布政教法令时,巡行振鸣此铃以引起众人注意。

【原文】25 子谓韶[1],“尽美矣[2],又尽善也[3]。”谓武[4],“尽美矣,未尽善也。”

【白话译文】

孔子论到韶时说:“音声美极了,而且意境也好极了。”论到武时说:“音声美极了,可是意境却不够好。”

【英语译文】

As for Shao music, Confucius commented, “The music is perfect concerning melody and artistic conception.” As for Wu music, Confucius commented, “The music is perfect concerning melody but not artistic conception.”

【注释】(1)韶:舜时的乐曲名。(2)美:指乐曲的声音而言。(3)善:指乐曲反映的内容而言。舜的天子之位是由尧“禅让”而来。故孔子认为“尽善”。周武王的天子之位是由讨伐商纣而来,乐章中大约有杀伐流血的音象,尽管是正义的战争,这是理性和平的孔子不愿欣赏的。故孔子认为“未尽善”。(4)武:周武王时乐曲名。

【原文】26 子曰:“居上不宽[1],为礼不敬[2],临丧不哀[3],吾何以观之哉?”

【白话译文】

孔子说:“身居上位不宽容下面的人,对待礼制礼节很粗暴,办丧事没有哀挽心情,我怎么继续观察他呢?”

【英语译文】

Confucius said, “If a person in high official post cannot forgive his subordinates, behaves rudely toward rites and has distressed feelings in funeral ceremony, how could I continue to observe him?”

【注释】(1)上:高位,上位。宽:宽容,宽厚。(2)为礼:对待礼制礼节。不敬:不尊重。(3)临丧:办丧事。不哀:心情轻松,不哀挽。

里仁篇第四(共二十六章)

前一篇的中心说“礼”,这一篇讲“仁”。孔子的核心思想是“仁”,“礼”只是

“仁”的表现形式。

【原文】1 子曰:“里仁为美[1]。择不处仁[2],焉得知[3]?”

【白话译文】

孔子说:“盛行仁风的住地是美好的。择居不与仁人君子为邻,哪能算聪明?”

【英语译文】

Confucius said, “A dwelling place with humanity is ideally beautiful. It's unwise not to live as neighbor of humane people.”

【注释】(1)里仁:里,可作名词讲,居住的地方。里仁,即风俗仁厚的居住地,也可作动词讲,指居住,为邻。里仁,也指居住在仁者所居之里,与仁者为邻。本译文取第一解。(2)择不处仁:择,指择居。处(chǔ),居住。择不处仁,意谓“择居不与仁人君子为邻”。(3)焉得:哪有。知:“智”的古字。

【原文】2 子曰:“不仁者不可以久处约[1],不可以长处乐[2]。仁者安仁[3],知者利仁[4]。”

【白话译文】

孔子说:“不仁的人不可以长久地居于贫困中,也不可以长久地居于安乐中。有仁德的人安于仁;有智慧的人利用仁。”

【英语译文】

Confucius said, “Inhumane people cannot lead poor life or comfortable life forever. People with humanity stick to humanity and wise people make use of humanity.”

【注释】(1)约:贫困。不仁之人。久约必滥。(2)乐:安乐,不仁之人久乐必淫。(3)安仁:安心于仁而不移。(4)利仁:利用仁以成事。

【原文】3 子曰:“唯仁者能好人[1],能恶人[2]。”

【白话译文】

孔子说:"只有仁人才能正确地喜爱人,正确地厌恶人。"

【英语译文】

Confucius said, "Only people with humanity can love and hate others correctly."

【注释】(1)好(hào):爱好,喜爱。(2)恶(wù):厌恶,憎恨。

【原文】4 子曰:"苟志于仁矣[1],无恶也[2]。"

【白话译文】

孔子说:"只要立志行仁德了,就将不会作恶了。"

【英语译文】

Confucius said, "If a person determined to do humane things, then he will not act evilly."

【注释】(1)苟(gǒu):假如,如果,只要。志于仁:立志行仁德。(2)无恶:无(wú),副词,表否定,犹"不"。恶(è),指凶暴,凶险,作恶。

【原文】5 子曰:"富与贵,是人之所欲也[1];不以其道得之[2],不处也[3]。贫与贱,是人之所恶也[4];不以其道得之[5]不去也[6]。去仁恶乎成名[7]?君子无终食之间违仁[8],造次必于是[9],颠沛必于是[10]。"

【白话译文】

孔子说:"发财和做官,是人们的欲望;不从正道得来,君子不接受。贫困和微贱,是人们的畏惧;不从正常规律袭来,君子不躲避。君子离开了仁德,怎么树立名声?君子没有吃完一餐饭的时间离开仁德,仓促匆忙时都一定和仁德同在,困顿挫折时都一定和仁德同在。"

【英语译文】

Confucius said, "A moral man won't accept fortune and official post, which are the desire of common people, obtained in a wrong way. A moral man never dodge being abnormally poor and humble, of which people are usually fearful. How could a moral man establish his reputation if he isn't humane and moral? A moral man never refuses being humane and moral, not even a short while of a meal. He always cherishes humanity and morality even in a hurry or frustration."

【注释】(1)所欲:欲望。(2)以:介词。这里表示行动或变化的起始。相当于"自""从""由"。下同。其道:指得富贵的正道(正常路径)。得之:受到。下同。(3)不处:不接受。(4)所恶:憎恨;畏惧。(5)其道:指受贫贱的正常规律。如出身贫贱,没有出仕,不会理财,健康状况等。此外,便是非正常规律,人祸,天灾,政治环境等。这里的"不以其道"指的即是"非正常规律"。(6)不去:挺着,不躲避。(7)去仁:抛弃仁德。恶乎:恶(wū),疑问代词,相当于"何""安""怎么"。乎:语气助词。成名:树立名声。(8)终食之间:吃完一餐饭的时间。违:离开。(9)造次:仓促,匆忙。必于是:一定同仁德在一起。颠沛:困顿挫折。

【原文】6 子曰:" 我未见好仁者[1],恶不仁者[2]。好仁者 ,无以尚之[3];恶不仁者,其为仁矣[4],不使不仁者加乎其身[5]。有能一日用其力于仁矣乎[6]? 我未见力不足者[7]。盖有之矣[8],我未之见也。[9]

【白话译文】

孔子说:"我没见过爱好仁德的人和厌恶不仁德的人。爱好仁德的人,没有别的人能超过。厌恶不仁德的人,他行仁德,只是避免不仁德的东西加在自己身上。有谁能一整天用力于仁德上呢? 我没见过力量不够的,大概这样的人还是有的,我没见到罢了。"

【英语译文】

Confucius said, "I've never seen a man who loves humanity and morality. Neither a man who hates inhumanity and immorality. No one can surpass a man who loves humanity and morality. A man who hates inhumanity and immorality just avoids inhumane and immoral things added upon himself when he acts humanely and morally. Who can focus on humanity and morality for a whole day? I've never seen a man without enough strength. Maybe there are such kind of men. I have just never seen them."

【注释】(1)好(hào):爱好,喜爱。(2)恶(wù):厌恶,憎恨。(3)无以尚之:没有什么能超过它。谓已至极限。义同无以复加。尚,超过的意思。(4)为仁:行仁德。矣:语气词,表停顿。(5)不仁者:不仁的思想行为。(6)有能一日用其力于仁矣乎:有谁能一整天用力于仁德上呢?(7)我未见力不足者:我没见过力量不够的。(8)盖:副词。大概。

【原文】7 子曰:“人之过也[1],各于其党:[2]。观过,斯知仁矣[3]。”

【白话译文】

孔子说:“人们的错误,都在各自的类别中。仔细观察人们的错误,就可知道他们的人品。”

【英语译文】

Confucius said, “Each person's faults fall into different categories. You can differentiate their different moral quality after you observe their faults carefully.”

【注释】(1)过:过失;错误。(2)于:在。党:类,同伙。(3)仁:通“人”。

【原文】8 子曰:“朝闻道[1],夕死可矣[2]。”

【白话译文】

孔子说:“早晨领会了天道真理,当晚就死去,也可以。”

【英语译文】

Confucius said, “It's alright and worthy to die at night after one has known the real Way and Truth in the morning.”

【注释】(1)闻道:领会某种道理。孔子所指的道,当是天道真理。(2)夕死:当晚死去。可矣:可以,无憾。

【原文】9 子曰:“士志于道[1],而耻恶衣恶食者[2],未足与议也[3],”

【白话译文】

孔子说:“读书人立志行大道,但是羞愧于穿破衣、吃粗粮的这种人,不足以给予评论了。"

【英语译文】

Confucius said, "A scholar should stick to great way. But those who are shameful of simple food and worn clothes do not deserve commenting."

【注释】(1)士:读书人。志于道:立志行大道。(2)而:转折连词,表反转关系,相当于"然而""但是""却"。耻:羞愧。恶衣恶食:穿破衣吃粗粮。(3)未足:不足以。与:给予。议:评论。

【原文】10 子曰:"君子之于天下也[1],无适也[2],无莫也[3],义之与比[4]。"

【白话译文】

孔子说:"君子对于天下的事,没有固定要怎么办,也没有固定不要怎么办,只要怎么按道义合理就怎么办。"

【英语译文】

Confucius said, "Facing things in this world, a moral man has no fixed thinking of how to do or how not to do. It's all right to do things only if it's consistent with the Way."

【注释】(1)于:对,对于。(2)适:亲厚。(3)莫:疏远。(4)义:恰当,合理。比(bì):接近,为邻。

【原文】11 子曰:"君子怀德[1],小人怀土[2];君子怀刑[3],小人怀惠[4]。"

【白话译文】

孔子说:"君子胸怀道德,小人胸怀权财;君子敬畏法度,小人贪念恩惠。"

【英语译文】

Confucius said, "A moral man cherishes way and virtue whereas a mean man cherishes power and fortune; a moral man respects law and regulation whereas a mean man clings to little favor."

【注释】(1)怀德:心中存德。(2)怀土:土地是权力和财产的依据。怀土,即心中存着权力财产的欲望。(3)怀刑:敬畏法度。(4)怀惠:贪念恩惠。

【原文】12 子曰:“放于利而行[1],多怨[2]。”

【白话译文】

孔子说:“依据个人私利而行事,招来的怨恨就很多。”

【英语译文】

Confucius said, “If a man behaves based on his own benefits, he will inccur much agony.”

【注释】(1)放(fǎng):依据。(2)多怨:怨恨。

【原文】13 子曰:“能以礼让为国乎[1]? 何有[2]? 不能以礼让为国,如礼何[3]?”

【白话译文】

孔子说:“能够用守礼谦让来治理国家吗? 有什么困难? 如果不能用守礼谦让来治理国家,又怎样来对待礼呢?”

【英语译文】

Confucius said, “Could a state be administrated by observing rites and modest declination? Is there any difficulty? If a state couldn't be administrated by observing rites and modest declination, how could rites be dealt with?”

【注释】(1)礼让:守礼谦让。为国:治国。(2)何有:用反问语气说明没有什么,这里表示不难。(3)如礼何:如何对待礼。

【原文】14 子曰:“不患无位[1],患所以立[2]。不患莫己知[3],求为可知也[4]。”

【白话译文】

孔子说:“不愁没有地位,愁立于那个地位的德能是否足够。不愁没有人知道自己,求诸己完善自身,具有可见知之实就行了。”

【英语译文】

Confucius said, "Don't worry about having no post but worry about whether you are virtue enough to hold the post. Don't worry about you are unknown. Just perfect yourself and make yourself deserve the reputation."

【注释】(1)位:地位;职位。(2)所以立:立于其位的德能。(3)莫己知:没有人知道自己。(4)求为可知:求诸己,完善自身,具有可见知之实。

【原文】15 子曰:"参乎[1]! 吾道一以贯之[2]。"曾子曰:"唯。[3]"子出,门人问曰[4]:"何谓也[5]?"曾子曰:"夫子之道忠恕而已矣[6]。"

【白话译文】

孔子说:"参呀! 我的道义,从万归一。由一统万。"曾子说:"是的。"孔子出去后,其他学生问道:"刚才老师和你讲的是什么意思?"曾子说:"他老人家的道义只是忠恕罢了。"

【英语译文】

Confucius said, "Zeng Shen! My way is that ten thousand induces to one and ten thousand governs one." Zeng Shen said, "Yes, it is." After confucius went out, other disciples asked, "What does the master mean just now?" Zeng Zi answered, "His way is loyalty and altruism."

【注释】(1)参:曾参,孔子的学生。下文的曾子,是对曾参的尊称。乎:语气助词,这里表感叹。(2)一:指孔子道义的出发点、行径和归宿浑然一体的"仁"。天下、人间,万象丛生,怎样做一个纯净的人,脱离兽性,大家都能和平安宁地生活,是孔子一生执着的追求。他采取中道,以身作则,劝说、教育、感化人们行善爱人。从不以救世主的姿态强迫人们怎么样、不怎么样而塞入自家"私货"甚至在血中"自立"。贯:贯穿;统摄。(3)唯(wěi):应答声。(4)门人:弟子,学生。(5)何谓:什么意思。(6)忠恕:忠恕,就是行仁的概括。朱熹集注:"尽己之谓忠,推己之谓恕。"如果天下有越来越多的人接受孔子,不互相倾轧,人间将会越来越文明清醒的。

【原文】16 子曰:"君子喻于义[1],小人喻于利[2]。"

【白话译文】

孔子说:“君子通晓道义,小人通晓私利。”

【英语译文】

Confucius said, “Moral man knows Way and Righteousness whereas mean man knows benefit.”

【注释】(1)喻:晓,通晓,懂得。义:道义。(2)利:利益。

【原文】17 子曰:“见贤思齐焉[1],见不贤而内自省也[2]。”

【白话译文】

孔子说:“看见贤人,就想向他看齐;看见不贤的人,就自己反省,有无同他类似的毛病。”

【英语译文】

Confucius said, “When you encounter a person of virtue, you should set him as an example; otherwise, if you don't encounter a person of virtue, you should try to find the same shortcomings like his.”

【注释】(1)思齐:希望看齐,希望相同。(2)内自省:在心中自我反省有无相似的“不好”。

【原文】18 子曰:“事父母几谏[1],见志不从[2],又敬不违[3],劳而不怨[4]。”

【白话译文】

孔子说:“侍奉父母,应该委婉地表达不同意见,如果自己的心意没被采纳,应该仍然恭敬,不触犯他们。虽然有所忧愁,但不埋怨。”

【英语译文】

Confucius said, “When you attend your parents, you should express different views euphemistically to them. If your suggestion hasn't been accepted by them, you should still be modest towards them, not offending them. Do not complain even though you're somewhat worried.”

【注释】(1)几(jī):轻微,婉转。几谏:委婉地劝止。(2)志:心意。不从:不依从,不采纳。(3)违:触迕,冒犯。(4)劳:忧愁,担忧。怨:埋怨。

【原文】19 子曰:“父母在[1],不远游,游必有方[2]。”

【白话译文】

孔子说:“父母在世时,不到远方去游历。如果必须远走时,一定要告诉父母准确的地址。”

【英语译文】

Confucius said, “Do not travel far away when your parents are still alive. And you should tell them the exact address if you have to travel to some place.”

【注释】(1)在:指活着。(2)有方:有一定的去向、处所。

【原文】20 子曰:“三年无改于父之道[1],可谓孝矣[2]。”

【白话译文】

孔子说:“三年不改变父亲的某些陈法,可称为孝了。”

【英语译文】

Confucius said, “If one hasn't changed his father's way of life for three years, then he will be called a filial son.”

【注释】(1)本章已见学而篇 11

【原文】21 子曰:“父母之年[1],不可不知也[2]。一则以喜[3],一则以惧[4]。”

【白话译文】

孔子说:“父母的年纪,不能不记在心里:一方面因父母高寿而喜欢,另一方面因父母寿高而增险,有所恐惧。”

【英语译文】

Confucius said, "We've to keep in mind our parents' ages. On the one hand, we're happy due to their longevity; on the other hand, we're fearing the adding dangers due to their being rather old."

【注释】(1)年:年龄。(2)知:记忆,记得。(3)一则:指一方面,一般多用于并列叙述两件事时。喜:喜高寿。(4)惧:惧寿高多险。

【原文】22 子曰:"古者言之不出[1],耻躬之不逮也[2]。"

【白话译文】

孔子说:"古时的君子不随便说话,就是怕做不到自己说的话。"

【英语译文】

Confucius said, "In ancient time, moral men didn't say anything casually because they feared that they could not keep what they had said."

【注释】(1)古者:古人。特指古之君子。言之不出:谓不随便说话。(2)耻:动词的意动用法,"以为可耻"的意思。躬:自身。逮(dài):及,赶上。躬之不逮,犹言自身跟不上言语;做不到自己说的话。

【原文】23 子曰:"以约失之者鲜矣[1]。"

【白话译文】

孔子说:"因约束自己而犯错误的很少。"

【英语译文】

Confucius said, "It is quite rare that one makes mistakes if he constrains himself."

【注释】(1)约:约束;节制。失(shī):错误,犯错误。鲜(xiǎn):少。

【原文】24 子曰:"君子欲讷于言而敏于行[1]。"

【白话译文】

孔子说:“君子情愿忍住嘴巴少说话,放开手脚多干活。”

【英语译文】

Confucius said, “Moral men are willing to practice more rather than doing much on articulation.”

【注释】(1)欲:愿意,情愿。讷(nè):忍住少说,慢开口。敏:敏捷,勤勉。行:行动,做事。

【原文】25 子曰:“德不孤[1],必有邻[2]。”

【白话译文】

孔子说:“有道德的人不会孤单,一定有同类相亲的人来做伴。”

【英语译文】

Confucius said, “A moral man will not be lonely and he is surely accompanied by same kind of people.”

【注释】(1)德:指有道德的人。孤:孤单,孤立。(2)邻:指亲近的人。

【原文】26 子游曰:“事君数[1],斯辱矣[2];朋友数[3],斯疏矣[4]。”

【白话译文】

子游说:“服侍君主过于烦琐,就会受侮辱了;结交友人过于烦琐,就会被疏远了。”

【英语译文】

Zi You said, “One will be insulted if he attended his monarch too complicatedly; and he will be estranged if he made friends too complicatedly.”

【注释】(1)数:一种动态过密、过快地重复出现。这种现象在人际间叫“烦琐”。(2)斯辱矣:就会被侮辱了。朋:用作动词。“结交”的意思。朋友,意谓“结交友人”。(3)斯疏矣:就会被疏远了。

公冶长第五(共二十八章)

《何晏集解》把第十章“子曰,始吾于人也”以下又分一章,题为二十九章;朱熹集注把第一、第二两章并为一。题为二十七章。此篇凡二十七章,皆论古今人物贤否得失,盖格物穷理之壹端也。胡氏以为疑多子贡之徒所记云。

【原文】1 子谓公冶长[1],“可妻也[2]。虽在缧绁之中[3],非其罪也。”以其子妻之[4]。

【白话译文】

孔子谈到公冶长时说:“是个可靠的男人。虽然被关过监狱,但不是他的罪过。”孔子把自己的女儿嫁给了公冶长。

【英语译文】

While mentioning Gongye Chang, Confucius said, “He is a truly reliable man. Although he has ever been imprisoned, he's not guilty.” After that, Confucius betrothed his daughter to Gongye Chang.

【注释】(1)谓:评论;说。公冶长:孔子学生,齐人。(2)妻(qì):嫁给;与之为妻。(3)缧绁(léi xiè):拴罪人的绳索,这里指代监狱。(4)子:古代兼指儿女,这里偏指“女”。

【原文】2 子谓南容[1],“邦有道不废[2],邦无道免于刑戮[3]。”以其兄之子妻之[4]。

【白话译文】

孔子谈到南容时说:“邦国政治清明,他不被废弃而得录用;邦国政治黑暗,也不致受刑罚或被处死。”所以孔子把自己的侄女嫁给南容。

【英语译文】

While mentioning Nangong Zirong, Confucius said, “He was hired without refusal when his state was governed wisely. And he was never punished or sentenced to death when his state was governed immorally." After that, Confucius betrothed his niece to Nangong Zirong.

【注释】(1)南容:孔子学生南宫适(kuò),姓南宫,字子容。(2)不废:不被废弃而得录用。邦有道:指邦国政治清明。(3)邦无道:指邦国政治黑暗。免于刑戮:不致受刑罚或被处死。(4)其兄:指孔子的哥哥孟皮。这时可能孟皮已死,所以孔子为他女儿主婚。

【原文】3 子谓子贱[1],"君子哉若人[2]!鲁无君子者[3],斯焉取斯[4]?"

【白话译文】

孔子谈到宓子贱时说:"真是个君子呀,这人!假如鲁国没有君子,这人从哪里取得这么好的品德?"

【英语译文】

While mentioning Nangong Zirong, Confucius said, "He's really a moral man. If there's no moral man in State Lu, then where does he obtain so moral quality?"

【注释】(1)子贱(公元前 521 年—?):孔子的学生,姓宓,名不齐,字子贱。春秋末鲁国人,比孔子小三十岁。以德行著称。曾为单(shàn)父宰,弹琴而治,政绩卓著。(2)若人:这人。若,义同"这,这个"。(3)鲁无君子者:者,助词,在这里表示因果、假设等关系。译文在句首,相当于"假设,如果。"译文在句末,相当于"的话。"(4)斯:近指代词,这人。焉:疑问代词,哪里,何处。斯:近指代词,这品德。

【原文】4 子贡问曰:"赐也何如[1]?"子曰:"女,器也[2]。"曰 :"何器也?"曰:"瑚琏也[3]。"

【白话译文】

子贡问孔子:"学生赐,怎么样?"孔子说:"你呀,是一个器皿。"子贡又问:"什么器皿呢?"孔子说:"宗庙里盛黍稷的瑚琏啦。"

【英语译文】

Zigong asked Confucius, "How do you think of me?" Confucius answered, "You are an utensil." Then Zigong continued to ask, "What kind of utensil am I?" Confucius said, "You are talented as the precious one used in temple for sacrifice."

【注释】(1)赐:子贡自报其名(请老师评说自己)。(2)女:同"汝"。器:根据下文指器皿。器皿,指饮食用具,如杯、盘及尊、彝(古代宗庙常用的礼器)之类。后泛指盛物的日常用具。(3)瑚琏(hú liǎn):瑚、琏都是古代宗庙盛黍、稷的礼器。以玉为装饰,十分珍贵。用以比喻治国安邦之才。

【原文】5 或曰:"雍也仁而不佞[1]。"子曰:"焉用佞[2]? 御人以口给[3],屡憎于人[4]。不知其仁[5],焉用佞?"

【白话译文】

有人说:"冉雍嘛,有仁德而没有口才。"孔子说:"哪里需用口才? 拿口才敏捷与人口头交锋,常常讨人厌恶。不了解他的仁德,干什么要有口才呢?"

【英语译文】

Somebody ever said, "As for Ran Yong, he's humane and moral but dumb in speaking." Confucius asked, "Is eloquence needed? It's disgusting when you confront with somebody just by means of eloquence. Why do you need eloquence if you don't know one's humanity and morality?"

【注释】(1)雍:冉雍(522—?)是孔子的弟子,姓冉,名雍,字仲弓,春秋末鲁国人。比孔子小二十九岁。佞(nìng):善辩,口才好。(2)焉用佞:哪里需要口才。(3)御人:指与人口头应对交锋。以:介词。用,拿。口给:口才敏捷,能言善辩。(4)屡憎于人:常常被人厌恶。屡(lǚ),指多次,常常。憎,指厌恶,憎恨。于人,指被人。(5)不知:不了解。

【原文】6 子使漆雕开仕[1]。对曰:"吾斯之未能信[2]。"子说[3]。

【白话译文】

孔子叫漆雕开去做官。他回答说:"我对做官还不能自信。"孔子听了很高兴。

【英语译文】

Confucius suggested that Qidiao Kai secure an official position. The latter replied, "I' m not self-confident in dealing with official affairs." Confucius became very glad after hearing this.

【注释】(1)漆雕开:漆雕是姓,开是名,字子开,孔子的学生。仕:从政,做官。(2)吾斯之未能信:"吾未能信斯"的倒装。之,结构助词。斯,近指代词,指代"仕"作信的宾语,为了强调宾语,用"之"把它提前。(3)说:同"悦"。

【原文】7 子曰:"道不行乘桴浮于海[1]。从我者其由与[2]?子路闻之喜。子曰:"由也好勇过我,无所取材[3]。"

【白话译文】

孔子说:"我主张的道路行不通时,就乘小筏漂流海外。跟随我的或许是仲由吧!"子路听到这话高兴得很。孔子说:"仲由啊,好勇之气超过了我,不能度量取舍。"

【英语译文】

Confucius said, "When my beheld way cannot go smoothly, I' ll float overseas. Isn't Zhong You who's willing to follow me?" Zilu was very happy after hearing this. Confucius said, "Zhong You, I cannot decide what to choose since you' re more courageous than me."

【注释】(1)道:主张的道路。不行:行不通。桴(fú):古代把竹子或木头编成簰当船用,大的叫筏,小的叫桴。(2)从(cóng):跟随。其:语气词,表推测。大概,或许。由:子路姓仲,名由,子路或季路是其字。与:语气助词,这里相当于"吧"。(3)无所取材:朱熹注:"材,与'裁'同,古字借用。"无所取材,即"无所取裁"。意谓"不能度量而定取舍"。

【原文】8 孟武伯问:"子路仁乎[1]?"子曰:"不知也。"又问。子曰:"由也[2],千乘之国可使治其赋也[3],不知其仁也。""求也何如[4]?"子曰:"求也,千室之邑[5],百乘之家[6],可使为之宰也[7],不知其仁也。""赤也何如[8]?"子曰:"赤也,束带立于朝[9],可使与宾客言也[10],不知其仁也。”

【白话译文】

孟武伯问:“子路可算仁德吗?”孔子说:“不晓得。”他又问。孔子说:“仲由嘛,一个拥有一千乘兵车的国家,可以叫他负责兵役和军政的工作。至于他仁德不仁德,我不晓得。”孟武伯问:“冉求怎么样?”孔子说:“求嘛,千户人口的大邑,可以叫他当县长;百辆兵车的大夫封地,可以叫他当总管。至于他仁德不仁德,我不晓得。”孟武伯问:“公西赤怎么样?”孔子说:“赤嘛,穿好礼服立于朝廷中,可以叫他接待外宾,办理交涉。至于他仁德不仁德,我不晓得。”

【英语译文】

Meng Wu Bo asked, “Is Zi Lu moral and kind?” Confucius answered, “I Don't know.” Meng Wu Bo asked again. Confucius said, “As for Zhong You, He could administrate corvee and army affairs in a state which owns one thousand sets of warrior carts. But I don't know whether or not he's moral and kind.” Meng Wu Bo then asked, “How about Ran Qiu?” Confucius answered, “As for Qiu, he can be empowered as a leader of a big county of one thousand households. He can administrate an area of one hundred warrior carts as well. But I don't know whether or not he's moral and kind.” Meng Wu Bo continued, “How about Gongxi Chi?” Confucius answered, “As for Chi, he can in his ritual gowns receive foreign guests and deal with foreign affairs in the court. But I don't know whether or not he's moral and kind.”

【注释】(1)孟武伯:即仲孙彘,春秋时鲁国人,孟懿子之子。(2)由:仲由。(3)千乘之国:拥有一千辆兵车的诸侯邦国。在孔子之时,千乘之国已不属大国了。赋:这里指兵赋。朱熹注:“赋,兵也。古者以田赋出兵,故谓兵为赋。”孔子认为子路可在千乘之国中掌管兵役和军政。(4)求:冉求。(5)邑:古代庶民聚居之所,除了房屋还有一些田地。千室之邑,指上千户人口的大邑。封建时代臣属的领地,也叫私邑。(6)百乘之家:卿大夫之家,拥有百辆战车。(7)之:代词,同“其”,表第三人称领属关系,他的。宰:古代官吏的通称。(8)赤:公西赤(公元前509—?)孔子弟子,姓公西,名赤字子华,亦称公西华。春秋末鲁国人。少孔子四十二岁。(9)束带:束紧腰带整饰衣着。朝:朝堂。(10)宾客:客人的总称。春秋、战国时多用来称他国派来的使者,本章中便是此义。亦指贵族的门客、策士等。又解:宾客分用时,“宾”指贵客;“客”指一般客人。

【原文】9 子谓子贡曰[1]:“女与回也孰愈[2]?”对曰:“赐也何敢望回[3]? 回也闻一以知十[4],赐也闻一以知二。”子曰:“弗如也;吾与女弗如也[5]。”

【白话译文】

孔子对子贡说:“你和颜回,哪一个强些?”子贡回答说:“赐怎么敢同回相比? 颜回他听到一件事,可以推演知道十件事;我呢,听到一件事只能推知两件事。”孔子说:“不及他;我同意你的话,是不及他。”

【英语译文】

Confucius said to Zi Gong, “Who is wiser, you or Yan Hui?” Zi Gong answered, “How can I be compared with Hui? Yan Hui is able to deduce ten things after hearing one thing; on the contrary, I' m just able to deduce two things after hearing one thing.” Confucius said, “I agree that you are not as able as him.”

【注释】(1)谓:对……说。(2)愈:胜过,更好。(3)望:比量,比拟。回:颜回。(4)闻一以知十:听到一件事可以推知十件事。(5)与(yǔ):动词,指同意,赞同。如:及,比得上。

【原文】10 宰予昼寝[1]。子曰:“朽木不可雕也,粪土之墙不可杇也[7];于予与何诛[3]?”子曰[4]:“始吾于人也[5],听其言而信其行[6];今吾于人也,听其言而观其行。于予与改是[7]。”

【白话译文】

宰予在白天睡觉。孔子说:“腐烂的木头不能雕刻,粪土一样的墙壁粉刷不得;对于宰予么,怎么责备呢?”孔子说:“以前,我对于别人,他怎么说,我就怎么信;现在,我对于别人,听到他的话,却要考察他的行为。是宰予的表现让我改变了态度的。”

【英语译文】

Zai Yu slept at day time. Confucius said, “Decayed wood can't be carved and dirty wall can't be painted. How should I scold Zai Yu?” Confucius said, “Long before when I get along with someone, I trust him by what he has said. Nowadays when I get along with someone, I will observe his actions even if I' ve heard what he said. It is Zai Yu who has changed my attitude."

【注释】(1)宰予:孔子学生,姓宰,名予,字子我,亦称宰我。春秋末鲁国人,小孔子二十九岁,能言善辩以言语著称。昼寝:白天睡觉。(2)粪土:污秽的泥土。杇(wū):同"圬",粉刷。(3)于:介词,指对,对于。与:语气词。何诛:怎么责备,责备什么。(4)子曰:这里表示下文是与上文有关的另一次谈话。(5)始:起初,以前。于:同注释3。(6)听其言而信其行:轻易相信人家言行一致。(7)是:代词,指上文所言对人的认识态度。

【原文】11 子曰:"吾未见刚者[1]。"或对曰:"申枨[2]。"子曰:"枨也欲[3],焉得刚[4]?"

【白话译文】

孔子说:"我还没有看见过坚强不屈的人。"有人回答说:"申枨坚强不屈。"孔子说:"申枨嘛,欲望太多,哪里能够坚强不屈?"

【英语译文】

Confucius said, "I' ve never encountered anyone who's as strong willed cos yielding to no one." Somebody replied, "Shen Cheng is a man just like this." Confucius said, "As for Shen Cheng, he has so much desire. How could he be so?"

【注释】(1)刚:坚强不屈。(2)申枨:孔子弟子,姓申名枨,春秋末年人。枨(chéng),史记仲尼弟子列传,有"申党字周"的记载。明代以后,大多以为申枨、申党各是一人;明代以后,从"枨""党"古音相近切入,以为申枨,申党实即一人。欲:"欲"的异体字,指过多的欲望,欲望过多,思想、行为必然扭曲。(4)得:达到,能够。

【原文】12 子贡曰:"我不欲人之加诸我也[1],吾亦欲无加诸人。"子曰:"赐也非尔所及也[2]。"

【白话译文】

子贡说:"我不愿别人欺侮我呢,我也不愿欺侮别人啦。"孔子说:"赐呀,这不是你能做到的。”

【英语译文】

Zi Gong said, “I am not willing to be bullied by anyone else and I don’t want to bully others either. ” Confucius said, “This is beyond your reaeh, Ci. ”

【注释】(1)欲:愿意,想要。之:结构助词。放在主语和谓语之间使句子转化为偏正词组(人之加诸我)。加:强加,侵凌。诸:语气助词,对单音节词“加”补凑音节。(2)尔:你。及:达到,做到。

【原文】13 子贡曰:“夫子之文章[1],可得而闻也[2];夫子之言性与天道[3],不可得而闻也。”

【白话译文】

子贡说:“老师的威仪文辞,我们能够知道;老师谈天性和天理,我们不可能知道。”

【英语译文】

Zi Gong said, “We may comprehend the awesome manners of your honorable moster but when you talk about the nature and principle of heaven, we cannot understand. ”

【注释】(1)夫子:老师,特指孔子。文章:朱熹注:“德之见乎外者,威仪文辞皆是也”。(2)可得:可能。而:语气助词。闻:知道。(3)性:指天性,人的本性。天道:天理。

【原文】14 子路有闻[1],未之能行[2],唯恐有闻[3]。

【白话译文】

子路具有新知,还没能实践;只怕又新知什么。

【英语译文】

Zi Lu has new knowledge but has not put into practice. And he’s afraid that he again obtains new knowledge.

【注释】(1)有:具有。闻:新知。(2)之:语气助词。(3)唯恐:只怕。有:又。

【原文】15 子贡问曰:"孔文子何以谓之"文也[1]?"子曰:"敏而好学,不耻下问,是以谓之文也。"

【白话译文】

子贡问道:"孔文子因什么谥号定为'文'?"孔子说:"他聪敏灵活,爱好学习,又谦虚下问,不以为耻,所以拿'文'字做他的谥号。"

【英语译文】

Zi Gong asked, "For what reason did Kong Yu get his posthumous name 'Wen'?" Confucius answered, "He's clever, witty and ready to learn. And he was modest, never ashamed of consulting minors. Therefore it's suitable to use 'Wen' as his posthumous name."

【注释】(1)孔文子:卫国的大夫孔圉。"文":谥号。

【原文】16 子谓子产[1],"有君子之道四焉[2]:其行己也恭[3],其事上也敬[4],其养民也惠[5],其使民也义[6]。"

【白话译文】

孔子评论子产,说:"他有四个方面是君子的道德:他为人做事庄严恭敬,他服侍君上认真负责,他教养人民注意恩惠,他役使人民讲求合理。"

【英语译文】

While commenting Zi Chan, Confucius said, "He's a moral man in four aspects: behaving himself modestly, serving monarch conscientiously, educating people mercifully and employing labors reasonably."

【注释】(1)谓:评论。子产:公孙侨,字子产,郑穆公之孙,为春秋时郑国的贤相。在郑简公、郑定公之时,执政二十二年。其时,于晋国当悼公、平公、昭公、顷公、定公五世;于楚国当共王、康王、郏敖、灵王、平王五世,这时晋楚两国争强,战争不息。郑国地位冲要,而周旋于两大国之间,子产却能不低声下气,也不妄自尊大,使国家得到尊敬和安全,的确是古代中国的一位杰出的政治家和外交家。(2)焉:代词。指君子之道。(3)行己:谓立身行事。(4)事上:指服侍君上。(5)养民:教养人民。(6)使民:役使人民。

【原文】17 子曰:"晏平仲善与人交[1],久而敬之[2]。"

【白话译文】

孔子说:"晏平仲善于和别人交往;交往越久,别人越敬重他。"

【英语译文】

Confucius said, "Yan Pingzhong was good at getting along with others. They spent together longer and they respected him more."

【注释】(1)晏平仲:齐国的贤大夫,名婴。现在流传的晏子春秋不是晏婴自己的作品,而是西汉以前的托名著作。交:交往。(2)久而敬之:之,代词。指晏平仲。

【原文】18 子曰:"臧文仲居蔡[1],山节藻棁[2],谄渎鬼神,何如其知也[3]?"

【白话译文】

孔子说:"臧文仲为安置占卜用的大龟,盖了一间华堂,有刻成山形的斗拱和绘着水藻的梁上短柱。他的聪明怎么是这样呢?"

【英语译文】

Confucius said, "In order to place the big turtle for divination, Zang Wenzhong set up a splendid hall consisting of complicatedly curved pillars. How could his wit go like this?"

【注释】(1)臧文仲:鲁国大夫臧孙辰(?—公元前617年)。居蔡:蔡国盛产大龟,蔡国君用以占卜的大龟叫蔡。后凡国君用以占卜的大龟都叫蔡;居蔡,谓安置占卜用的大龟。(2)山节藻棁:节,柱上的斗拱。棁(zhuō),指房梁上的短柱。山节藻棁,即把斗拱刻成山形,在房梁上的短柱上绘画水草花纹。这是古时装饰天子宗庙的做法。(3)知:同"智"。

【原文】19 子张问曰："令尹子文三仕为令尹[1]，无喜色；三已之[2]，无愠色[3]。旧令尹之政，必以告新令尹。何如？"子曰："忠矣。"曰："仁矣乎？"曰："未知[4]；焉得仁[5]？""崔子弑齐君[6]，陈文子有马十乘[7]，弃而违之[8]。至于他邦，则曰，'犹吾大夫崔子也[9]。'违之。之一邦[10]，则又曰：'犹吾大夫崔子也。'违之。何如？"子曰："清矣[11]。"曰："仁矣乎？"曰："未知；焉得仁？"

【白话译文】

子张问道："楚国的令尹子文三次做官当令尹，没有高兴的神色；三次被罢免，没有怨恨的脸色，而且还把一切旧政都告诉新令尹。这个人怎么样？"孔子说："可算尽忠于国家了。"子张道："算不算仁呢？"孔子说："还不知道他的内心和独处时的行为，怎么算仁呢？"子张又问："崔子杀了齐庄公，陈文子有马四十匹，舍弃不要，离开了齐国。他到了另一个国家，于是说道：'这里的执政者，和我们的崔子差不多。'再离开，再到了一个国家，再说道：'这里的执政者，和我们的崔子差不多。'于是再离开。这个人怎么样？"孔子说："可以算得上清高了。"子张说："算得上仁吗？"孔子说："还不知道他的内心和独处，怎么算仁呢？"

【英语译文】

Zi Zhang asked, "Zi Wen was elected as Prime Minister of Chu State for three times but he never showed glad appearance; and when he was dismissed from his post for three times, he never showed anger but told the new prime minister his own administrative methods. What do you think about this man?" Confucius answered, "He was loyal to his state." Zi Zhang asked, "Was he benevolent?" Confucius said, "Since I haven't known his inner-heart and his actions while being alone, how can he is regarded as a benevolent one?" Then Zi Zhang asked again, "Cui Zi killed Chu Zhuang Gong and he refused to own the forty horses belonged to Chen Wen Zi, he then left Qi State. While arriving at another state he said, 'Politicians here are just like Cui Zi.' Then he left again and arrived at still another state, saying once again, 'Politicians here are just like Cui Zi.' After that he left furthermore. What do you think about this man?" Confucius said, "He could be called lofty." Zi Zhang asked, "Was he benevolent?" Confucius said, "Since I haven't known his inner-heart and his actions whilebeing alone, how can he be regarded as a benevolent one?"

【注释】(1)令尹:春秋战国时楚国的执政官名,相当于宰相。子文:即鬬谷于菟(dòu gòu wū tú)。根据《左传》子文于鲁庄公三十年开始做令尹,到僖公二十三年让位给子玉,其中相距二十八年。在这二十八年中,可能有几次被罢免又被任命。三仕为令尹:三次做官当令尹。(2)三已之:三次被罢官。以上三仕、三已的"三"应是概数,犹言几次,多次。(3)愠色:愠(yùn),即含怒,怨恨。愠色,谓怨怒的神色。(4)未知:还不知道他的内心和独处。(5)焉得:怎么知晓,哪里明白。得,知晓、明白的意思。(6)崔子弑齐君:崔子,齐国的大夫崔杼;齐君,指齐庄公,名光。弑,古代在下的人杀掉在上的人叫作"弑"。"崔子弑齐君"的事,见《左传》襄公二十五年。(7)陈文子:也是齐国的大夫,名须无。十乘,即四十匹。(8)违之:离开齐国。(9)则:承接连词。犹:如同,好比。(10)之:往,至。(11)清:清高。

【原文】20 季文子三思而行[1]。子闻之,曰:"再,斯可矣[2]。"

【白话译文】

季文子办事,要考虑多次才行动。孔子听到这个传闻,说:"想两次,这就可以了。"

【英语译文】

Ji Wenzi usually takes actions after thinking over something for three times. After hearing this story, Confucius said, "It's alright for him to think twice."

【注释】(1)季文子:鲁国的大夫季孙行父,历仕鲁国文公、宣公、成公、襄公诸代。孔子生于襄公二十二年,大约在季文子死后十七年才出生。孔子说这话的时候,离季文子之死已是很多年了。三思:再三思考,反复思考。(2)再:两次,第二次,重复。斯:近指代词,这。

【原文】21 子曰:"宁武子[1],邦有道[2],则知[3];邦无道[4],则愚[5]。其知可及也[6],其愚不可及也[7]。"

【白话译文】

孔子说:"宁武子在国家政治清明时,就聪明;在国家政治混乱时,就学傻。他那聪明别人赶得上;他那傻气别人就赶不上了。"

【英语译文】

Confucius said, "Ning Wuzi is clever when politics goes on right way; he's stupid while politics goes on riots. Others could match his wit but couldn't catch up with his foolishness."

【注释】(1)宁武子:卫国的大夫,姓宁,名俞。(2)邦有道:国家政治清明。(2)则知:便聪明,不凸显自己。朱熹注:"无事可见。"(4)邦无道:国家政治混乱。(5)则愚:便学傻,不避艰险。尽心竭力周旋。朱熹注:"凡其所处皆知巧之士所深避而不肯为者。"(6)其知可及:他那聪明别人赶得上。(7)其愚不可及:他那傻气别人就赶不上。

【原文】22 子在陈[1]曰:"归与[2]! 归与! 吾党之小子狂简[3],斐然成章[4],不知所以裁之[5]。"

【白话译文】

孔子在陈国时,说:"回去吧! 回去吧! 我们的晚辈,志向高远,处事疏阔,富有文采,文章可观。我不知道拿什么去指导他们。"

【英语译文】

While in Chen State Confucius said, "Go home; let's go back home. Our juniors are ambitious, considerate, well-informed, intelligent and good wniters. I don't know how to instruct them."

【注释】(1)陈:古国名。公元前十一世纪周分封的诸侯国,妫姓。始封胡公(妫满),相传满为舜的后代。周武王灭商后,求舜的后代,得妫满封于陈,建都商丘(今河南淮阳)。有今河南东部和安徽一部分。公元前478年为楚所灭。孔子曾数度到陈。(2)归与:回去吧。(3)党:类,辈。吾党,意谓"我们"。小子:学生,晚辈。狂简:志向高远而处事疏阔。(4)斐然成章:富有文采,文章可观。(5)所以:介宾词组。"以"为介词,相当于"用""拿""凭;"所"为疑问代词作宾语,倒置于介词前面。相当于"何""什么"。裁:裁制;剪裁。引申为教育,栽培。之:代词。指"小子"。本句的主语承前省略了,应是第一人称"我",不是"吾党之小子"。

【原文】23 子曰:"伯夷、叔齐不念旧恶[1],怨是用希[2]。"

【白话译文】

孔子说:“伯夷、叔齐,这两兄弟,不记和别人过去的仇恨,因此别人对他们也很少怨恨。”

【英语译文】

Confucius said, “The two brothers, Bo Yi and Shu Qi, never kept in their mind others’ agonies. Therefore others seldom hated them.”

【注释】(1)伯夷、叔齐:孤竹君的两个儿子。父亲死了,两人互相让位,都逃到周文王那里。周武王起兵伐纣,他们拦住车马劝阻。周朝统一天下,他们以吃周朝的粮食为可耻,饿死于首阳山。旧恶:过去的仇恨。(2)怨是用:因此。希:少,罕有。

【原文】24 子曰:“孰谓微生高直[1]? 或乞醯焉[2],乞诸其邻而与之[3]。”

【白话译文】

孔子说:“谁说微生高这人直爽? 有人向他讨点醋,他不说自己没有,转向邻居讨来给那人。”

【英语译文】

Confucius said, “Who ever said that Weisheng Gao was generously upright? When somebody borrowed a little vinegar from him, he just refused but turned to his neighbor for help.”

【注释】(1)孰谓微生高:即尾生高,春秋时鲁国人。以守信闻名于当时。《庄子盗跖篇》,曾说其“与女子期于梁下(桥下),女子不来,水至不去,抱梁柱而死。”战国策淮南子等书中也有类似记载。(2)醯(xī):醋。(3)诸:代词“之”和介词“于”的合音。

【原文】25 子曰:“巧言、令色、足恭[1],左丘明耻之[2],丘亦耻之[3]。匿怨而友其人[4],左丘明耻之,丘亦耻之。”

【白话译文】

孔子说:“花言巧语,伪善的面孔,过分的恭顺,这些形态,左丘明认为可耻,我也认为可耻。内心藏着怨恨,表面上却同他要好,这种行为,左丘明认为可耻,我也认为可耻。”

【英语译文】

Confucius said, “Zuo Qiuming regarded flattery, hypocrisy, and extreme modesty as shameful things. So do I. One hates somebody in heart but pretends to befriend him. Zuo Qiuming regarded it as shameful. So do I.”

【注释】(1)巧言:表面上好听而实际上虚伪的话。令色:伪善、谄媚的脸色。足恭:过度谦恭。谓谄媚之色。足,旧读 jù,今读 zú,指过分。(2)左丘明:春秋时期鲁国的贤人。耻之:以之为耻。(3)丘:孔子自称其名。(4)匿怨:对人怀恨在心而不表现出来。匿(nì),即隐藏,隐瞒。而:转折连词,这里表反转关系。相当于“却”。友其人:和那(此)人交友。

【原文】26 颜渊、季路侍[1]。子曰:“盍各言尔志[2]?”子路曰:“愿车、马、衣、轻裘,与朋友共。敝之而无憾[3]。”颜渊曰:“愿无伐善,无施劳[4]。”子路曰:“愿闻子之志[5]。”子曰:“老者安之,朋友信之,少者怀之[6]。”

【白话译文】

孔子坐着,颜渊、季路站在孔子身边。孔子说:“何不各人说说自己的志向?”子路说:“我愿意把车、马、衣、轻裘和朋友共同使用。破损了也不在意。”颜渊说:“我愿意不夸耀自己的长处,不自夸功劳。”子路向孔子说:“希望听您的志向。”孔子说:“我愿意让老年人享受安乐,让朋友相互信任,让年轻人得到关怀。”

【英语译文】

Yan Yuan and Zi Lu stood beside Confucius while he's sitting. Confucius said, “Why don't you say something about your own ideal?” Zi Lu answered, “I'm willing to share my carts, horses, clothes and fur gowns with my friends. I don't care a little even if they were worn.” Yan Yuan answered instead, “I'm not willing to boast my advantages and achievements.” Zi Lu asked Confucius, “We want to know what your ideal is.” Confucius said, “I'm willing to see that elders enjoy their peaceful life, friends trust each other, and the youth are cared and protected."

【注释】(1)侍:论语中有侍、侍坐、侍侧等词语。大抵可作如下解释:侍,指孔子坐着,弟子站着;侍坐,指孔子和弟子都坐着;侍侧,或坐或立,不加肯定。(2)盍(hé):副词,表示反诘,犹何不。各言尔志:各自谈你的志向。(3)愿:愿意,情愿。车、马、衣、轻裘:都是名词。有人说,其中"轻"字是后人添上的,不当保留。可备一说。译注者,大都把"衣"解作动词,本注未从。共:共享。敝之:把这些使用坏了。之,代词。指车、马、衣、轻裘。无憾:不遗憾,不抱怨。(4)伐善:夸耀自己的长处。无施劳:不自夸功劳。一说,不施劳役于人。(5)愿闻:希望听说。(6)老者安之:使老年人享受安乐。朋友信之:使朋友相互信任。少者怀之:使年轻人得到关怀。

【原文】27 子曰:"已矣乎[1],吾未见能见其过而自内讼者也[2]。"

【白话译文】

孔子说:"算了吧!我还没有看见过能够看到自己的错误就扪心自责的人呢。"

【英语译文】

Confucius said, "Never mind it! I never encountered a man who could scold himself when he had found his own faults."

【注释】(1)已矣乎:已矣,叹词。意谓罢了、算了。乎,语气助词。表示感叹。相当于"啊"或"吧"。(2)内讼:内心自责。

【原文】28 子曰:"十室之邑[1],必有忠信如丘者焉[2],不如丘之好学也[3]。"

【白话译文】

孔子说:"十户人家的小地方,一定有像我这样又忠心又信实的人呢,只是不像我这样爱好学习罢了。"

【英语译文】

Confucius said, "In a place of ten households, there must be someone who is loyal and reliable. But surely there isn't anyone like me who is ready to learn."

【注释】(1)室:家,邑:人民聚居处。(2)焉:语气助词,表论断,一般去掉不译;也可译为“呢”“的”。

雍也篇第六(共三十章)

朱熹集注把第一、第二和第四、第五各并为一章,故作二十八章。共三十章。涉及“中庸之道”“恕”的学说、“文质”思想。

【原文】1 子曰:“雍也可使南面[1]。”

【白话译文】

孔子说:“冉雍这人啊,可以让他去当一个部门或一个地方的长官。”

【英语译文】

Confucius said, "As for Ran Yong, we can dispatch him to a department or a local place to be a leader."

【注释】(1)雍:冉雍(公元前522年—?)孔子弟子,姓冉,名雍,字仲弓。春秋末鲁国人。少孔子二十九岁。出生在“贱人”之家。南面:古人早就知道坐北朝南的方向最好。因此也以这个方向的位置为最尊贵。无论天子诸侯卿大夫,当他们作为长官出现时,总是南面而坐。

【原文】2 仲弓问子桑伯子[1]。子曰:“可也简[2]。”仲弓曰:“居敬而行简[3],以临其民[4],不亦可乎?居简而行简[5],无乃大简乎[6]?”子曰:“雍之言然[7]。”

【白话译文】

仲弓问子桑伯子这人怎么样。孔子说:“还可以,他很简约。”仲弓说:“修身严谨,行事简易不烦,拿这种作风来管理百姓,不也可以吗?若修身为人宽略又立身行事宽略,恐怕是太宽略吧?”孔子说:“你的话是对的。”

【英语译文】

Zhong Gong wanted to know Confucius' opinion about Zisang Bozi. Confucius answered, "He's good and lives shrift." Zhong Gong said, "If someone cultivates himself cautiously and does things simply, is it alright for him to govern common people? If cultivation and doing things are both too flexibly, aren't these too flexible?" Confucius said, "You are quite right there."

【注释】(1)仲弓:冉雍。子桑伯子称桑户、子桑户。春秋末年隐士,与孔子同时,生活崇尚简约。(2)可也简:可,表赞许,认可。犹言可以,可取,还行,不错。也,语气助词。表论断时,一般不译,也可译作"呢""的"。简,简约(节俭、简省)。(3)居敬:居,有"存""存心"的意思。居敬,直言就是"心中积存着敬畏"。正常人心中有敬畏的连锁反应,便是"持身恭敬(修身严谨)"。行简:指立身行事宽略(简易不烦,处事宽大不苛细)。(4)临:监视,监临。引申为统治,治理。(5)居简:指修身为人宽略(简易不烦,为人宽大不苛细)。(6)无乃:犹莫非、恐怕是,表示委婉反问的语气。大:"太"的古字。(7)然:犹"是"。相当于"对的""认为对的"。

【原文】3 哀公问[1]:"弟子孰为好学?"孔子对曰:"有颜回者好学,不迁怒不贰过[2]。不幸短命死矣[3],今也则亡,未闻好学者也[4]。"

【白话译文】

鲁哀公问:"你的学生谁好学?"孔子回答说:"有个叫颜回的学生好学,他不拿别人出气,不重犯同样的过失。不幸短命死了,现在就没有这样的人了,没听说过有好学的人了。"

【英语译文】

Ai Gong in Lu State asked, "Who is desirous for learning among your disciples?" Confucius answered, "A disciple named Yan Hui was ever desirous for learning. He never got angry at others and never made the same kind of mistakes. It's quite unfortunately that he was dead early. Nowadays I never hear anyone who is desirous for learning since there's no one like him."

【注释】(1)哀公:鲁国哀公。(2)迁怒:谓把对甲的怒气发泄到乙身上。不贰过:不重犯同样的过失。(3)不幸:不幸运,倒霉。短命:寿命短促。旧俗谓不足六十而死。关于颜回的生卒年与寿数有多说。有寿十八、二十九、三十一、四十一等诸说。根据《史记·仲尼弟子列传》记颜回"少孔子三十岁"推算,其生年当在鲁昭公二十一年(公元前521年)。其寿数依据李锴、毛奇龄、刘宝楠、钱穆等人的考辨,定为"四十一",则其卒年与《春秋·公羊传》《史记·孔子世家》所记的鲁哀公十四年(公元前481年)相合。未闻:未听说。

【原文】4 子华使于齐[1],冉子为其母请粟[2]。子曰:"与之釜[3]。"请益。曰:"与之庾[4]。"冉子与之粟五秉[5]。子曰:"赤之适齐也,乘肥马衣轻裘[6]。吾闻之也:君子周急不继富[7]。"

【白话译文】

公西子华被派遣到齐国去作使者,冉有替他的母亲请求小米。孔子说:"给他六斗四升。"冉有请求增加。孔子说:"再给他二斗四升。"冉有给了他八十石。孔子说:"公西华到齐国去,坐着肥马驾的车,穿着又轻又暖的皮袍;可见豪华。我听说过,君子只在雪里送炭,不去锦上添花。"

【英语译文】

Gongxi Zihua was sent to Qi State as ambassador and Ran You asked for millets in place of Zihua's mother. Confucius said, "Give him six *dou* four *sheng*." Ran You required more. Confucius said, "Give him two *dou* eight *sheng* more." Finally Ran You gave him eighty *dan*. Confucius said, "Zihua went to Qi State driving cart pulled by fat horses, wearing light fur clothes. It's quite extravagant. I've ever heard that moral man gives others timely assistance but he never adds a beautiful thing to a contrasting beautiful thing."

【注释】(1)子华:公西赤(公元前509年—?),孔子弟子。姓公西,名赤,字子华,亦称公西华。春秋末鲁国人,少孔子四十二岁。使:出使,子华被孔子派遣到齐国去作使者。(2)冉子:即冉有。其:代词指子华。请粟:请求小米。(3)釜(fǔ):古容量单位元。一釜,为六斗四升。(4)庾(yǔ):古容量单位元。一庾,为二斗四升,一说为十六斗。(5)秉(bǐng):古容量单位元,一秉为十六斛,十斗曰斛,故一秉即一百六十斗。五秉即八百斗(八十石 dàn)。(6)乘肥马衣轻裘:形容生活豪华。衣,读 yì,动词,指穿(衣,yī)。(7)周急:周济困急,援助正该援助的人。

不继富:不续有余,不助淫富。

【原文】5 原思为之宰[1],与之粟九百[2],辞[3],子曰:“毋![4]以与尔邻里乡党乎![5]”

【白话译文】

原思任孔子家的总管。孔子给他小米九百斗(或斛)。他不肯接受。孔子说:“不要推辞!有多的就给你地方上困急的人吧!”

【英语译文】

Yuan Si acted as Confucius' general house-keeper. Confucius gave him millets of nine hundred *dou*. But he refused. Confucius said, “Don't refuse it. You may use the surplus amount to help those people in urgent need in your locality.”

【注释】(1)原思:即原子思(公元前515年—?),孔子弟子,姓原,名宪,字子思,亦称仲宪。为之宰:之,代词,同“其”“他的”,这里指孔子的。(2)之:代词,他(指原思)。粟九百:百后面没有单位词。不好说。不过,有个习惯,古今大致相同,通常把最常用的单位略而不说。又根据上节,“与之粟”后,应当是容量单位元(不是重量单位)。而且最常用的单位斗比斛更优先。(3)辞:推辞,辞谢。(4)毋(wú):副词,表示禁止,莫,不可。(5)以与:给予。以,助词,补凑音节。尔:你。邻里乡党:都是古代地方单位的名称。朱熹集注:“五家为邻,二十五家为里,万二千五百家为乡,五百家为党。”

【原文】6 子谓仲弓[1],曰:“犁牛之子骍且角[2],虽欲勿用[3],山川其舍诸[4]?”

【白话译文】

孔子谈到冉雍时,说:“杂色牛生的红色而角正的小牛,虽然不想用它作祭祀的牺牲,山川之神难道会舍弃它吗?”

【英语译文】

When he commented on Ran Yong, Confucius said, “As for calf given birth by hybrid cow, it has red symmetric horns. Although we do not want to use them as sacrifice, will the gods of hills and rivers reject it?”

【注释】(1)谓:评论。(2)犁牛:杂色牛。骍(xīng):赤色。角:指牛角长得周正。(3)用:这里特指杀牲以祭。山川:山川之神。其:语气词,表反问,难道。诸:“之”“乎”两字的合音。

【原文】7 子曰:“回也,其心三月不违仁[1],其余则日月至焉而已矣[2]。”

【白话译文】

孔子说:“颜回呀,他的心长期不离开仁德,别的学生,只是断断续续地念到仁德罢了。”

【英语译文】

Confucius said, “As for Yan Hui, he never deviates from virtue and humanity. Other disciples just utter the two things intermittently.”

【注释】(1)三月:三个月,一年的四分之一,在日常生活中时间感觉不短,言者之意是说时间长、长期。违:离开。(2)其余:指除颜回外的学生。日月:犹言“某日某月”“或日或月”。至:通“志”,想念,念及。焉:近指代词,指“仁”。

【原文】8 季康子问[1]:“仲由可使从政也与[2]?”子曰:“由也果[3],于从政乎何有[4]?”曰:“赐也可使从政也与?”曰:“赐也达[5],于从政乎何有?”曰:“求也可使从政也与?”曰:“求也艺[6],于从政乎何有?”

【白话译文】

季康子问孔子:“仲由这人,可以用他管理政事么?”孔子说:“仲由果敢,有决断,让他管理政事,有什么困难呢?”又问:“端木赐呢,可用他管理政事么?”孔子说:“端木赐通晓事理,让他管理政事,有什么困难呢?”又问:“冉求呢,可用他管理政事么?”孔子说:“冉求多才多艺,让他管理政事,有什么困难呢?”

【英语译文】

Ji Kang Zi asked Confucius, “Can Zhong You be used as an administrative official?” Confucius answered, “Is there any difficulty if he is empowered as an official since he is decisive?” Ji Kang Zi continued, “Can Duanmu Chi be used as an administrative official?” Confucius answered, “Is there any difficulty if he is empowered as an official since he knows how things go on?" Ji Kang Zi asked once more, "Can Ran Qiu be used as an administrative official?" Confucius answered, "Is there any difficulty if he is empowered as an official since he has versatile abilities?"

【注释】(1)季康子:(? —公元前468年),春秋末鲁国大夫,季孙氏,名肥,季桓子之庶子,鲁哀公时为正卿。其父曾嘱"若相鲁,必召仲尼"(他的父亲曾经叮嘱"你做鲁国丞相时,必须召回仲尼")。鲁哀公十一年(公元前484年),齐攻鲁,他使冉有率师却之。又得知"冉有学之于孔子",遂"以币迎孔子"(见《史记·孔子世家》)。孔子周游列国十四年,于是回到了鲁国。孔子回鲁后,他曾多次问政于孔子。(2)也与:亦作"也欤",语气助词,这里表疑问,还可表感叹。(3)果:果敢,有决断。(4)何有:用于反问语气,说明没有什么。这里表示不难。(5)达:通晓事理。(6)艺:多才能。

【原文】9 季氏使闵子骞为费宰[1]。闵子骞曰:"善为我辞焉[2]!如有复我者[3],则吾必在汶上矣[4]。"

【白话译文】

季氏指派闵子骞作为他采邑费地的长官。闵子骞对来人说:"妥善地替我辞掉这个差事吧!如果有人再来找我,那我一定在汶水边了。"

【英语译文】

Ji has dispatched Min Ziqian to Prefecture Bi as a chancellor. Min Ziqian told the messenger, "Please help me to refuse this position skillfully. If somebody else comes to me I'll arrive at the Wen River."

【注释】(1)季氏:即季孙氏,鲁桓公之子季友的后裔,鲁国"三桓"之一。鲁宣公九年(公元前600年)与孟孙氏、叔孙氏轮流执政。自季文子始,季武子、季平子、季桓子、季康子相继掌握鲁国实力。闵子骞:(公元前536年—?)孔子弟子,姓闵,名损,字子骞(qiān),春秋末鲁国人,少孔子十五岁。在孔门中以德行与颜回并称,尤以孝行著称于世。相传他少年丧母,受继母虐待,其父欲驱逐继母,他劝阻说:"母在一子单,母去三子寒。"费(bì):同"鄪",季氏的采邑。(2)善为我辞焉:善,指妥善,好好地。在句子中作状语。为我,是指帮我、替我的意思。辞:推辞,辞谢。焉:代词,指"为费宰"。(3)复我者:再来找我的人。(4)汶上:汶水边,暗指齐国。汶水，今山东省大汶河，古时齐、鲁两国的界河。

【原文】10 伯牛有疾[1]，子问之[2]，自牖执其手[3]，曰："亡之[4]，命矣夫[5]！斯人也而有斯疾也[6]！斯人也而有斯疾也！"

【白话译文】

伯牛生了重病，孔子去问候他。从南面的窗口握着他的手，说："死亡啊，这就是命运了吗？这样的好人竟生这样的恶病！这样的好人竟生这样的恶病！"

【英语译文】

Confucius visited Bo Niu because he was seriously ill. Shaking his hand across the south window, Confucius said, "Death, is it fate? So kind a man got such kind of serious disease! So kind a man got such kind of serious disease!"

【注释】(1)伯牛：即冉耕(公元前544年—？)孔子弟子。姓冉，名耕，字伯牛，春秋末鲁国人，少孔子七岁，以德行著称。有疾：朱熹《四书集注》："有疾，先儒以为癞也。"癞(lài)，指恶疮，麻风。(2)子问之：孔子问候伯牛。(3)牖(yǒu)：窗口。朱熹《四书集注》："牖，南牖也。礼，病者居北牖下，君视之，则迁于南牖下，使君得以南面视己。时伯牛家以此礼尊孔子，孔子不敢当，不入其室，而自牖执其手，盖与之永诀也。"(4)亡之：死亡啊。之，语气助词。表停顿兼感叹。(5)命矣夫：命，命运。矣，语气助词，表已然或将然都相当于"了"。夫，助词，一般用在句末表感叹或疑问。命矣夫，意谓这就是命运了吗？(6)斯人：这样的人。而：转折连词，反而，竟然。有斯疾：生这样的病。

【原文】11 子曰："贤哉[1]，回也！一箪食[2]，一瓢饮[3]，在陋巷[4]，人不堪其忧[5]，回也不改其乐[6]。贤哉，回也！"

【白话译文】

孔子说："有德又有才呀，颜回啊！一筐饭，一瓢水，低矮狭小的住宅，别人都受不了那种穷困的忧愁，颜回却不改变那种穷困中自有的乐趣。有德又有才呀，颜回啊！"

【英语译文】

Confucius said, "Yan Hui was a man with talent and virtue! Others cannot bear the poor living situation where there're just a small amount of rice and water, and a shabby dwelling place. But Yan Hui can just enjoy the satisfaction in such kind of poverty. Yan Hui was a man with talent and virtue!"

【注释】(1)贤:有德行;有才能。(2)箪(dān):古代用来盛饭食的盛器。用竹或苇编成,圆形有盖。(3)瓢(piáo):以老熟的葫芦对半剖开制成的舀水器或盛酒器。饮:水、酒、饮料。(4)陋巷:简陋的巷子,狭小低矮的住宅。(5)堪(kān):能承受。其:远指代词。其忧,指箪瓢陋巷中那种穷困之忧。(6)其乐:指箪瓢陋巷中那种有所自悟不以穷困为累之乐。

【原文】12 冉求曰:"非不说子之道[1],力不足也。"子曰:"力不足者[2],中道而废[3]。今女画[4]。"

【白话译文】

冉求说:"不是我不喜欢您的立身行世的路,是我的力量不够。"孔子说:"如果真的是力量不够的话,走到半路会走不动的。现在你是主动划断不开步走。"

【英语译文】

Ran Qiu said, "It is not that I don't like your Way but that I lack strength." Confucius said, "You cannot move on in half way if you really lack strength. At present time it's you who actively refuse to move on in my Way."

【注释】(1)道:立身行世的路。(2)者:语气助词,可用在假设从句末,表假设语气的停顿。(3)中道:中途,半路。废:本义是房屋坍塌,引申为本身不能支持而停止,中止。今:现在。女(rǔ):通作"汝",你。(4)画:本义是划分界限,划分。引申为主动划断,截止。

【原文】13 子谓子夏曰:"女为君子儒[1]!无为小人儒[2]!"

【白话译文】

孔子对子夏说:"你要做个君子模式的儒,不要去做那小人模式的儒。"

【英语译文】

Confucius told Zi Xia, "You should become a moral-man-style Confucian scholar, but do not become a mean-man-style Confucian scholar."

【注释】(1)君子儒：与"小人儒"相对。春秋、战国时期有高度道德自觉和道德修养的儒，孔子于本章首次提出了"君子儒"与"小人儒"，把儒划分为君子与小人两个类型。君子原指统治者，小人原指被统治者，孔子把这两个概念运用到伦理学领域，赋予道德意义，以君子代表有道德觉悟、道德修养的儒，以小人代表没有道德觉悟、道德修养的儒。(2)小人儒：见前解。

【原文】14 子游为武城宰[1]。子曰："女得人焉耳乎[2]？曰："有澹台灭明者[3]，行不由径[4]，非公事，未尝至于偃之室也[5]。"

【白话译文】

子游做武城地方的长官。孔子说："你在这个地方得到什么人才没有？"他说："有一个叫澹台灭明的人，一贯走正路，不是公事，从不到我屋里来。"

【英语译文】

Zi You acted as chancellor in Wucheng. Confucius said, "Have you got any talented man here?" Zi You answered, "There is a man called Tantai, or Tantai Mieming who does things uprightly and never comes to me if he doesn't have official affairs."

【注释】(1)子游：即言偃(yǎn)(公元前506年—?)，孔子弟子，姓言、名偃、字子游，亦称言游，春秋末吴国人，少孔子四十五岁。与子夏、子张并为孔门晚期著名弟子，以文学著称，二十多岁即为武城宰(武城，今山东费县西南)。实行孔子关于"君子学道则爱人，小人学道则易使"的教诲，注重礼乐教化，致使孔子视察时，"满城闻弦歌之声"。(2)女：汝。得人：谓得到德才兼备的人。焉耳：亦作"焉尔"。于是。乎：语气助词。表疑问。(3)澹台灭明：(公元前552年—?)，孔子晚年弟子，姓澹(tán)台，名灭明，字子羽。春秋末鲁国武城人，少孔子三十九岁(或说四十九岁)。(4)径：小路，步道，比喻能达到某种目的的不正当门路。(5)未尝：不曾。

【原文】15 子曰:"孟之反不伐[1],奔而殿[2],将入门[3],策其马[4],曰:"非敢后也[5],马不进也[6]。"

【白话译文】

孔子说:"孟之反不自我夸耀,在抵御齐国的战役中,败退时走在后面掩护全军,将进城门,他打着马说道:"不是我敢于走在最后,是马不向前的缘故。"

【英语译文】

Confucius said, "Meng Zhifan never boasted himself. When retreating he lagged behind to guard other soldiers. While entering city gate, he hit his horse saying, 'It's not that I dare lagging behind but that my horse refuses to go ahead.'"

【注释】(1)孟之反:亦作"孟之侧",春秋时鲁国大夫,据左传哀公十一年记载,齐国伐鲁,鲁右翼之师溃退时,孟之反后入以为殿,掩护全军并"抽矢策其马,曰:'马不进也'以不伐其自功"。不伐:不自我夸耀。(2)奔而殿:奔,指败逃,败退。而,转折连词,指"却""但是"。殿,与下文"后"互文见义,殿后,走在后面掩护前面。(3)将入门:谓将进城门。(4)策:鞭打。(5)后:与上文"殿"互文见义。殿后。参见注2。(6)进:前进,向前。

【原文】16 子曰:"不有祝鮀之佞[1],而有宋朝之美[2],难乎免于今之世矣[3]"

【白话译文】

孔子说:"假如没有祝佗的口才,却有宋朝的美貌,在现在的社会上,难以避免不测了。"

【英语译文】

Confucius said, "If anyone isn't as eloquent as Zhu Tuo but is as beautiful as Song Zhao, it's very difficult to avoid mishaps in nowadays society."

【注释】(1)不有:这里表示假设语气。谓"假若没有"。祝鮀:一作"祝佗",春秋时卫国大夫,字子鱼,口才好。左传定公四年记载着他的外交辞令。鮀:音 tuó。佞:善辩,口才好。(2)而:转折连词,"却""但"。宋朝:宋国的公子朝,左传昭公二十年和左传定公十四年都记载着他因为美貌而惹起乱子的事情。(3)难乎:难于,难以。免:幸免,避免。于今:同“如今”,现在。世:世道。根据上下文的含义。这个“世道”即世道不好、乱世的婉辞。

【原文】17 子曰:“谁能出不由户[1]? 何莫由斯道也[2]?”

【白话译文】

孔子说:“谁能够走出屋外不经过屋门? 为何没有人从这条正路行走呢?”

【英语译文】

Confucius said, “Who can get out of his house not crossing doors? Why aren't there a man who walks through this right way?”

【注释】(1)户:单扇(门扉、门板)的叫户,双扇的叫门。后也泛指混用。(2)何莫:为何没有人。斯道:正道。朱熹《四书集注》引洪氏曰:“人知出必由户,而不知行必由道。道不远人,而人自远也。”这是说人们只要是到屋外去,就知道必须从门口走出去;但是不知道走路必须走正道。正道不会离开人,是人离开正道。

【原文】18 子曰:“质胜文则野[1],文胜质则史[2]。文质彬彬[3],然后君子[4]。”

【白话译文】

孔子说:“质朴超过文雅,就难免粗野;文雅超过质朴,就难免虚浮。文雅质朴兼备不偏,这样才算是君子,有道德又有修养。

【英语译文】

Confucius said, “It's rude if simplicity surpasses elegance; it's superficial if elegance surpasses simplicity. Both simplicity and elegance belong to a man, then the man can be called a moral man, both virtual and cultivated.”

【注释】(1)质:质朴。胜:掩盖,超过。文:文华,文雅。野:鄙俗,粗野。(2)史:虚饰,浮夸。(3)彬彬(bīnbīn):文质兼备的样子。(4)然后:表示接着某种动作或情况之后,犹言这样才是。

【原文】19 子曰:“人之生也直[1],罔之生也幸而免[2]。”

【白话译文】

孔子说:"人的生存正直不曲,不正直的人的生存是意外免除了祸害。

【英语译文】

Confucius said, "The existence of men is upright, and the existence of dishonest men is that they have unexpectedly dodged scourge."

【注释】(1)人之生:人的生存。在这个句子中作主语。也:语气助词,既作主语标志也表示停顿。直:正直。(2)罔:枉曲,不直。罔后省略了"人"。罔人:不直的人。幸:侥幸,意外获得成功或免除灾害。免:避免。

【原文】20 子曰:"知之者不如好之者[1],好之者不如乐之者[2]。"

【白话译文】

孔子说:"懂得"道"的人,不及喜爱"道"的人,喜爱"道"的人,不及耽乐"道"的人。

【英语译文】

Confucius said, "Those who understand Way don't match those who love Way; and those who love Way don't match those who enjoy Way."

【注释】(1)知:懂得,了解。之:代词,指学问、技艺、事业等。者:代词,用在形容词、动词、动词词组或主谓词组之后组成者字结构,用以指代人、事、物。这里是用在动词词组后的者字结构,指代人。好:喜爱,爱好。(2)乐:耽乐,以……为乐。

【原文】21 子曰:"中人以上[1],可以语上也[2];中人以下,不可以语上也。"

【白话译文】

孔子说:"中等水平及以上的人,可以同他谈论高深一层的学问;中等水平及以下的人,不可以同他谈论高深一层的学问。"

【英语译文】

Confucius said, "We could discuss learnings with those who are above intermediate level. And we couldn't discuss learnings with those who are below intermediate level."

【注释】(1)中人:中等水平的人。这类人继续努力,水平可以上升;不继续努力水平还会下降。所以可以语上有中等水平的人,不可以语上没有中等水平的人。(2)语:谈论。上:对于受众而言,高深一层的学问。

【原文】22 樊迟问知[1]。子曰:"务民之义[2],敬鬼神而远之[3],可谓知矣。"问仁。曰:"仁者先难而后获[4],可谓仁矣。"

【白话译文】

樊迟问怎么才算明智。孔子说:"专心致力于人民的正义事业,不冒犯鬼神,远远离开它,可以算是明智了。"又问什么是仁德。孔子说:"有仁德的人,首先努力克服困难做应做的事不废不止,然后达到成功。可以说是仁德了。"

【英语译文】

Fan Chi wondered how to be wise. Confucius told him, "It's wise for us to concentrate on people's righteous cause and not to offend ghosts, being far from them." Fan Chi asked for the meaning of humanity and virtue. Confucius said, "A man with humanity and virtue should first overcome difficulties and then focus on his own things, and finally attain his goal. That can be called humanity and virtue."

【注释】(1)樊迟:(公元前515年—?)孔子弟子,姓樊,名须,字子迟,亦称樊迟,春秋末鲁国人。少孔子三十六岁(一说四十六岁),好学广问,且敢于连续追问,直至通达。知:同"智",这里意谓明智。(2)务:专心致力。民:人民,人类。之:结构助词,用在定语和中心词之间,相当于"的"。义:正义,所当为。(3)敬:严谨对待,不冒犯。远之:离开它,避开它。远,读 yuàn。(4)仁者:有仁德的人。先难而后获:首先努力克服困难做应做的事,不废不止,然后达到成功。

【原文】23 子曰:"知者乐水[1],仁者乐山[2]。知者动[3],仁者静[4]。知者乐[5],仁者寿[6]。"

【白话译文】

孔子说:"聪明的人,喜好水乡;仁厚的人,喜好山林。聪明的人,好动;仁厚的人,好静。聪明的人,快乐;仁厚的人,高寿。”

【英语译文】

Confucius said, “Wise men love water and humane men love mountain. While wise men like actions, humane men like tranquility. Wise men are happy and humane men live long.”

【注释】(1)乐(yào):喜好。水:指江河湖海。(2)乐:同前。山:指山林。(3)动:好动。(4)静:好静。(5)乐(lè):快乐。(6)寿:高寿。

【原文】24 子曰:“齐一变[1],至于鲁[2];鲁一变,至于道[3]。”

【白话译文】

孔子说:“齐国的政治社会,一经改革,就可达到鲁国的现状;鲁国的政治社会,一经改革,就可合于大道。”

【英语译文】

Confucius said, “Upon reform the politics and society of Qi State can match with that of Lu State; and upon reform the politics and society of Lu State can concord with the Great Way.”

【注释】(1)齐:孔子之时,齐国风俗急于功利,喜欢夸诈,是霸政的余习。一变:谓假如一经改革。(2)至于:达到,合于。鲁:鲁国当时则重礼教,崇尚信义,还有先王的遗风。但人亡政息,不能没有废败。(3)道:先王之道,即孔子所继承发扬的大道。

【原文】25 子曰:“觚不觚[1],觚哉[2]! 觚哉!”

【白话译文】

孔子说:“觚没有棱角就不像觚了,这是觚吗! 这是觚吗!”

【英语译文】

Confucius said, “If a wine jug doesn't have edges and corners, then it's never called jug. Is it a jug? Is it a jug?"

【注释】(1)觚:gū,古代盛酒的器皿。腹部作四条棱角,足部也作四条棱角,这是觚的特征,没有这个特征就不是觚了。可是做出棱角比做圆的难,孔子所见的觚可能只是一个圆形的酒器,而不是上圆下方有四条棱角的了。却也称为觚。因此孔子慨叹当日事物名实不符,如"君不君,臣不臣,父不父,子不子"之类。觚不觚:觚不像觚。(2)觚哉:是觚吗?

【原文】26 宰我问曰:"仁者,虽告之曰[1],'井有仁焉[2]'其从之也[3]?"子曰:"何为其然也[4]?君子可逝也[5],不可陷也[6];可欺也[7],不可罔也[8]。"

【白话译文】

宰我问道:"有仁德的人,如果告诉他说:'井里掉下去一位仁厚的人啦!'他会跟着下去吗?"孔子说:"你为什么一定要这样做呢?君子可以叫他远去不回,但不可以陷害他。可以欺骗他,但不可以愚弄他。"

【英语译文】

Zai Wo asked, "If we told a man with humanity and virtue that an honest man had fallen into a well, would he follow him?" Confucius answered, "Why do you like that? We can tell a moral man leave forever but we cannot make a false charge against him. We can cheat him but not fool him."

【注释】(1)虽:假设连词,意谓假如、如果。(2)仁:即"仁人",和学而篇第一"泛爱众而亲仁"的"仁"用法相同。焉:语气助词,用在陈述句末,表动态的已然、将然或必然,和"矣"差不多。可译作"了""啦"。(3)其:代词,表第三人称。相当于他(她、它)或他(她、它)们。(4)何为(hé wèi):为什么。其然:必如此。也:语气助词,用在特指问句或选择问句末,表疑问语气。可译为"呢"。(5)逝:远去不回。(6)陷:陷害,设陷阱害人。(7)欺:欺骗。(8)罔:诬罔,犹言蒙骗,愚弄。

【原文】27 子曰:"君子博学于文[1],约之以礼[2],亦可以弗畔矣夫[3]!"

【白话译文】

孔子说:"君子广泛地学习文化知识,并用礼来约束这个学习,也可以不至于叛离正道的呀!”

【英语译文】

Confucius said, “Moral men learn knowledge extensively and restrain his learning by rites so that he won't be stoayed from the right way.”

【注释】(1)博学:广泛大量地学。文:文化知识。(2)约:约束,简约。之:代词,指代“博学于文”。礼:社会生活中由于风俗习惯而形成的行为准则、道德规范和各种礼节。朱熹《四书集注》:“程子曰:‘博学于文而不约之以礼,必至汗漫(漫无边际)。博学矣,又能守礼而由于(遵从)规矩,则亦可以不畔道矣。’”(3)畔:同“叛”。矣:语气助词,表肯定或判断,相当于“也”。一般不译,这里可译作“的”。夫:在这里作句末语气词,表感叹,可译作“呀”。

【原文】28 子见南子[1],子路不说。夫子矢之曰[2]:“予所否者[3],天厌之[4]!天厌之!”

【白话译文】

孔子去和南子相见,子路不高兴。孔子发誓说:“我如果有不正当行为的话,天弃绝我吧!天弃绝我吧!”

【英语译文】

Zi Lu became unhappy when Confucius went to see Nan Zi. Confucius pledged, “If I did any thing dishonest, the Heaven deserts me. The Heaven deserts me.”

【注释】(1)南子:卫灵公夫人。她把持着当日卫国的政治,而且有不正当的行为,名声不好。(2)夫子:这里是孔门对孔子的尊称,后因以特指孔子,后世又沿称老师为夫子。矢之曰:发誓说。之,在这里是助词,起调整音节的作用,没有实在意义。(3)所:连词,这里表示假设,相当于“如果”“假若”。古代常用于盟誓中。否:这里指违礼背道的行为。者:语气助词,用于表假设的分句末译作“的话”。从以上看来,予所否者,可译作“我如果有不正当行为的话,”(4)厌(yàn):弃绝,抛弃。

【原文】29 子曰:“中庸之为德也[1],其至矣乎[2]!民鲜久矣[3]。”

【白话译文】

孔子说:“中庸作为一种道德,也许是最高尚的了吧!人们缺乏这种道德很久了。”

【英语译文】

Confucius said,“As a kind of morality, doctrine of mean is perhaps the noblest one There has been the lack of it for a long time.

【注释】(1)中庸:孔子哲学、伦理思想的重要范畴。意谓不偏不倚地把握“中”这个事物运动的总准则。这个词始见于论语。但其思想渊源甚为久远。尧在让位于舜时即强调治理社会要“允执其中”,周公也倡力行“中德”,并强调在折狱用刑时要做到中正。尚中观念在周易中表现更明显,六十四卦中的每卦中爻(第二、五爻)爻词大多是吉利的。春秋时期中和观念得到发展,如晏婴提出五味调和成美羹,五色协和成文采,五声相和成美乐,君子听之“心平德和”。在上述基础上,孔子进一步提出中庸的概念,从而使中和观念哲理化。为德:作为(成为)道德。(2)其:副词,也许。至:最好的,最高超的。矣乎:了啊,了吧。(3)民:人们。鲜:缺乏,少有。

【原文】30 子贡曰:“如有博施于民而能济众[1],何如?可谓仁乎?”子曰:“何事于仁[2]!必也圣乎[3]!尧舜其犹病诸[4]!夫仁者[5],己欲立而立人,己欲达而达人。能近取譬[6],可谓仁之方也已[7]。”

【白话译文】

子贡说:“如果有人广泛地给人民以好处,又能帮助大家生活得很好,怎么样?可以说是仁德了吗?”孔子说:“这哪仅是仁德。一定是圣德了!尧、舜也许都难以做到呢!仁的含义是什么呢,自己想站得住,同时也使别人站得住;自己想行得通,同时也使别人行得通。能设身处地,推己及人,可以说是行仁德的方法了。

【英语译文】

Zi Gong said, “How about a man who shows mercy extensively on common people and help them to live well as well? Can that be called humane and virtue?” Confucius answered, “It's more than that. It is surely sage virtue. Yao and Shun might not do this. What is the real meaning of humanity? It means that if you want to establish yourself you should establish others; and if you want to do things smoothly, you should make others do things smoothly. It can be called methods of humanity and virtue if you can help others from your own standpoint."

【注释】(1)有:用同"或",这里是代词,意谓"有人"。博施:广泛施惠。济众:救助众人。(2)事:犹止,仅。于:语气助词。调整音节。(3)必:一定,肯定的判断。也:语气助词,表判断语气。圣:指聪明睿智的德行。乎:语气助词,表赞叹语气。(4)尧、舜:上古两位圣明的帝王,孔子心目中的榜样。其:也许。犹:还。病:难,不易。诸:语助词。表感叹。(5)夫:助词,表发端。谓提起要说的话,或提出主题来谈论。仁者:仁的含义。(6)能近取譬:谓能设身处地,推己及人。刘宝楠正义:"譬者,喻也;以己为喻,故曰近。"章炳麟菌说:"独夫为我,即曰贪贼,能近取譬,即曰仁义。"(7)仁之方:实践仁道的方法。也已:语气助词,表肯定或感叹。

述而篇第七(共三十八章)

《朱熹集注》把第九、第十两章并作一章,所以题为三十七章。本篇提出孔子的教育思想、学习态度、对仁德的阐释及其他思想主张,是研究孔子和儒家思想者常引篇章之一。

【原文】1 子曰:"述而不作[1],信而好古[2],窃比于我老彭[3]。"

【白话译文】

孔子说:"我只阐述而不创作,相信和爱好古人的伟大成就。我还私下与老彭相比。"

【英语译文】

Confucius said, "I just elaborate but not deliberately differ; I believe and cherish ancients' great achievement. Furthermore I privately compare myself with Lao Dan and Peng Zu."

【注释】(1)述:传述,讲述。不作:不标新立异。(2)信而好古:心服而且爱好古人事业的成绩。(3)窃:私下、私自,多用作谦辞。比:比方、比拟、比喻。于:介词,在……中(之间)。于我老彭,谓在我和老彭中(之间)。老彭:何晏集解引包咸曰:“老彭,殷贤大夫。”一说为老聃、彭祖的并称。郑玄、刘宝楠持此说。

【原文】2 子曰:“默而识之[1],学而不厌[2],诲人不倦[3],何有于我哉[4]?

【白话译文】

孔子说:“学问和见闻都暗暗记在心里,不断努力学习并且没有厌弃,教导别人没有厌倦,这三方面我还该做些什么呢?”

【英语译文】

Confucius said, “I keep in mind my learnings and knowledge; I try my best to study hard and never give up, and I never feel tired of instructing others. Besides these, what should I do?”

【注释】(1)默:暗暗,私下。而:副词、形容词词尾,粘附在描写声貌情态的词后和然焉差不多,有“……的样子”的意思。识(zhì):记住。之:代词,指学问、见闻。(2)学而不厌:努力学习并且没有厌弃。而:递进连词,并且。(3)诲人不倦:教导别人没有厌倦。(4)何有于我哉:本句想必是孔子在自我省视。

【原文】3 子曰:“德之不修[1],学之不讲[2],闻义不能徙[3],不善不能改[4],是吾忧也。

【白话译文】

孔子说:“品德不培养,学问不讲习;看到正义不能拥护,看到缺点错误不能改正。这些都是我的忧虑。”

【英语译文】

Confucius said, “I’m worried about the fact that people don’t cultivate morality, don’t practice learnings, don’t uphold justice and don’t correct faults and shortcomings.”

【注释】(1)德之不修:品德不培养。之,结构助词。(2)学之不讲:学问不讲习。之,结构助词。(3)闻义不能徙:看到正义不能拥护。徙(xǐ):改变意念相从。(4)不善不能改:缺点错误不能改正。

【原文】4 子之燕居[1],申申如也[2],夭夭如也[3]。

【白话译文】

孔子平时在家闲居,室内十分整洁清新,仪态十分平易舒展。

【英语译文】

When Confucius stayed casually at home, his rooms were neat and fresh and his manners were easygoing.

【注释】(1)燕居:闲居。(2)申申如:整饰的样子。如,形容词后缀,犹然。也:语气助词。(3)夭夭如:和舒的样子。参见前解。

【原文】5 子曰:"甚矣吾衰也[1]! 久矣吾不复梦见周公[2]!"

【白话译文】

孔子说:"我衰老得好厉害呀! 很长时间都没再梦见周公了!"

【英语译文】

Confucius sighed, "O, I' m seriously weak and old! I haven't dreamt Zhou Gong for ages!"

【注释】(1)甚(shèn):厉害、严重、很、极。在本句中作补语(置于衰后),或作状语(置于衰前)因强调而提。(2)久:时间长,长时间,在本句中的用法同"甚",参见前注。周公(?—约公元前1095年),姓姬,名旦,西周初政治家、思想家,周文王之子,周武王之弟,周成王之叔,鲁国之始祖,孔子心目中最敬服的古代圣人之一。

【原文】6 子曰:"志于道[1],据于德[2],依于仁[3],游于艺[4]。"

【白话译文】

孔子说:"立志行正道,执守善德,不背离仁厚之心,游憩于礼、乐、射、御、书、数六艺之中。"

【英语译文】

Confucius said, "We should set goal on right way, observe virtue, and do not go against humanity. We should always immerse in practicing rites, music, archery, calligraphy, and mathematics."

【注释】(1)志:目标、志向、立志。道:正道。(2)据:执守,依据。德:善德。(3)依:依从,不背离。仁:人己不背之心。(4)游:游览与休息。艺:礼、乐、射、御、书、数六艺。一说,即六经,指礼、乐、书、诗、易、春秋。

【原文】7 子曰:"自行束修以上[1],吾未尝无诲焉[2]。"

【白话译文】

孔子说:"只要是主动地给我十条干肉作见面礼,我从来没有不教诲的。"

【英语译文】

Confucius said, "Whoever presents me ten slices of dry meat as gift for first meating, I never refuse to instructing him."

【注释】(1)自行束修:修(xiū),是干肉,又叫脯(fǔ),每条脯叫脡(tǐng),十脡为一束。束脩就是十条干肉,古代用来作为初次拜见的礼物,这一礼物在当时是菲薄的。(2)诲:教诲。

【原文】8 子曰:"不愤不启[1],不悱不发[2],举一隅不以三隅反[3],则不复也[4]。"

【白话译文】

孔子说:"教导学生,不到他想弄懂而不得的时候,不去开导他;不到他想说出来却又说不出来的时候,不去引起他。讲东方,他不能联想到南、北、西三方,此时不可再授新课。"

【英语译文】

Confucius said, "When teaching student, don't enlighten him until he wants to, but cannot comprehend; don't arouse him until he wants to, but cannot speak out. New course cannot be presented at the moment students can't associate south, north and west after you talk about east."

【注释】(1)愤(fèn):郁结于心,心求通而未得。启:开导其意。(2)悱(fěi):想说而未能说出。发:引起。(3)举一隅不以三隅反:物之有四隅的,举一可知其三。反,回馈所领悟的事物或事理。(4)不复:意谓不能举一反三,即所学未能真的理解,此时不再上新课。

【原文】9 子食于有丧者之侧[1],未尝饱也。

【白话译文】

孔子在新逝亲属的人旁进餐,不曾吃饱过。

【英语译文】

Confucius was never full when he ate beside a person who had just lost his dearest one.

【注释】(1)食(shí):吃饭,进餐。有丧者:新逝亲属的人。

【原文】10 子于是日哭[1],则不歌[2]。

【白话译文】

孔子在碰上死者亲属这日,哭泣过,没有歌唱。

【英语译文】

Confucius cried and never sang a song when met a person who had lost his dearest one.

【注释】(1)是日:碰上死者亲属这日。(2)则:承接连词,即、就。不歌:没有歌唱。

【原文】11 子谓颜渊曰:"用之则行[1],舍之则藏[2],惟我与尔有是夫[3]!"子路曰:"子行三军[4],则谁与[5]?"子曰:"暴虎冯河[6],死而无悔者[7],吾不与也[8]。必也临事而惧[9],好谋而成者也[10]。"

【白话译文】

孔子对颜渊说:"用我就干,弃我就隐。只有我和你才能这样吧!"子路说道:"老师,您若指挥全军,将选用哪一个?"孔子说:"空手搏虎,徒步渡河,那样冒险行事、死不悔改的人,我是不取的。我要取的,一定是遇事谨慎戒惧、善于谋划成事的人了!"

【英语译文】

Confucius said to Yan Yuan, "I'll do things upon being hired and I'll retire upon being fired. Only you and I can be so!" Zi Lu asked, "Master, If one is to command armed forces, whom you'll choose?" Confucius said, "I'll never choose the man who bare-handedly fights against a tiger with bare hands, wades a river without a boat, does things riskily without changing a little. Whom I choose must be a man who's cautious and good at planning when carrying out a task."

【注释】(1)用之:用我。之,用作自称代词。即"我"。下同。则行:就干。(2)舍之:弃我。则藏:就隐。(3)惟:只有。有是夫:有,具有。是,近指代词。此,这种,这样。指代上文"用之则行,舍之则藏"这种品行。夫。句末语气词。表示感叹。(4)行(三)军:泛指用兵。行三军,犹言率领(指挥)全军。(5)则:承接连词。那么。谁与:即与谁,选拔哪个。与,选拔,举用的意思。(6)暴虎冯河:《诗·小雅·小旻》:"不敢暴虎,不敢冯河。"谓不敢空手搏虎,不敢徒步渡河。后以"暴虎冯河"喻冒险行事。冯,读 píng。(7)死而无悔者:死不悔改的人。(8)吾不与也:我不选用。(9)必也:"必须,必定要"的强调说法。临事而惧:遇事谨慎。(10)好谋而成者:善于谋划成事的人。

【原文】12 子曰:"富而可求也[1],虽执鞭之士[2],吾亦为之。如不可求,从吾所好[3]。"

【白话译文】

孔子说:"财富假若可以求得的话,就是拿着鞭子做下贱事,我也干。如果不可能求得,干我爱好的事。"

【英语译文】

Confucius said, "If wealth can be obtained, I will take action even if under threat of whip. And I will do what I like if wealth cannot be obtained."

【注释】(1)而:假设连词,用在复合句的前一分句的主语和谓语之间,同"如"差不多,可译为"假如""如果"。(2)虽:让步连词,译为"虽然""即使""纵然"。执鞭之士:士,通"事"。邢昺疏:"若富贵而于道可求者,虽执鞭贱职我亦为之。"执鞭之事,在古代大约有三个方面,一是帮人执鞭赶车;二是为君主出行,在前头执鞭清道;三是市场交易,执鞭看门。从吾所好:干我爱好的事。

【原文】13 子之所慎[1]:齐[2],战[3],疾[4]。

【白话译文】

孔子的慎重有三项:斋戒,战争,疾病。

【英语译文】

Cautions of Confucius: fast, war, and disease.

【注释】(1)所慎:慎重,名词。(2)齐(zhāi):同"斋",古代在祭祀前一定先做一番身心的整洁工作。这一番工作叫"斋"或者"斋戒",《乡党篇》第十说孔子"斋必变食,居必迁坐。"(3)战:关系国家的安危存亡,所以上文说领军作战,孔子表示必选"临事而惧,好谋而成"的人。(4)疾:关系个人的健康和生死,《乡党篇》描写孔子病了不敢随便吃药。

【原文】14 子在齐闻韶[1],三月不知肉味[2],曰:"不图为乐之至于斯也[3]。"

【白话译文】

孔子在齐国,多次听演奏舜时的韶乐,很长时间没感觉到菜里的肉味。他说:"没想到演奏乐曲竟然达到了这样好的境界。"

【英语译文】

When Confucius stayed in Qi State, he heard Shao Music many times and he didn't tast meat in his food. He said, "I never thought good music could elevate one to such good state."

【注释】(1)齐:齐国,诸侯中的大国与鲁国为邻。闻:反复多次听,含“欣赏”之意。韶:舜帝时的乐曲。(2)三月:谓时间长,不是两三天。不知:没感觉到。(3)不图:不料。为乐:奏乐(zòuyuè)。之:结构助词。至于斯:达到了这样好的境界。

【原文】15 冉有曰:“夫子为卫君乎[1]?”子贡曰:“诺;吾将问之[2]。”入[3],曰:“伯夷 叔齐何人也[4]?”曰:“古之贤人也。”曰:“怨乎[5]?”曰;“求仁而得仁[6],又何怨?”出,曰:“夫子不为也。”

【白话译文】

冉有说:“老师赞成卫君吗?”子贡说:“哦,我去问问老师。”子贡进入孔子屋里,说:“伯夷、叔齐是什么样的人呢?”孔子说:“古代的贤人呐。”子贡说:“他们后悔吗?”孔子说:“他们追求仁德,就有仁德,又后悔什么呢?”子贡出来,对冉有说:“老师不赞成卫君。”

【英语译文】

Ran You asked, "Is Master for Monarch Kuai Ze?" Zi Gong said, "I'll go to ask him." Zi Gong entered Confucius' room, asking, "What kind of men were Bo Yi and Shu Qi?" Confucius said, "They were ancient sages." Zi Gong asked, "Did they regret?" Confucius said, "They were humane and virtuous after they pursued humanity and virtue. What did they regret for?" Zi Gong came out and told Ran You, "Our Master isn't for Monarch Kuai Ze."

【注释】(1)为(wèi):帮助,赞成。卫君:指卫出公辄。辄是卫灵公之孙,太子之子。太子蒯聩得罪了卫灵公的夫人南子,逃在晋国。灵公死,立辄为君。晋国的赵简子又把蒯聩送回,借以侵略卫国。卫国抵御晋兵,自然也拒绝了蒯聩的回国。从辄和蒯辄是父子关系这一点来看,似乎是两父子争夺卫君的位置。和伯夷、叔齐两兄弟的互相推让,终于都抛弃了君位相比,是一鲜明对照。因之下文子贡引以发问,借以试探孔子对卫出公辄的态度。孔子赞美伯夷、叔齐,自然就是不赞成卫出公辄了。(2)诺(nuò):表示同意、遵命的应答声。吾之:代词,指代孔子。(3)入,曰:子贡进入孔子屋里,说。(4)何人也:什么样的人呢,那种人呢。(5)

怨:怨悔、后悔的意思。(6)求仁:追求仁德。而得:就有。

【原文】16 子曰:“饭疏食饮水[1],曲肱而枕之[2],乐亦在其中矣[3]。不义而富且贵,于我如浮云[4]。”

【白话译文】

孔子说:“吃粗饭,喝清水,弯着胳膊做枕头;乐趣也在这当中不会消失的。不正当的发财又升官,像浮云一样与我不相干。”

【英语译文】

Confucius said, “I surely find everlasting enjoyment in eating simple food, drinking water, and using my arms as pillow to sleep. It's unrelated to me and it's just like floating clouds to be wealthy and in official position through dishonest way.”

【注释】(1)饭:吃,吃饭。疏食:粗粝的饭食,糙米饭。饮(yǐn):喝。饮水,即喝水。(2)曲肱:弯着胳膊。肱(gōng):胳膊。曲肱而枕之,即弯着胳膊做枕头。(3)其:近指代词,相当于“这”,指代上文,“饭疏食饮水,曲肱而枕之。”浮云:飘逸的云。它在君子眼中,与晴、雨无关,过眼即逝。

【原文】17 子曰:“加我数年[1],五十以学易[2],可以无大过矣[3]。”

【白话译文】

孔子说:“但愿我能多活些岁月,用这一半或全部的时光努力学易,便可以不犯大的过错了。”

【英语译文】

Confucius said, “I wish I could live longer, and I'll spend half or all of my lifetime on learning the *Book of Changes*. As a result, I won't make great mistake.”

【注释】(1)加:古人认为各人的寿命长短各有定数,有的长,有的短。孔子希望能在自己的寿数上加长几岁。《史记》作“假”“借”或“给予”的意思。“加”“假”一声之转,用于此意义相通。“加(假)我数年”,谓但愿多活几年。(2)五十:五十,谓五分十分,五成十成,一半全部。以:用以。学易:易本为古代占筮书,发展演变到周代成为推天道以绝人事之学。

【原文】18 子所雅言[1]，诗、书、执礼[2]，皆雅言也。

【白话译文】

孔子的普通话，他读诗，读书，主持典礼仪式，都是普通话。

【英语译文】

Confucius' standard utterance was embodied while he read poetry and book, presided ritual ceremony. Those were all standard utterance.

【注释】(1)所：助词，相当于"之""的"。雅言：雅正之言。古时指通语（全国范围或全民族间的普通词语，也指几个地区内普遍使用的词语），相对方言而言。(2)执礼：主持典礼仪式。

【原文】19 叶公问孔子于子路[1]，子路不对[2]。子曰："女奚不曰[3]，其为人也[4]，发愤忘食[4]，乐以忘忧，[6]不知老之将至云尔[7]。"

【白话译文】

叶公向子路打听孔子的为人怎样，子路不回答。孔子知道后说："你怎么不这样说：'他的为人啊，勤奋用功，忘记吃饭。乐于求道，忘了忧愁，没感觉到衰老即将到来，如此而已。'"

【英语译文】

When Lord She asked ZiLu about Confucius' conduct, ZiLu refused to answer. After knowing this, Confucius said, "Why didn't you reply like this: 'As for his conduct, he's so diligent that he forgets eating and sleeping. And he's so fond of pursuing Way that he forgets sadness, not feeling that he's aging. It's just like this.'"

【注释】①叶(shè)：地名当时属楚，今河南叶(yè)县南三十里有古叶(shè)城。叶公是叶地方的长官，楚君称王，地方长官便称公。叶公叫沈诸梁，字子高。《左传》定公、哀公之间有一些关于他的记载，在楚国当时还算是一位贤者。②不对：不回答。③女：同"汝"。奚(xī)：为何，为什么。④其：代词，表第三人称领属关系,他(她、它)的,或他(她、它)们的。⑤发愤:勤奋用功。⑥乐:快乐。以:承接连词,相当于“而”。⑦不知:没感觉到。老之将至:衰老即将到来。云尔:云,指如此、这样。尔,同“耳”,指而已、罢了。

【原文】20 子曰:“我非生而知之者[1],好古[2],敏以求之者也[3]。”

【白话译文】

孔子说:“我不是生来就知事理的人,我是爱好古代文化、勤勉追求事理的人。”

【英语译文】

Confucius said, “I’m not a man who knows common sense. I’m a man who just loves ancient culture and persists on pursuing common sense.”

【注释】(1)知之者:知事理的人。(2)敏:勤勉。以:语气助词。求之者:追求事理的人。

【原文】21 子不语[1]怪、力、乱、神[2]。

【白话译文】

孔子不讲怪异、暴力、叛乱和鬼神。

【英语译文】

Confucius never talked about weird, violence, rebellion and ghosts.

【注释】(1)不语:不讲。(2)怪、力、乱、神:朱熹《四书集注》引谢氏曰:“圣人语常而不语怪,语德而不语力,语治而不乱,语人而不语神。”

【原文】22 子曰:“三人行[1],必有我师焉[2];择其善者而从之[3],其不善者而改之[4]。”

【白话译文】

孔子说:“三个人同路行走,必有我可取法的人;选取他的优点进行学习,对照他的缺点自我改正。”

【英语译文】

Confucius said, “When three people walk together, there must be a teacher from whom I can learn his merits and improve myself upon his shortcomings.”

【注释】(1)三人行:三个人同路行走,除了自己的另外两人,可能一恶一善,或均善或均不善,我从其善改其恶,如此这二人皆为我师。(2)必有我师焉:必有我可取法的人。(3)择其善者而从之:选取他的优点进行学习。(4)其不善者而改之:对照他的缺点自我改正。”

【原文】23 子曰:“天生德于予[1],桓魋其如予何[2]?”

【白话译文】

孔子说:“上天在我身上滋生了这样的品德品行,那桓魋将把我怎么样?”

【英语译文】

Confucius said, “The heaven bestows me such virtue; then how could Huan Tui do with me?”

【注释】(1)天生德:上天滋生品德品行,于予:在我身上。(2)桓魋:魋,读 tuí。桓魋,宋国的司马向魋,因为是宋桓公的后代所以又叫桓魋。其如予何:他把我怎么样。《史记·孔子世家》:“孔子去曹适宋,与弟子习礼大树下。宋司马桓魋欲杀孔子,拔其树。孔子去,弟子曰:‘可以速矣!’孔子曰:‘天生德于予,桓魋其如予何?’”

【原文】24 子曰:“二三子以我为隐乎[1]?吾无瘾乎尔[2]。吾无行不与二三子者[3],是丘也。[4]”

【白话译文】

孔子说:“你们这些学生认为我在保留什么吗?我对你们是没有保留的。我没有不帮助你们的行为。这就是我孔丘的为人。"

【英语译文】

Confucius said, "Do you think I've reserved anything? I have nothing reserved from you. I haven't intended not to help you. This is what I, Kong Qiu have done."

【注释】(1)二三子:诸君,几个人。以:认为。为隐:在隐瞒,进行隐瞒。(2)无瘾乎尔:对你们没有隐瞒。乎:介词,同"于"。(3)与:与,读 yǔ,帮助、援助。《战国策·秦策一》:"楚攻魏,张仪谓秦王曰:'不如与魏以劲之。'"(4)丘:孔子,名丘。

【原文】25 子以四教[1]:文,行,忠,信[2]。

【白话译文】

孔子用四门基本教育内容教育学生:文教用历代文章典籍进行,行教用社会生活实践进行,忠教用从事尽忠的品德进行,信教用交往守信的人格进行。

【英语译文】

Confucius educated his disciples through four basic elements: ancient classics cultivating humanities, social practice improving conducts, loyal virtue cultivating loyalty, creditable personality cultivating creditability.

【注释】(1)四教:四门基本教育内容,即文教、行(xíng)教、忠教、信教。(2)文行忠信:文教,主要是传授诗、书、礼、乐的各种专门知识。行教,主要是传修身的知识和提出躬行的要求。忠教,指培养忠的品德。信教,指培养守信的品德。

【原文】26 子曰:"圣人,吾不得而见之矣[1];得见君子者[2],斯可矣。"子曰:"善人,吾不得而见之矣[3];得见有恒者[4],斯可矣。亡而为有[5],虚而为盈,约而为泰[6],难乎有恒矣[7]。"

【白话译文】

孔子说:"圣人,我不能看见了;能看见君子,就可以了。"他又说:"善人,我不能看见了;能看见有一定操守的人,就可以了。本来没有,却假装有;本来空虚,却假装充实;本来穷困,却偏要奢侈。这种人就难于有善心了。”

【英语译文】

Confucius said, “I cannot meet sages but it’s alright that I can meet moral men.” Then he said, “I cannot meet well-doers but it’s alright that I can meet someone with integrity. People cannot become benevolent, who intend to have, to be full, and to be extravagant but actually have-not, to be empty, and to be poor.”

【注释】(1)圣人:指品德最高尚、智慧最高超的人。孔子心目中的圣人是尧、舜、禹、周文王、周武王、周公。不得而见之:不得,是不能的意思。而,是语气助词,起补凑音节的作用,没有实在意义。见之:之,代词,指代圣人。见之,见到圣人。(2)君子者:者,语气助词。用在名词后,表示停顿,没有实在意义。(3)善人:有道德的人,善良的人。(4)有恒者:常存善心的人,有一定操守的人。(者,用于形容词、动词、动词词组、数词或主谓词组后,构成“者”字结构,用以指代人、事、物。这里“有恒”是动词词组,后边加“者”就成了指代人的“者”字结构)。(5)亡(wú):无,没有。而为:却假装。(6)约:贫困。泰:奢侈。(7)难乎:难于。乎,介词,同“于”,引介补语。

【原文】27 子钓而不纲[1],弋不射宿[2]。

【白话译文】

孔子钓鱼,却不用网捕鱼;用带丝绳的箭射鸟,却不射归巢栖息的鸟。

【英语译文】

Confucius did fishing but never used fishing-net; he shot birds by arrows but never trapped nest-returning ones.

【注释】(1)钓:钓鱼。而不:却不。纲(gāng):提网的总绳。不纲,犹言不撒网或不用网拦河捕鱼。(2)弋(yì):用带丝绳的箭射。撂这里省略了宾语“鸟”。宿:宿后略了中心词“鸟”。宿鸟,归巢栖息的鸟。

【原文】28 子曰:“盖有不知而作之者[1],我无是也[2]。多闻择其善者而从之[3];多见而识之[4];知之次也[5]。”

【白话译文】

孔子说:"还真有一种自己又不懂就随意造作的人,我没有这样干。多多地听,选择其中好的接受过来;多多地看,全记在心里。这样的认知,比生而知之差一等。"

【英语译文】

Confucius said, "There are such kind of people who didn't understand anything but pretended to do so. I have never done like this. Listen to others more and accept those fine ones; observe others more and keep those useful things in mind. Such kind of cognition is only inferior to in-born cognition."

【注释】(1)盖:语气助词。用在句首或段落之首甚至整篇之首,作为提起话头的发语词。现代汉语没见这种用法,一般去掉不译。不知:无知,不懂。(2)无是:没有这样。(3)多闻:多多地听。(4)多见:多多地看。识之:全记在心里。(5)知:知识,智能。次:差一等,次一等。意谓"不是头等"。

【原文】29 互乡难与言[1],童子见[2],门人惑[3]。子曰:"与其进也[4],不与其退也,唯何甚[5]? 人洁己以进[6],与其洁也[7],不保其往也[8]。"

【白话译文】

互乡这里的人难于同他们交谈。一个少年进见了孔子,弟子们疑惑。孔子说:"赞成他来的行为,不是赞成他回去后的行为。何必十分要求呢? 人家端正干净地来,赞成他的端正干净,不记他过去的形象。"

【英语译文】

It's hard to talk with people living in the place of Hu Xiang. One day a young man came to meet Confucius. His disciples were confused. Confucius explained, "I agreed to his coming but it doesn't mean that I agreed to his previous actions. It's unnecessary to demand him too much. Since he came here with correct attitude, I agreed to his attitude and forget his previous actions."

【注释】(1)互乡:地名,不详其所在。难与言:难与人交谈。(2)童子:儿童,未成年的男子。见:谒见,晋见。指进见地位或辈分高的人。(3)门人:弟子。(4)与:赞成。(5)唯:语首助词。何甚:何必责备,何必十分要求。(6)洁己:使自己行为端正干净。(7)与:赞成。(8)不保:不保持,不保留。其往:他的过去。

【原文】30 子曰:"仁远乎哉[1]?我欲仁[2],斯仁至矣[3]。"

【白话译文】

孔子说:"仁德离我们很远吗?我想要仁德,这仁德就来啦。"

【英语译文】

Confucius said, "Does humanity stay far from us? As soon as I need it, it stays with me."

【注释】(1)乎哉:语气助词。乎,在句中舒缓语气,一般不译。哉,用在是非问句后,译作"吗""么"。(2)欲:想要,希望。(3)斯:指示代词,此。矣:语气助词用在陈述句末表行为的已然、将然或必然,译为"了""啦"。

【原文】31 陈司败问:"昭公知礼乎?"[1],孔子曰:"知礼。"孔子退[2],揖巫马期而进之[3],曰:"吾闻君子不党[4],君子亦党乎?君取于吴[5],为同姓[6],谓之吴孟子[7]。君而知礼孰不知礼[8]?"巫马期以告[9]。子曰:"丘也幸,苟有过,人必知之[10]。"

【白话译文】

陈司败问:"昭公懂不懂礼?"孔子说:"懂礼。"孔子离去后,陈司败向巫马期拱手行礼并请巫走近自己,说道:"我听说君子无所袒护,君子也袒护人吗?昭公从吴国娶了位夫人,吴和鲁是同性国家,不便叫她吴姬,便改叫吴孟子。昭公如果懂礼,谁不懂呢?"巫马期把这话转告给孔子。孔子说:"我啊,真幸运,假若有过错,人们必定知道。"

【英语译文】

Minister of justice in Chen State asked, "Does Duke Zhao know rituals?" Confucius answered, "He does." After Confucius left, he saluted to Wuma Qi with the hands folded, asking the latter to approach him, and he said, "I've heard that moral men don't take sides with anyone, Do they do so? Duke Zhao married a woman from

Wu State which surnamed the same as Lu state. It's inappropriate to call her Lady Wu but Wu Meng zi. If Duke Zhao has known rituals, whoever doesn't do so?" Wuma Qi retold these to Confucius, who responded, "Oh, I' m lucky that everybody knows if I have made any mistake."

【注释】(1)陈司败:朱熹《四书集注》:"陈,国名。司败,官名,即司寇也。"一说司败是人名。昭公:鲁昭公,名裯,襄公之庶子,继襄公而为君。(2)退:离去。(3)揖巫马期而进之:揖读 yī,拱手行礼。巫马期:孔子的学生,姓巫马,名施,字子期,又称巫马旗,小于孔子三十岁。而:进层连词,指"而且""并且"。进之,引进他(巫马期)。全句意谓:陈司败向巫马期拱手行礼并请巫走近自己。(4)党:相助匿非,袒护。(5)君取于吴:君,指鲁昭公。取,同"娶"。吴,当时的国名,拥有之地,相当于今天的淮水、泗水以南及浙江的嘉兴、湖州等地。哀公时为越王勾践所灭。(6)为同姓:鲁为周公之后姬姓;吴为太伯之后也是姬姓。(7)吴孟子:春秋时代,国君夫人的称号一般是所生长之国名加她的本姓。鲁娶于吴,这位夫人便应该称吴姬。但"同姓不婚"是周朝的礼法,鲁君夫人的称号若把"姬"字标明出来,便是很显明表示出鲁君违背了"同姓不婚"的礼制,因之改称为"吴孟子"。"孟子"可能是这位夫人的字。(8)而:如果、假如。(9)以告:"以此(陈司败所说的话)转告"的略语。(10)丘也幸:丘,孔子自称其名。可译作我或不译。也:语气助词。用在主语和谓语间,表提顿或停顿。可译作"啊""呀"或去掉不译。幸:幸运。苟:假如、如果、只要。

【原文】32 子与人歌而善[1],必使反之[2],而后和之[3]。

【白话译文】

孔子同别人一道唱歌,如果唱得好,一定跟随别人再唱一遍,然后相互应和而歌。

【英语译文】

When Confucius sang songs with others, he would repeated it once more with others and sang correspondently to others' singing if they sang well.

【注释】(1)歌而善:唱歌如果唱得好。而,指如果。(2)必使:必随从。《尔雅·释诂》:"使,从也。"反之:反,复。之,指代"歌"。反之,即再唱一遍。(3)而后:然后。和之:相互应和而歌唱。

【原文】33 子曰:“文莫吾犹人也[1]。躬行君子[2],则吾未之有得[3]。”

【白话译文】

孔子说:“努力向上、尽力而为,我和别人差不多。实行君子之道,那我所达到的程度还很不够。”

【英语译文】

Confucius said, “I have no difference with others in trying to be cheerful and to do things hardest. Whereas I haven’t done well in carrying out the way of being a moral man.”

【注释】(1)文莫:文,读 mín,通“忞”。指自强,勉力。《广雅·释诂》:“文,勉也。”莫,读 mò。《广雅·释诂》:“莫,强也。”朱熹《四书集注》:“莫,疑辞。”文莫,宜依前贤作为合成词解释,不宜读作两个单音词:意谓黾勉、努力、尽力而为。吾犹人也:我和别人差不多。(2)躬行:亲自实行。(3)则:转折连词。可译作“却”“那”。未之有得:未之,指犹未至,未达到。有得,指有所得,程度深,时间长。

【原文】34 子曰:“若圣与仁[1],则吾岂敢[2]?抑为之不厌[3],诲人不倦[4],则可谓云尔已矣[5]。”公西华曰[6]:“正唯弟子不能学也[7]。”

【白话译文】

孔子说:“说到圣和仁,那我怎么敢当?不过是学习仁圣之道不厌弃,教导别人不倦怠。就可说如此而已罢了。”公西华说:“这正是我们学不到的。”

【英语译文】

Confucius said, “As for a sage and humanistic man, how could I bear the title? It’s just that I never hate learning sage’s way and never feel tired of instructing others. It is just like this.” Gongxi Hua responded, “That’s just what we cannot reach.”

【注释】(1)若:连词,用在句首以引起下文,相当于“至于”“说到”。孟子公孙丑上提到子贡对这事的看法说:“学不厌,智也,教不倦,仁也,仁且智,夫子既圣矣。”可见当时学生就已把孔子看成圣人。(2)则:转折连词,却。岂敢:怎么敢。(3)抑:转折连词,指不过,只是。为之:学习仁圣之道。不厌:不厌弃。(4)诲人:教导别人。不倦:不倦怠。(5)则:承接连词,就。云尔:亦作“云耳”。用于句尾,表示“如此而已”。已矣:叹词,罢了。(6)公西华:见 6.4 注 1。(7)正唯:正是。唯,通“维”。

【原文】35 子疾病[1],子路请祷[2]。子曰:“有诸[3]?”子路对曰:“有之[4];诔曰:‘祷尔于上下神祇[5]。’”子曰:“丘之祷久矣。”

【白话译文】

孔子病得很重,子路请求向鬼神祷告。孔子说:“有这个道理吗?”子路回答说:“有啊,诔文上说:‘替你向天神地祇祈祷。’”孔子说:“我早就祈祷过了。”

【英语译文】

Confucius became seriously ill and Zi Lu offered to pray to ghosts. Confucius asked, “Is it reasonable?” Zi Lu responded, “It is. The eulogy reads like this ‘To pray to ghosts for you.’” Confucius said, “I have prayed long ago.”

【注释】(1)疾病:重病。(2)请祷:请求向鬼神祷告。邢昺疏:“孔子疾病,子路告请祷求鬼神,冀其疾愈也。”(3)有诸:朱熹《四书集注》:“有诸,问有此理否。”(4)有之:有此理。(5)诔(lèi):本应作“讄”,施于生者以求福。诔,施于死者以作谥,哀死而述其行之词也。上下:谓天地。天曰神地曰祇。祷:朱熹《四书集注》:“祷者悔过迁善,以祈神之佑也。无其理则不必祷,既曰有之,则圣人未尝有过,无善可迁,其素行固已合乎神明,故曰:‘丘之祷久矣。’”

【原文】36 子曰:“奢则不孙[1],俭则固[2]。与其不孙也,宁固[3]。”

【白话译文】

孔子说:“奢侈就显得不谦恭,俭约就显得寒碜,与其不谦恭,宁可寒碜。”

【英语译文】

Confucius said, “Extravagance means no humility and shrift means ugly. I’d rather to be ugly than not to be humble.”

【注释】(1)孙(xùn):同“逊”,谦恭。(2)固:固陋。(3)与其……宁:选择连词。与其,表不选。宁,表选取。

【原文】37 子曰:“君子坦荡荡[1],小人长戚戚[2]。”

【白话译文】
孔子说:“君子心胸开朗纯洁,小人经常忧惧伤怀。”

【英语译文】
Confucius said, “Moral men are broad-minded whereas mean men are always melancholy.”

【注释】(1)坦荡荡:平坦宽广,比喻胸襟开朗,心地纯洁。(2)长戚戚:经常忧惧伤怀。

【原文】38 子温而厉[1],威而不猛[2],恭而安[3]。

【白话译文】
孔子温和而严厉,有威仪而不猛烈,庄严而安详。

【英语译文】
Confucius was mild but severe, dignified but peaceful, sacred but calm.

【注释】(1)厉:严厉。(2)威:有威仪。不猛:不猛烈。(3)恭:庄严。

泰伯篇第八(共二十一章)

本篇主要涉及对尧、舜、禹等古代先王的评价、孔子教学方法和教育思想、孔子道德思想的具体内容以及曾子的赏析。

【原文】1 子曰:“泰伯[1],其可谓至德也已矣[2]!三以天下让[3],民无得而称焉[4]。"

【白话译文】

孔子说:"泰伯,那可以说品德最崇高了啊！再三把君位推让给小弟季历。老百姓找不到恰当的话来称赞他。"

【英语译文】

Confucius said, "Tai Bo, oh, He was the perfectly moral man. He yielded his position of monarchy to his younger brother, Ji Li. Common people couldn't find appropriate words to praise him."

【注释】(1)泰伯: 亦作"太伯"。周人祖先古公亶父的长子。古公有三个儿子太伯、仲雍、季历。传说,古公预见到季历的儿子姬昌(周文王)的圣德,想打破惯例不把君位传给长子太伯,而传给幼子季历从而传给姬昌。太伯为了实现父亲的愿望,便同仲雍出走至南边荒远之地,自号勾吴,和仲雍共同开创了吴国。(2)至德:至高的道德,最美好的道德。(3)三以天下让:三,指概言再三、多次。天下,古时多指中国范围内的全部土地,也指全国。古公至姬昌时段,领域很小,谈不上什么天下。这"天下"是引申义。指君位、君权。(4)无得:无从不能,

【原文】2 子曰:"恭而无礼则劳[1],慎而无礼则葸[2],勇而无礼则乱[3],直而无礼则绞[4]。君子笃于亲[5],则民兴于仁[6];故旧不遗[7],则民不偷[8]。

【白话译文】

孔子说:"毕恭毕敬,没有礼数,就会劳倦;只知小心,没有礼数,就会怯懦;敢作敢为,没有礼数,就会生乱;行为率直,没有礼数,就会急躁。在上位的人,对亲人感情深厚,老百姓就会走向仁德;在上位的人,不忘记老友、老同事,人间就会消解冷漠。"

【英语译文】

Confucius said, "People who are just modest but don't know etiquette will become tired; people who are just cautious but don't know etiquette will become coward; people who are just ambitious but don't know etiquette will cause chaos. People who are upright but don't know etiquette will become impatient. If people in leading places have affection, common people will become moral and benevolent; if people in leading places don't forget old friends, the society will become warm."

【注释】(1)礼:本章四个"礼"字,意义全同。指礼节,礼数。劳:烦劳,劳倦。(2)葸(xǐ):畏惧,胆怯。(3)乱:妄动,胡搞。(4)绞(jiǎo):急切,急躁。(5)君子:指在上位的人。笃于亲:对亲人感情深厚。(6)兴于仁:兴起仁德,走向仁德。(7)故旧:旧交,旧友。遗:忘记、遗弃。(8)偷:指人与人感情淡漠,社会风气浮薄。

【原文】3 有疾[1],召门弟子曰[2]:"启予足[3]!启予手!诗云:'战战兢兢,如临深渊,如履薄冰。[4]'而今而后[5],吾知免夫[6]!小子[7]!"

【白话译文】

曾子得了重病,把在身边的学生召集拢来,说道:"看看我的脚!看看我的手!《诗经》上说:'战兢兢肉麻心惊,好像走到深渊边,好像走上薄冰窟。'从今以后,我知道,只要像履薄临深一样戒惧,是可以免于祸害刑戮的了!年轻人!"

【英语译文】

Being gravlly ill, Zeng Zi summoned his disciples and said, "Look at my feet! Look at my hands! *The Book of Songs* reads, 'It seems we've reached cliff edge, it seems we've reached ice hole.' From today on, I know that we can avoid disasters, killing and legal punishment only if we do things just like reaching cliff edge and reaching ice hole! Young men!"

【注释】(1)有疾:病了。(2)门弟子:谓及门的弟子(在身边就学的学生)。亦省称"门弟"。(3)启:视,看。(4)诗云:三句诗,见《诗经·小雅·小旻》。诗意比喻身处险境,戒惧之至。履(lǚ),步行。(5)而今而后:从今以后。(6)吾知免夫:我知道只要像履薄临深一样戒惧是可以免于祸害刑戮的了。(7)小子:学生;晚辈。

【原文】4 曾子有疾,孟敬子问之[1]。曾子言曰[2]:"鸟之将死,其鸣也哀;人之将死,其言也善。君子所贵乎道者三[3]:动容貌,斯远暴慢矣[4];正颜色,斯近信矣[5];出辞气,斯远鄙倍矣[6]。笾豆之事[7],则有司存[8]。"

【白话译文】

曾子得了重病,孟敬子来探问病情。曾子主动说道:“鸟要死了,叫声是悲哀的;人要死了,说出的话是善意的。在上位的人,重视待人接物之法的三个要点是:举止仪容有感情,就可以避免别人的粗暴和怠慢;端正脸色,不带邪气,就容易让人相信;说话要有恰当的语气,这样就可以避免鄙陋粗野和错误。至于礼仪的细节,便是主管人员的事。”

【英语译文】

Prime Minister of Lu State, Zhongsun Jie once came to visit Zeng Zi due to the latter being gravly ill. Zeng Zi said voluntarily, “The cry of birds is sad when they're dying; the words of people are kind when they're dying. The three major points for people in leading places to get along well with others should be: if their manners show affection then they can avoid others' prudence and negligence; if their appearance is honest then they can easily make others believe them; if they utter in appropriate tone, they can avoid meanness, vulgarity and faults. As for the details of rituals and etiquette, they are up to the supervisor.”

【注释】(1)孟敬子:鲁国大夫仲孙捷。敬,是他的谥号。问之:探问病情。(2)言:话语,言辞。《书·盘庚上》:“迟任有言曰。”迟任说过。言,说过的话。《易·需》:“小有言。”招致小的口舌是非。言,闲言。朱熹《四书集注》:“言,自言也,”意谓不是回答孟敬子提问的话,而是自己阐明见解的话。所以,“言曰”,可译作“主动说道”。(3)君子:指在上位的人。所贵乎道者三:重视待人接物之法的三个要点。道,指在上位的人的待人接物之法。(4)动容貌:举止仪容有感情。斯:承接连词,指就,远:远离。暴慢:粗暴和怠慢。(5)正颜色:端正脸色,不带邪气。近信:亲近信任。(6)出辞气:说话要有恰当的语气。出辞:吐辞,说话。气:语气。鄙倍:鄙,是指粗野鄙陋。倍,同“背”,指不合理,错误。(7)笾豆之事:代表礼仪中的具体细节。笾,读 biān,古代的一种竹器。高脚,圆口。用以盛果实等食品。豆也是古代的一种像笾一样的器皿,用木料做成,有盖,用以盛有汁的食物。笾和豆都是古代用于宴会和祭祀的重要礼器。(8)则:承接连词,便。有司:主管其事的小吏。存:掌管,管理。

【原文】5 曾子曰:“以能问于不能,以多问于寡;有若无,实若虚,犯而不校[1]:昔者吾友[2],尝从事于斯矣[3]。”

【白话译文】

曾子说:“有能力却向无能力的人请教,知识丰富却向知识缺少的人请教;有学问像没学问一样,满腹知识像空无所有一样;纵被冒犯也不计较,从前我的一位朋友便曾经这样做了。”

【英语译文】

Zeng Zi said, “A capable man consults other incapable men and an informed man consults other uninformed men; a learned man is just like one without knowledge; a man never minds it even he is insulted. One of my friends long ago just did so.”

【注释】(1)犯:触犯,冒犯。校(jiào):计较。(2)昔者:从前。吾友:指颜回。(3)尝(cháng):曾经。从事:参与做(某种事情),致力于(某种事情)。斯:近指代词,指代上文“以能问于不能……犯而不校”。

【原文】6 曾子曰:“可以托六尺之孤[1],可以寄百里之命[2],临大节而不可夺也[3]:君子人与[4]?君子人也。”

【白话译文】

曾子说:“可以托付未成年的孤儿,可以托付国家的使命,面对生死存亡的大事毫不动摇:这种人是君子吗?是君子呢。”

【英语译文】

Zeng Zi said, “Very little orphan can be entrusted to him and state cause can also be entrusted to him. While facing life-death serious affairs, he never changes his determination. Can such kind of people be called moral men? Of course, he can.”

【注释】(1)六尺:有人计算过,古代六尺约合今日一百三十八厘米,相当于市尺的四尺一寸四分。身长六尺的人还是小孩,一般指十五岁以下的小孩。孤:孤儿。(2)寄:与上文“托”为互文,都是寄托的意思,即托付,委托。百里之命:国君的政令。百里,指诸侯国。(3)临大节:面对关系生死存亡的大事。夺:用强力使之动摇、改变。亦谓由于强力而动摇、改变。(4)君子人:即君子。与(yú):语气词,表疑问。

【原文】7 曾子曰:"士不可以不弘毅[1],任重而道远[2]。仁以为己任[3],不亦重乎?死而后已,不亦远乎?"

【白话译文】

曾子说:"有知识的人,不可以不宽宏坚强而有毅力,因为负担沉重,路途遥远。以实现仁德于天下为自己的责任,不也沉重吗?到死才止,不也遥远吗?"

【英语译文】

Zeng Zi said, "An informed man cannot be not broad-minded, not strong-will, and not perseverant. He has a great mission and a long way to go. He regards spreading morality and benevolence as his own obligation. Isn't it great? He'll not stop until death. Isn't it a long way to go?"

【注释】(1)弘毅:宽宏坚毅。谓抱负远大,意志坚强。(2)任重而道远:谓负担沉重,路途遥远。比喻担负的责任既重大又要经过长久的努力才能完成。(3)仁以为己任:以行仁德为自己的责任。

【原文】8 子曰:"兴于诗[1],立于礼[2],成于乐[3]。"

【白话译文】

孔子说:"学诗而振奋,学礼而立足,学乐而成人。"

【英语译文】

Confucius said, "People can become cheerful through learning poetry, and they can establish themselves in society through learning etiquette, and they can complete learning by music."

【注释】(1)兴于诗:诗可以使人振奋。(2)立于礼:礼可以使人立足于社会。(3)成于乐:乐可以使人所学得以完成。

【原文】9 子曰:"民可,使由之[1],不可,使知之[2]。"

【白话译文】

孔子说："百姓善良懂礼义，要让他们自由生息；那些不善良、不懂礼义的，要让他们知道如何向善、如何讲礼义。"

【英语译文】

Confucius said, "If common people are kindhearted and know about etiquette, let them live free; for those who aren't kindhearted and don't know about etiquette, let them know how to be kind and how to know about etiquette."

【注释】(1)民：百姓。可：对、善，用作表语。《书·尧典》："嚚讼可乎？……试可乃已。"意谓奸诈而好争讼好吗？……试用好便任用。使：让。由：树木生枝条叫由。引申为让百姓如树木生枝一样自由生长。之：语气助词。下同。(2)不可：承前省略了主语"民"字。知：了解，认识。

【原文】10 子曰："好勇疾贫[1]，乱也。人而不仁[2]，疾之已甚[3]，乱也。"

【白话译文】

孔子说："仗恃勇猛又厌恶贫困，是一种祸乱。对不仁的人恨得过分了，也是一种祸乱。"

【英语译文】

Confucius said, "It's catastrophy to demonstrate bravery and hate poverty. It is also catastrophy to extremely hate those unkind men."

【注释】(1)好勇：好，读 hào。好勇，好逞勇武。疾贫：厌恶贫困。(2)人而不仁：人却没有仁性，即不仁的人。(3)疾之已甚：痛恨不仁的人过分了。之，代词，代指"人而不仁"。

【原文】11 子曰："如有周公之才之美[1]，使骄且吝[2]，其余不足观也已[3]。"

【白话译文】

孔子说："如果具有周公那样的才能之美，假使又骄傲又吝啬，别的方面就不值一看了。"

【英语译文】

Confucius said, "If someone is as perfectly capable as Duke Zhou, and even if he's proud and stingy, it's unnecessary to observe other aspects of him."

【注释】(1)如:假设连词,假如,如果。周公之才之美:两个"之"都是结构助词。用在定语和中心词之间,相当于"的"。第一层,"周公"是定语,"才"是中心词。第二层,"周公之才"是定语,"美"是中心词。(2)使:假设连词,指假使,假如,如果。吝(lìn):吝啬、爱惜、舍不得。(3)其余:其他方面。不足观:不值得看。也已:语气助词,表肯定、表感叹。

【原文】12 子曰:"三年学[1],不至于穀[2],不易得也[3]。"

【白话译文】

孔子说:"学习了三年,没有想到做官,可贵呀。"

【英语译文】

Confucius said, "It's precious virtue for people not to think of becoming an official after studying for three years."

【注释】(1)三年学:学习了三年。(2)至:通"志"。想念,念及。穀:读 gǔ,古代以谷米为俸禄(相当于今日的工资),所以谷有禄的意义。禄,有做官的含义。(3)不易得:难得。引申为可贵。

【原文】13 子曰:"笃信好学[1],守死善道[2],危邦不入[3],乱邦不居[4]。天下有道则见[5],无道则隐[6]。邦有道[7],贫且贱焉[8],耻也;邦无道,富且贵焉[9],耻也。"

【白话译文】

孔子说:"坚信自己的道德和事业而勤奋学习,坚持正道至死而不改变。不安宁、不稳定的国家,不妄入。动乱的国家可以离开。天下太平就参与政事,不太平就隐退。国家政治清明,自己又贫又贱,是耻辱;国家政治混乱,自己又富又贵,也是耻辱。"

【英语译文】

Confucius said, "A moral man should firmly believe in his morality and cause so as to learn hard; and he should stick to right way and never change until death. He doesn't enter an unstable state aimlessly and he can leave a chaotic state. He participates administrative affairs while politics carries on smoothly, otherwise he'll retreat. It's shameful to be poor and humble when politics carries on purely and it's also shameful to be wealthy and noble when politics carries on chaotically."

【注释】(1)笃信好学:谓对道德和事业抱有坚定的信心并勤奋学习。(2)守死善道:谓坚持正道,至死而不改变。善道,即正道。(3)危邦:不安宁的或将倾覆的国家。(4)乱邦:动乱的国家。不居:犹言离去。(5)天下有道:国家或世界政治清明。见:读 xiàn,同"现"。与"隐"相对。指参与政事。(6)无道:承前省略了"天下"二字。谓国家或世界政治混乱。则隐:就隐退。(7)邦有道:国家政治清明。(8)贫且贱:又贫又贱。(9)富且贵:又富又贵。

【原文】14 子曰:"不在其位[1],不谋其政[2]。"

【白话译文】

孔子说:"不在那个职位上,就不谋虑那个政务。"

【英语译文】

Confucius said, "If you don't hold the post, then you needn't think about it's administrative affairs."

【注释】(1)位:指为官的职位。(2)政:政治事务。

【原文】15 子曰:"师挚之始[1],关雎之乱[2],洋洋乎盈耳哉[3]!"

【白话译文】

孔子说:"从太师挚开始独奏,到结尾合奏关雎的乐章,满耳都是响亮的音乐啊!"

【英语译文】

Confucius said, "What we heard are all cheerful music, from solo by Master musician Zhi at beginning to instrumental ensemble '*Fair Maid*' at the end."

【注释】(1)师挚之始:"始"指乐曲的开端。古代奏乐,当祭祀、宴会登堂时演奏的乐歌叫升歌。也叫升堂歌或登歌。一般由太师演奏。师挚,是鲁国的太师,名挚。师挚之始,谓师挚演奏的升歌。(2)关雎之乱:"始"指乐曲的开端,"乱"指乐曲的结束。由"始"到"乱"叫"一成"。"乱"是合乐,犹如今日的合唱。当合奏之时,奏关雎的乐章,所以有"关雎之乱"的说法。(3)洋洋:形容声音响亮,充满空间。

【原文】16 子曰:"狂而不直[1],侗而不愿[2],悾悾而不信[3],吾不知之矣[4]。"

【白话译文】

孔子说:"狂妄却不直率,幼稚无知却不诚实,样子诚恳却不讲信用,我不了解这些人为什么是这样。"

【英语译文】

Confucius said, "I do not know why those people are ambitious but not upright, outspoken but dishonest, pretentious but irreliable."

【注释】(1)狂:狂妄。而:转折连词,却。下文同。直:直率。(2)侗:读 tóng,幼稚,无知。愿:谨慎;诚实。(3)悾悾:悾,读 kōng。悾悾,诚恳的样子。信:诚信。(4)不知:不了解。

【原文】17 子曰:"学如不及[1],犹恐失之[2]。"

【白话译文】

孔子说:"学习好像抓不着一样,抓着了还怕丢掉了。"

【英语译文】

Confucius said, "To learn is like something unreached. People fear to lose it once it's reached."

【注释】(1)不及:赶不上;够不着。(2)犹恐:还怕。

【原文】18 子曰:“巍巍乎[1],舜禹之有天下也,而不与焉[2]!”

【白话译文】

孔子说:“真是崇高伟大呀!舜和禹拥有天下,他们没有结党营私,天下为公。”

【英语译文】

Confucius said, “It's really great! Yao and Shun owned the world but they didn't gang up for their own selfish interests. They administrated the world for public interest.”

【注释】(1)巍巍乎:崇高伟大呀。(2)禹:夏朝开国之君。传说他受虞舜禅让而即帝位,又是中国主持水利工程最早的功勋人物。而:代词,他(们)。不与:不,是“无”“没有”的意思。与,读 yǔ,是“党与”的意思。不与,即“无党与”,没有同党的人。犹言没结党营私,天下为公。

【原文】19 子曰:“大哉尧之为君也[1]!巍巍乎!唯天[2],唯尧则之[3]。荡荡乎[4],民无能名焉[5]。巍巍乎其有成功也[6],焕乎其有文章[7]!”

【白话译文】

孔子说:“真太伟大呀,尧这样做国君!真是崇高伟大呀!只有天才算大,只有尧能效法天之大。博大宽广啊!人民不能用语言表达诚挚的赞美。他创建的功绩真是特别崇高伟大呀!他的礼乐制度真是特别美好光明。”

【英语译文】

Confucius said, “It really great! It is really noble and great for Yao to be monarch. Only talent can be great and only Yao can follow heaven's greatness. Broad and spacious! No words can express people's honest praise. His achievement is especially noble and great! His systems of etiquette and music are bright and perfect.”

【注释】(1)尧:传说中古帝陶唐氏之号。《周易·系辞下》:“神农氏没,黄帝、尧、舜氏作。”为君:作为国君。巍巍:崇高伟大。(2)唯:只有。为大:算是大。(3)则之:仿效天。(4)荡荡乎:博大宽广啊,(5)名:形容,称说。(6)其有:他有。(7)焕:鲜明,明亮。文章:礼乐制度。

【原文】20 舜有臣五人而天下治[1]。武王曰:“予有乱臣十人[2]。”孔子曰:“才难,不其然乎[3]?唐虞之际,于斯为盛[4]。有妇人焉,九人而已[5]。三分天下有其二[6],以服事殷[7]。周之德,其可谓至德也已矣[8]。”

【白话译文】

舜有五位贤臣就使天下太平。武王曾说:“我有治国的贤臣十人。”孔子说:“人才难得,不是这样吗?唐尧和虞舜之间与周武王当年,人才最兴盛。”然而武王的十位贤臣中,还有一位女性。实有男性贤臣九人罢了。周文王得了天下的三分之二,仍然向商纣称臣,周朝的道德,那可以说是最高的了。”

【英语译文】

Yao made the world peaceful by using five able and virtuous courtiers. King Wu ever said, “ I have ten able and virtuous courtiers who can govern state. ” Confucius said, “They were precious talents, isn’t it? When Yao of Xia Dynasty and Shun of Shang Dynasty as well as King Wu of Zhou Dynasty were in power, talents are most abounded. ” However, among the ten courtiers of King Wu, there was a female. There were nine male courtiers. King Wen of Zhou Dynasty owned two thirds of the world and still surrendered to King Zhou of Shang Dynasty. Therefore the virtue of Zhou Dynasty can be the best. ”

【注释】(1)臣:指贤臣。天下治:天下太平。(2)乱臣:指善于治国的臣子。(3)才难:人才难得,难得的人才。其然:如此。(4)唐虞:唐尧和虞舜。际:际,指先后交接的时期。于斯:斯,指示代词,此。这里指代人才。盛:盛多。(5)有妇人:有位妇女。九人:九位男人。(6)三分天下有其二:《逸周书·程典篇》:“文王合九州岛之侯,奉勤于商。”相传当时分九州岛,文王得六州,占有三分之二。(7)服事殷:服事,五服之内所封诸侯定期朝贡,各依服数以事天子。亦泛谓尽臣道。服事殷,即向殷尽臣道。换句话说,向殷称臣。(附:所谓五服指古代王畿外围,以五百里为一区划,由近及远,分为侯服、甸服、绥服、要服、荒服,合称五服。服,服事天子之意。)(8)至德:最高的道德,盛德。已矣:语气词。用于句末与"矣"同义。

【原文】21 子曰:"禹,吾无间然矣[1]。而致孝乎鬼神[2],恶衣服而致美乎黻冕[3],卑宫室而尽力乎沟洫[4]。禹,吾无间然矣。"

【白话译文】孔子说:"禹,我对他是没有批评的。他自己吃粗劣的饮食,却把祭祀品办得很丰盛;他自己的穿着很粗劣,却把祭祀的礼服做得很华美,他的宫室低矮简陋,却集中力量修沟渠、兴水利。禹,我对他是没有批评的。"

【英语译文】

Confucius said, "Shun, I'll not criticize him. He himself ate coarse food but prepared plenty of sacrificial things; he himself wore raw clothes but made brilliant sacrificial gowns; his dwelling was shabby but he focused on constructing hydraulic engineering. Shun, I'll not criticize him."

【注释】(1)无间然矣:一解,读作"无间"然矣。间,朱熹《四书集注》:"间,罅隙也,谓指其罅隙而非议之也。"无间,没有非议。然,助词,在句中舒缓语气。矣,用在陈述句末表论断、决断语气。可译为"的"或去掉不译。又解,读作无"间然"矣。间然,谓非议,异议。然,用作词尾。(2)菲:读 fěi,微薄,使之微薄。菲饮食:粗劣的饮食。致孝:竭力办好祭祀。乎:同"于"。(3)恶衣服:粗劣的穿着。黻冕:读 fúmiǎn,古时祭服。朱熹《四书集注》:"黻,蔽膝也,以韦(去毛熟制的兽皮)为之;冕,冠也;皆祭服也。"(4)卑宫室:宫室低矮简陋。沟洫:读 gōuxù,田间水道。这里指农田水利工程。

子罕篇第九(共三十一章)

朱熹集注把第六、第七两章合并为一章,所以作三十。本篇为《公冶长》《雍也》两篇内容的引申,涉及孔子的思想、学问教育的观点和一般历史思想观念。

【原文】1 子罕言利[1],与命与仁[2]。

【白话译文】

孔子很少谈论“利”;他承认“命”,赞扬“仁”。

【英语译文】

Confucius seldom mentioned ‘material benefit’; but he admitted ‘fate’ and praised “humanity”.

【注释】(1)罕言:很少谈论。利:儒家的理论范畴指物质利益。孔子并不绝对排斥利,曾说:“因民之所利而利之,斯不亦惠而不费乎?”他提出利应符合义,主张见利思义,反对见利忘义。(2)与:承认;赞扬。命:指不以人的意志为转移的客观必然性。孔子主张“知命”,“不知命,无以为君子也。”仁:孔子思想体系的理论核心。尊重他人的价值,待人如待己。

【原文】2 达巷党人曰[1]:“大哉孔子! 博学而无所成名[2]。”子闻之,谓门第子曰:“吾何执[3]? 执御[4]乎? 执射乎[5]? 吾执御矣。”

【白话译文】达巷党那里有人说:“真伟大呀,那位孔先生! 知识渊博,技艺全面,却没有树立专长名声。”孔子得知这话后,对身边的学生说:“我干什么呢? 当车夫吗? 当射手吗? 我当车夫吧。”

【英语译文】

Country people in the place of Daxiang said, “Confucius is really great! He’s well informed and versatile but hasn’t established any special reputation.” Hearing this, Confucius said to his disciples nearby, “What will I do? To be a horse-cart driver? To be a archer? I’ll be a horse-cart driver.”

【注释】(1)达巷党人:达巷地方的乡里党人。一说指七岁而为孔子师的项橐。(2)博学:广泛学习,多方面学习;谓知识渊博,技艺全面;亦谓杂而不专。根据文意应当排除“杂而不专”的意思。无所成名:没有树立名声。(3)执:操持;从事。(4)执御:从事驾驭;当车夫。(5)执射:从事射击;当射手。

【原文】3 子曰:“麻冕[1],礼也;今也纯[2],俭[3],吾从众[4]。拜下[5],礼也;今拜乎上[6],泰也[7]。虽违众,吾从下[8]。”

【白话译文】

孔子说:“礼帽用麻布做,是传统礼制;现在用丝做,很省工,我遵从众人的办法。臣见君,先在堂下磕头,再升堂磕头,是传统礼制;现在都免了堂下磕头,只升堂后磕头,这是倨傲的表现。虽然违反众人,我坚持先在堂下磕头,再升堂磕头。”

【英语译文】

Confucius said, “It’s traditional ritual to make hemp hat; now I observe common method of making silk hat. It’s traditional ritual for courtiers to kowtow first below and then in the hall, while paying a formal visit to their monarch. It’s conceited now just to kowtow below the hall. I insist on kowtowing first below and then in the hall, although it violates common people’s doings.”

【注释】(1)麻冕:亦作“麻绕”。麻布帽。古时一种礼服。(2)今也:今天,现在。也,语气词。在这里表停顿。纯:指纯黑的丝。(3)俭:麻冕,用麻布做,依照规定要用二千四百缕经线的麻布,麻质较粗,必须织得非常细密,这很费工。若用丝,丝质细,容易织成。因而省俭些。(4)从众:遵从众人的做法。(5)拜下:指臣子对的行礼,先在堂下磕头然后升堂再磕头。(6)今拜乎上:犹言当今堂下不磕头,只在堂上磕头。(7)泰:骄纵。(8)从下:遵从“拜下”的礼。

【原文】4 子绝四[1]:毋意,毋必,毋固,毋我[2]。

【白话译文】

孔子不做四件事:没有凭空揣测,没有绝对肯定,没有拘泥固执,没有自以为是。

【英语译文】

Confucius doesn’t do four things, i. e. subjective speculation, absolute affirmation, stubborn perseverance, and self conceitedness.

【注释】(1)绝:杜绝,摒弃。(2)毋:同“无”,没有。意、必、固、我:分别指的是私意、期必、执滞、私己。

【原文】5 子畏于匡[1],曰:“文王既没[2],文不在兹乎[3]? 天之将丧斯文也[4],后死者不得与于斯文也[5];天之未丧斯文也[6],匡人其如予何[7]?”

【白话译文】

孔子在匡地被围困,他说:“周文王死了后,一切文化遗产不是都在我这里吗? 老天将要消灭这个文化嘛,我这个后死的人就不会在这个文化中活动了。老天不消火这个文化嘛,匡人他们把我怎么样?”

【英语译文】

Confucius was besieged in the place of Kuang, and he said, “Aren't all cultural heritage carried on by me after King Wen's death? If the Heaven extinguishes this culture, then what I, the follower of King Wen, will not act in it. If the Heaven doesn't intend to extinguish this culture, then what could people in the place of Kuang do with me?”

【注释】(1)畏于匡:匡,地名。在今河南省长垣县西南。畏,受到威胁。孔子离开卫国准备到陈国去,经过匡。匡人曾经遭受过鲁国阳货的掠夺和残杀,而孔子的相貌同阳货相像,便以为孔子就是阳货,于是拘禁了孔子。(2)文王:周文王,孔子心目中的尧、舜以来的道统传承人。文:文化遗产如礼乐制度等。兹:此。朱熹《四书集注》:“道之显者谓之文,盖礼乐制度之谓。不曰道而曰文亦谦辞也。(3)兹,此也,孔子自谓。”(4)之:结构助词。用在主语和谓语之间取消句子的独立性。丧:消灭。斯文:这些文化遗产。(5)后死者:孔子自谓。与:读 yù,干预,同“干预”“干豫”。谓过问或参与其事。于:介词,在……之中。斯文:这个文化遗产。(6)未:不。(7)如予何:奈我何,把我怎么样。

【原文】6 太宰问于子贡曰[1]:夫子圣者与[2]? 何其多能也[3]? 子贡曰:“固天纵之将圣,又多能也[4]。”子闻之[5],曰:“太宰知我乎[6]! 吾少也贱[7],故多能鄙事[8]。君子多乎哉[9]? 不多也。”

【白话译文】

太宰向子贡问道:“孔老先生是位圣人吗? 怎么这样多才多艺呢?”子贡说:“这本是上天要他成为圣人且又多技艺的。”孔子知道了这件事,说:“太宰知道我啊! 我年轻时,没钱财、没地位,学到了不少鄙人干的技艺。君子会有这么多技艺吗？不会的。”

【英语译文】

Tai Zai (the general assistant to monarch) asked Zi Gong, “Is Confucius a sage? How could he be so versatile?” Zi Gong answered, “It is the Heaven who orders him to be a sage and versatile.” After knowing this, Confucius said, “Tai Zai knows me well! When I was young, I had Neither position nor wealth but I learned many crafts of inferiors. Can a moral man own so many crafts? No, he can't.”

【注释】(1)太宰：相传殷置太宰。周称总宰，为天官之长，掌建邦之六典，以佐王治邦国。春秋列国亦多置太宰之官，职权不尽相同。秦、汉、魏皆不置。晋以避司马师讳，置太宰以代太师。北周文帝依周礼建六官，置天官大冢宰卿一人。隋、唐均无此官，宋崇宁间改左仆射为太宰，右仆射为少宰，靖康末复故。明清时一般称吏部尚书为太宰。(2)夫子：指孔子。与：语气助词，可表示疑问、感叹或停宕等语气。(3)多能：能，指才能、本领。多能，指的是多方面的才能(本领)。(4)固：原来，本来。纵：助长，促使。将：当，能。(5)闻之：听说。(6)知我乎：知道我啊。乎：语气助词，用于感叹句末，相当于“啊”。(7)少也：少，读 shào，指青年时期。也：语气助词，表提顿，可译为“啊”“呀”，也可去掉不译。贱：贫贱，谓没钱财，没地位。(8)鄙事：鄙人之事。旧多指各种技艺与耕种等体力劳动。(9)多乎哉：多后承前省略了“能”。乎哉，语气助词。在这里表示设问。

【原文】7 牢曰[1]：“子云：‘吾不试故艺[2]。’”

【白话译文】

牢说：“孔子说过：‘我不曾被国家所用，所以学了一些手艺。’”

【英语译文】

Qin Lao said, “Confucius ever said, ‘I had never been employed by any state, therefore I learned a few crafts.’”

【注释】(1)牢：孔子弟子，姓琴，字子开，一字子张。(2)试：用。故艺：所以学手艺。

【原文】8 子曰:“吾有知乎哉[1]?无知也。有鄙夫问于我[2],空空如也[3]。我叩其两端而竭焉[4]。”

【白话译文】

孔子说:“我有知识吗?没有呢。有个庸俗浅陋的人向我提问,我竟然一无所知。我从那个问题的首尾两端,反复细致探讨,然后才算晓得如何回答。”

【英语译文】

Confucius said, “Am I informed? No. When a thought-shallow man asked me a question, I knew nothing about it. After I thought over about its cause and effect for some time, I came to know how to answer him.”

【注释】(1)知:知识。(2)鄙夫:庸俗浅陋的人。问于我:向我提问。(3)空空如也:形容一无所知。后多指一无所有。(4)叩:探问、询问。叩其两端而竭焉,是指从问题的两端反复细致探讨,然后才知如何回答。

【原文】9 子曰:“凤鸟不至[1],河不出图[2],吾已矣夫[3]!”

【白话译文】

孔子说:“凤凰不出现,黄河不出图,没看见什么祥瑞气象,我这一生恐怕是完了吧!”

【英语译文】

Confucius said, “While phoenix didn't appear, no picture sprung from the Yellow River. I didn't see any auspicious sign so I will not see it forever in my life.”

【注释】(1)凤鸟:即凤凰。古代传说,凤凰是一种神鸟,祥瑞的象征。凤凰出现就表示天下太平。不至:不来,不出现。(2)河不出图:《易·系辞》上:“河出图,洛出书,圣人则之。”据汉儒孔安国、刘歆等解说:伏羲时有龙马出于黄河,背有旋毛如星点,称作龙图,伏羲取法以画八卦生蓍法;夏禹治水时有神龟出于洛水,背有裂纹如文字,禹取法而作《尚书·洪范》“九畴”。古代认为出现“河图洛书”是帝王受命的祥瑞。这里说“不出图”等于说“不祥瑞”。已矣:完了。

【原文】10 子见齐衰者[1]、冕衣裳者与瞽者[2]，见之[3]，虽少[4]，必作[5]；过之[5]，必趋[7]。

【白话译文】

孔子遇见穿丧服的人、穿戴着礼帽、礼服的人以及盲人，所遇见的即使是年轻人，孔子也一定站起来；经过他们身边时，一定小步快走以示敬意。

【英语译文】

Confucius would surely stand up when he met someone who wore funeral gown, ritual gown, or who was blind, even if they were young. While passing by them, Confucius walked fast in little pace to show respect to him.

【注释】(1)见：遇到；接触。齐衰(zīcuī)：古代丧服，五服之一。用粗麻布制成，以其将丧服下部的边折转缝起来而得名。服期有三年的，为继母、慈母；有一年的，为"齐衰期"，如孙为祖父母，夫为妻；有五月的，如为曾祖父母；有三月的，如为高祖父母。斩衰：旧时五种丧服中最重的一种。用粗麻布制成，左右和下边不缝。服制三年。子及未嫁女为父母、媳为公婆、承重孙(其人及父均系嫡长，而父先死，则祖父母丧亡时，其人称承重孙)为祖父母、妻为夫，均服。先秦诸侯为天子、臣为君亦服斩衰。(2)冕衣裳者：即衣冠整齐的贵族。冕是高等贵族所戴的礼帽，后来只有皇帝所戴才叫冕。衣是上衣，裳是下衣，相当现代的裙。瞽者：盲人。(3)见之：遇见的。(4)虽少：即使年少。(5)作：站起来。(6)过：经过。(7)趋：古代的一种礼节以"碎步疾行"表示敬意。

【原文】11 颜渊喟然叹曰[1]："仰之弥高[2]，钻之弥坚[3]。瞻之在前[4]，忽焉在后[5]。夫子循然善诱人[6]，博我以文[7]，约我以礼[8]，欲罢不能。既竭吾才[9]，如有所立卓尔[10]。虽欲从之[11]，末由也已[12]。"

【白话译文】

颜渊感叹地说："老师之道，越往上看，越觉得高，越钻研，越艰深，望见在前，忽然在后。老师最会一步一步有序地引导我们循步前进。用渊博的文化知识扩充我们的学问，用礼法界定我们的举止。使我们想停止学习都不可能。我已经用尽了我的才能，好像也取得了凸显的成就。本想于此继续前进，又不知怎样起步。"

【英语译文】

Yan Yuan ever sighed, "The Way of our teacher becomes more far-reached and more complicated as we look up and study carefully. We have been lagged behind once we notice it. He is adept in guiding us step by step to make progress gradually. He is knowledgeable in enlarging our learning and he uses ritual and etiquette to set boundaries of our manners. It's impossible for us to stop studying. I' ve used up my talent and seemly made obvious achievement. I planned to go on forward but did not know how to start off."

【注释】(1)喟然:喟,读 kuì,喟然,感叹的样子。(2)仰:抬头向上望。弥高:弥,读 mí,指益、更加。弥高,是指更高,越高。(3)钻:钻研。弥坚:更加坚深。坚深,同"艰深"。(4)瞻:看,望。(5)忽焉:忽然。(6)循循然善诱:循循,有顺序的样子。循循然善诱,然是词尾。"……的样子"的意义,没有恰当的词能够对译。(7)博我以文:博,扩充。文,文化知识。博我以文,用文化知识扩充我的学问。(8)约我以礼:约,界定。礼,礼法。约我以礼,是指用礼法界定我的举止。(9)既竭吾才:用完了我的才能。(10)如有:谦辞,似乎有。所立:名词,指成就、建树。卓尔:形容超群出众。训为"突出的",在这里是"所立"的后置形容词,起限制作用。(11)虽:读 suī,通"须",副词,指本,本来。从之:在成就上继续向前。之,指代"所立卓尔"。末由:无由,谓无从,无法。也已:语气助词,表肯定、感叹。

【原文】12 子疾病,子路使门人为臣[1]。病间[2],曰:"久矣哉,由之行诈也[3]!无臣而为有臣[4]。吾谁欺?欺天乎!且予与其死于臣之手也[5],毋宁死于二三子之手乎[6]!且予纵不得大葬[7],予死于道路乎[8]?"

【白话译文】

孔子病重,子路让同学充当家臣治理丧事。孔子病情好转后,说道:"很久了吧,仲由的欺骗行为呀!我没有家臣,硬要用装扮的家臣治丧,我哄谁呢?哄上天吗?我如果死在家臣掌握的环境里,不如死在学生的料理中了!即使不能隆重举行葬礼,我死在道路上了吗?"

【英语译文】

Due to Confucius' grave illness, Zi Lu asked his fellow to manage funeral affair as Confucius' servant. After becoming better, Confucius said, "Zhong You has cheated me for a long time! I don't have any servant but you pretended to make him do that. Whom I coaxed? Did I coax the Heaven? If I died being charged by servant I'd rather die being charged by my disciples! Did I die unfortunately at roadside eveh though grand funeral couldn't be held?"

【注释】(1)门人:弟子。为臣:当家臣。孔子当时已不是大夫,没有家臣,子路欲以家臣治其丧,意在尊敬圣人,未知违礼。古代诸侯死,才有家臣治丧,后大夫也有"僭"行此礼的。(2)病间:病情好转。(3)诈:欺骗。(4)为:装作。(5)与其:选择连词,常与"不如""哪及""宁肯"等词相呼应,表示两相比较择优而取的偏选关系。有"假如""如果"的意思,用于前一分句,引领不采取项。之手:手中,手里,指控制掌握的范围。(6)无宁:一作"毋宁"。选择连词,是指宁可,不如的意思。常同"与其"相应,用于第二分句,引领选择项。(7)大葬:按礼仪举行的隆重葬礼。(8)死于道路:自古以来认为的诸多原因的惨死。

【原文】13 子贡曰:"有美玉于斯,韫椟而藏诸[1]?求善贾而沽诸[2]?"子曰:"沽之哉!沽之哉!"

【白话译文】

子贡说:"这儿有一块美玉,把它放在柜子里藏起来呢?还是找一个识货的商人卖掉它呢?"孔子说:"卖掉它,卖掉它!我是在等待识货的人呢。"

【英语译文】

Zi Gong asked, "Here I have a fine jade. Shall I hide it in a cupboard or sell it to someone who knows its value?" Confucius answered, "Sell it! I'm waiting for that kind of man."

【注释】(1)韫椟:读 yùndú,藏在柜子里,珍藏,收藏。韫,谓藏、蕴藏、怀藏。椟,同"椟"。柜、函一类的藏物器。(2)贾:读 gǔ,商人,又同"价"。善贾,即"好价钱"。这里的语言环境当取第一义。善贾,即识货的商人。沽诸:沽,读 gū,卖。诸,语气助词,用在选择问句,特指问句,或者有所怀疑的推测或推论等句子末尾,表疑问语气,译为"呢"。(3)待贾者:等候买者;识货的人。

【原文】14 子欲居九夷[1]。或曰:"陋,如之何[2]?"子曰:"君子居之,何陋之有[3]?”

【白话译文】
孔子想去九夷居住。有人说:“那里偏僻落后,怎样对付那种环境?”孔子说:“君子住在那里,有什么偏僻落后?”

【英语译文】
Confucius wanted to live in Jiuyi. Somebody told him, “That place is backward. How can you deal with it?” Confucius answered, “If a moral man lives there, how could it be backward?”

【注释】(1)九夷:古代称东方的九种少数民族。亦称其所居之地。《后汉书·东夷传》:“夷有九种。曰:畎夷、于夷、方夷、黄夷、白夷、赤夷、玄夷、风夷、阳夷。”亦泛指少数民族。(2)陋:偏僻落后。如之何:怎么对付偏僻落后。(3)何陋之有:有什么陋。

【原文】15 子曰:“吾自卫反鲁[1],然后乐正[2],雅颂各得其所[3]。”

【白话译文】
孔子说:“我从卫国回到鲁国后,把音乐整理了一番,雅颂各归其位。”

【英语译文】
Confucius said, “I put *Songs* in order after I came back to Lu State from Wei State, with *Odes* and *Hymns* in right place.”

【注释】(1)自卫反鲁:据左转,事在鲁哀公十一年冬。(2)乐正:乐章乐曲得到了。(3)雅颂各得其所:雅颂间的错乱得到了廓清。

【原文】16 子曰:“出则事公卿[1],入则事父兄[2],有丧事不敢不勉[3],不为酒困[4],何有于我哉[5]?”
【白话译文】
孔子说:“离开自己的家,就服侍公卿,回到自己的家,就服侍父兄和长辈。有丧事不敢不守礼尽力,不被饮酒所困扰。这些事,我有什么成绩呀?”

【英语译文】

Confucius said, "On leaving home, I served lords and courtiers; on returning home, I attended parents, brothers and elders. During funeral I daren't disobserving rituals and I wasn't disturbed by drinking. Just things like these. What achievements have I made?"

【注释】(1)出:指离开自己的家。公卿:三公九卿的简称。三公,古代三种最高官职的合称。周以太师、太傅、太保为三公。九卿,古代中央政府的九个高级官职。周以少师、少傅、少保、冢宰、司徒、宗伯、司马、司寇、司空为九卿。(2)入:指回到自己的家。父兄:父亲与兄长。(3)丧事:泛指人死后殓奠殡葬等事宜,丧,读sāng。殓,读liàn。勉:尽力,努力。(4)困:困扰。(5)何有:用反问语气说明没什么。这里想必是孔子自省、自谦之词。"何有"应当读为"没有什么成绩。"

【原文】17 子在川上[1],曰:"逝者如斯夫[2]! 不舍昼夜[3]。"

【白话译文】

孔子在河边,叹道:"消逝的时光就像这流水一样啊! 日夜不停地流去不回来。"

【英语译文】

Confucius stood by riverside saying, "Passage of time is just like flowing river! It flows day and night, never stop and never come back."

【注释】(1)川上:河边。(2)逝者如斯:谓光阴如流水一去不返。夫:语气助词,这里表感叹。(3)不舍:不停止。

【原文】18 子曰:"吾未见好德如好色者也[1]。"

【白话译文】

孔子说:"我没看见过爱好道德,如同爱好美色一样的人。"

【英语译文】

Confucius said, "I never met a person who likes virtue as much as beauty."

【注释】(1) 好德:由敬人的心性养成,需要修养;较难。好色:由私欲发泄养成,无须修养;较易。

【原文】19 子曰:“譬如为山[1],未成一篑[2],止,吾止也[3]。譬如平地[4],虽覆一[5],进,吾往也[6]。”

【白话译文】

孔子说:“譬如堆土筑山,没有成功,是因为差一筐土,停止不筑,是我们自己停止的。譬如把坑洼填成平地,虽然才倒覆一筐土,继续不断倒覆一筐土,直到最后,是我们自己填平的。”

【英语译文】

Confucius said, “Things are just like piling earth into a hill. Failure is caused by shortage of a basket of earth and it's we who stopped doing that ourselves. Things are also like filling hollows into flat ground. It's we who managed doing that finally with continuous filling earth, till at last hollow were filled in.”

【注释】(1)为山:堆土筑山。(2)未成一篑:因为差一篑土没有成功。篑,读kuì,盛土的竹筐。(3)止:停止。(4)平地:填平地面,把坑洼填平。(5)覆一篑:倒进一篑土,覆盖一篑土。(6)进:继续。往:义同“进”。

【原文】20 子曰:“语之而不惰者[1],其回也与[2]!”

【白话译文】

孔子说:“给他讲解,他是从不懈怠的人,这便是颜回了!”

【英语译文】

Confucius said, “It was Yan Hui who was never sluggish while you taught him.”

【注释】(1)语:谈论,讲解。之:代词,代指他,他们。而:代词,代指他。不惰:懈怠,懒惰。者:人。(2)其:近指代词,代指这、此。也与:同“也欤”,语气助词,这里表感叹,也可表疑问。

【原文】21 子谓颜渊[1],曰:“惜乎[2]!吾见其进也,未见其止也[3]。”

【白话译文】

孔子谈到颜渊,说:“可惜呀!我只看到了他不断长进,从没看见他停滞不前。”

【英语译文】

When talking about Yan Yuan, Confucius said, “It's a pity! I just noticed his continuous progress but never noticed his hesitation.”

【注释】(1)谓:评论。(2)惜乎:可惜呀!(3)止:停滞不前。

【原文】22 子曰:“苗而不秀者有矣夫[1]!秀而不实者有矣夫[2]!”

【白话译文】

孔子说:“庄稼长了苗,却不开花吐穗的,还真有这样的呀!开花吐穗了,却不结出籽实的,也真有这样的呀!”

【英语译文】

Confucius said, “There really are crops which don't blossom but only grow sprouts! And there really are crops which don't bear grains but only blossom!”

【注释】(1)苗:用作动词,指长苗。而:转折连词,指却。秀:禾类植物开花抽穗,亦指花卉开花或开出的花朵。者:代词,代指“物”。有矣夫:有之夫。矣 :代词,与“之”字相当。夫:句末语气助词,表感叹,可译作“啊”“呀”。(2)实:果实;籽实。亦指结果实;结籽实。

【原文】23 子曰:“后生可畏[1],焉知来者之不如今也[2]?四十、五十而无闻焉[3],斯亦不足畏也已[4]。”

【白话译文】

孔子说:“年轻人令人敬畏,不可轻视。怎么知道后辈不及今天的人呢?人到四五十岁还没有名望,也就不值得敬畏了。”

【英语译文】

Confucius said, “Youths are awesome and we cannot feel contempt for them. How could we know that younger generations won’t surpass us today? People, who are near forty to fifty years old but without reputation, don’t deserve respecting.”

【注释】(1)后生:后辈,下一代。可畏:青年势必超过前辈,令人敬畏。(2)焉知:怎知。来者:将来的人,后辈。不如今:不及今天的人。(3)无闻焉:无闻,指没有名声,不为人知。焉,语气助词,用在陈述句末表论断、决断或终结的语气。有郑重其事以告人,使人深信不疑的意味,一般去掉不译。(4)也已:语气助词,这里表肯定。

【原文】24 子曰:“法语之言[1],能无从乎?改之为贵。巽与之言[2],能无说乎[3]?绎之为贵。说而不绎[4],从而不改,吾末如之何也已矣[5]。”

【白话译文】

孔子说:“合乎礼法的话,能够不遵从吗?改正错误更可贵。委婉附和的话,能够不喜悦吗?分析话的含义更可贵。盲目喜悦,不加分析,表面遵从,内心不改;这种人,我没有办法对付了。”

【英语译文】

Confucius said, “How can’t we observe ritual words? It’s more praiseworthy to correct mistakes. How can’t we be happy about euphemistic words? It’s more praiseworthy to analyze its meaning. I have no way to cope with those who are happy blindly, who are obedient superficially without analysis but never correct his mistakes in heart.”

【注释】(1)法语:合乎礼法的言语。(2)巽与:巽,读 xùn,巽与,即“顺从”“附和”。巽与之言,即委婉附和的话。(3)说:同“悦”。(4)绎(yì):寻绎,理出事物的头绪,引申为解析。为(wéi):在比较句中作谓语动词,含有“最”“更”的意思。后面形容词多为单音节,改之为贵,即“改之更”。末:代词,没有什么。如之何:怎么样,怎么办。

【原文】25 子曰:“主忠信[1],毋友不如己者[2],过则不惮改[3]。”

【白话译文】

孔子说:“君子不要结交不像君子的人。君子有了过错就不要怕难改正。”

【英语译文】

Confucius said, “A moral man should worship loyalty and honesty and not befriend immoral one. A moral man should be brave to correct his faults.”

【注释】(1)主:崇尚,注重。忠信:忠诚信实。(2)毋(wú):通“无 wú”,副词,表示禁止。犹“不可”“不要”。友:结交。不如己者:如,像。己,因主语是君子,“己”即是君子,“不如己者”即“不像君子的人”。(3)过:错误,过失。惮(dàn):畏惧、畏难。

【原文】26 子曰:“三军可夺帅也[1],匹夫不可夺志也[2]。”

【白话译文】

孔子说:“在实战中,三军的主帅,可以夺取;在社会生活中,平民男子汉的志向,不可以夺取。”

【英语译文】

Confucius said, “A general of armed forces can be decapitated in fight; but the aspiration of a common man cannot be taken away.”

【注释】(1)三军:军队的通称。周朝的制度,诸侯中的大国,可拥有军队三军。中军最尊上军次之下军又次之。一军一万二千五百人,三军合三万七千五百人。《周礼·夏官·司马》:“凡制军万有二千五百人为军王六军,大国三军,次国二军,小国一军。”可夺帅:可以夺取(除掉)其主帅。(2)匹夫:古代指平民中的男子。不可夺志:夺取(除掉)其志向。

【原文】27 子曰:“衣敝缊袍[1],与衣狐貉者立[2],而不耻者[3],其由也与?‘不忮不求[4],何用不臧[5]?’”子路终身诵之[6]。子曰:“是道也[7],何足以臧?”

【白话译文】

孔子说:“穿着破旧的、乱麻絮的袍,和穿着狐貉皮衣的人一块儿站着,不感觉有失体面的人,那就是仲由了吧?《诗经》上说:‘不嫉妒不贪求,为什么不好呢?’”子路老是念着这两句诗。孔子说:“仅仅这样做,怎么能够好呢?”

【英语译文】

Confucius said, “A man appears dignified even in worn cotton gown with another in leather-fur gown beside him should be Zhong You. *The Book of Songs* reads ‘Do not gain at expense of others. would it be right?’ ” Zi Lu always chants these two lines. Confucius said, “How can it be enough just chanting them ?”

【注释】(1)衣(yì):穿(衣服)。敝(bì):破旧。缊袍:以乱麻为絮的袍,古贫者所服。缊,读 yùn,乱麻、乱絮。(2)狐貉:指狐貉的毛皮制成的皮衣。朱熹《四书集注》:“以狐貉之皮为裘,衣之贵者。”貉,读 hé,兽名。形似狐,毛棕灰色,是一种重要的毛皮兽。(3)不耻者:不以为有失体面的人。(4)不忮不求:不嫉妒不贪求。忮,读 zhì,嫉妒。(5)何用不臧:为什么不好。以上两句见《诗经·邶风·雄雉》。(6)之:指上文两句诗。(7)道:方法,途径。

【原文】28 子曰:“岁寒[1],然后知松柏之后雕也[2]。”

【白话译文】

孔子说:“一年的最冷时节,才晓得松柏是最后落叶的。”

【英语译文】

Confucius said, “When it’s coldest in a year people realize that pines and cypresses have fallen leaves.”

【注释】(1)岁寒:一年的严寒时节。(2)雕:同“凋”,指植物的枯败零落,也指人或事物受到损伤或衰败穷困。

【原文】29 子曰:“知者不惑[1],不忧[2],勇者不惧[3]。”

【白话译文】

孔子说:“聪明的人不糊涂,仁德的人不忧愁,勇敢的人不害怕。”

【英语译文】

Confucius said, “A clever man isn't confused; a humane man isn't melancholy, and a brave man fears nothing.”

【注释】(1)惑:不明不白认识不清。(2)仁者:仁德的人,爱人助人,心怀广阔,极少愁虑,极少不愉。忧:心萌愁虑,有所不愉,郁闷。(3)惧:害怕。

【原文】30 子曰:“可与共学[1],未可与适道[2];可与适道,未可与立[3];可与立,未可与权[4]。”

【白话译文】

孔子说:“可以一起共同学习的人,未必可以一同归正道;可以一同归正道的人,未必可以一同依礼而行;可以一同依礼而行的人,未必可以一同通权达变。”

【英语译文】

Confucius said, “A man with whom one can learn together might not observe the right Way; a man who observes the right Way might not abide etiquette together; and a man who abides etiquette might not do things flexibly.”

【注释】(1)与:相与。谓相处,一道,共同。共学:一同学习。(2)适道:归从道统,谓走正道。(3)立:立于礼,依礼而行。(4)权:通权达变,变通而不离经违本。

【原文】31“唐棣之华[1],偏其反而[2]。岂不尔思[3]?室是远而[4]。”子曰:“未之思也[5],夫何远之有[6]?”

【白话译文】

“唐棣树啊花盛开,翩翩花朵随风歪。能说我不想你吗?家太远了难往来。”孔子说:“他没想念,真的想念,有啥遥远?”

【英语译文】

"Shadberry flowers blossom prime, flying flowers fall with wind. How could I say I'm not missing you? Distant hometown we've no exchange at all." Confucius said, "He didn't miss you. If he really missed you, how could hometown be far?"

【注释】(1)唐棣:植物名。又称"扶移""红枸子"。蔷薇科。落叶小乔木。唐棣古有二说:一是郁李,二是白杨类树木。(2)偏:通"翩"。其:顺承连词,相当于"而"。反:翻转。而:语气助词,表反问,译为"吗""么";表感叹译为"啊""呀""吧";表直陈终结,译为"呢""的"或去掉不要。(3)尔思:思尔,想你。(4)室:家。是:加重语气之词。(5)之:助词,补凑音节。(6)夫:语首助词。之:结构助词,表示"远",是前置宾语。

乡党篇第十

本是一章,今分为二十七节,记载孔子的容色言动、衣食住行,颂扬孔子是个符合礼的正人君子。

【原文】1 孔子于乡党[1],恂恂如也[2],似不能言者[3]。其在宗庙朝廷[4],便便言[5],唯谨尔[6]。

【白话译文】

孔子在他家乡那里,非常恭顺,好像不能说话的人。他在宗庙里、朝廷上,都能明白晓畅地谈吐,只是很谨慎而已。

【英语译文】

Confucius was so humbly cautious as not to speak at his hometown. However he could talk about anything fluently at temple or royal court, being only cautious.

【注释】(1)乡党:代称家乡。周制一万二千五百家为乡,五百家为党。(2)恂恂如:温顺恭谨的样子。恂,读 xún。如,形容词后缀,犹"然"表状态。(3)不能言者:不能说话的人。(4)宗庙朝廷:古代帝王、诸侯祭祀祖宗的庙宇称宗庙,接受朝见和处理政务的地方称朝廷。(5)便便(piánpián):善言的样子,语言流畅。(6)

唯谨尔：只是谨慎而已。

【原文】2 朝[1]，与下大夫言[2]，侃侃如也[3]；与上大夫言[4]，訚訚如也[5]。君在[6]，踧踖如也[7]，与与如也[8]。

【白话译文】

上朝时，同下大夫说话，神态和乐正直；同上大夫说话，神态和乐，善辩不阿；君主到堂了，神态恭敬又小心不安，举止有威仪，不卑不亢，合情合理。

【英语译文】

While waiting at court and talking with the senior officers of the lower grade, he spoke freely, but in a straightforward manner; and while talking with those of the higher grade, he did so blandly, but precisely. When the monarch was present, his manner displayed respectful uneasiness; it was grave, but self-possessed.

【注释】(1)朝：上朝的时候。(2)下大夫：古职官名。周在国君之下有卿、大夫、士三等，各等又分上、中、下三级，下大夫是大夫中的低级职官。侃侃如：犹侃侃然。谓神态和乐，一说神态刚直。侃，读 kǎn。(4)上大夫：大夫中的高级职官。(5)訚訚如：犹訚訚然，谓神态和悦，善辩不阿。訚，读 yín。(6)君在：君主临朝。谓君主到堂议事。(7)踧踖如：犹踧踖然，谓神态恭敬又小心不安。踧踖，读 cùjí。(8)与与如：犹与与然，谓神态有威仪又合度。

【原文】3 君召使摈[1]，色勃如也[2]，足躩如也[3]。揖所与立[4]，左右手[5]，衣前后[6]，襜如也[7]。趋进[8]，翼如也[9]。宾退，必复命曰："宾不顾矣[10]。"

【白话译文】

鲁君召见孔子，使令他接待宾客。他脸色庄重，脚步加快。向两旁的人作揖，左拱手，右拱手；衣服在前俯后仰时自然摆动，样子很整齐。他小步急速前行，像鸟儿展翅，自然飘逸开朗。贵宾辞别后，一定向君主回报，说："客人已经走远不回头了。"

【英语译文】

The monarch of Lu State summoned Confucius and made him receive guests. He walked with dignity and faster pace; he made a bow with hands folded in front to people at two sides. While doing so, his clothes swayed naturally and neatly. He walked forth cheerfully with little pace like flying bird. After guests left, he surely reported to monarch saying, "Guests have gone away never coming back."

【注释】(1)君召使摈:君主(鲁君),召见,使令。摈,通"傧",接待宾客。鲁君召见孔子,使令他接待宾客。(2)色:脸色,表情。勃如:勃然。兴起、振奋的状态。(3)足:脚。躩如:躩然,疾行的样子。躩,读 jué。(4)揖:拱手行礼。所与立:站在身边的人。(5)左右手:向左、向右拱手。(6)衣前后:衣服在前俯后仰时。(7)襜如:襜然。(衣服前后摆动)整齐的样子。襜,读 chān。(8)趋进:小步急速前行,表示敬意的一种动作。(9)翼如:翼然,鸟儿展翅的样子,形容自然飘逸,端好开张的状态。(10)顾:回头。

【原文】4 入公门[1],鞠躬如也[2],如不容[3]。立不中门[4],行不履阈[5]。过位[6],色勃如也[7],足躩如也[8],其言似不足者[9]。摄齐升堂[10],鞠躬如也,屏气似不息者[11]。出,降一等[12],逞颜色[13],怡怡如也[14]。没阶[15],趋进,翼如也。复其位,踧踖如也[16]。

【白话译文】

孔子进入朝廷的大门,神态恭敬谨慎,好像没有容身处。站立不在门中间,行走不踩门槛。经过国君的空座位前,脸色严肃,脚步也快,言语好像体弱者有气无声。提起衣边爬堂阶,神态恭敬谨慎,抑制着呼吸,如雕像一样没有气息。退出大门,才下一级台阶,脸色便放松了,安适自在。一步步下完台阶,脚步加快,如鸟展翅一样松活。回到自己的位置,神态恭敬又小心不安。

【英语译文】

When Confucius entered court gate, his manner was respectful and humble, for whom there seemed no place to occupy. He never stood amidst a gate and never stepped threshold. When he passed by the empty seat of monarch he displayed serious face, fast pace and spoke in very low voice like a weak man. While ascending steps, he pulled his gown humbly and cautiously holding his breath. While retreating court gate, he relaxed right away after descending one step. After descending all steps one by one, he hurried his pace just like flying birds. After returning his own seat, he looked respectfully and cautiously.

【注释】(1)公门:古称国君的外门为公门,也泛称官署、衙门。(2)鞠躬如:鞠躬然,恭敬谨慎的样子。(3)如不容:好像不能容纳、不能宽容。人对生疏的或不适应的环境,往往敏感,觉得自己没有置身处。(4)立不中门:这"中"字与《孟子·尽心》上:"中天下而立"的"中",用法相同,都是"居于(在)……中间"的意思。履阈:踩门槛。阈,读 yù,门槛。(6)过位:经过君主座位前。君主没在座位上。(7)色勃如:见 10.3 中注 2。(8)足躩如:见 10.3 中注 3。(9)不足者:体弱的人。足,指体质好。(10)摄齐:摄,提起;齐,读 zī,衣裳缝了边的下摆。(11)屏气:屏,bǐng,屏气即屏息,抑止呼吸。形容谨慎畏惧的样子。不息者:停止了呼吸的人。(12)降一等:下一级台阶。等,台阶的级。(13)逞颜色:脸色放松亮起来。逞,读 chěng,舒展。(14)怡怡如:怡怡然、安适自得的样子。(15)没阶:下完阶级。没,读 mò,尽。(16)踧踖如:见 10.2 中注 7。

【原文】5 执圭鞠躬如也[1],如不胜[2]。上如揖[3],下如授[4]。勃如战色[5],足蹜蹜如有循[6]。享礼[7],有容色[8]。私觌[9],愉愉如也[10]。

【白话译文】

孔子出使到外国,拿着圭,恭敬谨慎,好像举不动的样子。向上举好像在作揖,放下来好像在交给别人。满脸敬畏的神色。动脚便小步快走,好像有所遵循、不可偏离的样子。献礼物时,满脸和气。用私人身份和外国君臣会见时,显得和悦舒畅。

【英语译文】

As an ambassador to other state, Confucius held jade respectfully just like it's heavy. Holding it up, he seemed to make a bow with hands folded in front; while holding down, he seemed to give it to others. He looked awesome all the time. He walked in little pace like observing some appropriate regulations. While dedicating present, he looked friendly and harmoniously. While meeting monarch and courtiers of other states, he looked gentle and kind.

【注释】(1)执圭:古代帝王、诸侯,在朝聘、祭祀、丧葬等举行隆重仪式时所用的玉制礼器。长条形,上尖下方。其名称、大小因爵位及用途而异。(2)胜(shēng):能担负得了。(3)上、揖:上举、作揖。(4)下、授:下持、交付。(5)勃如战色:面部泛起敬畏的神色。战色,畏惧的神色。(6)蹜蹜(sùsù):小步快走的样子。如有循:好像有所遵循。(7)享礼:使臣向朝聘国的君主进献礼物的仪式。(8)有容色:有容貌神色,谓和颜悦色。(9)私觌:谓以私人身份拜会出使国的国君。觌,读 dí,指见、相见。(10)愉愉如:愉愉然,和悦舒畅。

【原文】6 君子不以绀緅饰[1],红紫不以为亵服[2]。当暑,袗絺绤[3],必表而出之[4]。缁衣,羔裘;素衣,麑裘;黄衣,狐裘[5]。亵裘长[6],短右袂[7]。必有寝衣[8],长一身有半[9]。狐貉之厚以居[10]。去丧[11],无所不佩。非帷裳[12],必杀之[13]。羔裘玄冠不以吊[14]。吉月[15],必朝服而朝[16]。

【白话译文】

君子不用近似黑色的天青色和铁灰色作镶边,近似朱色的红色和紫色不作平时居家的服色。暑天,穿细的或粗的葛布单衣,一定套着衬衫,露在外面。黑色衣配紫羔,白色衣配麑裘,黄色衣配狐裘。居家的皮袍比一般的衣服长些,但右手的袖子短些。狐貉毛深温厚,又用作坐垫暖体。丧服期满,什么佩带物都可佩带。不是上朝和祭祀的礼服,必先剪裁,然后缝合。不穿戴着紫羔和黑色礼帽去吊丧。每月初一,一定穿着上朝的礼服去朝见。

【英语译文】

A moral man doesn't trim his gown by dark and gray cloth; red and pink clothes aren't worn at home. At summer days thin and rough hemp coat should be covered by shirt. Black clothes match pink sheep fur; white clothes match lithe deer fur, and yellow clothes match wolf fur. Fur gown worn at home should be longer than common one but right sleeve is shorter. Wolf fur can be used as cushion to warm one's body. While mourning period comes to an end people can wear anything. People should first scissor and sew clothes which are not for the ceremonial robe in court or at sacrifice. Do not pay a condolence call in pink sheep fur and black ceremonial hat. At first day of each month, courtiers should go to court in their court ceremonial robe.

【注释】(1)绀緅饰:绀緅,读 gànzōu,都是表示颜色的名词。"绀"是深青中透红的颜色,相当于今天的"天青";"緅"是青多红少,比绀更暗,有人用铁灰色表示它。"饰"是绲边、镶边、缘边。在古代,黑色是正式礼服的颜色,绀緅这两种颜色都近于黑色,所以不用来镶边、为别的颜色做装饰。(2)红紫不以为亵:古代大红色叫"朱",是很贵重的颜色。红和紫都属朱色类,也连带被重视,不用来做家居便服的颜色。亵,读 xiè,指内衣、便服。(3)袗絺绤:袗,读 zhěn,指单衣,也指穿单衣。絺,读 chī,指细葛布。绤,读 xì,指粗葛布。(4)必表而出之:必须穿在衬衣面上。(5)缁衣,羔裘;素衣,麑裘;黄衣,狐裘:这三句表示内衣和外衣的颜色必须相称。古代穿皮衣毛向外,必须用罩衣遮住。这罩衣叫裼(xī)衣。这里的缁衣,素衣,黄衣的衣,正是这种裼衣。缁,黑色。古代所谓羔"裘",都是黑色的羊毛皮衣,就是今天的紫羔。麑,读 ní,指小鹿、毛色白。(6)亵裘长:亵裘,家居常穿的皮衣。为了保暖,做得较长,故曰亵裘长。(7)短右袂:袂,读 mèi,指衣袖。为了做事方便,右袖短一点较好。(8)寝衣:叫被子。不是睡衣。古代大被叫"衾",小被叫"被"。(9)长一身有半:人体长度的 1.5 倍。(10)狐貉之厚以居:狐貉之毛深长温厚,适用于家居暖体。(11)去丧:同"除丧"。指服丧的期限已满,亦指脱去居丧所穿的衣服。(12)帷裳:礼服,上朝和祭祀时穿。用整幅布做成,不加剪裁,多余的部分折叠着,犹如今天的百褶裙。(13)杀(shài):裁去(多余的)。"杀之"就是缝制之前裁去多余的布,不用折叠,省工省料。(14)羔裘玄冠不以吊:玄冠,古代朝服冠名,黑色。"羔裘玄冠",都是黑色的,古代都用作吉服。丧事是凶事,因此不能穿戴着去吊丧。(15)吉月:农历每月初一,或说大年初一。(16)必朝服而朝:一定穿着礼服去上朝。

【原文】7 齐[1],必有明衣[2],布[3]。齐必变食[4],居必迁坐[5]。

【白话译文】

斋戒时,沐浴完必须换上干净的内衣。斋戒时,必须改变饮食内容,不吃五辛。起居场所必须迁移,不和妻妾同房。

【英语译文】

While fasting, clean underwear must be put on after bathing. While fasting, pungent food should not be eaten. Living place should be changed and sexual intercourse should be prohibited.

【注释】(1)齐(zhāi):通作"斋"。指斋戒,古人在祭祀前沐浴更衣,整洁身心,以示虔诚。(2)明衣:古人在斋戒期间,沐浴后所穿的干净内衣。(3)布:用麻(或葛、丝、毛、棉等)的纤维,单独或混合织成的可制衣物的材料。(4)变食:改变饮食的内容。清夏炘学礼《管释·释斋》:"古人齐必变食,谓不食五荤(即五辛:小蒜、大蒜、韭、芸薹、胡荽),非不饮酒食肉。"(5)居必迁坐:改换平时起居的场所,不和妻妾同房。

【原文】8 食不厌精[1],脍不厌细[2]。食饐而餲[3],鱼馁而肉败[4],色恶,不食。臭恶[5],不食。失饪[6],不食。不时[7],不食。割不正[8],不食。不得其酱[9],不食。肉虽多,不使胜食气[10]。唯酒无量,不及乱[11]。沽酒市脯不食[12],不撤姜食[13],不多食。

【白话译文】

对于粮食不嫌把糠秕完全去尽。对于鱼和肉不嫌切得够细。饭食过久发生酸馊甚至腐臭,鱼和肉已现腐烂,都不吃。食物颜色难看,不吃。气味难闻,不吃。烹调不当,太过或不及,不吃。不到该当吃的时候不吃。不是正经宰杀合理切割的肉,不吃。即使肉很多,也不吃得超过吃主食。只有饮酒不限量,只要不醉到昏乱。买来的酒和肉干,不吃。每餐都要有姜,但不多吃。

【英语译文】

Grains are best with husk rid off; fish and meat are best with careful cutting. If rice get sour, and fish and meat are rotten, don't eat. If food looks in bad color, don't eat. If they smell terribly, don't eat. If they are cooked excessively or less, don't eat. If it is not dining time, don't eat. If the meat isn't cut correctly, don't eat. Meat shouldn't surpass main food. Drinking will not be limited only if drinkers won't be drunk. If wine and dry meat are bought, don't eat. Each meal we' d have ginger but not too much.

【注释】(1)食不厌精:粮食不嫌把糠秕去尽。(2)脍不厌细:脍,读 kuài,细切的鱼肉,亦指细切或切割。脍不厌细,意谓鱼和肉不嫌切得细。(3)食饐而餲:食,饭。饐,读 yì,饭食经久馊臭。餲,读 ài,食物经久而腐臭变味。(4)馁(něi):鱼类腐烂。败:腐烂,变质。(5)臭恶:气味难闻。(6)失饪:烹调不当,过熟。饪,读 rèn,熟。(7)不时:一指未成熟不宜食用的东西,又指未到进餐时。(8)割不正:割,用刀分解牲畜的骨肉,宰杀牲畜。没有正当理由宰杀牲畜和分解牲畜骨肉不规范,都叫"割不正"。(9)不得其酱:酱,用麦、面、豆等发酵制成的调味品。不得其酱,谓没有合适的调味品。(10)食气:吃饭。气,读 xì,"饩"的古字。(11)不及乱:不至醉到昏乱。(12)沽酒市脯:买来的酒和买来的肉食品。(13)不撤姜食:不撤,不撤除,不消除。姜食,用生姜做的咸菜或小菜,味道辛辣。

【原文】9 祭于公[1],不宿肉[2]。祭肉不出三日[3]。出三日,不食之矣。

【白话译文】
参与国家祭典,得到的祭肉,不保留到第二天。一般祭肉存留不过三天,过了三天,就不吃了。

【英语译文】
Sacrificial meat obtained from sacrificial ceremony on state level, Confucius never kept it for next day. He kept ordinary sacrificial meat for three days. And after three days, he didn't eat such meat.

【注释】(1)祭于公:参与国家祭祀典礼。公,指国家、朝廷。(2)不宿肉:古代大夫、士都有助君祭祀之礼。天子诸侯的祭礼,当天清晨宰杀牲畜,然后举行祭奠。第二天又祭,叫作“绎祭”。绎祭之后才令各人拿回自己带来助祭的肉。或者又依贵贱等级分别颁赐祭肉。这样,祭于公的肉,在颁赐时,至少已过了一两夜了,因之不能再存放一夜。(3)祭肉:指自家或者朋友送的祭肉。

【原文】10 食不语[1],寝不言[2]。

【白话译文】
吃饭时没有交谈,睡觉时没有交谈。

【英语译文】
He didn't talk about anything while eating and sleeping.

【注释】(1)食:吃饭。不:没有。下同。语:与下文“言”,互文见义。都是交谈,谈论的意思。(2)寝:睡觉。

【原文】11 虽疏食菜羹瓜祭[1],必齐如也[2]。

【白话译文】
即使是吃粗饭祭、喝小菜汤祭、尝新瓜祭,都一定同斋戒一样恭敬虔诚。

【英语译文】

He was pious the same as he fasted even if he ate rough rice, drank vegetable soup or tasted melon as sacrifice.

【注释】(1)瓜祭:或谓鲁论作“必祭”,瓜是错字。愚以为“瓜”不是错字,作“瓜”同样顺理成章而且更充实。因为“瓜”与疏食、菜羹是并列成分,读作“疏食,菜羹,瓜祭。”,实为“疏食祭,菜羹祭,瓜祭。”的探下省略句。《书舜典》云:“舜生三十,征庸三十,在位五十载。”杨树达按:“三十下并省‘载’字。”《孟子·滕文公上》云:“夏后氏五十而贡,殷人七十而助,周人百亩而彻。”杨树达按:“五十七十下并省亩字。”(2)齐如:斋戒然。内心外表恭敬虔诚的样子。

【原文】12 席不正[1],不坐[2]。

【白话译文】

座位不端正或不合礼制,纠正后才坐。

【英语译文】

He didn't take his seat until it was corrected if it wasn't right or inappropriate for rites.

【注释】(1)席不正:席,席的古字。古代没有椅、凳,都是在地面上铺席子,坐在席子上。这席子一般是用竹篾、苇蔑或草编织成的平片状物件。铺一张席就是安置一个座位。席不正的席,就是指用这种席子安排的座位、席位。席不正,有两层含义,一指席位摆放得不端正,又指席位的档次(排列的顺序,用料的贵贱)不合礼制。(2)不坐:纠正后才坐。

【原文】13 乡人饮酒[1],杖者出[2],斯出矣。

【白话译文】

举行乡饮酒礼后,等老年人都出去了,这才自己出去。

【英语译文】

After village drinking ritual ceremony, he would not retreat until the elders all went out.

【注释】(1)乡人饮酒:即行乡饮酒礼。《礼记·乡饮酒义》:"少长以齿。"以年龄大小为顺序。《礼记·王制》:"习鄉尚齿。"乡饮酒礼教民尊敬年长者。(2)杖者:指老年人。才,读 cǎi。

【原文】14 乡人傩[1],朝服而立于阼阶[2]。

【白话译文】
家乡本地人迎神驱鬼,穿着朝服站在东边的台阶上。

【英语译文】
When hometown fellows welcome gods to disperse ghosts, Confucius stood at eastern step in his court gown.

【注释】(1)傩(nuó):古代的一种风俗,迎神以驱逐疫鬼。多在腊日(农历十二月初八日)前举行。(2)阼阶:阼,读 zuò,大堂前东面的台阶,主人所立之地。

【原文】15 问人于他帮[1],再拜而送之[2]。

【白话译文】
托人向在外国的友人问好送礼,他拜了又拜才送行。

【英语译文】
When he asked somebody to send greetings or gift for his friends in other state, Confucius expressed his thanks once and again, then saw off.

【注释】(1)问:闻讯,问候。古人在问候时常赠送礼物表示情意。人:友人。于他帮:在外国。(2)再拜:拜了又拜,表示恭敬。

【原文】16 康子馈药[1],拜而受之[2],曰:"丘未达[3],不敢尝。"

【白话译文】

季康子送药给孔子,孔子行过礼,接下药来,说道:“我对这药性不大了解,不敢尝试。”

【英语译文】

Ji Kang zi gave medicinal herbs to Confucius. After receiving it and expressing thanks, Confucius said, “I don't know its quality and dare not taste it.”

【注释】(1)康子:季康子。馈药:赠药。(2)受之:接受所馈药。(3)达:通晓、明白。

【原文】17 厩焚[1]。子退朝,曰:“伤人乎?”不问马[2]。

【白话译文】

马房失火了。孔子从朝廷回来,问道:“伤人了吗?”没有问马怎么样。

【英语译文】

Once, the stable caught fire. When Confucius returned from the court, he asked, “Is anybody hurt?” He didn't care about horses.

【注释】(1)厩焚:厩,读 jiù,马房。厩焚,马房焚烧。(2)不:没有。

【原文】18 君赐食[1],必正席先尝之[2]。君赐腥[3],必熟而荐之[4]。君赐生[5],必畜之[6]。侍食于君[7],君祭,先饭[8]。

【白话译文】

国君赐给熟食,孔子一定摆正席位坐好先尝一尝。国君赐给生肉,一定弄熟了先进奉祖宗。国君赐给活物,一定养起来。陪侍国君进餐,在国君行饭前祭礼时,自己先吃饭为国君尝尝。

【英语译文】

When monarch bestowed cooked food, Confucius surely had a taste in his seat which was in order. When monarch bestowed raw meat, he surely sacrificed ancestors after cooking it. When monarch bestowed living animal, he surley raised it. When attending monarch to dine, he surley tasted first for monarch as monarch held before-meal-sacrificial rites.

【注释】(1)食:指饭菜等熟食。(2)正席:端正席位坐好。(3)腥:生肉。(4)熟而荐之:弄熟了请祖宗先尝。荐,读 jiàn,进奉。(5)生:生物;活物。(6)畜:饲养。(7)侍食:陪侍尊长进食。(8)先饭:侍食者在国君祭时先行吃饭,意在为国君尝饭。

【原文】19 疾,君视之,东首[1],加朝服拖绅[2]。

【白话译文】

孔子病了,国君来探问。他望着东方诚心迎接。把上朝的礼服盖在身上拖着大腰带。力遵君臣之礼。

【英语译文】

When monarch paid a visit to Confucius When he was iu, the monarck facing east, he honestly greeted. He covered his body with court gown with waist belt trying hard to observe the rites between courtier and monarch.

【注释】(1)东首:东向,朝东。古人卧榻一般设在南窗的西边,人在床榻上面,可以朝东。国君来看孔子 ,从东边台阶走上来(东阶即阼阶是主人之位。国君是全国的主人,到臣下的家中仍以主人姿态从东阶上下。)孔子能够面朝东来迎接他。(2)加朝服拖绅: 孔子卧病在床,不能穿朝服,只能盖在身上。绅,是束在腰间的大带,束了以后,两端都有一大段拖(下垂)着。

【原文】20 君命召[1],不俟驾行矣[2]。

【白话译文】

国君派人召唤孔子,不等驾好车马,他就动身先行。

【英语译文】

While monarch summoned hin, Confucius started off before his cart got ready.

【注释】(1)召:召见。(2)不俟驾:不等候驾车马。

【原文】21 入太庙[1],每事问[2]。

【白话译文】
孔子进入周公庙,每件事情都发问。

【英语译文】
Confucius asked about everything while he entered Zhou Gong's Temple.

【注释】本章已见于八佾篇 3. 15。

【原文】22 朋友死,无所归[1],曰:"于我殡[2]。"

【白话译文】
朋友死了,没有人安埋;孔子说:"这个丧葬事务,由我来料理。"

【英语译文】
One of his friends was dead and nobody buried it. And Confucius said, "This affair is up to me."

【注释】(1)无所归:义同"无所依归"。没有依靠和归宿。(2)于:语气助词。旧读 wū,今读 yú。用在句子或词语的前面,只起发语凑音的作用,可以去掉不译。殡(bìn):停放灵柩、埋葬,泛指丧葬事务。

【原文】23 朋友之馈[1],虽车马[2],非祭肉[3],不拜[4]。

【白话译文】
朋友赠送的礼物,即使是车马,只要不是祭肉,孔子在接受时不行拜礼。

【英语译文】
Upon receiving gifts given by friends, Confucius didn't express thanks-rites, even if the gifts were cart and horse except for sacrificial meat.

【注释】(1)朋友之馈:之,在这里是结构助词,前面的名词“朋友”是领属性定语,而不是主语,后面的动词“馈”是名词性词组的定语,而不是谓语。译时得把省略了的中心词“礼品”(或“东西”)补充出来。馈,读 kuì,赠送。(2)车马:属于重礼,但只用于享受。(3)祭肉:不及车马管钱,却是敬祖的礼物。(4)不拜:不行拜礼。

【原文】24 寝不尸[1],居不容[2]。

【白话译文】

孔子睡觉不像尸体一样直挺着;在家里不像奉祭祀待宾客一样讲求仪容。

【英语译文】

Confucius didn't look like a dead body while he was sleeping; and he cared less about his appearance and manners at home than at sacrificing or dining guests.

【注释】(1)不尸:不像尸体一般。(2)居:居家。不容:不像奉祭祀待宾客一样讲求仪容。或作“不客”,其说可供讨论。

【原文】25 见齐衰者[1],虽狎[2],必变[3]。见冕者与瞽者[4],虽亵[5],必以貌[6]。凶服者式之[7]。式负版者[8]。有盛馔[9],必变色而作[10]。迅雷风烈必变[11]。

【白话译文】

孔子看见穿孝服的人,即使是亲近的人,也免不了触动守孝的心情和仪容;看见戴礼帽的人和盲人,即使是常见的人,也一定有礼貌。乘车时看见穿丧服的人,就低着头,手伏在车前横木上。遇见背负国家图籍的人也手伏车前横木。一有丰富菜肴,一定神色变动,站起来。遇见疾雷大风,一定改变态度。

【英语译文】

Confucius would be moved when he saw somebody in funeral clothes, even an intimate one; he would be polite when he met blind man or a man in hat, even an ordinary one. He would lower his head and placed his hands at the bar of his cart when he saw a man in funeral clothes. He surely placed his hands at the bar of his cart when he met a man carrying state's map and census register material.

【注释】(1)齐衰者:穿孝服(亦称丧服)的人。齐衰,读 zīcuī,五种丧服之一,用粗麻布制成,下边折转缝着。(2)狎(xiá):亲近。(3)变:和原来不同。这里谓孔子因见齐衰者而触动守孝的心情和仪容。(4)冕者:戴着礼帽的人。瞽者:盲人。(5)亵:与“狎”同义。(6)貌:礼貌。(7)凶服:丧服。式:同“轼”。古代车前的横木。这里用作动词,式之,用手扶着轼的意思。(8)版:国家图籍(地图和户籍)。(9)盛馔:丰富的菜肴。馔,读 zhuàn。(10)变色:脸色变动。作:站立。(10)迅雷风烈:疾雷大风。必变,一定改变态度。

【原文】26 升车[1],必正立,执绥[2]。车中,不内顾[3],不疾言[4],不亲指[5]。

【白话译文】

孔子上车,一定先站立端正,然后抓住供拉着上车的索带登上。在车中,不回头看,不急急忙忙说话,不用手指指点点。

【英语译文】

While ascending his cart, Confucius surely first stood upright, then took hold of the string used for climbing up the cart. While in his cart, he never looked back nor hurried speaking, his finger not pointing casually.

【注释】(1)升车:登车。(2)执绥:抓住供拉着上车的索带。(3)内顾:回头看。(4)疾言:急遽地说话。(5)亲指:用手指指点点。

【原文】27 色斯举矣[1],翔而后集[2]。曰[3]:“山梁雌雉[4],时哉时哉[5]!”子路共之[6],三嗅而作[7]。

【白话译文】

孔子和子路来到山谷中,一片彩色片刻升空,盘旋一会儿,又一起停在山梁上;原来是野鸡。孔子赞叹道:“山梁上的母野鸡啊,时运好啊!时运好啊!”子路向它们拱了拱手。那些野鸡,反复张望嗅寻异味,最后飞走了。

【英语译文】

Confucius and Zi Lu came to a valley noticing a piece of colorful things flying up and then stopping at hill ridge. They were pheasants. Confucius praised, "She, pheasants on the ridge, good luck, good luck!" Zi Lu made an obeisance to them. Those pheasants finally flew away after searching for something once and again.

【注释】(1)色:物色。物体、物种各有特别颜色。人与鸟不同色,大概各种动物见到异色都有自己的反应。爱、恨、打、斗,消灭对方或逃避等。雉,俗称野鸡。羽毛鲜艳。一群野鸡集于山间,孔子和子路经过近旁。人鸟乍见,各有反应。鸟,选择逃避,人选择观望。人见一片彩色(野鸡)须臾升空,旋飞而后集于山梁。(2)翔:回旋而飞。(3)曰:孔子曰。(4)山梁:山涧上的桥。一解作"山脊",亦通。雌雉:母野鸡。(5)时哉时哉:形容时运很好(未曾碰上伤害者)。(6)共:同"拱"。(7)三嗅:嗅,读 xiù,用鼻子辨别气味,比喻刺探情况。鸟的鼻子外形与喙合二为一,鸟在徘徊张望中,就好像在用鼻子嗅寻有害的气味、刺探情况一样。三嗅而作,犹言经过反复张望、嗅寻最后飞走了。

先进篇第十一(共二十六章)

朱熹《四书集注》把第一、第二两章合并为一章。刘宝楠正义则把第十八和第十九、第二十和第二十一各并为一章。

【原文】1 子曰:"先进于礼乐[1],野人也[2];后进于礼乐[3],君子也[4]。如用之[5],则吾从先进[6]。"

【白话译文】

孔子说:"先学礼乐后做官的,往往是平民;做起官后,补学礼乐的,大多是达官子弟。如果选用人才,我倾向先学礼乐的。"

【英语译文】

Confucius said, "Those who first learn rites and music and then become officials are usually common people; and those who have become officials and try to make up learning rites and music are mostly descendants of high-rank officials. If selecting talents I'd prefer those who first learn rites and music."

【注释】(1)先进于礼乐:先学习礼乐,学好可出仕。(2)野人:郊外之民;没有爵禄的一般人。(3)后进于礼乐:从政做官后补习礼乐。(4)君子:卿大夫;这里指卿大夫的承袭子弟也。(5)用之:指用人才。(6)从:倾向。

【原文】2 子曰:"从我于陈、蔡:[1]。皆不及门也[2]。"

【白话译文】

孔子说:"跟随我在陈国、蔡国之间忍饥挨饿的人,都没在我这里了。"

【英语译文】

Confucius said, "Those who followed me and suffered starvation while in Chen State and Cai State are now far away from me."

【注释】(1)从我,跟随我。于,在。陈、蔡,皆古国名。鲁哀公三年(公元前492年),孔子离卫后,经曹、宋、郑至陈,住于司城贞子家。鲁哀公六年(公元前495年)吴侵陈,孔子避兵乱离陈去负函(楚地,今河南信阳市境)在陈、蔡间被困,绝粮七日,弟子饥馁皆病。依然讲诵,弦歌不止。者,同前面的"从我于陈、蔡"结合,是一种"者"字结构;"者"字结构可以指代人、事、物。这个"者"字结构指代人;相当于"……的人"。(2)不及门:现时不在门下。

【原文】3 德行[1]:颜渊、闵子骞、冉伯牛、仲弓。言语[2]:宰我、子贡。政事[3]:冉有、季路。文学[4]:子游、子夏。

【白话译文】

德行好的:颜渊、闵子骞、冉伯牛、仲弓。长于辞令的:宰我、子贡。能办理政事的:冉有、季路。通晓文章典籍的:子游、子夏。

【英语译文】

Those who are men of virtue are Yan Yuan, Min Ziqian, Ran Bo Niu, Zhong Gong. Those who are eloquent are Zai Wo and Zi Gong. Those who can deal with administrative affairs are Ran You and Ji Lu. Those who comprehend classics are Zi You and Zi Xia.

【注释】(1)德行(déxíng):指道德品行好。(2)言语:指善于辞令。(3)政事:指会处理政治事务。(4)文学:文章博学。主要指诗、书、易等经籍,与今日所谓文学有别。

【原文】4 子曰:“回也非助我者也[1],于吾言无所不说[2]。”

【白话译文】

孔子说:“颜回(啊)不是帮助我的人(呢)。他对我的话没有不喜欢的。”

【英语译文】

Confucius said, “Yan Hui isn't the man who has helped me. He doesn't like nothing of what I've said.”

【注释】(1)也:语气助词。用在主语、时间名词或副词性词语后面,表提顿或停顿,可译作“啊”“呀”;也可去掉不译。前一“也”字,就是用在主语后面的。后一“也”字,是用在复合句前一分句末,表提顿语气的,一般去掉不译,也可译作“啊”“呀”“呢”“的”。(2)于 :介词,指对、对于。

【原文】5 子曰:“孝哉[1],闵子骞!人不间于其父母昆弟之言[2]。”

【白话译文】

孔子说:“闵子骞真是孝顺呀!旁人对于他爹娘、兄弟称赞他的话没有指责。”

【英语译文】

Confucius said, “Min Ziqian is really a filial man! Others never scold what his parents and brothers praised him.”

【注释】(1)哉:语气词,表示感叹。(2)间(jiàn):非难,诽谤。昆弟:兄弟。

【原文】6 南容三复白圭[1],孔子以其兄之子妻之[2]。

【白话译文】

南容把“白圭之玷,尚可磨也;斯言之玷,不可为也。”这几句《诗经》上的诗,读了又读,孔子便把自己的侄女嫁给他。

【英语译文】

There were several lines in *The Book of Songs* like this, "If there are stains on the white jade, they can be rid of by grinding. If there're mistakes in your words, you cannot retell them once again." Nan Rong read these lines once again, to whom Confucius' niece was betrothed by Confucius.

【注释】(1)南容:见5.2中注1。三复白圭:《诗·大雅·抑》云:"白圭之玷,尚可磨也;斯言之玷,不可为也。"诗意是:白圭上的污点,还可磨掉;言语中的污点,没法去掉。南容读诗到这里,反复诵读。足见他很欣赏诗意,能谨慎言行。《论语·公冶长篇第五》的第二章载:"子谓南容'邦有道不废,邦无道免于刑戮。'"(2)以其兄之子妻之:其兄,孔子哥哥孟皮。子,古代兼指儿女,此处单指"女"。妻,读qì,指嫁给。之,指他(南容)。

【原文】7 季康子问[1]:"弟子孰为好学[2]?"孔子对曰:"有颜回者好学[3],不幸短命死矣,今也则亡[4]。"

【白话译文】

季康子问道:"哪个学生算最好学?"孔子回答说:"有个颜回好学,不幸短命死了,现在没有这样的人了。"

【英语译文】

Ji Kangzi asked, "Which disciple of yours is most fond of learning?" Confucius replied, "Yan Hui was most fond of learning but it's unfortunately that he's dead. Nowadays there isn't such kind of man."

【注释】(1)季康子问:鲁哀公也曾提过此问(6.3)。孔子的回答比这里的详细。(2)为:在比较句中作谓语动词,含有"最""更"的意思。(3)者:用在名词后,表示停顿,去掉不译。(4)今也:也,语气助词。用在主语、时间名词或副词性词语后面,表提顿或停顿,可以译为"啊""呀"。也可以去掉不译。亡:读wú,指无、没有。

【原文】8 颜渊死[1],颜路请子之车以为之椁[2]。子曰:“才不才[3],亦各言其子也。鲤也死[4],有棺而无椁。吾不徒行以为之椁[5]。以吾从大夫之后[6],不可徒行也。”

【白话译文】

颜渊死了,他父亲颜路请求孔子变卖车子来给颜渊置办套在棺外的大棺。孔子说:“一个有才一个无才,但各自都是自己的儿子。我的儿子鲤死了,也只有内棺没有外椁。我不能卖车步行来替他买椁。因为我也曾做过大夫,是不可以步行的。”

【英语译文】

After Yan Yuan's death, his father Yan Lu asked Confucius to sell his own cart to buy a big coffin for Yan Yuan. Confucius said, “Whether talented or not, everybody thinks highly of his own son. After Kong Li, my son's death, there was only small coffin but no big coffin. I could not sell my cart to buy a big coffin for him because I was ever a minister of law and couldn't walk on foot.”

【注释】(1)颜渊:即颜回。(2)颜路:颜回之父,名无繇(yóu),春秋末鲁国人,少孔子六岁,是孔子开始教学时的学生。请子:求孔子。之车:变卖车子。以为之椁:用来给颜回置办套在棺外的大棺。棺,读 guān,殓尸体的器具。多以木材制作。椁,读 guǒ,古代棺材有的有两层,内层叫棺,外层叫椁。(3)才不才:有才能或无才能。(4)鲤:孔鲤,字伯鱼,孔子的儿子,年五十死,那时孔子年七十。(5)徒行:步行。(6)以:连词,表原因或理由,相当于“因为”“由于”。吾从大夫之后:孔子在鲁国曾经做过司寇,是大夫之位。孔子不说“我曾为大夫”而说“吾从大夫之后”(我跟在大夫行列后面行走)是一种谦逊的说法。

【原文】9 颜渊死,子曰:“噫[1]!天丧予!天丧予[2]!”

【白话译文】

颜渊死了,孔子悲叹道:“唉,天灭我!天灭我!”

【英语译文】

After Yan Yuan's death, Confucius sighed, “O! The heaven abolishes me! The heaven abolishes me!”

【注释】(1)噫(yī):叹词,表示悲痛或叹息。(2)天丧予:丧,读 sàng,灭亡。《书·大诰》:“天惟丧殷。”

【原文】10 颜渊死,子哭之恸[1]。从者曰:“子恸矣!”曰:“有恸乎[2]? 非夫人之为恸而谁为?”

【白话译文】

颜渊死了,孔子哭得极其伤心。跟随孔子的人说:“您太伤心了!”孔子说:“我太伤心了吗? 不为这样的人伤心,又为谁伤心呢?”

【英语译文】

After Yan Yuan's death, Confucius cried sadly. Men accompanying him said, “You're too sad!” Confucius asked, “Am I too sad? If I'm not sad for him, who deserved my sadness?”

【注释】(1)恸(tòng):极其悲痛。(2)有:作有无的“有”解,与作呈现、产生或发生某种情状解都通。(3)非夫人之为恸:夫,读 fú,用作代词时,可表示第三人称、可表示近指、可表示远指。在本句中,表示近指。夫人,即此人(指颜渊),之,结构助词。作为宾语前置的标志。夫人是介词为的宾语,“非夫人之为恸即非为夫人恸”。而:承接连词,指那么,又。谁为:在古汉语中,如果介词或者动词的宾语是疑问代词,一般都放在介词或者动词之前。所以,谁为即为谁。

【原文】11 颜渊死,门人欲厚葬之[1]。子曰:“不可。”门人厚葬之。子曰:“回也视予犹父[2],予不得视犹子也[3]。非我也,夫二三子也[4]。”

【白话译文】

颜渊死了,孔子的学生们想要很丰厚地埋葬他。孔子说:“不可以。”学生们很丰厚地埋葬了颜渊。孔子说:“颜回呀! 你看待我好像看待父亲一样,我却不能够像对待儿子一般看待你。不是我要这样干啊,是你那些同学干的。”

【英语译文】

After Yan Yuan's death his classmates intended to bury him with heavy rites. Confucius said, "You can't do that." But they did so. Confucius said, "O, Yan Hui. You regard me as your father but I cannot regard you as my son. It is not I who did that but your classmates did."

【注释】(1)门人:弟子,学生。厚葬:谓不惜财力为死者经营丧葬。孔子主张丧事要与家庭财力状况相称,家庭富裕,不可越礼厚葬,家庭紧迫,只要衣衾能遮盖尸体,入殓后即可下葬。(2)回也:也,语气助词。用在主语"回"后,表提顿或停顿。可译作"啊""呀"或去掉不译。视予:看待我,对待我。犹父:谓如同父亲。(3)不得:不能,没能。犹子:谓如同儿子。(4)夫(fú):语首助词,表发端,有调理语气和音节的作用,没有一定的实义。二三子:几个人(同学)。

【原文】12 季路问事鬼神[1]。子曰:"未能事人,焉能事鬼?"曰:"敢问死[2]。"曰:"未知生,焉知死?"

【白话译文】

子路问如何服侍鬼神。孔子说:"还没能够服侍活人,怎么能够去服侍死人?"子路说:"请让我大胆问问,死是怎么回事。"孔子说:"生的道理还没有弄明白,怎么能够懂得死?"

【英语译文】

Ji Lu asked how to attend ghosts. Confucius answered, "Since you didn't attend living men, how could you attend ghosts?" Zilu continued, "Let me bravely ask you that what death means." Confucius said, "Since we didn't comprehend living, how could I tell you what death means?"

【注释】(1)季路:(公元前542年—公元前480年),姓仲,名由,字子路,一字季路,孔子弟子。春秋末鲁国之卞(今山东泗水县东)人,出身贫贱,少孔子九岁,为孔门弟子中年龄较长者,性耿直好勇。事:服侍。鬼神:鬼和神,亦偏指鬼。迷信者以为人死后魂灵不灭,还在冥冥中活动着,继续干涉人间的事情。那不灭的魂灵就是鬼。神,指世俗所谓的"神灵""神仙"和宗教与神话中所指的"超自然体"。孔子是现实生活中诚实的人,对于不着边际的东西,绝不妄断言,绝不盲从。(2)敢:谦辞,犹冒昧。

【原文】13 闵子侍侧[1],誾誾如也[2];子路,行行如也[3];冉有、子贡,侃侃如也[4]。子乐。"若由也[5],不得其死然[6]。"

【白话译文】

闵子骞陪在孔子身边,模样恭敬正直;子路呢,刚强气盛;冉有、子贡呢,温和快乐。孔子很高兴。但他说道:"像仲由嘛,怕不得好死呢。"

【英语译文】

Min Ziqian attended Confucius with respect; Zilu did that with high spirit; Ran You and Zi Gong did that with humidity and cheer. Confucius was very glad but he said, "If you did things like Zhong You you'll die awfully."

【注释】(1)侍侧:陪侍左右。下文子路、冉有、子贡后省略了"侍侧"。(2)誾誾如:誾誾,读 yínyín,誾誾如,恭敬正直的样子。如,形容词词尾,义同"然",表状态。(3)行行如:行行,读 hànghàng,行行如,刚强负气的样子。(4)侃侃如:侃侃读 kǎnkǎn,侃侃如,温和快乐的样子。(5)若由也:像子路这样。(6)不得其死然:得死,当时俗语,谓得善终(正常死亡)。然,语气助词。和"焉"差不多,有郑重其事以告人,使人深信不疑的意味。可译作"呢",或去掉不译。

【原文】14 鲁人为长府[1]。闵子骞曰:"仍旧惯[2],如之何?何必改作[3]?"子曰:"夫人不言,言必有中[4]。"

【白话译文】

鲁国重修国库。闵子骞说:"照老样子利用下去怎么样?为什么一定要改修呢?"孔子说:"这个人不爱谈论,一谈论就必然击中要害。"

【英语译文】

While Lu State rebuilding its treasury, Min Ziqian asked, "How about just use it in old way? Why must it be rebuilt?" Confucius said, "This man doesn't like commenting things. He'll hit the point as he does so."

【注释】(1)鲁人:"鲁人"的"人"指鲁国的执政大臣而言。这是"人"和"民"对称时的区别。民不含有官位的人。长府:藏财货武器的府库。长,读 cháng。

(2)仍旧贯:仍,指沿袭、依照。旧贯:原来的样子、旧制度、旧办法。(3)改作:更改,变更。(4)夫人:夫:代词,这里表近指,这、这个(这些)。此外还可表第三人称或远指。夫人,即这人、这个人。不言:不谈论。有中:犹言"中肯""中的"。有,于此用作动词词头。

【原文】15 子曰:"由之瑟奚为于丘之门[1]?"门人不敬子路。子曰:"由也升堂矣,未入于室也[2]。"

【白话译文】

孔子说:"仲由的瑟为什么拿到我孔丘门前来弹拨呢?"孔子的学生因此不尊敬子路。孔子说:"仲由么,德行和学问已经不错了,只是还不够精深罢了。"

【英语译文】

Confucius asked, "Why did Zhong You play his harp in front of my door?" Due to this, Confucius' disciples didn't respect Zhong You. Confucius said, "Zhong You has made achievement in learning and virtue but not so deep."

【注释】(1)瑟(sè):拨弦乐器。春秋时已流行,形似古琴,但无徽位(指示音节的标志),有五十弦,二十五弦,十五弦等种。今瑟有二十五弦、十六弦二种,每弦有一柱。奚(xī):为何,为什么。为:弹拨,演奏。丘:孔子自谓其名。门:门前,门口。(2)升堂矣未入于室也:这是一句比喻话。"堂"是正厅,"室"是内室。生活中总是先入门,次升堂,然后入室,这可用来表示做学问的几个阶段。今天民间还流行"他的手艺登堂了;他已经学到家了。"(登堂即升堂,犹言相当好;到家,犹言入室,意谓极好,没有缺陷。)

【原文】16 子贡问:"师与商也孰贤[1]?"子曰:"师也过[2],商也不及[3]。"曰:"然则师愈与[4]?"子曰:"过犹不及[5]。"

【白话译文】

子贡问:"子张与子夏谁更贤能?"孔子说:"子张做事过分,子夏做事分量不足。"子贡说:"那么,子张比子夏贤一些吧?"孔子说:"过分和分量不够是一样的,没恰到好处。"

【英语译文】

Zi Gong asked, "Who's more able and virtuous, Zi Zhang or Zi Xia?" Confucius said, "Zi Zhang does things excessively but Zi Xia does things insufficiently." Zi Gong said, "Then Zi Zhang should be more able and virtuous than Zi Xia." Confucius said, "Excessiveness just equals insufficiency, being not appropriateness."

【注释】(1)师与商也孰贤:师:孔子弟子,姓颛孙,名师,字子张,亦单称张,春秋末陈国阳城(今河南省淮阳)人,少孔子四十八岁。商:孔子弟子,姓卜,名商,字子夏。后亦称卜子夏。少孔子四十四岁。也:用在句子中间表示停顿。下面的"也"同。(2)过:过分,太甚。(3)不及:分量不够,赶不上。(4)然则:连词。连接句子,表示连贯关系。犹"如此,那么"或"那么"。愈(yù):贤,胜过。与:读 yú,同"欤",语气词。这里是表示商榷性的询问(或委婉的推测),可译为"吧"。(5)过犹不及:过分和分量不够是一样的没恰到好处。用"射击"或"秤轻重"为例,说明无论干什么,道理都一样"过犹不及"十分明显。

【原文】17 季氏富于周公[1],而求也为之聚敛而附益之[2]。子曰:"非吾徒也。小子鸣鼓而攻之[3]。"

【白话译文】

季氏比周公还富,而冉求还在替他搜刮钱财,使其增加更多的财富。孔子说:"冉求已不是我的学生了,同学们可以公开他的罪过,严厉地攻击他。"

【英语译文】

Ji Sun is wealthier than Duke Zhou but Ran Qiu is helping him to collect and accumulate more wealth. Upon this, Confucius said, "Ran Qiu isn't my disciple already and you disciples can disclose his guilt and attack him violently."

【注释】(1)季氏:即季孙氏。鲁桓公之子季友之后裔。周公:有两说:一指周公旦;也泛指在周天子左右做卿士的人,如周公黑肩、周公阅之类。(2)聚敛而附益之:谓急于敛取赋税以增加财富。事实可参阅左传哀公十一年和十二年文。季氏要用田赋制度增加赋税,使冉求征求孔子的意见,孔子则主张"施取其厚,事举其中,敛从其薄"。结果冉求仍旧听从季氏,实行田赋制度。《礼记·大学》说:"百乘之家,不畜聚敛之臣。与其有聚敛之臣,宁有盗臣。"可见儒家反对对人民的剥削。其思想渊源,可能本于此章。(3)小子:这里指学生等晚辈。鸣鼓而攻:谓宣布罪状而加以声讨。

【原文】18 子曰:“柴也愚[1],参也鲁[2],师也辟[3],由也喭[4]。”

【白话译文】

孔子说:“高柴愚笨,曾参迟钝,颛孙师偏激,仲由鲁莽。”

【英语译文】

Confucius said, “Gao Chai is stupid, Zeng Shen is wit-slow, Zhuansun Shi goes to excreme thought-sided, and Zhong You is rude.”

【注释】(1)柴:高柴(公元前521年—?),姓高,名柴,字子羔,孔子学生,少孔子三十岁。愚:愚昧。(2)参:(前505—公元前434),姓曾,名参,字子舆,少孔子四十六岁。鲁:笨拙。(3)师:参见11.16中注1。辟:读pì,偏执。(4)由:即子路。喭:读yàn,指鲁莽、粗俗。

【原文】19 子曰:“回也其庶乎[1],屡空[2]。赐不受命[3],而货殖焉[4],亿则屡中[5]。”

【白话译文】

孔子说:“颜回,他的学问道德差不多了吧,却是常常穷困。端木赐不认命,有求富意愿而去经商营利,料事常常准确。”

【英语译文】

Confucius said, “Yan Hui has achieved much in his learning but he's always in poverty. Duanmu Ci doesn't believe in fate and does business wishing to be rich and he always predicts things accurately.”

【注释】(1)其:代词。表第三人称领属关系,相当于他(她,它)的,或他(她,它)们的。庶:将近,差不多。(2)屡空:常常穷困。屡:读lǚ,多次,常常。空:读kòng,穷困;贫乏。赐:端木赐(公元前520年—公元前456年),姓端木,名赐,字子贡,也作子赣,亦称卫赐,春秋末卫国人,孔子学生,少孔子三十一岁。(3)不受命:不相信天命、不认命,有求富欲望。(4)货殖:谓经商营利。(5)亿:同“臆”,指臆测,揣度。亿则屡中:料事常常准确。

【原文】20 子张问善人之道[1]。子曰:“不践迹[2],亦不入于室[3]。”

【白话译文】

子张问做善人走什么路。孔子说:“做善人,不踩前人的足迹是不能到家的。”

【英语译文】

Zi Zhang asked how to be a philanthropic man. Confucius told him, “To be a philanthropic man, one cannot arrive at his goal if he doesn't follow footprint of predecessors.”

【注释】(1)善人:有道德的人,善良的人。道:方法,途径。(2)践迹:踩着前人的足迹。谓蹈袭,因袭。(3)入于室:义同“入室”,谓进入深奥精微之境,俗话说“到家”。

【原文】21 子曰:“论笃是与[1],君子者乎? 色庄者乎[2]?”

【白话译文】

孔子说:“言论忠诚老实的人受到推许,这种人是君子呢? 还是表面上严肃的人?”

【英语译文】

Confucius said, “A man whose words are loyal and honest is praised. Is he a moral man or a superficially serious man?”

【注释】(1)论笃:言论笃实(淳厚朴实,忠诚老实),亦指言论笃实的人。是:助词,用在宾语和它的动词之间,起着把宾语提前达到强调的作用。与:动词,指称赞、推许。“论笃是与”即“与论笃”这句借“是”字的作用,把宾语提到了前面。(2)君子者:者,用在名词后表停顿。色庄者:者,用在形容词后,组成者字结构,表示人、事、物。这里表示人。色庄者,谓面色严肃的人,面色严肃内心未必正经。

【原文】22 子路问:“闻斯行诸[1]?”子曰:“有父兄在,如之何其闻斯行之?”冉有问:“闻斯行诸?”子曰:“闻斯行之。”公西华曰:“由也问闻斯行诸,子曰,‘有父兄在';求也问闻斯行诸,子曰,'闻斯行之'。赤也惑,敢问[2]。"子曰:"求也退[3],故进之[4];由也兼人[5],故退之[6]。"

【白话译文】

子路问:"听说该干的事就干起来吗?"孔子说:"你有爸爸、哥哥活着,怎么能听说就干起来?"冉有问:"听说该干的事就干起来吗?"孔子说:"听说就干起来。"公西华说:"仲由问听说该干的事就干起来吗,您说他有爸爸、哥哥活着,不能这样做;冉求也问同样的问题,您却说'听说就干起来',我有些糊涂,冒昧地来问问。"孔子说:"冉求做事退缩,我要激励他;仲由胆量大,做事猛进,我要使他退一退,稳步而行。"

【英语译文】

Zi Lu asked, "Should I take action right away upon hearing something ought to be done?" Confucius said, "Since your father and elder brother are still alive how should you take action at once?" Ran You asked, "Should I take action right away upon hearing something ought to be done?" Confucius said, "Yes, you can do that." Gongxi Hua asked, "When Zi Lu asked for your opinion, you responded that he shouldn't do it since his father and elder brother are alive; but when Ran You asked the same question, you said he can take action right away. Now I'm confused. So I dare to ask you for the reason." Confucius said, "I will encourage Ran You because he's always reluctant to do things; whereas I will discourage Zi Lu because he's bold doing things, thus he can do things smoothly."

【注释】(1)闻斯行诸:闻,听说。斯,连词,则,指乃、就。行诸,行之(实行它,把它干起来)。诸,代词,用作宾语,相当于"之",用作定语相当于"其"。(2)敢问:大胆地问,冒昧地问。(3)退:畏缩,退缩。(4)进之:激励他。(5)兼人:胜过他人,能力倍于他人,行事猛进。(6)退之:使他退一退。

【原文】23 子畏于匡[1],颜渊后[2]。子曰:"吾以女为死矣[3]。"曰:"子在,回何敢死[4]?"

【白话译文】

孔子被匡地人错误围困,颜渊失散在后。孔子说:"我以为你已经死了呢!"颜渊说:“老师在,我怎么敢死?”

【英语译文】

Confucius was besieged mistakenly by people in Kuang with Yan Yuan lagging behind. Confucius said, “I thought you'd been dead!” Yan Yuan responded, “You are alive; how dare I to die?”

【注释】(1)畏:通“围”,围困。于:介词,“被”,表示被动。匡:古地名。这里匡后省略了“人”字。(2)后:朱熹《四书集注》:“后,谓相失在后。”(3)女:同“汝”。(4)何敢死:谓我怎么敢于死亡,碰到变故,应当与老师共存亡。

【原文】24 季子然问[1]:“仲由、冉求可谓大臣与[2]?”子曰:“吾以子为异之问[3],曾由与求之问[4]。所谓大臣者,以道事君,不可则止。今由与求也,可谓具臣矣。”曰:“然则从之者与[5]?”子曰:“弑父与君[6],亦不从也。”

【白话译文】

季子然问:“仲由和冉求可以说是大臣吗?”孔子说:“我以为你要提别的问题,竟然是问由和求。我们所说的大臣,他用公道、仁德辅佐君主,如果不行就不干。如今由和求,可算充数的臣子了。”季子然说:“那么,他俩便是听从我们季氏的人吗?”孔子说:“杀父亲、杀君主,他们也不会听从的。”

【英语译文】

Ji Ziran asked, “Can we say that Zhong You and Ran Qiu are courtiers?” Confucius answered, “I thought you asked other questions and it's about them. By courtiers we mean that they can assist their monarch by means of fairness and virtue. If they cannot do this, they can't be courtiers. Nowadays Zhong You and Ran Qiu can roughly be ranked among courtiers.” Ji Ziran said, “Then, they are the men who obey our order?” Confucius said, “They wouldn't obey any order to kill their monarch or parents.”

【注释】(1)季子然:季氏的子弟。(2)与:读 yú,语气词,同“欤”。(3)以子:认为你。为异之问:提出别的问题。为,行为动词,随上下文含义很活。异,指其他,别的。之,助词,一般用在定语和中心词之间,相当于现代汉语的助词“的”。问,名词,指问题。(4)曾:读 zēng,副词,指乃,竟。与:读 yǔ,连词,和。之:结构助词,标志宾语前置。问,这里是动词。(5)具臣:充数之臣。(6)然则:那么。从之者:听从季氏的人。(7)弑:读 shì,古代卑幼杀死尊长叫弑。多指臣子杀死君主,子女杀死父母。

【原文】25 子路使子羔为费宰[1]。子曰:"贼夫人之子[2]。"子路曰:"有民人焉[3],有社稷焉[4],何必读书,然后为学?"子曰:"是故恶佞者[5]。"

【白话译文】

子路叫子羔去做费邑官长。孔子说:"这是害别人的儿子。"子路说:"那里有老百姓,有土神和谷神,为何一定要读书才算做学问呢?"孔子说:"所以我讨厌狡辩的人。"

【英语译文】

Zi Lu asked Zi Gao to be magistrate in Fei District. Confucius said, "You are doing harm on other's son." Zi Lu said, "In that place there are subjects and gods of land and grain, and why should he just read books and then conduct study?" Confucius said, "That's why I hate people who excuse himself."

【注释】(1)子羔:即高柴。费宰:费邑官长。(2)贼:害,伤害。夫(fú):语气助词,舒缓语气,一般去掉不译。(3)民人:人民,百姓。社稷:古代帝王、诸侯所祭的土神和谷神。社,土神;稷,谷神。社稷一般沿用为国家的代称。(5)是故:连词,指因此,所以。佞者:狡辩的人。

【原文】26 子路、曾皙、冉有、公西华侍坐[1]。子曰:"以吾一日长乎尔,毋吾以也[2]。居则曰[3]:'不吾知也!'如或知尔,则何以哉[4]?"子路率尔而对曰[5]:"千乘之国摄乎大国之间[6],加之以师旅[7],因之以饥馑[8];由也为之,比及三年[9],可使有勇,且知方也[10]。"夫子哂之[11]。"求!尔何如?"对曰:"方六七十[12],如五六十[13],求也为之,比及三年,可使足民。如其礼乐,以俟君子[14]。""赤!尔何如?"对曰:"非曰能之,愿学焉。宗庙之事,如会同,端章甫,原为小相焉[15]。""点!尔何如?"鼓瑟希,铿尔,舍瑟而作[16],对曰:"异乎三子者之撰[17]。"子曰:"何伤乎[18]?亦各言其志也[19]。"曰:"莫春者,春服既成[20],冠者五六人,童子六七人,浴乎沂[21],风乎舞雩[22],咏而归。"夫子喟然叹曰[23]:"吾与点也[24]!"三子出曾皙后。曾皙曰:"夫三子者之言何如?”子曰:“亦各言其志也矣。”曰:“夫子何哂由也?”曰:“为国以礼,其言不让,是故哂之。”“唯求则非邦也与[25]?”“安见方六七十如五六十而非邦也者?”“唯赤则非邦也与?”“宗庙会同,非诸侯而何? 赤也为之小,孰能为之大[26]?”

【白话译文】

子路、曾皙、冉有、公西华四个人陪着孔子坐在一块儿。孔子说:“由于我年纪比你们都稍大一点,不要为这个而拘束吧。平时,你们说没人了解自己,如果有人了解你们,你们将怎么样呢?”子路急忙答道:“一千辆兵车的国家,夹处于大国之间,外面有军队侵犯,国内又加以饥荒;我去治理,大约三年,可使人人有勇气,个个懂道义。”孔子微微笑了笑。又问:“冉求,你怎么样?”回答说:“方圆六七十里或者五六十里的地方,我去治理,大约三年,可使人人富足,但是振兴礼乐,这就要等待贤人君子了。”又问:“公西赤,你怎么样?”回答说:“不是说我能干,我愿意学习这样干:祭祀活动或者盟会活动,我愿意穿着礼服带着礼貌做一个赞礼和司仪的小官。”又问:“曾点,你怎么样?”他弹瑟逐渐稀疏,铿的一声停止了弹拨,站起来回答说:“我和他们三位的才能不同。”孔子说:“那有什么妨碍呢? 只是各谈各的志向而已。”曾皙说:“暮春三月,春天的衣服都穿定了,邀五六位成年人,带六七个小孩,到沂水里洗洗澡,在舞雩台下乘乘凉,一路唱着歌走回来。”孔子大声长叹说:“我赞同曾点的想法呀。”子路、冉有、公西华三人退出了,曾皙后走。曾皙问道:“三位同学的话怎么样?”孔子说:“只是各谈各的志向而已呀。”曾皙再问:“您为什么对仲由微笑呢?”孔子说:“治国讲求礼让,可是他的话一点也不谦虚,所以笑笑他。”曾皙又问:“冉求所讲的不是国家吗?”孔子说:“怎样见得纵横六七十里或者五六十里的土地就不是一个国家呢?”曾皙又问:“公西赤所讲的不是国家吗?”孔子说:“有宗庙,有国家间的盟会,不是国家是什么? 如果公西赤只能做小傧相,谁能做大傧相呢?”

【英语译文】

Zi Lu, Zeng Xi, Ran You and Gongxi Hua were sitting together with Confucius. Confucius said, “Don't be restrained because I' m older than you. You usually say that nobody knows you. But if somebody has known you what will you do?” Zi Lu hurried to reply, “If a state of one thousand fighting carts was besieged among big states while evasion outside and famine inside took place at the same time, I' ll just spend three years on making its people brave and rites-aware.” Confucius just smiled a little bit. Then he asked, “How about you, Ran You?” Ran You answered, “As for a state about four thousand square *li*, if I administrate it, I'll use three years to make everyone well off. But in order to spread rites and music, I should invite able and virtuous man." Then Confucius continued, "How about you, Gongxi Hua?" Gongxi Hua answered, "It's not that I can but I'll learn to do like this: I'm willing to wear ritual gown and hat to attend sacrificial and alliance activities, being a small official to host the ceremony." Confucius continued, "Zeng Dian, how about you?" On fading of his playing *se* gradually, he stood up slowly, then answered, "I have different abilities from theirs." Confucius said, "It doesn't matter. Just talk about your own ambition." Zeng Xi sid, "In late spring, after putting on spring clothes, I will invite five or six adults leading six or seven kids to bathe in Yi River and enjoy coolness under Wuyu Altar. After doing these we'll come back singing songs." Confucius sighed loudly, "I agree to Zeng Dian' idea." Zi Lu, Ran You and Gongxi Hua retreated with Zeng Xi lagging behind. Zeng Xi asked, "How about three classmates' words?" Confucius answered, "They just talk about their own ambition." Zeng Xi asked again, "Why did you smile at Zi Lu?" Confucius said, "It needs rites to administrate a state but Zi Lu knows little about it. Therefore I smile at him." Zeng Xi asked once more, "Isn't a state what Ran You talked about?" Confucius said, "How can we say that a place about four thousand square *li* isn't a state?" Zeng Xi continued, "Isn't a state what Gongxi Hua talked about?" Confucius answered, "There are temple and alliance activities, how can we say it isn't a state? If Gongxi Hua can be just a small official to host the ceremony, who can be a big one?"

【注释】(1)曾晳:姓曾,名点(又作蒧),字子晳,曾子父亲,也是孔子学生。公西华:即公西赤(公元前 509 年—?),孔子弟子,姓公西,名赤,字子华,亦称公西华,春秋末鲁国人。少孔子四十二岁。侍坐:在尊长近旁陪坐;也指尊长坐着,己站立侍候。(2)以:由于,因为。一日长:犹"一日之长",年龄比别人稍大。乎:相当于介词"于"。尔:你,你们。毋(wú):副词,指莫、不可,表禁止。以:认为。(3)居则曰:平素家居时即说。则,副词。即,就。(4)不吾知也:本句宾语提前,加以强调,还原为"不知吾也!"如或:如果,如果有。则:连词,指就、那么。何以:用什么,怎么。(5)率尔(shuàiěr):不经心而急速的样子。(6)摄乎:夹处于。(7)师旅:古代军队编制,借指军队或战事。(8)因:增添,累积。饥馑(jījǐn):庄稼收成极差或颗粒无收。(9)比及:及至,等到(指将来);未及,未等到(指已往)。(10)知方:知礼法,知道正确的行为方向。(11)哂(shěn):微笑。(12)方六七十:方,古时计量用语,表示纵横若干长度。"方六七十"犹言纵横六七十里(或方圆六七十里)。(13)如五六十:如,连词,表示选择关系,是或者的意思。如五六十,犹言或者纵横五六十里(或方圆五六十里)。如其礼乐:如,连词,表示转折关系,相当于"然如""至于""但是"。以俟:以,代词,此,这。(14)俟,读 sì,动词,指等待。(15)宗庙之事:祭祀活动。如会同:如,连词,表示并列关系,指和、与。端章甫:端,指玄端,古代一种黑色礼服。祭祀时,天子、诸侯、士大夫,都穿这种礼服。章甫,商代的玄冠,古人沿用为礼貌。"端章甫"是个修饰句,在古代可以不用动词。如果添上动词当为"穿端戴章甫"。小相:相,读 xiàng,傧相,祭祀和会盟时主持赞礼和司仪的官;相有卿、大夫、士三级,小相是士这一级。(16)希:同"稀",指弹瑟的速度放慢,节奏逐渐稀疏。铿尔(kēngěr):象声词,形容金石玉木等所发出的洪亮的声音。舍瑟:停止拨瑟。作:起,起立。(17)异乎:不同于。撰(zhuàn):才具,才能。(18)伤:妨碍。(19)亦:副词,指仅仅、只是。(20)莫春者:莫春,即暮春。春末,多指农历三月。者,用于名词后表停顿。春服:春日穿的衣服。既成:已经完成,已经成为。这里是说春日的衣服已经穿定了。(21)冠者:冠,读 guàn,冠者,二十岁以上的成年人。浴乎沂:沐浴于沂水中。沂,古水名,源出山东省曲阜市东南的尼山,西流至滋阳县合于泗水。(22)风乎舞雩:风,读 fèng,被风吹,受风。引申为"乘凉"。舞雩,读 wǔyú,指舞雩台。《水经注》:"沂水北对稷门。……杜预曰:本名稷门,僖公更高大之,今犹不与诸门同,改名高门也。……亦曰雩门。门南隔水,有雩坛。坛高三丈,曾点所欲风舞处也。"此台(坛)当在今曲阜市南。(23)喟然:大声长叹的样子。(24)与:赞同。(25)唯:语首助词。(26)之:代词,同"其"。

颜渊篇第十二(共二十四章)

本篇共计 24 章,主要是孔子的几位弟子问他怎样才是仁,这些内容是经常被引用的。孔子还谈到怎样算是君子等问题。

【原文】1 颜渊问仁。子曰:"克己复礼为仁[1]。一日克己复礼[2],天下归仁焉[3]。为仁由己[4],而由人乎哉[5]?"颜渊曰:"请问其目[6]。"子曰:"非礼勿视,非礼勿听,非礼勿言,非礼勿动。"颜渊曰:"回虽不敏,请事斯语矣。[7]"

【白话译文】

颜渊问什么是仁。孔子说："抑制一己之私、复兴礼制和礼节就是仁。如果有一天复兴了礼制和礼节,天下众人都会称许你是仁人。行仁全凭自己,还能凭别人吗?"颜渊说:"请问行仁有哪些条目?"孔子说:"不合礼的不看,不合礼的不听,不合礼的不说,不合礼的不动。"颜渊说:"我虽然迟钝,请让我实践您这话。"

【英语译文】

Yan Yuan asked what humanity is. Confucius said, "To restrain one's own interest and to revive rites can reach humanity. As soon as rites are revived some day, all common people will praise that you are humane. To practice humanity depends on yourself not on others." Yan Yuan asked, "What are the essentials to do that?" Confucius said, "Don't do indecorous things, don't listen to indecorous things, don't say indecorous things and don't act upon indecorous things." Yan Yuan said, "Even though I am stupid let me practice your words."

【注释】(1)克己:抑制一己之私。复礼:复兴礼制和礼节。为:算作,算是。(2)一日:一旦,如果有一天。(3)天下:指天下众人。归仁:称许为仁人。(4)为仁:行仁,实践仁。(5)而由人乎哉:而,读 néng,通"能"。乎哉,语气助词,这里表示设问。(6)请问:敬辞,用于请求对方解答问题。目:条目,要目,纲目,细目。(7)请事:请,敬辞,这里表示自己愿意做某事而请求对方允许。事:实践,从事。

【原文】2 仲弓问仁[1]。子曰:"出门如见大宾[2],使民如承大祭[3]。己所不欲[4],勿施于人[5]。在邦无怨[6],在家无怨[7]。"仲弓曰:"雍虽不敏,请事斯语矣。"

【白话译文】

仲弓问什么是仁。孔子说:"走出自家门,就像会见国宾一样庄敬不苟,使唤百姓就像承办重大祭祀一样严肃认真。自己不情愿的事物,不要扔与他人。在国家工作岗位上没有怨恨,居于家没有国家工作,也没有怨恨。"仲弓说:"我虽迟钝,请让我践行您这话。"

【英语译文】

Zhong Gong asked what humanity is. Confucius said, "Going out of home, you should behave seriously like meeting state guest; and summoning common people, you should act gravely as hosting important sacrificial ceremony. Don't force others what you don't desire. You should not complain or hate anything while you are in official post or just at home." Zhong Gong said, "Even though I am stupid, let me practice your words."

【注释】(1)仲弓:即冉雍。参见6.1中注1。(2)出门:外出,走出门外。大宾:泛指国宾(国家的贵重客人)。(3)大祭:古代的重大祭祀,包括天地之祭、禘祫(dìxiá)之祭(帝王祭祀祖先的隆重礼仪)等。(4)所不欲:不情愿的事物。(5)施:施加;扔与。(6)在邦:在国家工作岗位上。(7)在家:居于家,没有国家工作。

【原文】3 司马牛问仁[1]。子曰:"仁者,其言也讱[2]。"曰:"其言也讱,斯谓之仁矣乎?"子曰:"为之难[3],言之得无讱乎[4]?"

【白话译文】

司马牛问什么是仁。孔子说:"有仁德的人,说话谨慎迟缓。"司马牛说:"说话谨慎迟缓,这就叫作仁了吗?"孔子说:"做事包括行仁不容易,说话能不谨慎迟缓吗?"

【英语译文】

Sima Niu asked what humanity is. Confucius said, "A man of humanity speaks cautiously and slowly." Sima Niu said, "Is it regarded as humanity to speak cautiously and slowly?" Confucius said, "It isn't easy to do things humanistically. So how shouldn't one speak cautiously and slowly?"

【注释】(1)司马牛:孔子弟子。姓司马名耕字子牛,亦称司马牛。春秋末宋国人。《史记·仲尼弟子列传》:"司马耕,字子牛。牛多言而躁,问仁于孔子。"(2)讱(rèn):出言谨慎迟缓。(3)为之难:做事包括行仁不容易。(4)言之:说话。得无:能不。

【原文】4 司马牛问君子。子曰:"君子不忧不惧。"曰:"不忧不惧,斯谓之君子矣乎?"子曰:"内省不疚[1],夫何忧何惧[2]?"

【白话译文】

司马牛问怎样做一个君子。孔子说:"君子不忧愁,不恐惧。"司马牛说:"不忧愁、不恐惧就是君子了吗?"孔子说:"没有过失,问心无愧,有什么忧愁、什么恐惧呢?”

【英语译文】

Sima Niu asked how to become a moral man. Confucius said, “A moral man doesn't worry or fear anything.” Sima Niu asked, “Does a moral man not worry or fear anything?” Confucius said, “He has no errors and isn't regretful for anything. What on earth will he worry or fear?”

【注释】(1)内省:内心自我反省。不疚:没有愧疚。不,没有。疚,读 jiù,因有过失而感到内心惭愧痛苦。(2)夫:助词,用于句首,表示发端。何忧何惧:有什么忧愁、什么恐惧呢?

【原文】5 司马牛忧曰:“人皆有兄弟,我独亡[1]。”子夏曰:“商闻之矣[2]:生死有命[3],富贵在天[4]。君子敬而无失[5],与人恭而有礼[6]。四海之内[7],皆兄弟也:君子何患乎无兄弟也[8]?”

【白话译文】

司马牛忧愁地说:“别人都有兄弟,只是我没有。”子夏说:“我听说过:生死由命运把关,富贵凭机遇开门。君子尊重别人和万事万物的价值,不出差错,待人接物不傲慢,有礼节,天下到处,都是兄弟:君子怎么会担心有到没有兄弟呢?”

【英语译文】

Sima Niu said sadly, “Other people have brothers but I don't have.” Zi Xia said, “I have heard the following words: life or death is controlled by fate and being wealthy and noble depends on natural laws. A moral man respects value of other people and of things doesn't make mistakes and he unconceitedly deals with people and affairs according to rites. He has brothers everywhere-how could he worry that he has no brothers?”

【注释】(1)亡(wú):无,没有。(2)子夏、商:子夏姓卜,名商,字子夏,后亦称卜子夏、卜先生,孔子弟子,少孔子四十四岁。(3)生死有命:生死,指人的出生死亡和寿年。有,同下文“在”同义。命,与下文“天”互文见义,即“天命”。(4)富贵在天:富贵,富裕而显贵,犹言有财有势。在天,依存于天命。所谓“天命”除开神话和迷信,实际是大自然和人类社会发展的千变万化的规律,这个规律不是一个人可以随心所欲的。(5)敬:尊重人和事物的价值。(6)与人:对待别人。(7)四海之内:古代以中国四境有海环绕,四海之内,犹言天下,全国各地。(8)患:忧虑;担心。乎:于。

【原文】6 子张问明[1]。子曰:"浸润之谮[2],肤受之愬[3],不行焉[4],可谓明也已矣。浸润之谮,肤受之愬,不行焉,可谓远也已矣[5]。"

【白话译文】

子张问怎样才叫明白人。孔子说:"像水逐渐浸润一样隐缓传播的谗言,和像皮肤受到刺激一样恶毒的诽谤,都在你这里行不通,那你可算明白人了。像水逐渐浸润一样隐缓传播的谗言,和像皮肤受到刺激一样恶毒的诽谤,都在你这里行不通,那你可算见识高远的人了。"

【英语译文】

Zi Zhang asked how to be a sensible person. Confucius said, "You are a sensible person if slander cannot reach you, which spreads like water invasion and which causes pain like your skin being stang. You are an insightful person if slander cannot reach you, which spreads like water invasion and which causes pain like your skin being stang."

【注释】(1)明:明白。(2)浸润之谮:谮,读 zèn,指谗毁、诬陷。(3)肤受之愬:像皮肤受到刺激一样恶毒的诽谤。愬,读 sù,指诽谤、控告。不行:犹言行不通。(5)远:指见识高远。

【原文】7 子贡问政。子曰:"足食,足兵[1],民信之矣[2]。"子贡曰:"必不得已而去[3],于斯三者何先[4]?"曰:"去兵。"子贡曰:"必不得已而去,于斯二者何先?"曰:"去食。自古皆有死,民无信不立[5]。"

【白话译文】

子贡问怎样治理政事。孔子说:"充足粮食,充足军备,让百姓信任吧。"子贡说:"如果必须,不得不舍弃一项,在这三项中,先舍弃哪一项?"孔子说:"舍弃军备。"子贡说;"如果必须,不得不舍弃一项,在粮食和百姓的信任两项中,舍弃哪一项?"孔子说:"舍弃粮食。自古以来,谁都免不了死亡。如果百姓不相信政府,国家是站立不住的。”

【英语译文】

Zi Gong asked how to deal with administrative affairs. Confucius answered, “Let common people trust administration by means of plenty armaments and plenty food.” Zi Gong asked, “If one of the three things needs to be abandoned; which will go first?” Confucius answered, “Armaments.” Zi Gong asked, “If one of the two things, food and people's trust, needs to be abandoned; which will go first?” Confucius answered, “Food. Nobody could dodge death ever since ancient time. A state couldn't establish itself if people don't trust the government.”

【注释】(1)足兵:充足军备。(2)民信之矣:百姓相信政府吧。(3)必不得已:“必”和“不得已”同义复用,表示强调,犹言必须,出于无奈不能不。而:结构助词,用于状语和中心词之间表示偏正关系。去:舍弃,去掉。(4)何先:省略了动词“去”,“何”是宾语前置。“何先去”相当于现代汉语“先去哪一个”。(5)民无信:百姓不相信政府。不立:指国家立不住。

【原文】8 棘子成曰[1]:“君子质而已矣[2],何以文为[3]?”子贡曰:“惜乎,夫子之说[4]!君子也,驷不及舌[5]!文犹质也,质犹文也[6]。虎豹之鞟犹犬羊之鞟[7]。”

【白话译文】

棘子成说:“君子只要有好的本质就够了,要那些表面文采干什么?”子贡说:“很遗憾,先生这个说法不对!君子啊,一言既出,驷马难追。本质和文采,同时存在。虎豹犬羊的文采是各自皮上的毛;去了毛的虎豹犬羊皮,不好辨认。因为它们已经不是虎豹犬羊的质与文了。君子的文采与君子的本质同在。”

【英语译文】

Ji Zi cheng said, “For a moral man only good essence is enough; and what's the use of grace?” Zi Gong said, “It's a pity that your opinion is wrong! For a moral man, if he utters words, four horses cannot catch up with it. Essence and grace coexist at the same time. The grace of tiger, puma, dog and goat is their hair; if they are unhaired, it's hard to recognize them. Because they don't have the essence and grace of tiger, puma, dog and goat any more. Therefore essence and grace of a moral man coexist at the same time."

【注释】(1)棘子成:卫国大夫。(2)君子:古代,君子所指有两类人,一类是统治者和贵族男子,一类是泛称才德出众的人。质:朴实,淳朴,本质,性能。(3)何以文为:要文干什么。文,指文华、文采。人的外表、风度、仪节。惜乎:可惜呀,表示遗憾。(4)夫子:古代对男子的敬称。这里是子贡面对棘子成的指称。说:评论,言论。"惜乎,夫子之说!"是倒装句。夫子之说,是主语,惜乎,是谓语。(5)君子也:是主语部分。也,是语气助词,用在主语后表提顿或停顿,可译作啊、呀,也可去掉不译。驷不及舌,是谓语部分;驷,这里代指四匹马所驾的车。不及,赶不上。舌,代指语言。(6)文犹质也,质犹文也:谓文与质同在。有质即有文,有文即有质;无文即无质,无质即无文。不可偏废。(7)虎豹之鞟,犹犬羊之鞟:去了毛的虎豹皮看上去和去了毛的犬羊皮相像,都不是原来的虎豹犬羊了;难于区别。因为虎豹犬羊之鞟的质与文已经不是虎豹犬羊的质与文了。鞟,读 kuò,去了毛的皮、皮革。

【原文】9 哀公问于有若曰[1]:"年饥[2],用不足如之何[3]?"有若对曰:"盍彻乎[4]?"曰:"二,吾犹不足[5],如之何其彻也[6]?"对曰:"百姓足,君孰与不足?百姓不足,君孰与足?"

【白话译文】

鲁哀公问到有若:"年成不好,国家用度不够,应该怎么办?"有若回答道:"为何不实行十分抽一的税率呢?"哀公说:"十分抽二,我还不够用,怎么能十分抽一呢?"有若回答道:"如果百姓够用,您怎么会不够?如果百姓不够用,您怎么会够?"

【英语译文】

Aigong of Lu State asked You Ruo, "What should I do when my state lacks supplies in a famine year?" You Ruo answered, "Why don't you implement the policy of taxing at the rate of one tenth?" Aigong said, "How can I do that if I don't have enough supplies even taxing at the rate of two tenths?" You Ruo answered, "How could you lack anything if common people have enough supplies? How could you have enough supplies if they lack much?"

【注释】(1)哀公:鲁国君主。有若:(公元前518年—?)孔子晚年弟子,姓有,名若,字子有,春秋末鲁国人,少孔子三十三岁,身高体伟,状似孔子,有勇力。他发挥孔子的仁礼统一学说,特别重视"孝"与"礼",首先提出孝悌为仁之本。孔子死后被众弟子共立为师。(2)年饥:亦作"年饥",年成荒歉。(3)用不足:指国家用度不够。(4)盍(hé):副词,表示反诘,犹何不。彻(chè):周代的田税制度。何晏集解引郑玄曰:"周法十一而税,谓之彻。"即税率为百分之十(10%)。(5)二:犹言十分之二(20%)。(6)如之何:怎么,为什么。

【原文】10 子张问崇德辨惑[1]。子曰:"主忠信,徙义,崇德也[2]。爱之欲其生,恶之欲其死。既欲其生,又欲其死,是惑也。'诚不以富,亦祇以异[3]。'"

【白话译文】

子张问怎样提高品德、明辨昏乱。孔子说:"崇尚忠信,见义勇为,就是提高品德。爱一个人时,希望他长寿;厌恶他时,恨不得他马上死去。既要他长寿,又要他短命,这就是昏乱。诗上说:'忠信不够,也会欺诈。'"

【英语译文】

Zi Zhang asked how to improve one's integrity and ability to get rid of confusion. Confucius answered, "It's improving integrity to worship loyalty and credibility and to bravely help those in difficulty and danger. While loving a person you wish him live long; while disliking him, you wish him die at once. It's confused thought to wish him live long and die at once. *The Book of Songs* reads, 'To me she has nothing superior. You have just changed loyalties.'"

【注释】(1)崇德:提高品德。辨惑:明辨昏乱,解除糊涂。(2)主:崇尚,注重。徙义:谓见义即改变意念而跟从。(3)诚不以富,亦祇以异:引自《诗经·小雅·我行其野》。意谓诚德不至丰厚充实,也只会滑向反面,不免欺诈惑乱。诚,义同上文"忠信"。以,义同"及""至"。富,谓丰厚充实。亦祇,也只有。异,异端。这里指与"忠信"相反的欺诈惑乱。

【原文】11 齐景公问政于孔子[1]。孔子对曰:"君君,臣臣,父父,子子[2]。"公曰:"善哉!信如君不君,臣不臣,父不父,子不子[3],虽有粟[4],吾得而食诸[5]?"

【白话译文】

齐景公向孔子咨询为政问题。孔子回答道:“君是君,臣是臣,父是父,子是子,不可乱来。”景公说:“对呀!如果真的君不是君,臣不是臣,父不是父,子不是子,都乱来,即使粮食很多,我吃得着吗?”

【英语译文】

Duke Jing of Qi State asked Confucius about administrative affairs. Confucius answered, “Monarch is monarch; courtier is courtier; father is father; and son is son.” Duke Jing of Qi State said, “It's right! Could I get food even there's plenty of them if monarch isn't monarch, if courtier isn't courtier, if father isn't father, and son isn't son?”

【注释】(1)齐景公:名杵臼,鲁昭公末年,孔子去过齐国。问政:咨询或讨论为政之道。(2)君君,臣臣,父父,子子:这是四个省略了联系动词“是”的并列句。(3)信如:如果真是。君不君,臣不臣,父不父,子不子:其中四个“不”都是“非,不是”的意思。(4)有粟:粮食多。有,意思是多、丰收、富足。(5)诸:代词,相当于“之”,这里代“粟”。

【原文】12 子曰:“片言可以折狱者[1],其由也与[2]?”子路无宿诺[3]。

【白话译文】

孔子说:“只凭一方面的诉词即可判决案件的,大概是仲由了?”子路没有不及时兑现的诺言。

【英语译文】

Confucius said, “A man making judgment about a case based on sided evidence may be Zhong You.” Zi Lu always keeps his promise without delay.

【注释】(1)片言:简短的文字或语言,也指诉讼时一方的语言。折狱:判决狱讼,片言可以折狱,谓只听一方面的诉词即可判决狱讼。形容听狱者能取信于人,人不敢欺。亦谓用简洁的语言断案,形容听狱者眼明心亮、判断精准。(2)其:副词,表推测、估计、大概,或许。(3)无宿诺:没有不及时兑现的诺言。宿诺,指拖延着没践行的诺言。“片言可以折狱”和“无宿诺”勾画出一个精明能干,爽朗清新,为民办事,没有贪腐的好官。

【原文】13 子曰:"听讼[1],吾犹人也。必也使无讼乎[2]!"

【白话译文】

孔子说:"审理诉讼,我和别人差不多。我以为做官一定要使诉讼事件逐渐减少,直到没有才好!"

【英语译文】

Confucius said, "I have no difference from others while scrutinizing lawsuit cases. I think an official should make effort to reduce cases until none."

【注释】(1)听讼:审理诉讼,审案。孔子在鲁定公时,曾为大司寇。司寇就是治理刑事的官。(2)必也:强调状语"必",一定要。

【原文】14 子张问政。子曰:"居之无倦[1],行之以忠[2]。"

【白话译文】

子张问如何执行政事。孔子说:"在政治职位上,不要疲倦懈怠,使用权力,处理事务,要忠实,不三心二意。"

【英语译文】

Zi Zhang asked Confucius about administrative affairs. Confucius answered, "One in his position cannot be tired and while dealing with affairs by means of his power, he should be loyal."

【注释】(1)居之:之,代词,指代上文"政"。下文中"之"同。居之即居政,谓在政治职位上。无倦:不要疲倦懈怠。(2)行之:谓行政,执掌国家政权,管理国家事务(今也指机关、企业、团体等内部的管理工作或管理领导。)。以忠:要忠实,不三心二意。

【原文】15 子曰:"博学[1]于文,约[2]之以礼,亦可以弗畔[3]矣夫!"

【白话译文】

孔子说:“君子广泛地学习文化知识,并用礼来约束这个学习,也可以不至于叛离正道的呀!”

【英语译文】

Confucius said, “Moral men extensively learn knowledge and restrain his learning by rites so that he won't betray the right way.”

【注释】(1)博学:广泛大量地学。文:文化知识。(2)约:约束,简约。之:代词,指代“博学于文”。礼:社会生活中由于风俗习惯而形成的行为准则、道德规范和各种礼节。朱熹《四书集注》:“程子曰:‘博学于文而不约之以礼,必至汗漫(漫无边际)。博学矣,又能守礼而由于(遵从)规矩,则亦可以不畔道矣。’”(3)畔:同“叛”。矣:语气助词,表肯定或判断,相当于“也”,一般不译,这里可译作“的”。夫:在这里作句末语气词表感叹,可译作“呀”。

【原文】16 子曰:“君子成人之美[1],不成人之恶。小人反是[2]。”

【白话译文】

孔子说:“君子成全他人为善,不方便他人为恶。小人与这相反。”

【英语译文】

Confucius said, “A moral man helps others accomplish good things but not evil things. A mean man just does oppositely.”

【注释】(1)成人:成全他人,方便他人。(2)是:代词,指此、这。

【原文】17 季康子问政于孔子。孔子对曰:“政者正也[1]。子帅以正孰敢不正[2]?”

【白话译文】

季康子向孔子问政事。孔子回答道:“政字的意思就是端正。您自己拿端正带头,谁敢不端正?”

【英语译文】

Ji Kang Zi asked Confucius about administrative affairs. Confucius answered, "The meaning of administration is uprightness. If you initiate everything uprightly, who dare not do so?"

【注释】(1)政者正也:者,助词,用于名词后表停顿。正:端正。(2)子:代词,表示第二人称,相当于"您"。帅:引导,带头。

【原文】18 季康子患盗[1],问于孔子[2]。孔子对曰:"苟子之不欲[3],虽赏之不窃[4]。"

【白话译文】

季康子厌苦盗贼,向孔子请教。孔子回答道:"假若您不贪求财货,即使奖励偷窃,他们也不会干。"

【英语译文】

Ji Kang Zi hated theft and asked Confucius for advice. Confucius answered, "People won't steal even facing reward on condition that you don't lust after wealth."

【注释】(1)患盗:厌苦偷盗。(2)问:询问,请教。(3)苟:假如,如果,只要。欲:贪欲,贪求。(4)窃(qiè):盗窃。

【原文】19 季康子问政于孔子曰[1]:"如杀无道[2],以就有道[3],何如?"孔子对曰:"子为政焉用杀[4]?子欲善而民善矣[5]。君子之德风[6],小人之德草[7]。草上之风[8],必偃[9]。"

【白话译文】

季康子向孔子请教政治,说道:"假如杀掉坏人而主动亲近好人,怎么样?"孔子回答道:"您治理政事,怎么用得杀戮呢?您爱好善良,百姓也就爱好善良。领导人的行为操守像风。老百姓的行为操守像草。风去吹草,草就顺风倒。"

【英语译文】

Ji Kang Zi asked Confucius about administrative affairs, "How about killing an evil man and then being on intimate terms with kind man?" Confucius answered, "Why do you need to kill anyone when you deal with administration? People will love kindness if you love it. Leader's action is just like wind and people's actions are like grasses. Grasses will fall at one side upon wind blowing."

【注释】(1)问政:请教政治。(2)无道:指不行正道的坏人或暴君。(3)以就:而主动亲近。有道:指行正道的好人。(4)焉:疑问代词,指怎么、哪里。(5)欲:愿意,爱好。(6)德风:德,指行为操守,句子的主语;风,句子的谓语。意谓行为操守如风。(7)德草:行为操守如草。(8)上:加,添。草上之风(草加之风),犹"以风吹草"。(9)偃(yǎn):倒伏。

【原文】20 子张问:"士何如斯可谓之达矣[1]?"子曰:"何哉,尔所谓达者[2]?"子张对曰:"在邦必闻,在家必闻[3]。"子曰:"是闻也非达也。夫达也者,质直而好义[4],察言而观色[5],虑以下人[6]。在邦必达,在家必达。夫闻也者,色取仁而行违[7],居之不疑[8]。在邦必闻,在家必闻。"

【白话译文】

子张问:"读书人要怎样才叫显达了?"孔子说:"你所说的显达是什么意思?"子张答道:"做国家的官时一定要有名,做卿大夫的家臣时一定要有名。"孔子说:"这个叫有名,不叫显达。常说的显达,就是朴实正直而处事公平。观察言语脸色,揣度对方的心意,一般情况都对人谦让。做国家的官时一定显达,做卿大夫的家臣时一定显达。常说的有名,就是表面上主张仁德,实际行动却背道而驰。处于这种骗局还不知犹豫,做官时必定会骗名,做家臣时也必定会骗名。"

【英语译文】

Zi Zhang asked, "How can a scholar be called illustrious and influential?" Confucius asked, "What do you mean by being illustrious and influential?" Zi Zhang answered, "One must be well. known when he is an official of both state and courtiers." Confucius said, "This can be called famous but not illustrious and influential. By being illustrious and influential, we mean one should be upright and do things fairly. He can judge others' words and guess others' intention and he's always modest towards others. He is illustrious and influential when he is an official of both state and courtiers. By being famous, we mean that one advocates superficial humanity and morality but his real actions go against this. In this situation he never hesitates and he surely obtains fame by cheating when he is an official of both state and courtiers."

【注释】(1)士:智者,贤者,泛指读书人。斯:承接连词,指则、乃。也可译作就、便。达:贵显,显达。(2)何哉:谓语前置,尔所谓达者,是主语。(3)在邦:在诸侯国内做官。闻:有名,著称。在家:在卿大夫家做家臣。(4)夫:句首助词。下同。质直:朴实正直。好义:处事公平。(5)察言而观色:而,是并列连词,可以省略,作"察言观色"。观察言语脸色,以揣度对方的心意。(6)虑以下人:虑,大概,一般情况。以,语气助词。舒缓语气,调整节奏。下人,对人谦让。(7)色取仁而行违:表面上主张仁德,实际行动却背道而驰。色,外表。取,求索,采取。(8)居之不疑 :居,处于。之,近指代词,指代"色取仁而行违"。不疑,不迟疑,不犹豫。

【原文】21 樊迟从遊于舞雩之下[1],曰:"敢问崇德,修慝,辨惑[2]。"子曰:"善哉问[3]!先事后得[4],非崇德与?攻其恶[5],无攻人之恶[6],非修慝与[7]?一朝之忿,忘其身[8],以及其亲[9],非惑与?"

【白话译文】

樊迟陪着孔子在舞雩台下游览,说道:"请问怎样提高品德,怎样改正过错,怎样解除糊涂。"孔子说:"问得好!先付出劳动后收获,不是提高品德了吗?指责自己的过错,不指责别人的过错,不是改正过错了吗?因为一时的愤怒,便舍弃自己,甚至舍弃爹妈,不是糊涂了吗?"

【英语译文】

Fan Chi, accompanying Confucius, was sightseeing under WuYu Altar and he said, "Dare I ask you a question, how to improve one's integrity, how to correct one's mistakes, and how to avoid being confused?" Confucius said, "Good question! Isn't it improving one's integrity to gain after pain? Isn't it correcting one's mistakes to just scold one's own faults instead of not others'? Isn't it being confused to give up oneself, even one's parents, just because of agony for a while?"

【注释】(1)樊迟:即樊须。孔子弟子。姓樊,名须,字子迟,亦称樊迟。舞雩:指舞雩台。参见先进篇第十一 11.26 中注 22。(2)敢问:谦辞。犹冒昧问问;请问。崇德:提高品德。修慝:改正过错。修,治理。慝,读 tè,邪恶。辨惑:辨明昏乱;解除糊涂。(3)善哉问:倒装句。(4)先事后得:先做事后取报酬;先付出劳动后收获。(5)攻其恶:指责自己的过错。其,己称代词。(6)无:不。人:别人。(7)与:同欤。(8)一朝之忿:一时的愤怒,并非大不了的事。朝,读 zhāo,早晨。忘:遗弃;不顾念。其身:自身,自己。(9)以及其亲:甚至双亲。

【原文】22 樊迟问仁。子曰:"爱人。"问知[1]。子曰:"知人[2]。"樊迟未达[3]。子曰:"举直错诸枉[4],能使枉者直。"樊迟退,见子夏曰:"乡也吾见于夫子而问知[5],子曰,'举直错诸枉,能使枉者直'何谓也[6]?"子夏曰:"富哉言乎[7]!舜有天下选于众[8],举皋陶[9],不仁者远矣[10]。汤有天下选于众[11],举伊尹[12],不仁者远矣。"

【白话译文】

樊迟问怎样叫仁。孔子说:"爱人。"又问怎样叫智,孔子说:"善于鉴别人物。"樊迟没能明白。孔子说:"提拔正直的人,不任用邪曲的人,能让邪曲的人转变正直。"樊迟退了出来,遇见子夏,说道:"刚才我去见老师,问怎样叫智,老师说:'提拔正直的人,不任用邪曲的人,能让邪曲的人转变正直。'这是什么意思呢?"子夏说:"这话的意义丰富呀!舜治理天下,在众人中挑选,把皋陶提拔出来,小人离开不见了。汤治理天下,在众人中挑选,把伊尹提拔出来,小人离开不见了。"

【英语译文】

Fan Chi asked what is called humanity. Confucius said, "Loving people." Fan Chi asked again what is called wisdom and Confucius answered, "Being good at differentiating persons." Fan Chi didn't understand it. Confucius said, "You can change an evil person into an upright one if you promote an upright person, not an evil one." Fan Chi retreated and encountered Zi Xia, saying, "Just now, I met Master and I asked him what wisdom is. Master said that 'You can change, evil person into an upright one if you promote an upright person but not an evil one.' What does it mean?" Zi Xia said, "It has complicated meanings! When Shun administrated his kingdom, he selected Gao Yao from masses, and then mean men were all gone. When Tang administrated his kingdom, he selected Yi Yin from masses, and then mean men were all gone."

【注释】(1)问知:问智慧。知,读 zhì,智的古字。智慧,聪明。(2)知人:谓能鉴察人的品行、才能。知,读 zhī,认识,辨别。(3)未达:还没明白。达,指通晓、明白。(4)举直:提拔正直的人。错诸枉:不任用邪曲人。错,读 cù,同"措",指舍弃、置而不用。诸:语气助词,用在句中舒缓语气。枉:邪曲。(5)乡(xiàng):同“向”,有“先”“刚才”“原来”“从前”等义,指“现在前”,时间可长可短。见于:拜见到了。(6)何谓也:是什么意思呢。(7)富哉言乎:倒装句。(8)舜:人名。五帝之一,传说为我国父系氏族社会后期部落联盟的贤明首领。姚姓有虞氏,名重华,史称虞舜或舜。见《书·尧典》《史记·五帝本纪》。有:治理。选于众:在众人中挑选。(9)皋陶(gāoyáo):亦作皋繇,虞舜时的司法官,见《书·舜典》。(10)不仁者:指小人。远(yuàn):离开,避开。(11)汤:商朝开国之君,又称成汤、成唐、武汤、武王、天乙等。《书·汤誓》:“伊尹相汤伐桀。”(12)伊尹 :商汤大臣。名伊,一名挚,尹是官名。相传生于伊水,故名。是汤妻陪嫁的仆人隶,后助汤伐夏桀,被尊称为阿衡。(阿衡,商代官名。即师保之官。任辅弼帝王和教导王室子弟之职,有师有保,统称“师保”。)

【原文】23 子贡问友。子曰:“忠告而善道之[1],不可则止[2],毋自辱焉[3]。”

【白话译文】

子贡问如何交友。孔子说:“真诚劝告,好好引导,他不接受,也就算了,不要自找侮辱。”

【英语译文】

Zi Gong asked how to make friends. Confucius said, “You can do that by loyal advice and tactful enlightenment. If he doesn’t accept your words, it doesn’t matter. Don’t get self insult.”

【注释】(1)忠告:真诚劝告。善道:善加诱导。道,读 dǎo。(2)不可:不认可,不听。(3)自辱:自找侮辱。

【原文】24 曾子曰[1]:“君子以文会友[2],以友辅仁[3]。”

【白话译文】

曾子说:“君子通过文字结交朋友,通过朋友切磋培养仁德。”

【英语译文】

Zeng Zi said, “A moral man makes friends by means of literary works and improves integrity through friends."

【注释】(1)曾子:即曾参(公元前505年—公元前434年),孔子弟子。姓曾,名参,字子舆。春秋末鲁国南武城(原属山东费县现属平邑县)人,少孔子四十六岁,其先祖虽为贵族,但至其父已降为平民,其父曾点也受业于孔子。(2)以文会友:通过文字结交朋友。(3)以友辅仁:通过朋友切磋培养仁德。

子路篇第十三(共三十章)

本篇共30章,涉及治理国家的政治主张,孔子的教育思想,个人的道德修养与品格完善,"和而不同"的思想等。

【原文】1 子路问政。子曰:"先之劳之[1]。"请益[2]。曰:"无倦[3]。"

【白话译文】

子路问如何实施政治。孔子说:"在政事中起引导带头作用,勤奋做事。"子路请求进一步讲讲。孔子说:"不要懈怠。"

【英语译文】

Zi Lu asked how to carry out administration. Confucius said, "You should set an example in administrative affairs and do things diligently." Zi Lu requested further explanation and Confucius said, "Never slacken your effort."

【注释】(1)先之:在政事中引导带头。劳之:在政务中勤奋做事。(2)请益:益,增加。引申为进一步或进一层。(3)无倦:不要懈怠。

【原文】2 仲弓为季氏宰[1],问政。子曰:"先有司[2],赦小过[3],举贤才[4]。"曰:"焉知贤才而举之?"举尔所知;尔所不知,人其舍诸[5]?

【白话译文】

仲弓做季氏的总管,向孔子请教政事。孔子说:"要引导下属人员做事,宽免小过错,提拔有德才的人。"仲弓问:"怎么知道谁有德才而去提拔他?"孔子说:

"提拔你所知道的,你不知道的,别人会埋没他们吗?"

【英语译文】

When Zhong Gong acted as house steward in Ji's, he asked Confucius' advice for administration. Confucius said, "You should make subordinates do things, forgive trivial mistakes, and promote the man with virtue and ability." Zhong Gong then asked, "How can I know who is the man with virtue and ability and deserves promotion?" Confucius said, "Promote those whom you know well. Will others neglect those whom you don't know?"

【注释】(1)仲弓:即冉雍。宰:古代指家臣之长,一般译作总管。(2)先有司:引导下属官吏。先,引导。有司,分管部门工作的官吏。(3)赦(shè):有"舍弃""释放""宽免罪过""减免租税"等用义。赦小过,即宽免管辖范围内的小过。(4)举:提拔。(5)人其舍诸:人,别人。其,副词,表推断。舍,舍弃。诸,代词,相当于"之",这里代指贤才。

【原文】3 子路曰:"卫君待子而为政[1],子将奚先[2]?"子曰:"必也正名乎[3]!"子路曰:"有是哉,子之迂也[4]! 奚其正[5]?"子曰:"野哉,由也[6]! 君子于其所不知,盖阙如也[7]。名不正,则言不顺;言不顺,则事不成;事不成,则礼乐不兴;礼乐不兴,则刑罚不中[8];刑罚不中,则民无所措手足[9]。故君子名之必可言也[10],言之必可行也[11]。君子于其言,无所苟而已矣[12]。"

【白话译文】

子路说:"卫国君主等待您去治理国政,您首先干什么?"孔子说:"一定是纠正名实不符了。"子路说:"有这样的做法吗? 您离事情太远了! 为什么要纠正名实不符?"孔子说:"太粗野了,由啊! 君子对于不懂的事情或道理就不张口议论。名分不正,是名实不符的严重乱象,说起话来就不顺理;说话不顺理,事情就办不成。事情办不成,礼乐就不能复兴;礼乐不能复兴,刑罚就不会公正;刑罚不公正,老百姓连手脚怎么搁就不知道。所以君子称谓事物必定能说清道理。君子讲的话必定能通行。君子对于他自己要讲的话一点也不马虎罢了。"

【英语译文】

Zi Lu said, "Since the monarch of Wei State is awaiting you to administrate his state, then what will you do firstly?" Confucius answered, "I'll surely correct the unconformity of name and being." Zi Lu asked, "Is there such doing? You are too far from reality! Why do you correct the unconformity of name and being?" Confucius said, "You are too mean, Zhong You. A moral man never comments on things or ideas he doesn't know. It's serious chaotic phenomenon of incorrect name, which leads to unsmooth speech; unsmooth speech leads to unachievable things; unachievable things leads to the failure of revitalizing of rites and music; the failure of revitalizing of rites and music leads to unfairness of penalty and punishment; unfairness of penalty and punishment leads to people being at a loss on taking actions. Therefore a moral man can elaborates clearly ideas while naming things. What a moral man says must be reasonable. A moral man is never careless about what he says."

【注释】(1)卫君:卫出公辄。朱熹集注:"是时出公不父其父而祢(nǐ,父死,神主入庙,称祢。)其祖,名实紊矣,故孔子以正名为先。谢氏曰:'正名虽为卫军而言,然为政之道,皆当以此为先。"(2)奚先:什么先干,先干什么。奚,疑问词。何事,什么事。(3)正名:宇宙的本质是物。物的动、静,成化、成事。物、化、事,都实际存在着。人是堪与天地并称的主体物之一。所谓社会、历史、文化、文明,人是主角。人对物、化、事的称谓表述有约定俗成的符号。符号叫"名",实际存在叫"实"。名实相符滋生安宁,名实不符,乱象横生。正名,就是使名实相符。(4)迂:曲折,走远路。比喻干非当务之急的事。(5)奚其正:奚,疑问词。为何,为什么。其,副词,表将来时。正,犹正名。(6)野:鄙俗,粗野。(7)盖阙如也:盖,读gài,承接连词,和"则"差不多。用在复句或紧缩句之间,前此说明原因、理由或情况,后此说明相应的措施或结果。可译作"于是"或"就""便"。阙,读quē,空缺着。阙如也,谓存疑不言了或空缺不书了。(8)不中,不合适,不恰当。(9)错:同"措",指放,置。错手足,指摆放手足,比喻日常行动。(10)君子名之:君子给事物命名必可言也:必定能说清道理。(11)言之:指君子讲的话。(12)苟:随便,马虎。

【原文】4 樊迟请学稼[1]。子曰:"吾不如老农[2]。"请学为圃[3]。子曰:"吾不如老圃[4]。"樊迟退出。子曰:"小人哉,樊须也[5]! 上好礼,则民莫敢不敬[6];上好义则民莫敢不服;上好信,则民莫敢不用情[7]。夫如是,则四方之民襁负其子而至矣[8],焉用稼[9]?"

【白话译文】

樊迟请求学种庄稼。孔子说:“我不如老农。”请求学种菜。孔子说:“我不如会种菜的农民。”樊迟退出。孔子说:“识见浅狭呀,樊须这人!居上位的人讲礼,有礼节,百姓就没有谁敢不尊敬;居上位的人讲正义,行为不苟,百姓就没有谁敢不服从;居上位的人讲诚恳信实,百姓就没有谁敢不真情相待。做到这样,四方的百姓就会背着小儿女来依靠,哪里要自己种庄稼?”

【英语译文】

Fan Chi requested to learn farming. Confucius said, "I' m less skilled than veteran peasants." He requested learning method of planting vegetables. Confucius said, "I' m less skilled than veteran florists." Then Fan Chi retreated. Confucius sighed, "Shallow is Fan Chi! If upper men do things according to rites, no one dares not to be respectful; if upper men are righteous, no one dares not to be obedient; if upper men are loyal and credible, no one dares not to treat others disloyally. If so, people anywhere will follow and depend on you by carrying their babies. Is it necessary for you to farm yourself?"

【注释】(1)稼:种粮食作物。(2)老农:会种庄稼的农民。(3)圃:种植蔬菜、花果或苗木的园地。(4)老圃:会种菜的农民。(5)小人:识见浅狭的人。(6)莫敢:没有谁敢。莫,代词,指没有谁,没有什么。(7)用情:以真情相待。(8)襁负:用襁褓背负。襁褓,读 qiǎngbǎo,背负婴儿用的宽带和包裹婴儿的小被子。(9)焉用:哪里需要,怎须。焉,疑问代词,指怎么、哪里。用,指须、需要。

【原文】5 子曰:“诵诗三百[1],授之以政[2],不达[3];使于四方[4],不能专对[5];虽多[6],亦奚以为[7]?”

【白话译文】

孔子说:“熟读《诗经》通本三百篇,把政治任务交给他,却达不到从政水平、办不好事;派他出使外国,又不能独立应对、谈判,虽然读得多,又有什么用呢?”

【英语译文】

Confucius said, "A man who can recite *The Book of Songs* is endowed with a task of administration but he cannot administrate affairs well; when he is empowered as an envoy to foreign states, he cannot deal with such affairs as negotiing independently. What's the use of him although he has read so much?"

【注释】(1)诵:朗读,背诵,熟读。诗三百:诗,指诗经。三百,三百篇。现存的版本,三百零五篇。三百(三百篇),是口头概数。(2)授之以政:把政治任务交给他。(3)不达:达不到(从政水平办不好事)。(4)使于四方:出使外国。(5)专对:谓任使节时独自随机应答。古代的使节只接受使命,如何去交涉应对,只能随机应变独立行事,更不能事事请示或者早就在国内一切安排好。春秋时代的外交往来和谈判,多半是背诵诗篇来代替语言;所以诗是外交人才的必读书。(6)虽多:指读的诗虽多。(7)亦奚以为:"亦",又。"奚",何。"以",动词,用。"为",语气词,用在句末,表疑问,常与"奚""何"搭配。

【原文】6 子曰:"其身正[1],不令而行[2];其身不正,虽令不从[3]。"

【白话译文】

孔子说:"居上位者的行为端正,不发命令,办事也能通行。居上位者的行为不端正,即使三令五申,也没人听从。"

【英语译文】

Confucius said, "Upper men could execute policy smoothly without orders if they are upright. Nobody will observe them upon repeated orders if they are not upright."

【注释】(1)其身正:其,代词,表第三人称领属关系,即居上位者的。身正,行为端正。(2)不令而行:不发命令。而行,能够通行。而,读 néng,指能、能够。(3)虽令:即使三令五申。不从:(众人百姓)不听从。

【原文】7 子曰:"鲁卫之政[1],兄弟也。"

【白话译文】

孔子说:"鲁国和卫国的政治,像兄弟一般的相似。"

【英语译文】

Confucius said, "The administrative situation in Lu State and Wei State is as same as the relationship of two brothers."

【注释】(1)鲁卫之政:朱熹《四书集注》:"鲁,周公之后,卫,康叔之后;本兄弟之国,而是时衰乱,政亦相似,故孔子叹之。"

【原文】8 子谓卫公子荆[1]:"善居室[2]。始有[3],曰:'苟合矣[4]。'少有[5],曰:'苟完矣。[6]'富有[7],曰:'苟美矣[8]。'"

【白话译文】

孔子谈到卫国的公子荆时说:"他很会居家过日子,刚有一点生活资料,他就说:'就这样,足够了。'稍多有点生活物资,他又说:'就这样,完备了。'财物较多了,他便说:'就这样,美满了。'"

【英语译文】

When talking about the son of monarch of Wei State, Confucius said, "He's apt at living. When he just has a little subsistence he says, 'It's enough like this.' When he has a little more materials he says, 'It's perfect like this.' When he has still much more wealth, he says, 'It's satisfactory like this.'"

【注释】(1)卫公子荆:卫国一个名叫荆的公子(卫国君的庶子)。当时的称谓叫公子荆(不叫荆公子)。吴季札曾把他列为卫国的君子。(2)善居室:善于居家过日子。(3)始有:有,与"无"相对。始有,这里指刚有一点生活资料。(4)苟合:就这样够了。苟,暂且,勉强。可译作"就这样"。合,通"给",足够的意思。(5)少有:稍多有点生活物资。少,读 shǎo,指稍、略。(6)完:完备。(7)富有:财物较多了。(8)美:美满。

【原文】9 子适卫[1],冉有仆[2]。子曰:"庶矣哉[3]!"冉有曰:"既庶矣,又何加焉[4]?"曰:"富之。"曰:"既富矣,又何加焉?"曰"教之。"

【白话译文】

孔子到卫国,冉有驾车。孔子说:"人烟好稠密呀!"冉有说:"人烟稠密,人口已经众多了,又该怎么办呢?" 孔子说:"使他们富裕起来。"冉有说:"已经富裕了,又该怎么办呢?"孔子说:"教育他们。"

【英语译文】

Confucius went to Wei State with Ran You driving cart. Confucius said, "It's so populous here!" Ran You asked, "How should we do since the state is populous?" Confucius answered, "We should make people rich." Ran You asked, "How should we do since people are already rich?" Confucius answered, "We should educate them."

【注释】(1)适:往,至。(2)仆:用作动词谓驾驭车马,用作名词谓驾驭车马的人。(3)庶:指人口众多。(4)又何加焉:又,副词,表重复或继续。何加,增加什么。焉,近指代词,相当于"此",用作补语(或宾语,有这里、这时、这事、这东西含义供选用)。

【原文】10 子曰:"苟有用我者,期月而已可也[1],三年有成[2]。"

【白话译文】

孔子说:"假如有用我的人,国家政事,一年就一定初见成效,三年便会大有成就。"

【英语译文】

Confucius said, "If someone empowers me to administrate state affairs, I can make preliminary achievement within one year; moreover, I can make great achievement within three years."

【注释】(1)而:承接连词,指就、然后。已可也:已经可以了,一定可以了。期月:期,读 jī,同"朞"。期月,指一年。(2)有成:成功、有成效、有成就。

【原文】11 子曰:"'善人为邦百年[1],亦可以胜残去杀矣[2]。'诚哉是言也[3]!"

【白话译文】

孔子说:"'有道德的人、善良的人连续长久治国行仁政,也可以使残暴的人化而为善,不须严惩,终于废除刑杀。'这话真实可信呀!"

【英语译文】

Confucius said, "'A moral and philanthropic monarch governs a state by means of humanistic strategies; and he can also move brutal men to change into kind men without penalty and capital punishment.' This is really believable!"

【注释】(1)善人:有道德的人,善良的人。为邦:治理国家。百年 :为时间长久。(2)亦可:也可。(3)胜残去杀:实行仁政使残暴的人化而为善因而可以废除刑杀。(4)诚哉 :真实可信呀。

【原文】12 子曰:"如有王者[1],必世而后仁[2]。"

【白话译文】

孔子说:"如果有行王道的人兴起,三十年后仁政必定大见成效。"

【英语译文】

Confucius said, "If there arises someone who implements kingly way, then thirty years later he'll surely make great achievement in humanistic administration."

【注释】(1)王者:指帝王,天子。儒家反对霸道,认为帝王、天子是行王道仁政的最高统领:王者。世:三十年。

【原文】13 子曰:"苟正其身矣[1],于从政乎何有[2]? 不能正其身,如正人何[3]?"

【白话译文】

孔子说:"假若端正了自己,对于做官执政有什么困难? 不能正自己,怎么去端正别人?"

【英语译文】

Confucius said, "Isn't it difficult for anyone to hold official post if he makes himself upright? How could he make others upright if he cannot make himself upright?"

【注释】(1)其身:自身,自己。(2)从政:参与政事,处理政事,做官执政。乎:语气助词,舒缓语气。何有:有何难。(3)如正人何:把端正别人怎样进行。

【原文】14 冉子退朝[1]。子曰:“何晏也[2]?”对曰:“有政[3]。”子曰:“其事也[4]。如有政,虽不吾以[5],吾其与闻之[6]。”

【白话译文】

冉有下班回来。孔子说:“怎么这样晚?”回答说:“有政务。”孔子说:“那只是事务呢。若是有政务,虽然不用我了,我还可参与和知情。

【英语译文】

Ran You came back after one day's work. Confucius asked, “Why do you come back so late?” He replied, “Due to affairs.” Confucius said, “Just due to affairs. I can participate in and be informed about administration even though I' ve not empowered doing these things.”

【注释】(1)冉子:即冉有,又叫冉求,当时为季氏宰。退朝:古代君臣朝见礼毕而退。这里的“朝”是季氏的私朝。(2)晏(yàn):晚,迟。(3)有政:有国政。(4)其事也:那是家事呢。(5)不吾以:不用吾。以,用。吾其与闻之:其,副词,相当于“尚”,“还”。与闻,谓参与其事并且得知内情。与,读yù。

【原文】15 定公曰[1]:“一言而可以兴邦,有诸[2]?”孔子对曰:“言不可以若是其几也[3]。人之言曰[4]:‘为君难,为臣不易。’如知为君之难也,如果唱不几乎一言而兴邦乎[5]?”曰:“一言而丧邦,有诸? 孔子对曰:“言不可以若是其几也。人之言曰:‘予无乐乎为 君,唯其言而莫予违也。’如其善而莫之违也,不亦善乎? 如不善而莫之违也,不几乎一言而丧邦乎?”

【白话译文】

鲁定公问:“一句话就可以兴盛国家,有这样的事?”孔子回答说:“说话的效果不可以如此期望。人们的话说:‘做君主难,做臣子不易。’如果知道做君主的困难了,不接近于一句话就可以兴盛国家么?”鲁定公又问:“一句话就可以丧失国家,有这样的事?”孔子回答说:“说话的效果不可以如此期望。人们的话说:‘我做君主没有快乐,唯一的快乐是我的话没有人违抗。’如果说的话正确、很好,没有人违抗,不也是很好吗? 如果说的话不正确、不好,没有人违抗,不接近于一句话就可以丧失国家么?”

【英语译文】

Ding Gong of Lu State asked, "Is there such kind of thing that a word can make a state prosperous?" Confucius answered, "We cannot expect the effect of a word like this. People say, 'It's both difficult for monarch and courtiers.' If someone gets to know monarch's difficulties, isn't it the same as that spoken can make a state prosperous?" Ding Gong asked once more, "Is there such kind of thing that a word can make a state lost?" Confucius answered, "We cannot expect the effect of a word like this. People say, 'I'm not happy to be monarch and I'm only happy that nobody objects my words.' Isn't it a good thing that nobody objects words which are spoken appropriately? If words are spoken inappropriately and nobody objects, isn't it the same as that a word can make a state lost?"

【注释】(1)定公:鲁国君主。(2)有诸:诸,代词,相当于"之"。历来多作兼词'之乎'解释,但有所不通。(3)几(jì):通"冀",期望。(4)人之言曰:人,泛指一般人,犹言有人,人们。(5)几乎:接近于。

【原文】16 叶公问政[1]。子曰:"近者悦,远者来。"

【白话译文】

叶公问政治管理。孔子说:"做到近处的人喜欢你,远处的人投靠你。"

【英语译文】

The magistrate in the region of She asked about administrative affairs. Confucius answered, "You should make people nearby like you, and make people far away go and seek refuge in your place."

【注释】(1)叶公:叶,读shè,地名当时属楚,今河南叶(yè)县南三十里有古叶(shè)城。叶公是叶地方的长官,楚君称王,地方长官便称公。叶公叫沈诸梁,字子高。《左传》定公、哀公之间有一些关于他的记载,在楚国当时还算是一位贤者。(参见7.19)

【原文】17 子夏为莒父宰[1],问政。子曰:"无欲速,无见小利。欲速则不达;见小利则大事不成。”

【白话译文】

子夏做莒父邑的长官,向孔子问政治治理。孔子说:“不要求快,不要着眼小利。求快就达不到目的;着眼小利就办不成大事。”

【英语译文】

While being leading official in Ju Fu in Lu State, Zi Xia asked Confucius how to perform political administering. Confucius answered, “Not in haste and not on trivial benefit. More haste, less speed; focusing on trivial benefit leads to failure of important things.”

【注释】(1)莒父:鲁国的一个邑,已不确知其所在。《山东通志》认为在今山东高密市东南。莒,读 jǔ。

【原文】18 叶公语孔子曰[1]:“吾党有直躬者[2],其父攘羊[3],而子证之[4]。”孔子曰:“吾党之直躬者异于是:父为子隐[5],子为父隐。直在其中矣[6]。”

【白话译文】

叶公告诉孔子说:“我那里有个直率的人,他父亲偷了只羊,他就告发了。”孔子说:“我们那里直率的人和你们的不同,父亲替儿子隐瞒,儿子替父亲隐瞒。直率就在这里面。”

【英语译文】

She Gong told Confucius, “In my hometown, there is a straightforward man. After his father stole a sheep, he informed against his father.” Confucius said, “In my hometown, straightforward men are different from yours: father and son conceal things for each other: that's the real meaning of straightforwardness.”

【注释】(1)语:告诉。(2)党:古代一种地方基层组织,五百家为党。吾党,或译作“家乡”。作“我(们)那里”似更贴近。直躬者:以直道立身的人,直率的人。(3)攘(rǎng):盗窃,窃取。朱熹《四书集注》:“有因而盗曰‘攘’。”言非“惯盗”。(4)证:告发,检举。(5)隐:隐瞒。(6)直在其中矣:孔子伦理哲学的基础在于

“孝”和“慈”,父子相隐算是直行亲情,故言“直在其中矣”。

【原文】19 樊迟问仁。子曰:“居处恭[1],执事敬[2],与人忠[3]。虽之夷狄[4],不可弃也。”

【白话译文】

樊迟问什么是仁。孔子说:“平日的仪容言行要端正庄严,从事工作要严肃认真,对人民百姓要真心实意。就是到外国去,也不可抛弃这些品德。”

【英语译文】

Fan Chi asked Confucius what humanity is. Confucius answered, “One should act uprightly and appear dignified, and he should work seriously and conscientiously; and he should treat people sincerely and wholeheartedly. Even in other states, he should not abandon these virtues.”

【注释】(1)居处:处读 chǔ,平日的仪容举止。(2)执事:从事工作。(4)与人:对待百姓。(5)之:动词,指至,到。夷狄:泛称除华夏族以外的各族,外国。

【原文】20 子贡问曰:“何如斯可谓之士矣[1]?”子曰:“行己有耻[2],使于四方[3],不辱君命[4],可谓士矣。”曰:“敢问其次[5]。”曰:“宗族称孝焉[6],乡党称弟焉[7]。”曰:“敢问其次。”曰:“言必信,行必果,硁硁然小人哉[8]!抑亦可以为次矣[9]。”曰:“今之从政者何如?”子曰:“噫[10]!斗筲之人[11],何足算也[12]?”

【白话译文】

子贡问道:“怎样才可以叫作‘士’?”孔子说:“处世为人,知道羞耻,出使外国,很好地完成君主的使命,可以叫作‘士’了。”子贡说:“请问次一等的。”孔子说:“同族人孝顺父母,同乡人称赞他有老有少,有大有小。”子贡又说:“请问再次一等的。”孔子说:“说话一定诚实,做事一定果断,这是没有分寸的小人物啊!但也可以算作再次一等的‘士’。”子贡又问:“现在那些执掌政权的人怎么样?”孔子说:“唉!一些见识短浅器量狭小的人,算个什么?”

【英语译文】

Zi Gong asked, “How can a person be called a scholar?” Confucius said, “He could be called a scholar if he has sense of shame in his being and doing and accomplishes monarch's mission as convey to other states." Zi Gong said, "Could you say something scholar of lower levels?" Confucius answered, "Clansmen are filial to their parents and fellows in hometown praise him for knowing brotherly rituals." Zi Gong then asked, "Could you say something about the scholar of much lower levels?" Confucius answered, "It is a minor man who speaks sincerely and does things decisively! But he can also be called a scholar of much lower levels." Zi Gong continued, "How about those in administrative posts?" Confucius answered, "Oh! They are short-sighted and narrow-minded men. How can they be scholars?"

【注释】(1)士:智慧贤能的人。(2)行己:做人做事,处世为人。有耻:谓有知耻之心;知道羞耻。(3)四方:指外国。(4)不辱:不玷辱,不辜负。君命:君主的使命。(5)其次:指次第较后、第二,不是"次要的"。(6)宗族:同宗同族的人。(7)乡党:同乡,乡亲,乡里。弟(tì):后作"悌",顺从和敬爱兄长。(8)硁硁(kēng kēng):硁,是象声词,形容刚劲有力的击石声。硁硁,在这里则是形容浅陋固执。译文用"没有分寸"来表示"浅陋固执"。分寸,指说话或做事应掌握的尺度、界限。(9)抑亦:但也。抑,转折连词。但是,然而。(10)噫(yī):叹词,表示悲痛或叹息。(11)斗筲之人:斗筲,读dǒushāo,斗容十升,筲,竹器,容一斗二升,都是小容器。斗筲之人,喻指才识短浅,气量狭窄的人。(12)何足算也:算不上了。

【原文】21 子曰:"不得中行而与之[1],必也狂狷乎[2]!狂者进取,狷者有所不为也。"

【白话译文】

孔子说:"相交不到行为合乎中庸之道的人,就一定要同志高勇进的人和洁身自守的人相交,志高勇进的人一意向前,洁身自守的人不肯做坏事。"

【英语译文】

Confucius said, "If we cannot befriend men whose doings accord with doctrine of mean, we must befriend those who are ambitious and those who are innocent. Ambitious men head forward bravely and innocent men refuse doing evil deeds."

【注释】(1)不得:得不到。中行(xíng):行为合乎中庸之道的人。与(yí)之:

和他交往。(2)狂狷(kuáng juàn):指志高勇进的人和洁身自守的人。

【原文】22 子曰:"南人有言曰[1]:'人而无恒[2],不可以作巫医[3]。'善夫[4]!""不恒其德,或承之羞[5]。"子曰:"不占而已矣[6]。"

【白话译文】

孔子说:"南方人有句话说:'人没有恒心,不能当巫医。'这话很好啊!"《易经·恒卦·九三爻辞》说:"不经常保持美德,有时会受到羞辱。"孔子说:"这样看来,没有恒心的人,用不着去占卦了。"

【英语译文】

Confucius said, "Southerners say 'people who hasn't the sense of perseverance cannot be witch doctor.' It's quite right!" *The Book of Changes* reads: "If a man doesn't retain his virtues, sometimes he will be insulted." Confucius said, "Therefore people without perseverance needn't to practice divination."

【注释】(1)南人:南方的人。(2)人而无恒:而,结构助词,和"之"相同,用在主语和谓语之间使句型转为偏正词组。可译作"的,也可去掉不译。"(3)巫医:用卜筮祈祷之术替人治病的人。(4)善夫:夫,读 fú,句末语气词。这里表示感叹。(5)不恒其德,或承之羞:这两句出自《易经·恒卦·九三爻辞》,意谓不经常保持美德,有时会受到羞辱。或,代词,指有时。(7)不占:不要占卦。

【原文】23 子曰:"君子和而不同[1],小人同而不和[2]。"

【白话译文】

孔子说:"君子讲和谐,没有抵触悖谬之心,也没有偏袒勾结之意。小人讲同伙既有偏袒勾结之意,又有抵触悖谬之心。"

【英语译文】

Confucius said, "Moral men haven't intents for either going against fallacy or preferring collusion. In contrast mean men have intents for both going against fallacy or preferring collusion."

【注释】(1)和而不同:朱熹《四书集注》:"和者无乖戾之心。同者有阿比之意。"乖戾,有抵触、不一致、悖谬、不合情理等意思。阿比,指偏袒勾结。(2)同而不和:偏袒勾结之意,抵触悖谬之心。"

【原文】24 子贡问曰:"乡人皆好之[1],何如?"子曰:"未可也[2]。""乡人皆恶之[3],何如?"子曰:"未可也;不如乡人之善者好之[4],其不善者恶之。"

【白话译文】

子贡问道:"同乡的人都喜欢他,这个人怎么样?"孔子说:"不可以就说他好。"子贡又问:"同乡的人都讨厌他,这个人怎么样?"孔子说:"不可以就说他坏。比不上同乡的好人都喜欢他,同乡的坏人都讨厌他。"

【英语译文】

Zi Gong asked, "If a man is liked by all of his hometown fellows, how about him?" Confucius said, "We cannot say he is good." Zi Gong asked again, "If a man is disgusted by all of his hometown fellows, how about him?" Confucius said, "We cannot say he is bad. It is not so good as the situation where all good men like him and not so bad as all bad men disgust him."

【注释】(1)乡人:同乡的人。好(hào):喜欢。(2)未可:不可以。(3)恶(wù):讨厌,憎恨。(4)不如:比不上。

【原文】25 子曰:"君子易事而难说也[1]。说之不以道,不说也;及其使人也,器之[2]。小人难事而易说也。说之虽不以道,说也;及其使人也,求备焉[3]。"

【白话译文】

孔子说:"在君子下面工作很容易,讨他欢喜却难。不以正当方式讨他欢喜,他不会欢喜;到他使用人时,能衡量德才分配任务。在小人下面工作很难,讨他欢喜却容易。用不正当的方式讨他欢喜,他欢喜。到他使用人时,总是百般挑剔,要求完美无缺。"

【英语译文】

Confucius said, "It's quite easy to work, led by a moral man, but it's hard to please him. He'll not happy if you please him improperly; and when he uses you, he'll allot task appropriately. It's quite hard to work, led by a mean man, but it's easy to please him. He'll be happy if you please him improperly; and when he uses you, he always find faults with you and demand perfection."

【注释】(1)事:共事;服侍 。难说(yuè):难于取悦,难讨欢喜。(2)器:谓量才使用。(3)求备:求全责备,对人对事要求完美无缺的意思。

【原文】26 子曰:"君子泰而不骄[1],小人骄而不泰。"

【白话译文】

孔子说:"君子安详舒坦,却不骄傲凌人;小人骄傲凌人,却不安详舒坦。"

【英语译文】

Confucius said, "Moral men are peaceful or at ease but not arrogant or conceited; on the contrary, mean men are arrogant or conceited but not peaceful or at ease."

【注释】(1)泰、骄:指为人处事的两种相互对立的心情、风度。

【原文】27 子曰:"刚、毅、木、讷近仁[1]。"

【白话译文】

孔子说:"刚强、果决、朴质、话不轻易出口,有这四种品德的人接近于仁德。"

【英语译文】

Confucius said, "Steel-mindedness, decisiveness, simplicity and reluctance to speak make a man approach humanity and virtue."

【注释】(1) 刚、毅、木、讷:是人品表现出来的四种形象。

【原文】28 子路问曰:"何如斯可谓之士矣?"子曰:"切切偲偲[1],怡怡如也[2],可谓士矣。朋友切切偲偲,兄弟怡怡。"

【白话译文】

子路问道:“怎么样才可以叫作“士”了?”孔子说:“互相敬重切磋勉励,共同向善,和睦相处,可以叫作“士”了。朋友之间,互相敬重切磋勉励,共同向善 ;兄弟之间,和睦共处。”

【英语译文】

Zi Lu asked, “How can people be called scholars?” Confucius answered, “If they respect and encourage each other, trying to be kind all together and get along harmoniously, they can be called scholars. Friends respect and encourage each other, trying to be kind all together. Brothers get along harmoniously.”

【注释】(1)切切偲偲:偲,读 sī。偲偲,也是互相勉励。切切,指互相敬重切磋勉励的样子。(2)怡怡如也:和顺的样子,安适自得的样子,特指兄弟和睦的样子。

【原文】29 子曰:“善人教民七年[1],亦可以即戎矣[2]。”

【白话译文】

孔子说:“有道德的善良人教导人民达到了七年,也能够让他们作战。”

【英语译文】

Confucius said, “If a kind man with virtue educates people for seven years, he can send them to fight in a war.”

【注释】(1)善人:有道德的善良人。七年:指培养人才成型所需的时间。时间长短,视情况和需要而定。(2)即戎:用兵,作战。

【原文】30 子曰:“以不教民战[1],是谓弃之[2]。”

【白话译文】

孔子说:“用未受过训练的民众去作战,这叫抛弃他们。”

【英语译文】

Confucius said, “You are discarding them if you send untrained common men to fight in a war."

【注释】(1)以不教民战:以,用。不教民:没有受过教练的民众。战:作战。(2)是谓:这叫。弃之:抛弃他们。

宪问篇第十四(共四十四章)

朱熹集注把第一章自"克、伐、怨、欲"以下别为一章。把第二十章自"曾子曰"以下别为一章,又把第三十七章自"子曰作者"以下别为一章,所以题为四十七章。

【原文】1 宪问耻[1]。子曰:"邦有道,谷[2];邦无道,谷,耻也。""克伐怨欲不行焉[3],可以为仁矣[4]?"子曰:"可以为难矣[5],仁则吾不知也[6]。"

【白话译文】

原宪问如何叫耻辱。孔子说:"国家政治清明,做官领俸禄;国家政治黑暗,也做官领俸禄,这就叫耻辱。"原宪又问:"好胜、自夸、愤恨、贪欲这四种毛病都没有患,可以算是仁人吗?"孔子说:"可以算是难能可贵而已,若说是仁人,我不了解实际情况。"

【英语译文】

Yuan Xian asked what a shame is. Confucius said, "People act as paid official when politics is purely bright. They also do so when politics is dark. This is called a shame." Then Yuan Xian asked, "Could a man be called humanistic one if he isn't ambitiows, self-boastful, indignant and greedy?" Confucius said, "It's hard for a man to be like this. But I don't know the real situation as for being humanistic."

【注释】(1)宪:即原宪,参见6·5中注1。(2)谷(gǔ):官俸,古时常以谷物计禄。(3)克伐怨欲:好胜,自夸,愤恨,贪欲。(4)为仁矣:可以算是仁人吗。(5)为难矣:为,指算是、算作。矣,语气助词。前"矣"用在是非问句中译为"吗""么"。后"矣"用在陈述句中,表限止语气,相当于"耳",译为"而已"、"罢了"。(6)不知:不晓得,不了解。

【原文】2 子曰:“士而怀居[1],不足以为士矣。”

【白话译文】

孔子说:“读书人〔以天下为己任〕留恋自己的家庭生活,就不够为读书人了。”

【英语译文】

Confucius said, “If a man only cares about his household life, he cannot become a scholar who regards world's affairs as his own responsibility.”

【注释】(1)怀居:怀恋居所。

【原文】3 子曰:“邦有道,危言危行[1];邦无道,危行言孙[2]。”

【白话译文】

孔子说:“国家政治清明,说话正直,行为正直;国家政治黑暗,行为正直,说话谦恭。”

【英语译文】

Confucius said, “When politics is pure and bright, we speak and do things uprightly; when politics is dark we act uprightly and speak modestly.”

【注释】(1)危言危行:正直言论和正直行为。(2)言孙:孙,读 xùn,通“逊”。谦恭。言孙,说话谦恭。

【原文】4 子曰:“有德者必有言[1],有言者不必有德。仁者必有勇[2],勇者不必有仁。”

【白话译文】

孔子说:“有道德的人一定有名言,有名言的人不一定有道德。有仁德的人一定有勇气,有勇气的人不一定有仁德。”

【英语译文】

Confucius said, "A man with virtue must have famous sayings but a man having famous sayings isn't necessarily a man with virtue. A man with virtue must have courage but a man having courage isn't necessarily a man with virtue."

【注释】(1)有德者必有言:德,指道德、美德。必,副词,指一定、必然。言,指著名的言论或话语。(2)仁者必有勇:仁者,即仁人、有仁德的人。勇,指"勇气"。勇气,即随心而至之气,气至力亦至,所以勇敢、勇猛。

【原文】5 南宫适问于孔子曰[1]:"羿善射[2],奡荡舟[3],俱不得其死然[4]?禹、稷躬稼而有天下[5]?"夫子不答。南宫适出,子曰:"君子哉若人!尚德哉若人[6]!"

【白话译文】

南宫适向孔子问道:"羿善于射击,奡不仅擅长水战,还能陆上运舟。两人却都没得到好死样?禹和稷都亲自种田,却都能治理天下?"孔子没有回答。南宫适退出后,孔子说:"这个人,好一个君子呀!这个人,多么崇尚道德呀!"

【英语译文】

Nangong Kuo asked Confucius, "Hou Yi was adept at archery and Ao was adept at boating in land as well as fighting in water, however, they both died unnaturally. Yu and Ji did farming themselves but owned the world. Why?" The Master didn't answer him. After his retreating, Confucius said, "This man is really a moral man! He really worships virtue!"

【注释】(1)南宫适:适,读 kuò,亦作"括"。南宫适(即南宫括),姓南宫,名适(括),字子容,故亦称南容。孔子弟子,又为侄女婿。春秋末鲁国人,崇尚道德,处事谨慎。(2)羿(yì):在古代传说中有三个羿,都是射箭能手。一为帝喾的射师,见于说文;二为唐尧时人,传说当时十日并出,羿射落了九个,见《淮南子·本经训》;三为夏代有穷国的君主,见《左传·哀公四年》。这里所指的和《孟子·离娄篇》所载的逄蒙学射于羿的羿,据说都是夏代的羿。(3)奡(ào):字亦作"浇",古代传说中人物,夏代寒浞(zhuó)荡(dàng)舟:以手推舟行于陆地。一说以舟船冲锋陷阵。(4)得其死:活到生命终止,善终。(5)禹、稷躬稼而有天下:躬稼,亲自种田。有天下,治理天下。(6)君子……尚德哉若人:若人,犹这人,这个人。南宫适借古事问孔子,意指当今尚力不尚德,考察历史,尚力者不得善终,尚德者终有天下。所以孔子称赞他。

【原文】6 子曰:“君子而不仁者有矣夫[1],未有小人而仁者也[2]。”

【白话译文】

孔子说:“执政者中不仁的人是有的吧。缺乏道德的人中不会有仁人的。”

【英语译文】

Confucius said, “There are men in power who are not humanistic. Men without virtue cannot be humanistic ones.”

【注释】(1)君子:指执政者。(2)小人:泛指缺乏道德的人(无论其执政或在野)。

【原文】7 子曰:“爱之,能无劳乎[1]? 忠焉,能无诲乎[2]?”

【白话译文】

孔子说:“爱他,能不叫他操劳吗? 忠于他,能不教诲他吗?”

【英语译文】

Confucius said, “If you love someone, how couldn't you make him busy working? If you are loyal to someone, how couldn't you instruct him?”

【注释】(1)劳:使动用法。使……操劳。《国语·鲁语下》:“夫民劳则思,思则善心生;逸则淫,淫则亡善,亡善则恶心生。”(2)焉:代词,同“之”。

【原文】8 子曰:“为命[1],裨谌草创之[2],世叔讨论之[3],行人子羽修饰之[4],东里子产润色之[5]。”

【白话译文】

孔子说:“郑国政令的制定,裨谌拟稿,世叔评论,外交官子羽修改,使生动,东里子产修饰文字,使有文采。”

【英语译文】

Confucius said, "The decree of Zheng State was drafted by Bi Chen and commented by Si Shu. Then it was modified rendered more vividly by diplomat Zi Yu. Finally it was polished and deliuered with more literary elegance by Zi Chan in Dongli."

【注释】(1)为命:制定政令。(2)裨谌(bì chén):郑国大夫。草创:起草,拟稿。(3)世叔:左传作子太叔,即游吉,郑国大夫。讨论:研究、评论。(4)行人:掌管朝觐聘问的官。古代的外交官。子羽:公孙挥的字。修饰:修改润饰,使文字生动。(5)东里:地名,在今郑州市,子产所居。子产:即公孙侨(约前580年—公元前522年)。春秋时政治家、思想家,字子产,又字子美,谥号成子。因居东里亦称东里子产,在郑简公、郑定公之时执政二十二年推行作封洫、制丘赋、立谤政、铸刑书等一系列改革政策,使郑国国力大增。润色:修饰文字使有文采。

【原文】9 或问子产[1]。子曰:"惠人也。"问子西[2]。曰:"彼哉!彼哉[3]!"问管仲。曰:"人也[4]。夺伯氏骈邑三百[5],饭疏食[6],没齿无怨言[7]。"

【白话译文】

有人向孔子探问子产的为人。孔子说:"是宽厚慈祥的人。"问子西怎样。孔子说:"他呀!他呀!"问管仲怎样。孔子说:"这个人哪,齐桓公剥夺伯氏骈邑七千五百户封地给予他,伯氏只能吃粗劣的食物,一直到死也没有怨恨的话。"

【英语译文】

Someone asked Confucius about how Zi Chan bears himself. Confucius answered, "He's really an amiable man." The man asked about Zi Xi of Zheng State. Confucius said, "O, he, O, he!" The man asked about Guan Zhong. Confucius answered, "O! This man. Duke Huan in Qi State took away 7 500 households of the minister Bo Shi in Pian Yi and gave them to him. And Bo Shi could only eat rough food without complaint until his death."

【注释】(1)或问子产:问,指考察、过问。下同。(2)子西:春秋时有三个子西,一是郑国的公孙夏,生当鲁襄公之世,为子产的同宗兄弟,子产便是继他而主持郑国政务的;二是楚国的斗宜申,生当鲁僖公、文公之世;三是楚国的公子申,和孔子同时。曾经拥立楚昭王,也有政绩,但不能革除楚国“僭王”之号。楚昭王曾经要起用孔子,子西又从中阻挠。后来又因为子西而导致楚国内乱。因此孔子对这个人一时不好评价(郑汝谐认为这个“子西”应该是郑国的子西,而非楚国的子西)。(3)彼哉:他呀。是当时表示轻视的习惯用语,含有不愿、不便或不值评说之意。(4)人也:朱熹《四书集注》:“人也,犹言此人也。”意谓这个人啊。夺:剥夺。(5)伯氏:齐国大夫。骈邑:地名。骈邑三百 :朱熹《四书集注》:“盖桓公夺伯氏之邑以与管仲,伯氏自知己罪,而心服管仲之功,故穷约以终身而无怨言。荀卿所谓‘与之书社三百,而富人莫之敢拒’者,即此事也。” 据此,“骈邑三百”是“骈邑书社三百”之省文。古制,二十五家立社,把社内人名登录簿册,谓之“书社”。书社三百,即七千五百户。(6)饭疏食:吃粗劣的食物。(7)没齿(mòchǐ):终身,老年,死。

【原文】10 子曰:“贫而无怨难[1],富而无骄易[2]。”

【白话译文】

孔子说:“贫穷却没有怨恨很难;富贵却不骄傲容易做到。”

【英语译文】

Confucius said, “It's quite difficult to be poor without complaint; but it's very easy to be rich without pride.”

【注释】(1)而:转折连词,指然而、却。下同。(2)无:表存在与“有”对,即“没有”;表否定,犹非、不是、不。

【原文】11 子曰:“孟公绰为赵魏老则优[1],不可以为滕薛大夫[2]。”

【白话译文】

孔子说:“孟公绰当晋国诸卿赵氏或魏氏的家臣总管,力有余裕;却没有才能做滕、薛这种小国的大夫。”

【英语译文】

Confucius said, “Meng Gong chuo was quite qualified to be general steward fo Zhao's and Wei's families in Jin State; but he wasn't capable to be minister of small states such as Teng or Xue State."

【注释】(1)孟公绰为赵魏老则优:孟公绰 ,鲁国大夫。《左传》与《史记》都有关于他的记载。赵魏,晋国诸卿赵氏和魏氏。朱熹《四书集注》:"老,家臣之长。"犹家臣总管。优,宽绰,有余力。(2)滕、薛:当时的小国。在鲁国附近,滕的故城在今山东藤县西南十五里。薛的故城在今山东藤县南四十四里。朱熹《四书集注》:"大夫,任国政者。滕、薛国小政繁,大夫位高责重。然则公绰盖廉静寡欲而短于才者也。"

【原文】12 子路问成人[1]。子曰:"若臧武仲之知[2],公绰之不欲[3],卞庄子之勇[4],冉求之艺,文之以礼乐[5],为成人矣[6]。"曰:"今之成人者何必然?见利思义,见危受命,久要不忘平生之言[7],亦可以为成人矣。"

【白话译文】

子路问怎样才是完美的人。孔子说:"像臧武仲的智慧,孟公绰的清心寡欲,卞庄子的勇敢,冉求的多才多艺,再用礼乐使他们富有文采,都可以成为完美的人了。"接着又说:"现在的完美人哪里一定要这样?看到利益能想到该不该得到它,遇到危难能舍身拯救,就是衰老了也不忘当年的约言,都可以成为完美的人了。"

【英语译文】

Zi Lu asked how to become a perfect man. Confucius said, "A man can become perfect if is as wise as Zang Wuzhong, if he desires for nothing as Meng Gongchuo did, if he is as brave as Bian Zhuangzi, if he was versatile as Ran Qiu and if rites and music make him cultivated." Confucius continued, "Nowadays a man need not to do so. Only if he can think about whether or not he deserves obtaining benefit on noticing it, only if he can give hand on seeing dangers, only if he keeps promise on aging, he can be called perfect man."

【注释】(1)成人:德才兼备的人,犹如完人。(2)臧武仲:鲁大夫臧孙纥。他很聪明,逃到齐国后能遇见齐庄公的被杀而设法辞去庄公给他的田。(3)公绰:即孟公绰,参见上章。(4)卞庄子:鲁国的勇士。(5)文:使动用法,使……有文采(文化)。(6)亦可以:都可以。(7)久要(yāo):旧约(从前的约言)。久要不忘平生之言,何晏集解引孔安国曰:"久要,旧约也。平生犹少时。"邢昺疏:"言与人少时有旧约,虽年长贵达,不忘其言。”晋葛洪抱朴子·行品:“守一言于久要,历岁衰而不渝者,信人也。”

【原文】13 子问公叔文子于公明贾曰[1]:“信乎,夫子不言不笑不取乎[2]?”公明贾对曰:“以告者过也[3]。夫子时然后言[4];人不厌其言;乐然后笑,人不厌其笑;义然后取,人不厌其取。”子曰:“其然? 岂其然乎[5]?”

【白话译文】

孔子向公明贾问公叔文子的情况,说:“老先生不说,不笑,不收钱财,是真的吗?”公明贾回答道:“这是告诉你的人把话说过头了。他老人家到该说话的时候才说话,人家不厌恶他的话;高兴了才笑,人家不厌恶他的笑;该收受时才收受,人家不厌恶他收受。”孔子说:“是这样吗? 难道是这样吗?”

【英语译文】

Confucius asked Gongming Jia about Gongshu Wenzi, “Is it true that the reverend doesn't speak, laugh and accept money?” Gongming Jia answered, “It has been exaggerated by the man who told you. He didn't speak until it's time for him to do so and others didn't detest his words; he didn't laugh until he's happy and others didn't detest his laughter; he didn't accept money until it's time for him to do so and others didn't detest his acceptance.” Confucius asked, “Is it so? Isn't it so?”

【注释】(1)公叔文子:卫国大夫。檀弓载有他的故事。公明贾:卫人。姓公明名贾。贾,读 jiǎ。(2)信乎:真的吗。不取:不收受,不索取。(3)以:代词,指此、这。(4)时:指适当的时候。(5)其然:其,代词,表近指,指公明贾所说的情况。然,代词,指如此,这样。

【原文】14 子曰:“臧武仲以防求为后于鲁[1],虽曰不要君[2],吾不信也。”

【白话译文】

孔子说:“臧武仲凭借他的采邑防城要求鲁君立其后代为卿大夫,虽然有人说他不是要挟国君,我是不信的。”

【英语译文】

Confucius said, "Zang Wuzhong demanded the Monarch of Lu State to set his son as successor using his feoff Fang as a prop. Although some peopce said he didn't threat the monarch, I still don't believe it."

【注释】(1)臧武仲:即臧孙纥,又称臧纥,鲁国大夫。防,臧武仲的封邑,在今山东费县东北六十里之华城,离齐国边境很近。(2)要(yāo):要挟,胁迫。

【原文】15 子曰:"晋文公谲而不正[1],齐桓公正而不谲[2]。"

【白话译文】

孔子说:"晋文公诡诈,耍手段,不正派。齐桓公正派,不诡诈,不耍手段。"

【英语译文】

Confucius said, "Wen Gong of Jin State, Chong Er played tricks and was not upright. Huan Gong of Qi State, Xiao Bai was upright and did not play tricks."

【注释】(1)晋文公:名重耳,春秋五霸之一。谲(jué):诡诈,欺诳。(2)齐桓公:名小白,春秋五霸之一。

【原文】16 子路曰:"桓公杀公子纠,召忽死之,管仲不死[1]。"曰:"未仁乎?"子曰:"桓公九合诸侯[2],不以兵车[3],管仲之力也。如其仁,如其仁[4]。"

【白话译文】

子路说:"桓公杀掉公子纠,召忽自杀表示追随不舍,管仲却没有自杀。"停了一下又说:"管仲没有仁德吧?"孔子说;"齐桓公多次主持诸侯盟会,制止了战争,都是管仲的力量,这便是他的仁德,这便是他的仁德。"

【英语译文】

Zi Lu said, "After Huan Gong killed Jiu, his brother, Zhao Hu committed suicide to show his loyalty; whereas Guan Zhong did not do so." Then Li Lu asked, "Was Guan Zhong not a man with virtue and humanity?" Confucius answered, "Huan Gong hosted alliance conferences several times to hold back wars. It's the result of Guan

Zhong's effort. This is his virtue and humanity. This is his virtue and humanity."

【注释】(1)管仲不死:齐桓公和公子纠都是齐襄公的弟弟,齐襄公无道,两人都怕受牵累,于是,桓公由鲍叔牙侍奉逃往莒国,公子纠由管仲和召忽侍奉逃往鲁国。襄公被杀后,桓公先回齐国立为君,兴兵伐鲁逼迫鲁国杀了公子纠,召忽自杀以殉,管仲反而做了桓公的宰相(参见《左传庄公八年和九年》)。(2)九合诸侯:桓公纠合诸侯共计十一次,这一"九"字是"多"的意思,非指实数。(3)不以兵车:不,副词。表示禁止。勿,不要。以,用。兵车,战车;喻指兵威;武力。(4)如其仁:如,副词,指乃、是。

【原文】17 子贡曰:"管仲非仁者与?桓公杀公子纠,不能死又相之。"子曰:"管仲相桓公,霸诸侯,一匡天下,民到于今受其赐[1]。微管仲[2],吾其被发左衽矣[3]。岂若匹夫匹妇之为谅也[4],自经于沟渎而莫之知也[5]。"

【白话译文】

子贡说:"管仲不是仁人吧?齐桓公杀死公子纠,他不能为公子纠殉死,又辅助齐桓公。"孔子说:"管仲辅佐齐桓公,称霸诸侯,使天下得到匡正,人民到今天还受到他的恩惠。没有管仲,我们都要披着头发,向左边掩衣襟,接受外族统治了。难道他该像普通老百姓,持守小节小信,自杀于困厄之境却没有人去过问一样吗?"

【英语译文】

Zi Gong asked, "Isn't Guan Zhong a humanistic man? After Huan Gong of Qi State killed Xiao Bai, he didn't die to show loyalty but assisted Huan Gong." Confucius answered, "Guan Zhong assisted Huan Gong to become leader of Dukes and correct the whole political order. Even today common people benefit from his efforts. Without him, we still wear long hairs and wear clothes as those uncultivated being governed by minorities. Should he do as common people do to hold trivial rites and commit suicide when facing troubles without anyone knowing him?"

【注释】(1)赐:给人的恩惠或财物。(2)微管仲:微,无,没有。只用于和既成事实相反的假设句首。(3)吾其披发左衽:吾,我们。其,语气助词。被:同"披"。左衽:衽,读 rèn,指衣襟。左衽前襟向左掩。我国古代某些少数民族的服装。因以指受少数民族的统治。(4)匹夫匹妇:平民男女。谅:诚信,诚实。(5)自经:自缢。经,指系缢、悬吊。沟渎:犹"沟洫"。田间水道,(借指农田水利)泛指田野,比喻困厄之境。莫:代词,指没有谁。之知:去管,去过问。

【原文】18 公叔文子之臣大夫僎与文子同升诸公[1]。子闻之,曰:"可以为'文'矣[2]。"

【白话译文】

公叔文子的家臣大夫僎,和文子同时提升于朝廷中为官,孔子听到这事,说:"公叔文子是可以谥为'文'的。"

【英语译文】

Gongshu Wenzi's family courtier Zhuan and Wenzi were both promoted to posts of court officials. On hearing it, Confucius said, "Gongshu Wenzi deserved posthumous titlk 'Wen'."

【注释】(1)公叔文子之臣大夫僎:臣,家臣。大夫,这里是任官职者之称。僎,读 zhuàn,指家臣的名。诸,用法同"于"。公,公朝。古代官吏在朝廷治事之所,借指朝廷。(2)"文":谥号,表其人生前为人处世顺理成章。

【原文】19 子言卫灵公之无道也[1],康子曰[2]:"夫如是,奚而不丧[3]?"子曰:"仲叔圉治宾客[4],祝鮀治宗庙[5]。王孙贾治军旅[6]。夫如是奚其丧[7]?"

【白话译文】

孔子谈到卫灵公的昏庸无道,季康子说:"既然是这样,他因为什么不败亡?"孔子说:"他有仲叔圉接待宾客,祝鮀管理祭祀,王孙贾统帅军队,像这样,怎么会败亡?"

【英语译文】

When Confucius mentioned that Ling Gong of Wei State was muddle-headed, Ji Kangzi said, "Since he was like this, why wasn't he defeated?" Confucius said, "Under him, Zhong Shu Yu received guests and Zhu Tuo administrated sacrifice and Wang Shun Jia led army. With these how could he be defeated?"

【注释】(1)卫灵公:卫国的昏君,但能任用人才。(2)康子:季康子。(3)奚而:疑问词。犹为何,如何。丧:失位,垮台。(4)仲叔圉:圉,读 yǔ。仲叔圉,即孔文子,卫国大夫。(5)祝鮀:一作祝佗,卫国大夫。(6)王孙贾:卫国大夫。朱熹《四书集注》:"三人皆卫臣,虽未必贤,而其才可用。灵公用之,又各当其才。"(7)奚其:疑问词,犹言为何、为什么。

【原文】20 子曰:"其言之不怍[1],则为之也难[2]。"

【白话译文】

孔子说:"一个人说话不羞惭,实践起来很困难。"

【英语译文】

Confucius said, "If a man speaks without shame, it's hard for him to conduct practice."

【注释】(1)怍(zhuò):羞惭。(2)为:行为。

【原文】21 陈成子弑简公[1]。孔子沐浴而朝[2];告于哀公曰:"陈恒弑其君,请讨之[3]。"公曰:"告夫三子[4]!"孔子曰:"以吾从大夫之后,不敢不告也[5]。君曰'告夫三子'者!"之三子者,不可。孔子曰:"以吾从大夫之后,不敢不告也。"

【白话译文】

陈恒杀了齐简公。孔子斋戒沐浴而后朝见鲁哀公,报告道:"陈恒杀了他的君主,请您出兵问罪。"哀公说:"你去向仲孙、叔孙、季孙三位大夫报告罢!"孔子退出后自言自语道:"因为我也曾在大夫之列,不敢不报告。国君却说'去报告那三位揽权大夫!'"孔子去报告那三位揽权大夫,不肯问罪。孔子说:"因为我也曾在大夫之列,不敢不报告。"

【英语译文】

Chen Heng killed Jian Gong of Qi State. After fast and showering, Confucius paid respect to Ai Gong of Lu State, reporting, "Chen Heng killed his monarch. Please send army to condemn him." Ai Gong said, "Please report this to three ministers,

Zhong Sun, Shu Sun and Ji Sun." Confucius said to himself after retreating, "I daren't not to report because I was ever ranked among ministers. However He said 'Go and report to the three ministers!'" Confucius went and reported to those powered ministers but they would not send army. Confucius said, "I daren't not to report because I was ever ranked among ministers."

【注释】(1)陈成子:就是陈恒。齐国大夫。弑(shì):下杀上。简公:齐国君主,名壬。(2)沐浴而朝:朱熹《四书集注》:"是时孔子致仕居鲁,沐浴斋戒以告君,重其事而不敢忽视也。"(3)讨:出兵问罪。(4)告夫三子:夫,读 fú,语气助词,音义都与异于大夫的"夫(fū)"不同。三子,即三桓。三桓是春秋后期执掌鲁国国政的三卿,即孟孙氏(一作仲孙氏)、叔孙氏、季孙氏,他们是鲁桓公之子仲庆父(亦称孟氏)、叔牙、季友的后裔,故称。(5)孔子曰……:这是孔子退朝后的话。

【原文】22 子路问事君。子曰:"无欺也[1],而犯之[2]。"

【白话译文】

子路问如何服侍君主。孔子说:"不要阳奉阴违地欺骗,却可直谏冒犯。"

【英语译文】

Zi Lu asked how to attend monarch. Confucius answered, "You cannot cheat him by compliame in appearance but opposition in heart. However you can remonstrate him directly."

【注释】(1)无:副词,表示禁止、不要、不可。(2)而犯之:而,转折连词,指然而、但是、却。犯,指触犯、冒犯。

【原文】23 子曰:"君子上达[1],小人下达[2]。"

【白话译文】

孔子说:"君子向上追求仁义,小人向下追求财利"

【英语译文】

Confucius said, "A moral man pursues humanity but a mean man pursues benefit."

【注释】(1)上达:追求仁义。(2)下达:追求财利。

【原文】24 子曰:"古之学者为己[1],今之学者为人[2]。"

【白话译文】

孔子说:"古之学者治理自己,修养自己的学问道德,去非求是。今之学者治理他人,挑剔攻击他人之不备,夺其席,挡其路。"

【英语译文】

Confucius said, "In old days scholars governed themselves, cultivating his own learning and morality, searching for truth and ridding off fallacies. However, nowadays scholars governed others, finding faults with others, attacking others suddenly and hindering others' development."

【注释】(1)学者:做学问的人,求学的人,学术上有造诣的人。为己:治理自己,修养自己的学问道德,去非求是。(2)为人:治理他人,挑剔攻击,夺其席挡其路。

【原文】25 蘧伯玉使人于孔子[1]。孔子与之坐而问焉[2],曰:"夫子何为?"对曰:"夫子欲寡其过而未能也[3]"。使者出。子曰:"使乎!使乎[4]!"

【白话译文】

蘧伯玉派一位使者往见孔子。孔子给他座位。然后问他:"蘧老干些什么?"使者回答道:"他老人家想使自己减少些过错却还没能做到。"使者告辞退出。孔子说道:"好一位使者呀!好一位使者呀!"

【英语译文】

Qu Boyu sent a messenger to visit Confucius. Confucius made him seated and then asked, "What is elder Qu doing now?" The messenger responded, "The elder wants to make less mistake but he fails." Then the messenger bade farewell. Confucius said, "How good a messenger he is! How good a messenger he is!"

【注释】(1)蘧伯玉:春秋时卫国的大夫,姓蘧(qú)名瑗。相传他年五十而知四十九年非,是一个求进甚急并善于改过的贤大夫。孔子在卫国时,曾经住过他家。于:往。(2)坐:同“座”,指座席、座位。而焉:代词,代指他。(3)寡:使减少。(4)使乎:赞美使言行得体。

【原文】26 子曰:“不在其位,不谋其政[1]。”曾子曰:“君子思不出其位[2]。”

【白话译文】

孔子说:“不在那个职位上,就不谋虑那个政务。”曾子说:“君子所思虑的不超出自己的工作岗位。”

【英语译文】

Confucius said, “If you don’t hold the post, you needn’t to think about the administrative affairs of that post.” Zeng Zi said, “What a moral man thinks doesn’t go beyond one’s post.”

【注释】(1)不在其位,不谋其政。见泰伯篇8·14。(2)位:职位、工作岗位。

【原文】27 子曰:“君子耻其言而过其行[1]。”

【白话译文】

孔子说:“君子羞耻自己说的话超过了自己的行为。”

【英语译文】

Confucius said, “A moral man feels ashamed when his words have gone beyond his actions.”

【注释】(1)而:结构助词,和“之”相同,用在句子的主语、谓语间,使句子在形式上转化成偏正词组(尽管语意并没有多大改变),不再有独立性,从而做句子成分。可以译为“的”也可去掉不译。

【原文】28 子曰:“君子道者三[1],我无能焉[2]:仁者不忧,知者不惑,勇者不惧。”

子贡曰:“夫子自道也[3]。”

【白话译文】

孔子说:“君子的道德三个方面,我没有达到:仁不忧,智不惑,勇不惧。”子贡说:“这是老师的自评。”

【英语译文】

Confucius said, “I haven't reached the standard of being a moral man, i. e. , being humanistic without worry, being wise without confusion, and being brave without fear. ” Zi Gong said, “This is the master's self-evaluation. ”

【注释】(1)道:道德。者:助词,用在名词后,表明语音上的停顿,并引出下文,常表示判断。由于古代汉语判断句一般不用联系动词,而现代汉语一般都得用联系动词,翻译时可以去掉不译或适当添上联系动词“是”或“为”。下三“者”同此。(2)能:够到,达到。焉:代词,代指他(们)、它(们)。(3)自道:自己谈自己。

【原文】29 子贡方人[1]。子曰:“赐也贤乎哉[2]? 夫我则不暇[3]。”

【白话译文】

子贡比较他人而较其短长。孔子说:“赐,你够贤了? 我就没有这些闲工夫。”

【英语译文】

Zi Gong compared himself with others to find shortcomings. Confucius said, “You are able and virtuous enough. I haven't time to do so. ”

【注释】(1)方人:朱熹《四书集注》:“比方人物而较其短长也。”(2)乎哉:语气助词,这里表疑问。朱熹《四书集注》:“乎哉,疑辞。比方人物而较其短长虽亦穷理之事。然专务为此,则心驰于外而所以自治者疏矣。故褒之而疑其辞,复自贬以深抑之。”一说表感叹(还可表设问或反诘、表祈使)夫(fú):发语词。

【原文】30 子曰:“不患人之不己知[1],患其不能也[2]。”

【白话译文】

孔子说:"不担心别人不知道自己,担心自己没有能力。"

【英语译文】

Confucius said, "Don't worry about that others haven't known you but worry about that you are not capeble enough."

【注释】(1)患:担心,忧虑。(2)其:己称代词。

【原文】31 子曰:"不逆诈[1],不亿不信,[2]抑亦先觉者[3],是贤乎!"

【白话译文】

孔子说:"不事先猜疑别人存心欺诈,不揣度别人不诚实,然而还是及早发觉者,这样的人是贤者吧!"

【英语译文】

Confucius said, "A man doesn't suspect that others deliberately cheat him and do things dishonestly towards him, however he can notice those behavious beforehand. Such kind of man is surely able and virtuous!"

【注释】(1)逆诈:谓事先即猜疑别人存心欺诈。(2)亿:臆测,揣度。不信:不诚实。(3)抑:转折连词,指但是、然而。

【原文】32 微生亩谓孔子曰[1]:"丘何为是栖栖者与[2]? 无乃为佞乎[3]?"孔子曰:"非敢为佞也,疾固也[4]"

【白话译文】

微生亩对孔子说:"丘,你为什么这样忙忙碌碌的呢? 莫非玩口才么?"孔子说:"我不敢玩口才,我憎恶那些世俗鄙陋。"

【英语译文】

Weisheng Mu asked Confucius, "Qiu, why are you so busy all day long? Are you showing your eloquence?" Confucius answered, "I dare not show my eloquence and I detest those worldly insights and things."

【注释】(1)微生亩:即尾生晦。姓微生,名亩。朱熹认为其为"年长的隐者"。王夫之认为其为"老庄之徒"。(2)何为:何为(wèi),为什么。何为(wéi),干什么;是什么。是:用作副词,"如此","这么"的意思。栖栖(xīxī):忙碌不安的样子。者:代词,代指忙碌的情形。与:语气助词,表疑问。(3)无乃:犹莫非,恐怕是。为佞:玩口才,耍嘴皮子。(4)疾固:憎恶那些世俗鄙陋。

【原文】33 子曰:"骥不称其力[1],称其德也[2]。"

【白话译文】

孔子说:"对于骏马不是称赞它的力量,而是称赞它驯服于人的善良。"

【英语译文】

Confucius said, "We never prefer strength of fine horse, on the contrary we prefer its being tame and kind."

【注释】(1)骥(jì):骏马。(2)德:骥之德在于"调良",即驯服善良。

【原文】34 或曰[1]:"以德报怨[2],何如?子曰:"何以报德?以直报怨,以德报德。"

【白话译文】

有人对孔子说:"用恩惠回答怨恨,怎么样?"孔子说:"用什么报答恩惠呢?用正直公平回答怨恨,用恩惠报答恩惠。"

【英语译文】

Someone said to Confucius, "How about repaying resentment with virtue?" Confucius replied, "What will it be for repaying virtue? We should respond to resentment by means of fairness and uprightness, virtue for virtue."

【注释】(1)或:有人。(2)以德报怨:《老子·第六十三章》:"大小多少,报怨以德。"可能当日流行"以德报怨"这话。

【原文】35 子曰:“莫我知也夫[1]! 子贡曰:“何为其莫知子也[2]? 子曰:“不怨天不尤人[3],下学而上达[4]。知我者其天乎[5]!”

【白话译文】

孔子说:“没有人知道我呀!”子贡说:“为什么还没有人知道您呢?”孔子说:“不怨恨天,不怪罪人,下学人事知识,上知天命道理,知道我的只有天吧!”

【英语译文】

Confucius said, “Nobody knows me!” Zi Gong asked, “For what reason nobody knows you?” Confucius said, “I' ll never rcomplain about Heaven and common people. I' ll learn secular knowledge and get to know Heaven's decree. Then only the Heaven knows me.”

【注释】(1)莫我知:莫知我。也夫:语气助词,表感叹。(2)其:副词,指尚、还。(3)尤:责备,怪罪。(4)下学而上达:《何晏集解》《邢昺疏》都作“下学人事,上知天命”解。(5)其:乃,只。

【原文】36 公伯寮愬子路于季孙[1]。子服景伯以告[2],曰:“夫子固有惑志于公伯寮[3],吾力犹能肆诸市朝[4]。”子曰:“道之将行也与,命也[5];道之将废也与,命也。公伯寮其如命何!”

【白话译文】

公伯寮向季孙毁谤子路。子服景伯把这事告诉孔子,并且说:“季孙氏他老人家早已被公伯寮所迷惑了,可是我的力量还能把公伯寮的尸首放在街头示众。”孔子说:“我的主张将会实现吗?听从命运。我的主张将永远不会实现吗?也听从命运。公伯寮能把我的命运怎么样呢!”

【英语译文】

Gongbo Liao slandered Zi Lu in front of Ji Sun. Zifu Jingbo reported it to Confucius saying, “The elder Ji Sun has already been confused by Gongbo Liao, but I' m strong enough to display his body in the street.” Confucius said, “Can my political insight be realized? I' ll obey fate. Will my political insight never be realized? I' ll obey fate. How can Gongbo Liao deal with my fate?"

【注释】(1)公伯寮:《史记·仲尼弟子列传》作"公伯僚"云"字子周" 愬:"诉"的异体字,谗毁。(2)子服景伯:鲁大夫,名何。(3)夫子固有惑志:夫子,指季孙。固有,指本来就有。惑志,这里指惑乱之心。(4)市朝:市场和朝廷。在用法上,有时偏指市场或朝廷。古时把罪人的尸体示众,或置于市场(集),或置于朝廷。命:天命,命运。

【原文】37 子曰:"贤者辟世[1],其次辟地[2],其次辟色[3],其次辟言[4]。"子曰:"作者七人矣[5]。"

【白话译文】

孔子说:"贤明的人,避开浊乱的社会。比贤明次一点的人,迁地以避灾祸,再次一点的人,离开藐视自己的上司,再次一点的人,回避恶言恶语。"孔子又说:"像这样做的人,已经有七位了。"

【英语译文】

Confucius said, "An able and virtuous man escapes from corrupted society. A less able and virtuous man flees to dodge catastrophes. A still less able and virtuous man leaves his superordinate who contempts him. A still much less able and virtuous man keeps himself from slanders." Confucius said again, "There were seven persons who had ever done like this."

【注释】(1)辟世:逃避尘世,躲避乱世。辟,指退避、躲避。(2)辟地:迁地以避灾祸。(3)辟色:离开藐视自己的上司。(4)辟言:回避恶言。(5)作者:承接上文谓这样做的人。

【原文】38 子路宿于石门[1]。晨门曰[2]:"奚自?"子路曰:"自孔氏。"曰:"是知其不可而为之者与?"

【白话译文】

子路在石门住了一夜。第二天清早,掌管城门的人说:"你从哪儿来?"子路说:"从孔家来。"管门人说:"就是那位明知不行却一定要去那么干的人吗?"

【英语译文】

Zi Lu stayed overnight outside of capital gate. Next morning the doorkeeper asked, "Where did you come from?" Zi Lu answered, "I came from Confucius." The doorkeeper asked, "Is that one who always did on his will while knowing obvious obstacles?"

【注释】(1)石门:鲁国都城的外门。(2)晨门:掌管城门开闭的人。

【原文】39 子击磬于卫[1],有荷蒉而过孔氏之门者[2],曰:"有心哉,击磬乎!"既而曰[3]:"鄙哉,硁硁乎[4]!莫己知也,斯已而已矣[5]。深则厉[6],浅则揭[7]。"子曰:"果哉[8]!末之难矣[9]。"

【白话译文】

孔子在卫国击磬赏乐时,一个挑着草筐子的人经过门前,说道:"这个敲磬人有心思啊,在击磬吗!"隔一会儿又说道:"执着浅俗呀,硁硁地响!哀叹没有人知道自己。这就罢休算了。水深就连衣涉过,水浅就提起衣服涉过。"孔子说:"真果断坚决呀!不要去责难他。"

【英语译文】

When Confucius played *qing* and appreciated music in Wei State a man carrying grass basket passed by the gate and said, "The *qing*-players was obsessed with something! He's playing *qing*!" After a while he said again, "He's stubborn and shallow playing it! He sighs nobody knows him. It's alright stopping. If the water is deep, we wade with clothes on. And if the water is shallow, we wade plucking clothes." Confucius said, "He is really decisive! Don't scold him."

【注释】(1)磬(qìng):古代打击乐器,状如曲尺,用玉、石或金属制成。悬挂于架上,敲击而鸣。(2)荷蒉:荷,读 hè,指肩负、扛。蒉,读 kuì,指草织的盛器。(3)既而:时间副词,犹不久。(4)鄙哉:固执浅陋啊。硁硁(kēngkēng):象声词。(5)斯已而已矣:这就罢休算了。(6)深则厉:水深连衣涉过。(7)浅则揭:水浅提起衣服涉过。揭,读 qì。以上两句见《诗·邶风·匏有苦叶》。(8)果:果断,坚决。(9)末:副词。表示禁戒,相当于"不要"。难:责难(nàn)。

【原文】40 子张曰:“书云:‘高宗谅阴[1],三年不言。’何谓也?”子曰:“何必高宗,古之人皆然。君薨[2],百官总已以听于冢宰三年[3]。”

【白话译文】

子张说:“《尚书》说:‘殷高宗守孝,住在凶庐,三年不言语。’这是什么意思?”孔子说:“不仅是高宗,古人都是这样:国君死了,继承的君王,三年不问政治,各部门的官员都总管自己的政事,听命于总宰三年。”

【英语译文】

Zi Zhang asked, “According to *The Book of History*, ‘while observing mourning for his parent Gao Zong in Shang Dynasty lived enclosed for three years without any utterance.’ What does it mean?” Confucius said, “Not only Gao Zong but all ancient people did so. Upon king's death, the successor didn't care about administration for three years. Every official in every post cares about his own affairs under the guidance of the Prime Minister.”

【注释】(1)高宗:殷高宗武丁。谅阴:居丧时所住的房子,又叫“凶庐”。这两语见《书·无逸篇》。(2)薨(hōng):死的别称,从周代始,人的死亡有尊卑之分,“薨”以称诸侯之死。(3)总已:谓总摄已职。冢宰:官名,朝廷百官之首。

【原文】41 子曰:“上好礼[1],则民易使也[2]。”

【白话译文】

孔子说:“君主崇尚礼治,民众就容易接受治理。”

【英语译文】

Confucius said, “If the monarch worships governance by rites, common people are easily administrated.”

【注释】(1)上:君主,皇帝。好礼:崇尚礼治、礼制。(2)使:使用,引申为“治理”。

【原文】42 子路问君子。子曰:“修己以敬[1]。”曰:“如斯而已乎?”曰:“修己以安人[2]。”曰:“如斯而已乎?”曰:“修己以安百姓。修己以安百姓,尧舜其犹病诸[3]?”

【白话译文】

子路问怎样才能成为君子。孔子说:“自我修养而严肃恭谨,不狂妄。”子路说:“这样就行了吗?”孔子说:“自我修养而使他人安宁。”子路说:“这样就行了吗?”孔子说:“自我修养而使老百姓都安宁。使老百姓都安宁,尧和舜也还未能做到。”

【英语译文】

Zi Lu asked how to become a moral man. Confucius answered, “To cultivate oneself and to be humble, not being conceited.” Zi Lu said, “Is that alright?” Confucius said, “Self-cultivation makes others peaceful.” Zi Lu asked, “Is that alright?” Confucius said, “Self-cultivation makes all common people peaceful. But Yao and Shun didn’t make all common people peaceful”

【注释】(1)修己:修身,自我修养。以:承接连词。相当于“而”。敬:严肃,恭谨。不狂妄。(2)安人:为他人谋安宁。朱熹《四书集注》:“人者对己而言,百姓则尽乎人矣”(3)病:难,不易。诸:近指代词。代“修己以安百姓病”。

【原文】43 原壤夷俟[1]。子曰:“幼而不孙弟[2],长而无述焉[3],老而不死,是为贼[4]。”以杖叩其胫[5]。

【白话译文】

原壤伸出双腿,像个簸箕,坐在地上。孔子说:“你幼小时不恭顺兄长,长大了没有学业成就,老了还不死,是在为害社会。”说完用拐杖敲敲他的小腿。

【英语译文】

Yuan Rang stretched his legs which are like dust pans, and then sat on ground. Confucius scolded him, “While young, you didn’t respect elders; while aging, you didn’t achieve anything. Being old, you don’t die and you are doing harm to society.” After saying so, Confucius beat his calf slightly with stick.

【注释】(1)原壤春秋时鲁人。孔子的老朋友。不拘礼法。《礼记·檀弓下》第八十八节,说他母亲死后,孔子去帮他治丧,他却站在棺材上唱起歌来。故有人称他为"方外圣人"(皇侃),一说大概是一位另有主张而立意反对孔子之人(杨伯峻)。夷俟(yísì):伸两足箕踞而坐。古人视为倨傲无礼之态。邢昺疏:"夷,踞也,俟,待也。"(2)孙弟:同"逊悌",指敬顺兄长。(3)无述:没有记述或叙述,犹言无学业成就。(4)为贼:做祸害。(5)杖:拐杖,叩:敲,打。胫(jìng):人的小腿。

【原文】44 阙党童子将命[1]。或问之曰:"益者与?"子曰:"吾见其居于位也,[2]见其与先生并行也[3]。非求益者也,欲速成者也。"

【白话译文】

阙党一个少年在乡人和孔子间传达信息。有人问孔子:"这是一个求上进的人吗?"孔子说:"我看见他坐在成年人的座位上,看见他和长辈并肩而行。他不是一个肯求上进的人,只是一个急于求成的人。"

【英语译文】

In the place of Que, a youngster sent message between hometown fellows and Confucius. Somebody asked Confucius, "Is this a person who pursues progress?" Confucius answered, "I saw that he sat on a seat of adult, and I saw that he walked side by side with elders. He's not a man who pursues progress but a man who is hurry to make achievement."

【注释】(1)阙党:即阙里孔子幼时所居之地。在今曲阜孔庙东墙外。童子:未过二十岁的孩子。将命:传命,传宾主之言。(2)居于位:坐在座位上。据《礼记·玉藻》的记载,"童子无事则立主人之北,南面。"则"居于位"不合当日礼节。(3)与先生并行:《礼记·曲礼上篇》说:"五年以长,则肩随之(古时年幼者事年长者之礼。并行时斜出其左右而稍后。)"童子的年龄相差甚远不能和先生(成人、长辈)并行。

卫灵公篇第十五(共四十二章)

《朱熹集注》把第一第二两章并为一章,故曰凡四十一章。涵盖孔子的"君子小人”观、教育思想和政治思想等言行。

【原文】1 卫灵公问陈于孔子[1]。孔子对曰:“俎豆之事[2],则尝闻之矣[3];军旅之事,未之学也[4]。”明日遂行。

【白话译文】

卫灵公问孔子如何布阵打仗。孔子回答道:“有关祭祀、礼仪的事,那么我从前听说过;关于军队打仗的事,我从来没有学习过。”第二天便离开卫国。

【英语译文】

Duke Ling of Wei State asked Confucius how to deploy troops. Confucius replied, "I have ever heard things about sacrifice and etiquette; but I have never learned anything about troops and fight." The next day he left Wei State.

【注释】(1)陈:同“阵”。问陈,即问如何布阵打仗。俎豆之事:俎和豆是古代祭祀、宴飨时盛食物的两种礼器。(2)俎豆之事,犹言礼仪之事。(3)则:连词,表承接。(4)未之:之,语气助词,补凑音节。

【原文】2 在陈绝粮[1],从者病,莫能兴[2]。子路愠见曰[3]:“君子亦有穷乎?”子曰:“君子固穷[4],小人穷斯矣[5]。”

【白话译文】

孔子在陈国断了粮食,跟从的人饿得病了,不能起身站立。子路怨恨地说:“君子也穷困吗?”孔子说:“君子再穷都持节不变,小人一穷就胡作非为。”

【英语译文】

While in Chen State Confucius and his followers had nothing to eat. His followers were so hungry that they couldn't stand up. Zi Lu said with anogy, "Are moral men so poor that they do things unsmoothly?" Confucius said, "Even poor and unsmoothly moral men never divert their morality, however mean men will do evil thing while being poor and doing things unsmoothly."

【注释】(1)绝粮:断粮,吃不上粮食。(2)兴:起身。(3)愠见(yùnxiàn):怨恨显露。(4)固穷:固守于穷,再穷持节不变。滥(làn):过度,没有节制。引申为没有操守,胡作非为。

【原文】3 子曰:“赐也,女以予为多学而识之者与[1]?”对曰:“然,非与?”曰:“非也,予一以贯之[2]。”

【白话译文】

孔子说:“赐啊,你认为我是多方面学习又能记得住的吗?”子贡回答说:“对呀,不是这样吗?”孔子说:“不是这样的,我用真正的根本贯通全面。”

【英语译文】

Confucius asked, “Ci, do you think I learn all-round knowledge and keep them in mind?” Zi Gong answered, “Yes, isn't it?” Confucius said, “No. I reach knowledge concerning each aspect withesserce.”

【注释】(1)识(zhì):记注。(2)一以贯之:一,即初始、根本。以,指用。贯,即贯通。之,指治学的全过程。

【原文】4 子曰:“由!知德者鲜矣[1]。”

【白话译文】

孔子对子路说:“由呀!掌握道德的人可少啦。”

【英语译文】

Confucius said to Zi Lu, “You! There are few people who know about morality.”

【注释】(1)知:主管,掌握。《易·系辞上传》:“干知大(太)始,坤作成物。”

【原文】5 子曰:“无为而治者其舜也与[1]?夫何为哉?恭己正南面而已矣[2]。”

【白话译文】

孔子说:“以德化民,不用刑治的人,这便是舜了吧?他做了什么呢?他恭谨以律己,不偏不倚地坐在帝位上做领导和表率罢了。”

【英语译文】

Confucius said, "Wasn't Shun, the sage who civilized people not by penalty but by virtue? What did he do? He disciplined himself cautiously and set example at his throne facing south."

【注释】(1) 无为而治:以德化民,不用刑治。(道家主张顺应自然,无须作为)。(2)恭己:谓恭谨以律己,正:不偏不倚。南面:古代以坐北朝南为尊位,古帝王诸侯见群臣,或卿大夫见僚属,皆面向南而坐,因用以指居帝王或诸侯、卿大夫之位,也泛指居尊位或官位。

【原文】6 子张问行[1]。子曰:"言忠信,行笃敬[2],虽蛮貊之邦[3],行矣。言不忠信,行不笃敬,虽州里[4],行乎哉?立则见其参于前也[5],在舆则见其倚于衡也[6],夫然后行。"子张书诸绅[7]。

【白话译文】

子张问怎样才能通行无阻。孔子说:"言语忠诚老实,行为忠厚恭肃。纵然到了别的部族国家,也行得通。言语欺诈,行为刻薄轻浮,就是在本乡本土行得通吗?站立的时候,如见'言忠信,行笃敬'六字并立在前面。在车厢里如见这六字靠在车辕前头的横木上;做到这样时刻不忘,才能通行无阻。"子张把这些话写在了衣外大带上。

【英语译文】

Zi Zhang asked how to carry out oneself smoothly. Confucius answered, "He should utter words honestly and act out modestly. Even though, he went to other states he could carry out smoothly. Could he do so if he uttered dishonestly and acted out frivolously in his notherland? While standing, he noticed "honest words and modest action"; while in carriage, he noticed these words on the bar. Keeping these words in his mind and never forgetting make him carry himself out smoothly." Then Zi Zhang wrote these words on his coat robe.

【注释】(1)行:谓通行无阻。(2)行笃敬:行为忠实厚道、恭谨端肃。(3)蛮貊之邦:古代指南方和北方落后部族,亦泛指四方落后部族。(4)州里:古代二十五家为里,二千五百家为州,后泛指乡里或本土。(5)其:代词,指代“言忠信,行笃敬”。参:罗列,并立。(6)倚于衡:靠在车辕前头的横木上。(7)书诸绅:书,写。诸,近指代词,相当于“之”。又解,代词“之”和介词“于”的合音。绅,古代士大夫束于衣外腰间一头下垂的大带。

【原文】7 子曰:“直哉史鱼[1]!邦有道,如矢;邦无道,如矢。君子哉蘧伯玉[2]!邦有道,则仕;邦无道,则可卷而怀之[3]。”

【白话译文】

孔子说:“好一个刚直不屈的史鱼!政治清明像箭一样直,政治黑暗也像箭一样直。好一个君子蘧伯玉!政治清明就答应做官,政治黑暗就可以把自己收卷着藏起来。”

【英语译文】

Confucius said, “How upright and unyielding Shi Yu was! He's arrow-like straight in times when politics was pure as well as dark. What a moral man Qu Boyu was! While in time of pure politics, he promised to be official. But he hid himself in time of dark politics.

【注释】(1)史鱼:亦称史鳅,春秋时卫国大夫,字子鱼,曾为公孙文子谋避祸之计,以刚直不屈著称,临死时,他嘱咐儿子不要“治丧正室”以此劝告卫灵公进用蘧伯玉,斥退弥子瑕。古人称这为尸谏。(2)蘧伯玉:见14·25中注1。

【原文】8 子曰:“可与言而不与之言[1],失人[2];不可与言而与之言,失言[3]。知者不失人[4],亦不失言。”

【白话译文】

孔子说:“可同他说而不同他说,是错过人才;不可同他说而同他说,是白说或误说。聪明人既不错过人才,也不白说或误说。”

【英语译文】

Confucius said, “One will miss a talent when he can talk with someone but he refuses doing so; it's nonsense for him to talk with someone when he should not do so.

A wise man doesn't miss a talent or speak nonsense."

【注释】(1)与言:是探下面的"与之言"而省略了"之"字。(2)失人:错过人才。(3)失言:谓不该对某些人讲某些话。(4)知:"智"的古字。

【原文】9 子曰:"志士仁人[1],无求生以害仁有杀身以成仁[2]。"

【白话译文】

孔子说:"有远大志向的人和有德行的人,没有为求生路而损害仁德,只有舍弃生命来成就仁德。"

【英语译文】

Confucius said, "A man with virtue and great ambition won't harm humanity and morality for surviving but will sacrifice himself to achieve humanity and virtue."

【注释】(1)志士仁人:志士和仁人,即有远大志向的人和有德行的人。(2)求生:设法活下去,谋求生路。害仁:损害仁德。杀身:舍生,丧生。成仁:成就仁德。

【原文】10 子贡问为仁[1]。子曰:"工欲善其事,必先利其器[2]。居是邦也[3],事其大夫之贤者,友其士之仁者。"

【白话译文】

子贡问怎样实行仁德。孔子说:"工匠要把工做好,必须先使工具精良。处于任何一个邦国,都要侍奉大夫中的贤人,结交士人中的仁人。"

【英语译文】

Zi Gong asked how to carry out humanity and virtue. Confucius said, "A craftsman should perfect his tools in order to finish his job perfectly. While in any state, one should attend able and virtuous ministers and befriend humanistic men among scholars."

【注释】(1)为仁:实行仁德。(2)利其器:使工具精良。(3)是邦:此邦,此国,任何一个邦国。

【原文】11 颜渊问为邦[1]。子曰:“行夏之时[2],乘殷之辂[3],服周之冕[4],乐则韶舞[5]。放郑声[6],远佞人[7]。郑声淫,佞人殆。”

【白话译文】

颜渊问如何治理邦国。孔子说:“用夏朝的历法,坐殷朝款式的车子,戴周朝款式的礼帽,音乐采用韶和武。弃绝郑国的乐曲,斥退巧言谄媚的人。郑国的乐曲靡丽淫秽,巧言谄媚的人危险。”

【英语译文】

Yan Yuan asked how to govern a state. Confucius said, “You may govern it by using Xia Dynasty calendar, driving Yin Dynasty carriage, wearing Zhou Dynasty hat, playing Shao and Wu music. And you should rid of music in Zheng State and flattering persons because music in Zheng State is wanton and flattering persons are very dangerous.”

【注释】(1)为邦:治理邦国。(2)行夏之时:时,特指历法。夏朝用自然曆,以建寅之月(旧历正月)为每年的第一月,春、夏、秋、冬合乎自然现象。周朝则以建子之月(旧历十一月)为每年的第一月,而且以冬至日为元日。这个在观测天象方面虽然比以前进步,但不及夏历方便农业生产。就在周朝也有许多国家仍旧使用夏历。(3)乘殷之辂:辂,读 lù,商代的车子,比周代的车子自然朴质些。(4)服周之冕:周代的礼帽自然,又比以前的华美。孔子不反对礼服的华美。曾赞美禹“致美乎黻冕”。(5)乐则韶舞:舜时乐舞名。何晏集解:“韶,舜乐也。尽善尽美,故取之。”一说,“韶舞,即韶武,武、舞,古字通用。韶,相传为舜乐曲名,歌颂虞舜能继承尧的盛德而致太平;武,相传为周武王乐曲名,歌颂周武王能伐纣而致太平。”(6)放郑声:弃绝郑国的音乐。(7)远佞人:斥退巧言谄媚的人。

【原文】12 子曰:“人无远虑,必有近忧[1]。”

【白话译文】

孔子说:“一个人没有长远的考虑,必然会有眼前的忧患。”

【英语译文】

Confucius said, "If a man doesn't think of his future, he will have worries at the moment."

【注释】(1)忧:忧患。

【原文】13 子曰:"已矣乎[1]! 吾未见好德如好色者也。"

【白话译文】

孔子说:"完了啊! 我没看到过爱好美德如爱好美貌一样的人。"

【英语译文】

Confucius said, "It's doom! I have never met a person who loves virtue the same as he loves beauty."

【注释】(1)矣乎:语助词。

【原文】14 子曰:"臧文仲其窃位者与[1]? 知柳下惠之贤而不与立也[2]。"

【白话译文】

孔子说:"臧文仲是个才德不称而窃据官位的人么? 知道柳下惠贤良,却不同他并立于朝。"

【英语译文】

Confucius said, "Was Zang Wenzhong an immoral man who took over post? He did know Liu Xiahui was an able and virtuous man but refused to stand together with him in court."

【注释】(1)臧文仲:(? —公元前617年),春秋时鲁国执政,臧孙氏名辰,历仕鲁庄公、闵公、僖公、文公四君。曾废除关卡以利通商。窃位:谓才德不称窃取名位。(2)柳下惠 :即展禽。春秋时鲁国大夫,展氏名获字禽。食邑柳下,私谥惠,故又称柳下惠。与立:朱熹《四书集注》:"与立,谓与之并立于朝。"俞樾《群经平议》认为“立同位”。因而一些译文把“而不与立”译作“却不给他官位”。按《石经春秋》:“公即位”作“公即立”。《周礼·春官》:小宗伯掌“神位”,故书“位”作“立”。东汉郑司农云:“古者立、位同字。”由此可见“立”在篡“位”。后逐渐明晰分清。这里孔子的话共十九个字,“位”和“立”中间隔十一个字,不远也不近,清晰明白。假如当作“位”,又何必分写为“立”。在故弄玄虚吗?接下来,“与”在此是介词,后面省略了代词“之”,不是动词。再说,君主时代,弄臣要权,给某人官位,大都要打君主的招牌。孔子怎么会给人以话柄。

【原文】15 子曰:“躬自厚而薄责于人[1],则远怨矣[2]。”

【白话译文】

孔子说:“对自己重责,对别人轻责,就远离怨恨了。”

【英语译文】

Confucius said, “One is far away from hatred if he lays much obligation on himself and less on others.”

【注释】(1)躬自:自己,亲自。厚:对下文“薄”。“厚”后面省略了“责”。“厚责、薄责”犹言“重责、轻责”。(2)远(yuàn):离开,避开。

【原文】16 子曰:“不曰‘如之何[1],如之何’者,吾末如之何也已矣[2]。”

【白话译文】

孔子说:“不讲‘怎么办,怎么办’的人,不动脑筋,我没法对他怎么办了。”

【英语译文】

Confucius said, “For those who don’t say ‘how to do’, I have no way to treat them.”

【注释】(1)如之何:怎么办。(2)末:副词。相当于“未”“没有”“不”。

【原文】17 子曰:“群居终日,言不及义,好行小慧,难矣哉[1]!”

【白话译文】

孔子说:“大伙儿整天在一起,不说一句同道德义理沾边的话,喜欢耍小聪明,事情难料啊!”

【英语译文】

Confucius said, “People stay together all day long, never talking about morality but playing tricks. It's hard to predict things!”

【注释】(1)难矣哉:疑虑、为难的感叹。

【原文】18 子曰:“君子义以为质[1],礼以行之[2],孙以出之[3],信以成之[4]。君子哉!”

【白话译文】

孔子说:“君子以义为人格本质,以礼行义休现君子本质,以谦逊出现行义举止,以诚信完成一生行义。真是君子了!”

【英语译文】

Confucius said, “A moral man regards righteousness as essence of his trait, practices righteousness through rites conducts righteous actions through modest, and accomplishes righteousness through honesty and credibility.”

【注释】(1)质:性质,本质。(2)之:代词,指代义。下文两个“之”同此。(3)孙:同“逊”。出:出现。(4)信以成之:以诚信完成一生行义。

【原文】19 子曰:“君子病无能焉[1],不病人之不己知也。”

【白话译文】

孔子说:“君子忧虑自己没有能力,不忧虑别人不知道自己。”

【英语译文】

Confucius said, “A moral man worries that he is capable enough but doesn't worry that others don't know about him.”

【注释】(1)病:忧虑。

【原文】20 子曰:“君子疾没世而名不称焉[1]。”

【白话译文】
孔子说:“君子恨,到死而名声不被人称述。”

【英语译文】
Confucius said, “A moral man hates the fact that no one praises his fame until his death.”

【注释】(1)疾:忧虑;恨。没世:没读 mò,死。

【原文】21 子曰:“君子求诸己[1],小人求诸人。”

【白话译文】
孔子说:“君子追究自己,小人追究别人。”

【英语译文】
Confucius said, “A moral man finds fault with himself but a mean man with others.”

【注释】(1)求:责求,追究。诸:介词,同“于”。

【原文】22 子曰:“君子矜而不争[1],群而不党[2]。”

【白话译文】
孔子说:“君子端庄而不争执,合众而不偏私勾结。”

【英语译文】
Confucius said, “A moral man is dignified without quarrel and he is gregarious without camouflage.”

【注释】(1)矜(jīn):端庄。争:争执。(2)群:合众,会合。党:偏私勾结。

【原文】23 子曰:“君子不以言举人[1],不以人废言。”

【白话译文】

孔子说:“君子不凭言语中听,就推举、提拔人;不凭人有污点,就鄙弃他的合理言语。”

【英语译文】

Confucius said, “Moral men don't recommend or promote anyone due to lovely words; and they don't contempt anyone's reasonable words due to his bad conducts.”

【注释】(1)举人:推举、选拔人才。(2)废言:抛弃有理的话。

【原文】24 子贡问曰:“有一言而可以终身行之者乎?”子曰:“其恕乎[1]! 己所不欲,勿施于人。”

【白话译文】

子贡问道:“有没有一句话可以终身奉行的呢?”孔子说:“有,是推己及人吧! 自己不想要的任何事物,不要施加于别人。”

【英语译文】

Zi Gong asked, “Is there a saying observed life long?” Confucius answered, “Yes, love others! Don't hand over others those things you don't like yourself.”

【注释】(1)其:副词,表论断。犹乃。恕:推己及人,仁爱待物。

【原文】25 子曰:“吾之于人也[1],谁毁谁誉[2]? 如有所誉者,其有所试矣[3]。斯民也[4],三代之所以直道而行也[5]。”

【白话译文】

孔子说:“我对待别人,诋毁了谁? 称赞了谁? 若有所称赞,我就有所考验。

夏、商、周的老百姓都这样,所以三代能按正道行事。”

【英语译文】

Confucius said, “As for others whom I have slandered and whom I have praised? If I praised someone, I had tested him already. Common people in dynasties of Xia, Shang and Zhou all did like this so they could do things in Right Way.”

【注释】(1)吾之于人也:之,结构助词,使句子词组化。于人,对人。(2)谁毁谁誉:犹毁谁誉谁。(3)其,代词,代指我。试,考验。(4)斯民:老百姓。(5)三代:夏、商、周。直道而行,按正道行事。

【原文】26 子曰:“吾犹及史之阙文也[1]。有马者借人乘之[2],今亡矣夫[3]!”

【白话译文】

孔子说:“我还能看到史书上的有意存疑而未写出的文句。有马的人把马借给别人乘坐,现在没有这种精神了罢!”

【英语译文】

Confucius said, “I can still notice that in historic book, there're unwritten words of suspicion. Nowadays, are there people who have horses and lend them to others to ride?”

【注释】(1)阙(quē)文:原指有疑暂缺的字,后亦指有意存疑而未写出的文句。(2)借人:借给别人。(3)亡矣夫:没有了吧。亡,读 wú,指无、没有。

【原文】27 子曰:“巧言[1]乱德。小不忍,则乱大谋。”

【白话译文】

孔子说:“花言巧语搅乱道德。在小事情上不忍耐,就会搅乱大谋略。”

【英语译文】

Confucius said, “Blandishments confuse morality. If somebody cannot tolerate trivia, he'll be confused with great tact.”

【注释】(1)巧言:花言巧语。

【原文】28 子曰:“众恶之,必察[1]焉;众好之,必察焉。”

【白话译文】
孔子说:“众人都厌恶的,一定要考察;众人都喜爱的,也一定要考察。”

【英语译文】
Confucius said, “We should investigate things all people ddetest; and we should also investigate things all people like.”

【注释】(1)察:考察。

【原文】29 子曰:“人能弘道[1],非道弘人。”

【白话译文】
孔子说:“人能弘扬大道,不是大道弘扬人。”

【英语译文】
Confucius said, “People can expand great way but great way cannot expand people.”

【注释】(1)弘(hóng):廓大。弘道,即弘扬大道或正道。

【原文】30 子曰:“过[1]而不改,是谓过矣。”

【白话译文】
孔子说:“有了过错不改,过错就继续存在真是过错了。”

【英语译文】
Confucius said, “If you don't correct faults, they will continue to exist. Then you really have faults.”

【注释】(1)过:过错。

【原文】31 子曰:"吾尝终日不食终夜不寝,以思,无益[1],不如学也。"

【白话译文】

孔子说:"我曾经整日整夜不吃不睡,苦苦地进行思考,没有收益,不如踏实学习。"

【英语译文】

Confucius said, "I ever didn't eat anything all day long and thought over but without any gains. Therefore I'd rather learn conscientiously."

【注释】(1)无益:没有收益。

【原文】32 子曰:"君子谋道不谋食[1]。耕也,馁在其中矣[2];学也,禄在其中矣[3]。君子忧道不忧贫[4]。"

【白话译文】

孔子说:"君子用心力于学术,不用心力于衣食。耕田,也常常挨饿;学习常常得俸禄。君子担忧正道不张,不担忧受贫困。"

【英语译文】

Confucius said, "Moral men focus wholeheartedly not on subsistence but on academic. They often starve even though farming but they often get living supplies while learning. Moral men worry about failure of Right Way and they don't worry about being poor."

【注释】(1)谋道:探求事理道义等。谓用心力于学术。(2)馁(něi):饥饿,使挨饿。(3)禄:俸禄。(4)贫:缺少财物,贫困。与"富"相对。

【原文】33 子曰:"知及之[1],仁不能守之;虽得之必失之。知及之,仁能守之。不庄以莅之[2],则民不敬。知及之,仁能守之,庄以莅之,动之不以礼,未善也。"

【白话译文】

孔子说:“聪明才智足以得到的那个职位,仁德不能保持它,就是得到了,也一定会失掉。聪明才智足以得到的那个职位,仁德也能保持它。不端庄治理政事,老百姓就不会敬重。聪明才智足以得到的那个职位,仁德能保持它。又能端庄治理政事,但动员群众不合礼制,是不够好的。

【英语译文】

Confucius said, “The post, which has been obtained by wisdom, will lose if it cannot be kept by humanity and virtue. The post will not be respected by common people, which has been obtained by wisdom and kept by virtue and humanity but where administrative affairs cannot be conducted with grandeur. The post isn't good enough, which has been obtained by wisdom and kept by virtue and humanity and where administrative affairs cannot be conducted with solomnity but people aren't summoned by rites.”

【注释】(1)知及之:知,指聪明才智。之,代词,泛指治理政事的职位,职位高低大概都一样。(2)莅(lì):亦作“莅”,指亲临省视、治理。

【原文】34 子曰:“君子不可小知而可大受也[1],小人不可大受而可小知也。”

【白话译文】

孔子说:“君子不可以用小事情考验他,他可以接受重大任务。小人不可以接受重大任务,却可以用小事情考验他。”

【英语译文】

Confucius said, “A moral man should not be tested by trivial things because he could shoulder great mission. A mean man isn't able to accept great mission but might be tested by trivial things.”

【注释】(1)小知(zhī):从细事上察知。大受:承担重任,委以重任。

【原文】35 子曰:“民之于仁也[1],甚于水火[2]。水火,吾见蹈而死者矣[3],未见蹈仁而死者也。"

【白话译文】

孔子说:"百姓依靠仁德,超过依靠水火。我看见过趋赴水火而死的;没见过践履仁德而死的。"

【英语译文】

Confucius said, "Common people depend on humanity and virtue more than water and fire. I have seen people who died from treading in fire and water but I have never seen a single man who died from carrying out humanity and virtue."

【注释】(1)于:依靠。(2)甚:超过,胜过。水火:《孟子·尽心上》说:"民非水火不生活。"(2)蹈:践踏,趋赴。

【原文】36 子曰:"当仁[1],不让于师[2]。

【白话译文】

孔子说:"以仁为己任,不谦让给老师。"

【英语译文】

Confucius said, "Regarding humanity as one's own obligation, one isn't necessarily subordinated toone's teacher."

【注释】(1)当仁:以仁为己任。(2)不让于师:虽师亦无所逊。

【原文】37 子曰:"君子贞而不谅[1]。"

【白话译文】

孔子曰:"君子操守坚定不移,却不固执己见,不拘泥细节。"

【英语译文】

Confucius said, "A moral man sticks to integrity but never sticks to his own idea and is never confined to trivia."

【注释】(1)贞:操守坚定不移。谅:固执;拘泥。

【原文】38 子曰:“事君[1],敬其事而后其食[2]。”

【白话译文】
孔子说:“服侍君主,先认真做好差事,然后领俸禄。”

【英语译文】
Confucius said, “When somebody attends his monarch, he should first perform his tasks and then gets his living supplies.”

【注释】(1)事君:服侍君主。(2)敬其事:认真做好差事。后其食:后领俸禄。

【原文】39 子曰:“有教无类[1]。”

【白话译文】
孔子说:“无论贵贱贤愚都给以教育。”

【英语译文】
Confucius, “I'll educate those no matter how noble, humble, clever, or foolish they are.”

【注释】(1)有教(jiào):只有教育。无类:没有类别,不分类。

【原文】40 子曰:“道不同,不相为谋。”

【白话译文】
孔子说:“主张不同,不互相商议。”

【英语译文】
Confucius said, “We needn't collude with those with different viewpoint.”

【注释】(1)道:主张。

【原文】41 子曰:“辞达而已矣[1]。”

【白话译文】

孔子说:“言辞能够表达意思就行了。”

【英语译文】

Confucius said, “It is alright when words are expressed smoothly.”

【注释】(1)辞:言辞。

【原文】42 师冕见[1],及阶,子曰:“阶也。”及席,子曰:“席也。”皆坐,子告之曰:“某在斯[2],某在斯。”师冕出。子张问曰:“与师言之道与[3]?”子曰:“然;固相师之道也。”

【白话译文】

师冕来见孔子。走到阶沿边,孔子说:“这是阶沿啦。”走到座席旁,孔子说:“这是座席啦。”都坐定了,孔子告诉他说:“某人在这里,某人在这里。”师冕告辞后,子张问:“这是跟瞎了乐师讲话的方式吗?”孔子说:“是的;这本来是帮助瞎子乐师的方式。”

【英语译文】

Blind musician, Shi Mian, visited Confucius. When he reached the step, Confucius told him, “It's the step.” When he reached his seat, Confucius told him, “It's your seat.” After all people were seated, Confucius told the musician, “Somebody is here; somebody is here.” And when Shi Mian bade farewell, Zi Zhang asked, “Is this the way to talk with a blind man?” Confucius answered, “Yes. This is the way to help blind musician.”

【注释】(1)师冕:师,乐师。冕,这人的名。古代的乐师一般是瞎子。(2)某:在文章或口语中,古今惯例都是把无须说出的现场人名用“某”或“某人”或“某某”代替。(3)道:方法,方式。

季氏篇第十六（共十四章）

本篇主要包括孔子及其学生的政治活动、与人相处和结交时注意的原则、君子的三戒、三畏和九思等。

【原文】1 季氏将伐颛臾[1]。冉有、季路见于孔子曰[2]："季氏将有事于颛臾[3]。"孔子曰："求！无乃尔是过与[4]？夫颛臾，昔者先王以为东蒙主[5]，且在邦城之中矣，是社稷之臣也[6]。何以伐为"？冉有曰："夫子欲之[7]，吾二臣者皆不欲也"。孔子曰："求！周任有言曰[8]：'陈力就列[9]，不能者止[10]。'危而不持，颠而不扶，则将焉用彼相矣[11]？且尔言过矣[12]，虎兕出于柙[13]，龟玉毁于椟中[14]，是谁之过与？"冉有曰："今夫颛臾，固而近于费[15]。今不取，后世必为子孙忧。"孔子曰："求！君子疾夫舍曰欲之而必为之辞[16]。丘也闻有国有家者，不患寡而患不均[17]，不患贫而患不安。盖均无贫[18]，和无寡，安无倾。夫如是，故远人不服[19]，则修文德以来之[20]。既来之，则安之。今由与求也，相夫子，远人不服，而不能来也；邦分崩离析，而不能守也；而谋动干戈于邦内。吾恐季孙之忧，不在颛臾，而在萧墙之内也[21]。"

【白话译文】

季氏准备攻打颛臾。冉有、子路二人一同谒见孔子，说道："季氏将要对颛臾动武了。"孔子说："冉求！恐怕你们是错了吧？颛臾，从前上代君王用它主持东蒙山的祭祀，而且他的国土早在我们初封的疆域内，是与鲁国共安危的重要藩属，为什么要攻打它？"冉有说："季孙要这么干，我们两个当臣子的都不想这么干。"孔子说："冉求！周任有句话说：'在职位上能恪尽职守就干，不能就辞职。'瞎子遇到危险或将摔倒，漫不经心，不扶不持，哪里还用那牵瞎子的人呢？你的话错了。虎、兕从笼子里逃走了，龟壳、宝玉在匣子里毁坏了，这是谁的过失呢？"冉有说："现在颛臾，城墙完好坚固，离季孙的采邑费又很近，现今不占领，以后一定是子孙的祸害。"孔子说："冉求！君子很讨厌那种不说自己的贪心，反而一定找借口遮掩的歪风。我听说过：诸侯或大夫不必着急人民太少，只需着急不能各得其所应得；不必着急财富不多，只需着急境内不安。理由是：各得其所应得就没有贫穷，和平相处人民就多，境内安宁就没有倾危。做到这样，还有远方的人不归服，就进一步搞好礼乐教化来招致他们。他们既然来了，就得使他们安心。如今仲由和冉求两人辅佐季孙，远方的人不归服，却不能招致；国家支离破碎，却不能保全；反而想在国境内使用兵力,我恐怕季孙的忧患不在颛臾,而在他自己的宫廷内呢。"

【英语译文】

Ji's group prepared to attack Zhuan Yu. Ran You and Zi Lu paid a visit to Confucius together and said, "Ji's group are going to invade Zhuan Yu." Confucius said, "Ran Qiu! I'm afraid you're wrong. Long ago monarchs chose Dong Meng Mount in this state, Zhuan Yu, as the place for sacrifice. Furthermore its land already belongs to Lu State's territory and we should face dangers and threats together. Why should they attack this state?" Ran You answered, "Ji Sun wants to do so but we courtiers don't want to do so!" Confucius suggested, "Ran Qiu! Zhou Ren ever said 'A person in his post should do his duty. But he should resign if he cannot.' It isn't necessary to lead a blind man if the leader cares little about the blind man's falling down. You are wrong. If tigers and bears escaped from their cages and if turtle shell and jade were broken in their boxes, whose faults?" Ran You answered, "At present time, city walls of Zhuan Yu are solid and it's near feoff Fei of Ji's group. If they didn't occupy it then it will be scourge of their offspring." Confucius said, "Ran Qiu, a moral man detests those who doesn't expose his greed but hide it by any excuse. I ever heard: marquis or minister needn't worry bout too few subjects but worry about that people cannot obtain what they want; they needn't worry about Little wealth but worry about unpeaceful land. The reason is that there is no poverty if people obtained what they wanted, and there are more people if they live peacefully, and there is no danger in the land if the territory is calm and quiet. If doing so and people far away aren't willing to yield, we should attract them by means of rites, music and education. We should calm them if they have come. Nowadays Zi Lu and Ran You assisted Ji Sun but people far away aren't willing to yield and the broken state cannot be united. On the contrary, you want to resort to arm forces. Consequently I'm afraid that Ji Sun's scourge doesn't lie in Zhuan Yu but in his own court."

【注释】(1)颛臾:读 zhuānyú,鲁国的附庸国家,现在山东省费县西北八十里有颛臾村,当是古颛臾之地。(2)季路:即仲由,又叫子路。(3)有事:祭祀、盟会、兵戎是天子、诸侯的国家大事。这"有事",当是"用兵"的意思。(4)无乃尔是过与:无乃,犹莫非、恐怕是。表示委婉反问的语气。尔,代词,代指你们、你。是过与,即"是错了吧"。(5)东蒙主:东蒙山主祭人。(6)社稷之臣:指一身系国家之安危的重臣。(7)夫子:指“季孙”。(8)周任:古代一位史官。(9)陈力就列:指在所任职位上能恪尽职守。(10)不能者止:即“不能则止”。者,用作连词,相当于“则”。(11)相:引导盲者的人。(12)且:语气助词,和“夫”差不多,用在句首,表议论的开始。现代汉语中没有相应的词,可以去掉不译。(13)虎兕出于柙:兕,读sì,古代犀牛一类的动物。皮厚可制铠。柙,读xiá,指关野兽、牲畜的笼子。(14)龟玉:指龟甲和宝玉。古代认为是国家的宝器。椟:读dú,指柜子、匣子一类的藏物器。(15)固:指城墙完好坚固。费:指季氏的私邑。(16)疾夫舍曰欲之而必为之辞:疾,厌恶;憎恨。夫,语气助词。舍曰,不说,不讲。欲之,谓贪欲其利。为之辞:为贪欲找借口。(17)不患寡而患不均……安无倾:朱熹《四书集注》:“寡,谓民少。贫,谓财乏。均,谓各得其分。安,谓上下相安。季氏之欲取颛臾,患寡与贫耳。然是时季氏据国,而鲁公无民,则不均矣。君弱臣强,互生嫌隙,则不安矣。均则不患于贫而和,和则不患于寡而安,安则不相疑忌,而无倾覆之患。”(18)盖:因果连词,表示原因或理由。(19)故远人不服:还有远方的人不归服。故,义同“尚”“仍”。(20)文德:指礼乐教化,与“武功”相对。来:招致,招之使来。(21)萧墙:古代宫室内作为屏障的矮墙,借指内部。

【原文】2 孔子曰:“天下有道[1],则礼乐征伐自天子出[2];天下无道,则礼乐征伐自诸侯出。自诸侯出,盖十世希不失矣[3];自大夫出,五世希不失矣[4];陪臣执国命[5],三世希不失矣。天下有道,则政不在大夫。天下有道,则庶人不议[6]。”

【白话译文】

孔子说:“国家政治清明,制礼作乐、出兵征讨都由天子决定;国家政治黑暗,制礼作乐、出兵征讨便由诸侯决定。由诸侯决定,大概传到十代,很少还能继续的;由大夫决定,传到五代,很少还能继续的;大夫的家臣把持国家的政权,传到三代,很少还能继续的。国家政治清明,国家的最高政治权力就不会掌握在大夫手中。国家政治清明,老百姓就不会非议纷纷。

【英语译文】

Confucius said, “When politics is pure and bright the King decides things concerning rites, music, armaments and war; while politics is dark dukes do that. If dukes do these things, a state can last for ten generations with rare exceptions; if ministers do these things, a state can last for five generations with rare exceptions; if family courtiers of ministers do these things, a state can last for three generations with rare exceptions. When politics is pure and bright, the utmost power cannot be owned by ministers. When politics is pure and bright, common people won't have controuersial comment on it. "

【注释】(1)天下有道:国家政治清明。(2)自天子出:礼乐征伐由天子决定。孔子认为尧、舜、禹、汤及西周是如此的。(3)盖十世希不失矣:盖,副词,指大概。十世,即十代。希,即稀少、罕有。失,即失掉、丢失。自齐桓公以后,周天子已无发号施令的力量了。齐自桓公称霸,歷孝公、昭公、懿公、惠公、灵公、庄公、景公、悼公、简公十代,简公被陈恒所杀。晋自文公称霸,历襄公、灵公、成公、景公、厉公、平公、昭公、顷公八代,六卿专权。所以说十世希不失矣。(4)五世希不失矣:鲁自季友专政,歷文子、武子、平子、桓子而为阳虎所执,所以说五世希不失矣。(5)陪臣执国命:陪臣,古代天子以诸侯为臣,诸侯以大夫为臣,大夫又自有家臣。大夫对于天子,大夫的家臣对于诸侯称。本文中的陪臣是指大夫的家臣。国命,指国家的政权。鲁季氏家臣南蒯、公山弗扰、阳虎之流都当身而败,不曾到过三世。当时各国家臣也有专政的,"三世希不失"是宽仁的说法。(6)庶人不议:老百姓不非议。

【原文】3 孔子曰:"禄之去公室五世矣[1],政逮于大夫四世矣[2],故夫三桓之子孙微矣[3]。"

【白话译文】

孔子说:"国家政权离开鲁君已经五代了,政权落到大夫手中已经四代了,所以桓公的三房子孙已经衰落了。

【英语译文】

Confucius said, "In Lu State, sovereign power has left from its monarch for five generations; and it's controlled by ministers for four generations. Therefore the descendants of Duke Huan have already declined."

【注释】(1)禄:俸禄,引申为"政权"。去:离开。公室:君主的家族,王室。五世:自鲁君丧失政治权力到孔子说这段话时,经历了宣公、成公、襄公、昭公、定公五代。(2)逮(dài):及,及至。四世:自季氏最初把持鲁国政治到孔子说这段话时,经历了文子、武子、平子、桓子四代。(3)三桓:鲁国三卿仲孙(一称孟孙)、叔孙、季孙都出于鲁桓公,故称“三桓”。微:衰微,衰落。

【原文】4 孔子曰:“益者三友[1],损者三友。友直,友谅[2],友多闻,益矣。友便辟[3],友善柔[4],友便佞[5],损矣。”

【白话译文】

孔子说:“有益的朋友三种,有害的朋友三种。和正直的人交朋友,和诚信的人交朋友,和见识多的人交朋友,就有益了。和谄媚逢迎的人交朋友,和阿谀奉承面善心恶的人交朋友,和巧言善辩、阿谀逢迎的人交朋友,就有害了。

【英语译文】

Confucius said, “There are three kinds of beneficial friends and three kinds of harmful friends. It's beneficial for us to make friends with upright men, honest men, and knowledgeable men. However it's harmful for us to make friends with creeps, heart-evil, and voluble men.”

【注释】(1)三友:三种朋友。友,作名词解。(2)友谅:同信实的人交朋友。友,作动词解。谅,有“信”“小信”两义,视上下文而定。(3)便辟(piánpí):亦作“便僻”“便嬖”。谄媚逢迎。(4)善柔:阿谀奉承,面善心恶。(5)便佞(piánnìng):巧言善辩,阿谀逢迎。

【原文】5 孔子曰:“益者三乐[1],损者三乐。乐节礼乐[2],乐道人之善,乐多贤友,益矣。乐骄乐[3],乐佚游[4],乐宴乐[5],损矣。”

【白话译文】

孔子说:“有益的爱好三种,有害的爱好三种。爱好调节礼节和音乐。爱好称道他人的善德善行,爱好多交贤友,就有益了。爱好骄纵享乐,爱好游荡而不节制,爱好宴饮欢乐,就有害了。

【英语译文】

Confucius said, “There are three beneficial preferences and three harmful preferences. Preferences mediate rites and music. It's beneficial for someone to prefer to praise others' morality and kind deeds, and to make friends with able men. It's harmful for someone to prefer to wallow without restraint, and to seek pleasure while dining. ”

【注释】(1)三乐(yào):三种爱好。(2)礼乐(yuè):礼节和音乐。(3)骄乐(lè):骄纵享乐。(4)佚(yì)游:亦作“佚游”,放纵游荡而无节制。(5)宴乐(yànlè):安乐,宴饮欢乐。

【原文】6 孔子曰:“侍于君子有三愆[1]:言未及之而言谓之躁[2],言及之而不言谓之隐[3],未见颜色而言谓之瞽[4]。”

【白话译文】

孔子说:“伺候尊长,说话有三种过失:不该说话的时候说话,叫作急躁;该说话的时候不说话,叫作隐瞒;没看见脸色就说话,叫作昏昧。

【英语译文】

Confucius said, “There are three faults while attending elders. If someone speaks on wrong occasion, he's impatient. If someone doesn't speak, when it's time to do so, he's concealing something. If someone speaks when he dosen't notice others' reactions, he's stupid. ”

【注释】(1)侍:陪从或伺候尊长、主人。君子:泛指有德位的人。三愆(qiān):三种过失。(2)言未及之:不该说话的时候。躁:急躁。(3)言及之:该说话的时候。隐:隐瞒。(4)颜色:脸色。瞽(gǔ):昏昧,不明事理。

【原文】7 孔子曰:“君子有三戒[1]:少之时,血气未定[2],戒之在色;及其壮也,血气方刚[3],戒之在斗;及其老也,血气既衰,戒之在得。”

【白话译文】

孔子说:“君子有三项警戒:少年时,血气未充分稳定,要警戒女色;到壮年时,血气正旺,要警戒争斗;到老年时,血气已衰,要警戒贪得无厌。

【英语译文】

Confucius said, “A moral man has three things to guard against. While young, he should guard against sex since his vigor isn't stable; while grown-up, he should guard against Physical confrontations since his vigor becomes ripe; while old, he should guard against greed since his vigor has waned."

【注释】(1)三戒:三项警戒。(2)血气:血液气息,元气精力。未定:未充分稳定。(3)方刚:谓人在壮年时体力精神正当旺盛。

【原文】8 孔子曰:"君子有三畏:畏天命[1],畏大人[2],畏圣人之言[3]。小人不知天命而不畏也,狎大人[4],侮圣人之言[5]。"

【白话译文】

孔子说:"君子有三怕:怕天命,怕王公大人,怕圣人说的话。小人不懂天命,所以不怕它;轻视王公大人,侮蔑圣人说的话。"

【英语译文】

Confucius said, "A moral man has three things to fear, that is, fear for Heaven's decree, fear for men in high posts, and fear for sage's words. A mean man doesn't fear for Heaven's decree since he doesn't understand it; and he contempts men in high posts and slanders sage's words."

【注释】(1)天命:上天的意志,由天主宰的命运。(2)大人:指在高位的人。(3)圣人:指道德极高的人。(4)狎:轻忽,轻慢。(5)侮:侮蔑。

【原文】9 孔子曰:"生而知之者上也,学而知之者次也;困而学之,又其次也;困而不学,民斯为下矣。"

【白话译文】

孔子说:"生来就知道的是上等,学习后知道的就次一等;遇到困难才学习的,又次一等;遇到了困难也不学,这种老百姓算下等了。"

【英语译文】

Confucius said, "A man who's informed on birth belongs to first class and a man who's informed after learning belongs to second class. A man who learns while facing difficulties belongs to third class and a man who doesn't learn while facing difficulties belongs to last class."

【注释】(1)民 :指遇到困难不学的老百姓。

【原文】10 孔子曰:"君子有九思[1]:视思明,听思聪,色思温,貌思恭,言思忠,事思敬,疑思问,忿思难,见得思义。"

【白话译文】

孔子说:"君子有九种思考:看时,思考看明白没有;听时,思考听清楚没有;自己的脸色,思考是不是温和;自己的姿态,思考是不是恭敬;自己说的话,思考是不是忠诚老实;自己做的事,思考是不是认真负责;遇到疑难,思考怎样请教;将要发怒,思考会不会引发祸患;将要得到什么,思考该不该得。"

【英语译文】

Confucius said, "A moral man has nine kinds of thinking. While seeing, he thinks whether he sees carefully; while listening, he thinks whether he listens clearly; he thinks whether his looking is fine; he thinks whether his manner is modest; he thinks whether his words are honest; he thinks whether his deeds are responsible; he thinks how to seck advice upon meeting difficulties; he thinks whether it leads to disaster while he's bursting into anger; he thinks whether he deserves it while he's going to obtain something."

【注释】(1)九思:九种思考。

【原文】11 孔子曰:"见善如不及,见不善如探汤[1]。吾见其人矣[2],吾闻其语矣。隐居以求其志[3],行义以达其道[4]。吾闻其语矣,未见其人也。"

【白话译文】

孔子说:"见到善良,好像比不上,尽力追赶;见到邪恶,好像摸到了沸水,使劲避开。我看见过这样的人,也听见过样的话。避世隐居来保全自己的意志,依正义行事来实现自己的理想。我听过这样的话,没见过这样的人。"

【英语译文】

Confucius said, "On seeing good and kind and feeling unmatched, one tries to catch up; on seeing bad and evil and feeling heated by boiling water, one tries to dodge quickly. I have seen such kind of person and heard such kind of words. Someone sticks to his will by living in seclusion and he realizes his ideal by conducting upright deeds. I have heard such kind of words and never seen such kind of person."

【注释】(1)探汤:探试沸水。(2)其人:这样的人。其,近指代词,代指这样、如此。其语的"其"同此解。(3)其志:自己的意志。其,己称代词。其道的"其"同此解。(4)行义:依正义而行。

【原文】12 齐景公有马千驷[1],死之日,民无德而称焉[2],伯夷叔齐饿于首阳之下[3],民到如今称之。其斯之谓与[4]?

【白话译文】

齐景公有马四千匹,他死的时候,老百姓说他坏,没有品德。伯夷、叔齐,耻食周粟,饿死于首阳之下,老百姓到现在还称颂他们。两条记载的史实绝然不同吧?

【英语译文】

Jing Gong of Qi State owned four thousand horses. Upon his death, people said that he was an immoral man. Bo Yi and Shu Qi starved to death at the foot of Shou Yang Mountain due to refusing the food of Zhou Dynasty. Nowadays people still speak very highly of them. Are the two recorded deeds absolutely different?

【注释】(1)驷:量词。马四匹曰驷。(2)民无德而称焉:民,主语是老百姓。无德,前置补语,强调"没有德行"。而,结构助词。称,谓语,指述说,声称。焉,代词,相当于"之",指代齐景公。(3)伯夷、叔齐:商末孤竹君的两个儿子。相传其父遗命要立次子叔齐为继承人。叔齐让位给伯夷,伯夷不受,叔齐也不愿登位,先后都逃到了周国。周武王伐纣,二人叩马谏阻。武王灭商后,他们耻食周粟,采薇而食,饿死首阳山中。首阳:山名,现在何地,古今传说纷纭,已经难于确指。(4)其斯之谓与:其斯,都是代词。犹言"彼此",谓这个和那个,双方。常用以指"不一致""不同"的事物或概念。

【原文】13 陈亢问于伯鱼曰[1]:“子亦有异闻乎[2]?”对曰:“未也。尝独立,鲤趋而过庭[3]。曰:‘学诗乎?’对曰:‘未也。’‘不学诗,无以言。’鲤退而学诗。他日,又独立,鲤趋而过庭。曰:‘学礼乎?’对曰:‘未也。’‘不学礼,无以立’ 鲤退而学礼。闻斯二者。”陈亢退而喜曰:“问一得三,闻诗闻礼,又闻君子之远其子也。”

【白话译文】

陈亢对孔子的儿子伯鱼问道:“您在老师那里也得到不同的传授吗?”答道:“没有。他曾经一个人站在庭中,我小步快行地经过,他问我:‘学诗没有?’我说:‘没有。’‘不学诗没有凭据讲话。’我退回来学诗。过了些日子,他又一个人站在庭中,我又小步快行地经过,他问我:‘学礼没有?’我说:‘没有。’他说:‘不学礼没有凭据立足社会。’我退回来学礼,只听过这两次教诲。”陈亢回去高兴地说道:“我问一样知道了三样。知道诗,知道礼,知道君子对儿子并不优于对学生。”

【英语译文】

Chen Gang asked Kong Li, “Are you educated by master differently?” Kong Li answered, “No. He ever stood admist yard himself and I hurried past him. He asked, ‘Did you learn poems?’ I said, ‘Not yet.’ He said, ‘You have no evidence to speak without learning poems.’ I came back to learn poems. Several days later, once more he stood amidst the yard himself and I hurried past him. He asked, ‘Did you learn rites?’ I said, ‘Not yet.’ He said, ‘You cannot establish yourself in society without learning rites.’ I came back to learn rites. And I have ever heard his instruction twice.” After going back Chen Gang said happily, “Upon asking once I have known three things. I have known poems, rites and that the master treated his son and his disciples equally.”

【注释】(1)陈亢(gāng):孔子弟子,姓陈,名亢,字子亢,一字子禽。伯鱼 :孔子之子孔鲤之字。(2)有异闻:得到不同的传授。有,指取得、占有。异,即不同的。闻,指传授、传布。(3)趋(qū):碎步疾行表示恭敬。过庭:走过厅堂。

【原文】14 孔子曰:“邦君[1]之妻,君称之曰夫人,夫人自称曰小童[2];邦人称之曰君夫人,称诸[3]异邦曰寡小君;异邦人称之亦曰君夫人。”

【白话译文】

孔子说:"国君的妻子,国君称她为夫人,夫人自称为小童;国内的人称她为君夫人,但对外国人便称她为寡小君;外国人称她也为君夫人。

【英语译文】

Confucius said, "As for the wife of the monarch of a state, the monarch himself calls her madam, and the madam calls herself xiaotong; people within the state calls her madam of monarch, and introduce hercas less monarch to foregners; people of foreign states call her monarch's madam."

【注释】(1)邦君:指诸侯国的国君。(2)小童:谦称。犹说自己无知如童子。(3)诸:"之于"的合音。寡:即"寡人",古代帝王、国君对自己的谦称。

阳货篇第十七(共二十六章)

《汉石经》同。《何晏集解》把第二、第三两章以及第九、第十两章各并为一章,所以只有二十四章。介绍了孔子的道德教育思想、孔子对仁的进一步解释,还有关于为父母守丧三年问题,也谈到君子与小人的区别等。

【原文】1 阳货欲见孔子[1],孔子不见,归孔子豚[2]。孔子时其亡也[3],而往拜之。遇诸涂[4]。谓孔子曰:"来!予与尔言。"曰[5]:"怀其宝而迷其邦[6],可谓仁乎?"曰:"不可。好从事而亟失时可谓知乎?[7]"曰:"不可。日月逝矣,岁不我与。"孔子曰:"诺[8];吾将仕矣。"

【白话译文】

阳货想要孔子来拜见自己,孔子不去;他派人送孔子一头蒸熟了的小猪,好让孔子登门答谢。孔子等候他不在家时去拜谢。两人在路上遇着了。阳货对孔子说:"来!我跟你说话。"他接着说:"自己拥有一身本领,却听任国事混乱,可以叫作仁爱吗?"停了一会儿又说:"不可以。一个人又喜欢做官任职,却又累累错过机会,可以叫作聪明吗?"停了停又说:"不可以。""时光一去就永不回来了呀。"孔子说:"哦,我打算做了。"

【英语译文】

Yang Huo wanted Confucius to visit him but Confucius refused doing so. He dispatched a man to present Confucius a steamed piglet so that Confucius could say thanks to him. Confucius visited him when he wasn't at home. They met on the road. Yang Huo uttered, "Come on, I'll say something to you." He then said, "Could it be called humanistic that a man with versatile abilities let state affairs in disorder?" After a moment he said again, "No. Could it be called clever that a man loves to be official but misses chances repeatedly?" After a pause, he said again, "No. Time and tide wait for no man." Confucius said, "O! I decided to be an official."

【注释】(1)阳货:又叫阳虎,季氏的家臣。季氏几代人把持鲁国的政治,阳货当时又把持季氏的权柄,是一个乱臣。因企图削除三桓而未成,逃往晋国。欲见:在人与人交往活动中的"见"大概是三个角度,上接见下,下拜见上,平辈相见、会见。阳货欲见孔子,前人都作"想令孔子来拜见"解。(2)归(kuì):通"馈",赠送。豚(tún):做成熟食的小猪。(3)时其亡:等他不在家。时,通"伺",等候。亡,出门。(4)遇诸涂:遇于路上。诸,介词,同"于"。涂,即道路。(5)曰:自此以下的几个"曰"字都是阳货自问自答。(6)怀其宝:喻自藏其才,怀才。迷其邦:指不肯从政,隐居不仕。(7)好从事:喜欢做官任职。而:转折连词,却。亟(qì):累次,一再。失时:错过时机。(8)诺(nuò):表示同意、遵命的答应声。

【原文】2 子曰:"性[1]相近也,习相远也。"

【白话译文】

孔子说:"人生成的本性是差不多的,生活习惯的差异引起了较大的性格差距。"

【英语译文】

Confucius said, "Man's inborn traits have no difference. However, differences in living habits cause great differences in traits."

【注释】(1)性:本性。

【原文】3 子曰:"唯上知[1]与下愚[2]不移。"

【白话译文】

孔子说:“只有最聪明的人和最愚蠢的人不会变动。

【英语译文】

Confucius said, “Only those who are cleverest and most stupid will never change.”

【注释】(1)上知:最聪明的人。(2)下愚:最愚蠢的人。

【原文】4 子之武城[1],闻弦歌之声[2]。夫子莞尔而笑曰[3]:“割鸡焉用牛刀?”子游对曰:“昔者偃也闻诸夫子曰:‘君子学道则爱人,小人学道则易使也。’”子曰:“二三子[4]!偃之言是也。前言戏之耳。”

【白话译文】

孔子到了武城,听到了依琴瑟而咏歌的声音,他微笑着说:“杀鸡哪里用得上杀牛的刀?”子游回答道:“以前我听老师说过,做官的通过学习就会有仁爱的心,老百姓通过学习,就容易听指挥。”孔子对学生们说:“小子们!言偃这话说得正确。我刚才那句话不过同他开个玩笑罢了。”

【英语译文】

Confucius heard song-singing to harp tune as he reached Wu Cheng. He said with a smile, “Needn't we use bull-knife to butcher a chick?” Zi You answered, “In the past, we heard you said that an official could become humanistic through learning, and that people could become obedient through learning.” Confucius said to his disciples, “Young men, his words is right. Just now I played a joke.”

【注释】(1)武城:古邑名。又名“南武城”。春秋鲁地。在今山东费县西南。当时子游为武城宰,按孔子礼乐之治的思想治理,满城皆为弦歌之声。(2)弦歌:依琴瑟而咏歌。(3)莞(wǎn)尔:微笑的样子。二三子:犹言诸君,诸位,几个人。

【原文】5 公山弗扰以费畔[1],召[2],子欲往。子路不说[3],曰:“末之也已[4]!何必公山氏之之也[5]?”子曰:“夫召我者而岂徒哉[6]?如有用我者,吾其为东周乎[7]?”

【白话译文】

公山弗扰利用费邑图谋造反,诡引人才。孔子想去。子路不高兴,他说:“没有地方去啦!为什么一定要去公山氏那里呢?”孔子说:“那个找我去的人,难道竟是白白地召我吗?假若有人用我,我将使周文王、武王的大道在东方复兴。”

【英语译文】

Gongshan Furao plotted to rebel in Fei Yi. He attracted talents. Confucius wanted to go but Zi Lu was unhappy, saying, “No place to go? Why do you want to go to Gongshan's place?” Confucius answered, “Doesn't the man who has attracted me hire me vainly? If someone empowers me to do things, I will revive the Great Way of Kings Wen and Wu in the East.”

【注释】(1)公山弗扰:即公山不狃。春秋末鲁国执政大臣季氏私邑费之宰。以费畔:据费谋叛。(2)召:招引。(3)说:同“悦”。(4)末之:没有地方去的意思。也已:语气助词,这里表感叹,可译为“啦”“了”。(5)何必公山氏之之也:“何必之公山氏也”的宾语前置句式。(6)夫(fú):代词,表示远指,指那、那个、那些。召我者而岂徒哉:而,连词。用在主语和谓语之间起强调主语的作用。岂徒哉,是“岂徒召我哉”的省略。(7)为东周:犹言“兴周道于东方”。

【原文】6 子张问仁。孔子曰:“能行五者于天下为仁矣。”“请问之。”曰:“恭[1]、宽[2]、信[3]、敏[4]、惠[5]。恭则不侮[6],宽则得众,信则人任焉,敏则有功,惠则足以使人。”

【白话译文】

子张问孔子怎样才算仁。孔子说:“能够在天下实行五种美德,就算仁了。”子张说:“请问哪五种?”孔子说:“庄重、宽厚、诚实、勤敏、慈惠。庄重就不会互相侮辱,宽厚就能互相支持,诚实就能互相信任,勤敏就能事业有成,慈惠就能使用别人。”

【英语译文】

Zi Zhang asked Confucius how to become humanistic. Confucius said, “It can be called humanity if five kinds of morality can be realized.” Zi Zhang asked, “May I ask what they are?” Confucius said, “Solemnity, generosity, honesty, diligence, mercifulness. People with solemnity won't insult each other; people with generosity will support each other; people with honesty will trust each other; people with diligence will succeed in cause; and people with mercifulness will use others."

【注释】(1)恭:庄重。(2)宽:宽厚。(3)信:诚实。(4)敏:勤敏。(5)惠:慈惠。(6)侮:侮辱。

【原文】7 佛肸召[1],子欲往。子路曰:"昔者由也闻诸夫子曰:'亲于其身为不善者,君子不入也。'佛肸以中牟畔[2],子之往也如之何?"子曰:"然,有是言也。不曰坚乎[3],磨而不磷[4],不曰白乎,涅而不缁[5]。吾岂匏瓜也哉[6]?焉能系而不食[7]?"

【白话译文】

佛肸招引孔子,孔子打算去。子路说:"从前我听老师说过,'亲自做坏事的人那里,君子不进去。'如今佛肸占据中牟谋反,您却要去,怎么说呢?"孔子说:"对,我说过这话。可是,磨也磨不平的东西,你不认为它坚硬吗?染也染不黑的东西,你不认为它洁白吗?我难道是匏瓜吗?怎么能只挂在那里不给人吃呢?"

【英语译文】

Bi Xi summoned Confucius, who wanted to go there. Zi Lu said, "I ever heard that you said 'A moral man never joins a group where people do evil things themselves.' Nowadays Bi Xi occupied Zhong Mou and intended to rebel, but you want to go. How can you explain it?" Confucius answered, "Yes, I've said this. But don't you think that an ungrihdable thing is hard? Don't you think that an anti-undyeable object is white? Am I a gourd which is just hung there but not eatable?"

【注释】(1)佛肸(bìxī):人名,春秋末年,晋大夫范氏、中行氏的家臣,为中牟的县宰。(2)中牟:古邑名,春秋晋地。当时在黄河东岸,在今河南南乐、河北大名、山东聊城之间。鲁定公九年(前501年)晋国范氏家臣佛肸在中牟举兵对抗晋国权臣赵简子,召孔子即此时。(3)不曰:犹"不谓",即"不以为""不认为"的意思。(4)磨而不磷:谓极坚之物,磨也磨不薄。磷,读lìn,指薄、减损。(5)涅而不缁:谓极白之物,染也染不黑。涅,读niè,指染黑、染污。缁,读zī,指黑色。(6)匏(páo)瓜:一年生草本植物,果实比葫芦大。古有甘、苦两种,苦的不能吃,成熟后比水轻,可以系于腰用来泅渡。(7)系而不食:悬挂着不吃,参看注6。系:读xì,悬挂。

【原文】8 子曰:"由也!女闻六言六蔽矣乎[1]?"对曰:"未也。""居[2]!吾语女[3]。好仁不好学,其蔽也愚[4];好知不好学,其蔽也荡[5];好信不好学,其蔽也贼[6];好直不好学,其蔽也绞[7];好勇不好学,其蔽也乱[8];好刚不好学,其蔽也狂[9]。"

【白话译文】

孔子说:"仲由!你听说过六种品德和六种弊端吗?"子路回答道:"没有。"孔子说:"坐下!我告诉你。爱好仁德不爱好学问,弊端就是容易被愚弄;爱好聪明不爱好学问,弊端就是放荡不羁;爱好诚实不爱好学问,弊端就是容易被利用而受害;爱好直率不爱好学问,弊端就是急切尖刻,不通情达理;爱好勇敢不爱好学问,弊端就是容易坏秩序、生祸事;爱好刚强不爱好学问,弊端就是狂妄自大。

【英语译文】

Confucius asked, "Zhong You, have you ever heard six merits and six demerits?" Zhong You answered, "No, I haven't heard about that." Confucius said, "Sit down and I'll tell you about it. The demerit is that he is easy to be fooled if someone loves humanity but not learning. The demerit is that he is wanton if someone loves intelligence but not learning. The demerit is that he is easy to be made use of if someone loves sincerity but not learning. The demerit is that he is unreasonable if someone loves frankness but not learning. The demerit is that he is easy to make trouble if he loves courage but not learning. The demerit is that he is self-conceited if someone loves strength but not learning."

【注释】(1)六言:这里是六句话的意思,不是六个字。每句话说了一种美德;同时围绕"不好学就不明事理"这个主题指出了所带来的六种弊端。六蔽:六种弊端。有弊端就有缺失,本来的美德,就损失了。(2)居:坐。(3)语(yù):告诉。(4)愚:若可陷可罔之类。(5)荡:放荡不羁。(6)贼:被利用受害。(7)绞:急切尖刻。(8)乱:坏秩序,生祸事。(9)狂:狂妄自大。

【原文】9 子曰:"小子何莫学夫诗[1]?诗,可以兴[2],可以观[3],可以群[4],可以怨[5]。迩之事父[6],远之事君[7],多识于鸟兽草木之名[8]。"

【白话译文】

孔子说:“学生们为什么没有人研究诗？好诗,可以启发意志,放飞联想;可以观察世风,了解人情;可以推动交流,促进和谐;可以讽刺邪恶,呼唤善良。近处,可以用来侍奉父母;远处,可以用来服侍君上。而且还可以在鸟兽草木的名称上增长常识。”

【英语译文】

Confucius asked, “Why don't you disciples study poetry? Poetry can be used to enlighten your intelligence and association; it can be used to enable you to observe worldly things and custom; it can be used to enhance communication and harmony among people; it can be used to attack evils and call for goodness. In one's family it can be used to serve parents; in a country it can be used to serve the monarch. Furthermore it can be used to increase one's common knowledge concerning names of birds, beasts, plants and trees.”

【注释】(1)小子何莫学夫诗:小子,指学生们。何莫,指为何没有人。学夫诗,即研究诗。夫,是句中语气助词。(2)兴:启发意志,放飞联想。(3)观:观察世风,了解人情。(4)群:推动交流,促进和谐。(5)怨:讽刺邪恶,呼唤善良。(6)迩之:近处。(7)远之:远处。(8)多识:增长常识。

【原文】10 子谓伯鱼曰:“女为周南、召南矣乎[1]？人而不为周南、召南[2],其犹正墙面而立也与[3]?”

【白话译文】

孔子对伯鱼说:“你研究过周南和召南了吗？人如果不研究周南和召南,那会像把脸贴近墙壁站立着,看不见前方又走不过去。”

【英语译文】

Confucius asked Bo Yu, “Have you ever studied *Zhou Nan and Shao Nan*? If a person didn't study them, he will not see and pass place in front of him just like facing against a wall.”

【注释】(1)女:同“汝”。为:学习,研究。周南、召南:《诗经》篇名。是国风的

第一、二这两部分。(2)而:假设连词,用在复合句的前一分句的主语和谓语之间,与"如"差不多,可译作"假如""如果"。(3)正墙面而立:朱熹《四书集注》:"言即其至近之地,而一物无所见。"

【原文】11 子曰:"礼云礼云[1],玉帛云乎哉[2]? 乐云乐云,钟鼓云乎哉?"

【白话译文】

孔子说:"礼呀礼呀,难道仅是指玉帛等礼物说的吗? 乐呀乐呀,难道仅是指钟鼓等乐器说的吗?"

【英语译文】

Confucius said, "As for *li*, we don't just refer to gifts such as jades and silks. As for *yue*, we don't just refer to musical instruments such as bells and drums."

【注释】(1)礼云礼云:这两个"云"字和下文"乐云乐云"的两个"云"字,都是语气助词。同"焉""也"差不多,用以表停顿语气,可译为"啊""呀",也可去掉不译。(2)玉帛云乎哉:这个"云"字同下文"钟鼓云乎哉"的"云"字两个都是动词,说。乎哉,语气助词,这里表设问或反诘。

【原文】12 子曰:"色厉而内荏[1],譬诸小人[2],其犹穿窬之盗也与[3]"?

【白话译文】

孔子说:"外表强硬而内心怯懦,比如坏人,那就好像挖墙洞和爬墙头的小偷罢?"

【英语译文】

Confucius said, "A man is like a devil if he is strong outwards but coward inwards. Isn't he like a thief who digs hole in a wall and climbs it?"

【注释】(1)色厉而内荏:外表强硬而内心怯懦。色,即外表、脸色。厉,指严厉、猛烈。内,即内心。荏,读 rěn,指柔弱、怯弱。(2)譬诸:譬之于,譬如。小人:这里指坏人。(3)其犹:那就如同。穿窬:挖墙洞和爬墙头。窬,读 yú,同"踰",指翻越。(4)譬诸:譬之于,譬如。

【原文】13 子曰:“乡愿[1],德之贼也[2]。”

【白话译文】

孔子说:“乡里中表面像是谨慎厚道而实际和流俗合污的伪善人,是败坏道德的贼。”

【英语译文】

Confucius said, “A hypocrite in countryside is a thief of degraded and immoral man.”

【注释】(1)乡愿:孟子作“乡原”,指乡中貌似谨厚而实与流俗合污的伪善者。(2)德之贼:败坏道德的小人。贼,把杀人、抢劫、偷盗的人叫“贼”比较常见,对国家、人民、社会道德风尚造成严重危害的小人也叫“贼”。

【原文】14 子曰:“道听而途说[1],德之弃也[2]。”

【白话译文】

孔子说:“从道路上听到,在道路上传说,违背了道德。”

【英语译文】

Confucius said, “It violates morality to hear and spread anything on the road.”

【注释】(1)道听而途说:道与途同义。(2)德之弃也:是“弃德也”的倒装句式。弃,抛弃;违背。

【原文】15 子曰:“鄙夫可与事君也与哉[1]?其未得之[2],患得之[3]。既得之,患失之[4]。苟患失之,无所不至矣。”

【白话译文】

孔子说:“庸俗浅薄的人能够服侍国君吗?在未谋得职位时,忧虑如何才能得到;得到后,忧虑如何才能不失掉。假如忧虑如何才能不失掉,没有什么手段使不出来。”

【英语译文】

Confucius said, "Can a vulgar and shallow man serve his monarch? While not empowered, he always worries about how to be empowered; while empowered, he always worries about how to keep the power. If he always does so, then he will employ every means to keep it. "

【注释】(1)鄙夫:庸俗浅薄的人。可与:可以。与,介词。可以,意谓"可能"或"能够"。(2)其未得之:之,指事君的职位。下文四个"之"字同此。(3)患得之:为如何才能得到而忧虑。(4)患失之:为如何才能不失掉而忧虑。

【原文】16 子曰:"古者民有三疾[1],今也或是之亡也[2]。古之狂也肆[3],今之狂也荡[4];古之矜也廉[5],今之矜也忿戾[6];古之愚也直,今之愚也诈而已矣[7]。"

【白话译文】

孔子说:"古代的人民有三种缺点,现在呢,也许都没有了。古代的狂人不受拘束直言奉送,现在的狂人放荡不羁了;古代自己矜持的人还有逊让的礼节,现在自己矜持的人蛮横无理,动辄发怒。古代的愚人很直率,现在的愚人欺骗作假罢了。"

【英语译文】

Confucius said, "Ancient people had three shortcomings while nowadays perhaps people don't have. Ancient frantic persons spoke straightforwardly while those in present days are unconventional and uninhibited; ancient reserved men observed rites while those in present days are irritable and unreasonable; ancient fools were frank while those in present days are cheats and frauds. "

【注释】(1)三疾:三样缺点。(2)或是:或许,也许是。之:代词,指三疾。亡:无,没有了。(3)肆:不受拘束;纵恣,放肆。(4)荡:放荡不羁。(5)廉:收敛。见《释名·释言语》。引申为"逊让"。(6)忿戾(fèn lì):蛮横无理,动辄发怒。(7)诈(zhà):欺骗,作假。

【原文】17 子曰:"巧言[1]令色鲜矣[2]仁。"

【白话译文】

孔子说:“言语好听脸色谄媚,仁德很少啊!”

【英语译文】

Confucius said, “A man who speaks superficially and shows flattery is seldom a moral one.”

【注释】(1)巧言:表面上好听而实际上虚伪的话。令色:伪善、谄媚的脸色。(2)矣:语气助词,表感叹,犹“啊”。鲜矣仁:犹“仁鲜矣”。

【原文】18 子曰:“恶紫之夺朱也[1],恶声之乱雅乐也[2],恶利口之覆邦家者[3]。”

【白话译文】

孔子说:“讨厌把正色服装换成杂色服装,讨厌邪曲的声音搅乱典雅的音乐,讨厌伶牙俐齿颠覆国家的人。”

【英语译文】

Confucius said, “I hate colorful clothes replacing clothes of formal color; I hate evil music upsetting elegant one; and I hate eloquent man who overthrows one's country.”

【注释】(1)紫:杂色。夺:压倒,胜过。朱:正色。(2)郑声:春秋战国时郑国的音乐,任性情,不端肃,被斥为淫声。雅乐:古代帝王祭祀天地、祖先及朝贺宴飨时所用的舞乐。(3)利口:能言善辩;能言善辩的人。

【原文】19 子曰:“予欲无言。”子贡曰:“子如不言,则小子何述焉?”子曰:“天何言哉?四时[1]行焉,百物生焉[2],天何言哉[3]?”

【白话译文】

孔子说:“我不想说什么话了。”子贡说:“如果老师什么话都不说,那么我们这些学生传述什么呢?”孔子说:“老天爷说了什么话呢?春夏秋冬四季照常运行,万物照常生长,老天爷说了什么话呢?”

【英语译文】

Confucius said, "I don't want to speak anymore." Zi Gong said, "If you master don't speak anything, what could we disciples retell?" Confucius answered, "What did the Heaven say? However four seasons operate normally, and all things grow normally. But what did the Heaven say?"

【注释】(1)四时:春夏秋冬四季。(2)百物生焉:万物照常生长。(3)天何言哉:老天爷说了什么话呢?

【原文】20 孺悲欲见孔子[1],孔子辞以疾。将命者出户[2],取瑟而歌,使之闻之。

【白话译文】

孺悲想见孔子,孔子推说有病,传话人出门去拒绝,孔子取下瑟来边弹边唱,让孺悲听见。

【英语译文】

Ru Bei wanted to meet Confucius but Confucius rejelted by saying he's ill. Messenger went out to refuse him and Confucius played musical instrument *se* to let Ru Bei hear him.

【注释】(1)孺悲:春秋末鲁国人。孔子弟子,《礼记·杂记》载:"恤由之丧,哀公使孺悲之孔子学士丧礼,士丧礼于是乎书。"本章所谈是孺悲未学礼之事。(2)将命者:传达命令的人。

【原文】21 宰我问[1]:"三年之丧[2],期已久矣。君子三年不为礼,礼必坏;三年不为乐,乐必崩。旧谷既没,新谷既升,鑽燧改火[3],期可已矣[4]。"子曰:"食夫稻[2],衣夫锦,于女安乎?"曰:"安。""女安,则为之[6]! 夫君子之居丧,食皆不甘,闻乐不乐,居处不安[7],故不为也。今女安则为之!"宰我出。子曰:"予之不仁也! 子生三年,然后免于父母之怀。夫三年之丧,天下之通丧也,予也有三年之爱于其父母呼!"

【白话译文】

宰我提出问题说道:"守孝三年,这个期限太久了。君子三年不习礼,他必定荒废礼仪;三年不习乐,他必定荒废音乐。老谷子吃完了,新谷子已经登场了,取火用的燧木也轮流了一周。守孝一周年可以了。”孔子说:“父母死后不到三年,就吃那白米饭,穿那花缎衣,你心里安不安呢?”宰我说:“安。”孔子说:“你心里安,你就这么干吧。君子的守孝,吃美味不觉得甜,听音乐不感到快乐,日常生活没有一项安宁,才不这样干。如今你既觉得心安,你去干好了。”宰我退出后,孔子说:“宰我真是不仁啊!儿女生下来三年,才能脱离父母的怀抱。守孝三年,天下都是这样。难道宰予没有从他父母那里得到三年怀抱的爱吗?”

【英语译文】

Zai Wo asked, “Three years of mourning for one's parent is too long. A moral man will surely neglect rites if he didn't practice rites for three years; he' ll surely neglect music if he didn't practice music for three years. While old rice was used up, new rice has grown up and for another round wood for getting fire by friction has been used. It's alright to mourn just for one year. ” Confucius asked “Are you comfortably calm if you eat good rice and wear gauze clothes just one year after your parent's death?” Zai Wo said, “I' m calm. ” Confucius said, “You may do that if you feel calm. While a moral man's mourning, he doesn't taste delicious even if he eats delicious foods, and he doesn't feel happy even if he listens to music. In everyday life, nothing can makes him comfortably calm. Therefore he doesn't do anything like these. Now that you feel calm doing so then you may do so. ” After Zai Wo retreated Confucius sighed, “Zai Wo is really a man without humanity! Three years after a baby was born can it leave away from parents' hug. All people mourn their parent's death for three years. Hasn't Zai Wo been loved by his parents for three years?”

【注释】(1)宰我:孔子弟子,姓宰,名予,字子我,亦称宰我。春秋末鲁国人,少孔子二十九岁,能言善辩,以“言语”著称,从孔子周游列国,其间常受孔子排遣。(2)三年之丧:犹守孝三年,是古代服大丧之礼。服丧者在三年时间里(实际只有两年)必须穿着孝服,摒弃一切日常的饮食娱乐。(3)鑽燧改火:古时钻木取火,因季节不同而用不同的木材。何晏《集解》引马融曰:“周书·月令有更火之文:春取榆柳之火,夏取枣杏之火,季夏取桑柘之火,秋取柞楢之火,冬取槐檀之火。一年之中,钻火各异,故曰改火也。”(4)期可已:期,读 jī,同“朞”,这里指一周年。可已,即“可以”。已,同“以”。(5)稻:dào 同“稻”,古代北方以稷(小米)为主要粮食,水稻和粱(精细的小米)是珍品,而稻的耕种面积更小。所以这里特别提出来和锦为对文。(6)则为之:指缩短服丧期。(7)居处(chǔ):日常生活。

【原文】22 子曰:"饱食终日,无所用心,难矣哉!不有博弈者乎[1]?为之犹贤乎已[2]。"

【白话译文】

孔子说:"一天到晚吃得饱饱的,什么心思都不用一点,难有出息呀!不是有掷骰子和下围棋的游戏吗?干一干,总比闲着不动好。"

【英语译文】

Confucius said, "If someone is fall and leads an idle life without thinking anything, he cannot achieve anything. Aren't there games of throwing the dice and playing chess? It's much better to play these games than doing nothing."

【注释】(1)博:局戏。具体玩法,传说不一。弈:围棋。(2)已:读 yǐ,停止不动。

【原文】23 子路曰:"君子尚勇乎[1]?"子曰:"君子义以为上[2],君子有勇而无义为乱,小人有勇而无义为盗。"

【白话译文】

子路说:"君子把勇放在上头吗?孔子说:"君子以义为上头,君子有勇无义就会犯上作乱,小人有勇无义就会做盗贼。"

【英语译文】

Zi Lu asked, "Does a moral man rank bravery above all?" Confucius answered, "A moral man ranks righteousness, above all. If a moral man has bravery without righteousness, he'll offend his superior and do evil things. If a mean man has bravery without righteousness, he'll become a thief."

【注释】(1)尚勇:古字"上""尚"通。尚 ,在此用作动词。尚勇,谓把"勇"推到上头(前面)。(2)义以为上:上,在此用作名词。义以为上,谓以义为上头(前面)。

【原文】24 君子亦有恶乎[1]?”子曰:“有恶:恶称人之恶者[2],恶居下流而讪上者[3],恶勇而无礼者,恶果敢而窒者[4]。”曰:“赐也亦有恶乎?”“恶徼以为知者[5],恶不逊以为勇者,恶讦以为直者[6]。”

【白话译文】

子贡说:“君子也有厌恶吗?”孔子说:“有厌恶:厌恶宣扬别人过错的人,厌恶身居下位而毁谤上位的人,厌恶勇敢而不讲理的人,厌恶果敢而顽固的人。”孔子说:“赐!你也有厌恶吗?”子贡说:“我厌恶抄袭他人以为聪明的人,厌恶不谦逊认为勇敢的人,厌恶揭发别人隐私以为正直的人。”

【英语译文】

Zi Gong asked, “Does a moral man hate anything?” Confucius answered, “Yes, he does. He hates those who spread other's faulti he hates those who are in low rank but slander men in high rank; he hates those who are brave but unrreasonable; he hates those who are decisive but stubborn.” Confucius said, “Do you hate anything either?” Zi Gong answered, “I hate those who copy others but think clever themselves; I hate those who aren't modest but think brave themselves; I hate those who uncover other's privacy but think upright themselves.”

【注释】(1)有恶(wù):厌恶。有恶,谓有厌恶的性情。恶,在此是名词。(2)恶称人之恶者:第一个恶字,读 wù,内动词,指厌恶。称:述说,声称。第二个恶字,读 è,名词,指缺失、丑陋。(3)恶居下流而讪上者:从这个“恶”字起以下皆读 wù,指下流,本义为河流的下游,引申为与上位相对的下位。(4)果敢:果决勇敢。窒:读 zhì,指乖戾,执拗。(5)徼(jiāo):抄袭。知:同“智”。(6)讦(jié):揭发、攻击他人隐私过错或短处。

【原文】25 子曰:“唯女子与小人为难养也[1],近之则不孙,远之则怨。”

【白话译文】

孔子说:“只有女子和小人最难培养上路啊,接近他们,他们缺少礼节,疏远他们,他们又怨恨。”

【英语译文】

Confucius said, "Only women and mean men are hard to be cultivated. If you approach them, they know little about rites; if you keep away from them, they become resentful."

【注释】(1)养:培养。培养为"相处"者,大概是下文有"远之近之"的说法。不错,人与人、父与子、师与生等,都有远之、近之的时候。这是交往接触的一般表层现象,实际上是什么关系还得深入具体分析。窃以为孔子是从教育培养的角度说这话的,在当时要把女子和小人按照儒家理念来培养,确实难度最大。应该说孔子讲的是大实话,没有掩饰也没有歧视。

【原文】26 子曰:"年四十而见恶焉[1],其终也已[2]。"

【白话译文】

孔子说:"四十岁了,还被人厌恶,他的成就可能不大了吧。"

【英语译文】

Confucius said, "If a man is still disgusted while forty years old, his achievement may not be great."

【注释】(1)年四十:四十岁,成就品德之时。见恶:被厌恶。(2)其:副词,或、或许、也许,推测事物具有某种可能性。终:结局,终点。也已:语气助词。

微子篇第十八(共十一章)

本篇共计11章。主要包括孔子的政治思想主张,孔子弟子与老农谈孔子、孔子关于塑造独立人格的思想等。

【原文】11 微子去之[1],箕子为之奴[2],比干谏而死[3]。孔子曰:"殷有三仁焉[4]。"

【白话译文】

微子离开了纣王,箕子给纣王当奴隶,比干进谏纣王被剖心而死。孔子说:

“殷商末年有三位仁人呢。”

【英语译文】

Wei Zi left King Zhou and Ji Zi became slave of King Zhou. Bi Gan remonstrated but was pierced through heart to death by King Zhou. Confucius commented, “At the end of Shang Dynasty, there were three men with humanity.”

【注释】(1)微子:名启,纣王的同母兄。启出生时,他的母亲还是妾。纣出生时,他们的母亲已经立为妻了。所以纣得嗣位而启不得立。因见纣王淫乱将亡,多次进谏,纣不听,最后出走。(古书中唯《孟子·告子篇》认为微子是纣的叔父。)之:代词,指殷纣王。下同。(2)箕子:纣的叔父。纣王无道,他多次进谏,纣不听,便被发佯狂,被降为奴隶。(3)比干:纣的叔父。力谏纣王,纣王说,听说圣人的心有七个孔,便被剖心而死。(4)仁:有德者之称,指仁人。

【原文】2 柳下惠为士师[1],三黜[2]。人曰:“子未可以去乎?”曰:“直道而事人[3],焉往而不三黜[4]? 枉道而事人[5],何必去父母之邦[6]?”

【白话译文】

柳下惠做高级法官,多次被贬降。有人对他说:“你不可以离开鲁国吗?”他说:“按正道充任下属到哪里去不多次被贬降? 违背正道充任下属,为什么一定要离开祖国呢?”

【英语译文】

Liu Xiahui acted as higher judge but was demoted for three times. Someone said to him, “Why didn’t you leave Lu State?” He answered, “ If you do things as an inferior man obeying right way, how can you not be demoted wherever you go? But if you do things as an inferior man violating right way, why do you leave your country?”

【注释】(1)士卿:掌刑狱的官。(2)黜(chù):贬降,罢退。(3)直道:正道。事人:谓充任下属(下级官职)。(4)焉:疑问代词,代指哪里。(5)枉道:违背正道。(6)父母之邦:犹言祖国。

【原文】3 齐景公待孔子曰[1]:“若季氏则吾不能[2];以季、孟之间待之[3]。”曰:“吾老矣,不能用也。”孔子行[4]。

【白话译文】

齐景公谈到如何对待孔子时说:“像鲁君对待季氏那样对待孔子,那我做不到,只能用低于季氏、高于孟氏的职位对待他。”不久又说:“我老了,不能用他了。”孔子离开了齐国。

【英语译文】

While talking about how to treat Confucius, Duke Jing of Qi State said, “I cannot treat him the way Monarch of Lu state treated Ji Shi, and I can only give him a position which is lower than that of Ji Shi but higher than that of Meng Shi.” Not long after that he said once more, “I cannot use him since I'm old.” Then Confucius left Qi State.

【注释】(1)齐景公:齐国国君。(2)季氏:鲁国的大夫。位居上卿。(3)季、孟之间:犹言低于季氏高于孟氏。鲁国的大夫。位居下卿。(4)行:去,离开。

【原文】4 齐人归女乐[1],季桓子受之[2],三日不朝[3],孔子行。

【白话译文】

齐国官方选一批歌舞女艺人赠送到鲁国去,鲁国执政大夫季孙斯接受了;多日不理朝政。孔子便离开了鲁国。

【英语译文】

When Qi State enrolled a group of dancing girls and dedicated them to Lu state and Ji Sun Si, the executive minister of Lu State accepted them all and didn't care about court affairs. Then Confucius left Lu State.

【注释】(1)齐人:指齐国执政当局。归:同“馈”。女乐:歌舞伎(歌舞女艺人)。(2)季桓子:鲁国执政大夫季孙斯。(3)不朝:不理朝政。

【原文】5 楚狂接舆歌而过孔子曰[1]:“凤兮[2]!凤兮!何德之衰?往者不可谏[3],来者犹可追[4]。已而,已而[5]!今之从政者殆而[6]!”孔子下欲与之言。趋而辟之[7],不得与之言。

【白话译文】

楚国的狂人接舆经过孔子的车旁,边走边唱:“凤凰呀!凤凰呀!为何道德这么衰败?过去的不可挽回,未来的还可补救。算了吧!算了吧!如今的官场十分危险!”孔子下车想同他谈谈。他急忙快走避开,孔子没法同他谈。

【英语译文】

The lunatic Jie Yu of Chu State walked by Confucius' cart and sang, “O! Phenix! O! Phenix! Why did morality degrade so much? We cannot recover things in past but we can recompens in the future. Forget it! Forget it! The official circles nowadays become very dangerous!” Getting off his cart, Confucius wanted to talk with Jie Yu. But he walked away in a hurry and Confucius had no way to talk with him.

【注释】(1)楚狂:楚国的狂人。接舆:楚国人。相传他披髪佯狂,亦称楚狂接舆。(2)凤兮:这里以凤喻指孔子。(3)谏:匡正;挽回。(4)追:补救;改正。(5)已(yǐ):停止,算了。(6)而:语助词。(7)辟(bì):退避,躲避。

【原文】6 长沮桀溺耦而耕[1],孔子过之,使子路问津焉[2]。长沮曰:“夫执舆者为谁[3]?”子路曰:“为孔丘。”曰:“是鲁孔丘与?”曰:“是也。”曰:“是知津矣。”问于桀溺。桀溺曰:“子为谁?”曰:“为仲由。”曰:“是鲁孔丘之徒与?”对曰:“然。”曰:“滔滔者天下皆是也[4],而谁以易之[5]?且而与其从辟人之士也[6],岂若从辟世之士哉[7]?”耰而不辍[8]。子路行以告[9]。夫子怃然曰[10]:“鸟兽不可与同群,吾非斯人之徒与而谁与[11]?天下有道,丘不与易也。”

【白话译文】

长沮、桀溺两人一同耕田,孔子从那儿经过,叫子路去请问渡口。长沮问子路:“那位驾车的是谁?”子路说:“是孔丘。”他又说:“是鲁国那位孔丘吗?”子路说:“是的。”他说道:“他是知道渡口的呀。”子路问桀离,桀离说:“您是谁?”子路说:“我是仲由。”桀离说:“您是鲁国孔丘的弟子吗?”子路说:“对的。”他说道:“像洪水一样狂乱的人到处都是,你们同谁去改革局面呢?你与其跟着避开坏人的人,不如跟着逃避整个社会的人好吧?”说完,继续干活不停。子路回来把情况告诉孔子。孔子失望地说:“我们不可以同飞禽走兽合群共处,若不同这些人群共处又同什么去共处呢?天下如果太平,我就不和你们一起来从事改革了。”

【英语译文】

Confucius passed the place where Chang Ju and Jie Ni ploughed together. He then dispatched Zi Lu to ask where the port was. Chang Ju asked Zi Lu, "Who is the man driving the cart?" Zi Lu answered, "He's Kong Qiu." Chang Ju asked again, "Is the Kong Qiu in Lu State?" Zi Lu said, "Yes, he is." Chang Ju said, "He does know where port is!" Zi Lu then asked Jie Ni and the latter asked, "Who are you?" Zi Lu answered, "I'm Zhong You." Jie Ni said, "Are you the disciple of Kong Qiu in Lu State?" Zi Lu said, "Yes, you are right." Jie Nie then said, "Everywhere are people who are as lunatic as flood and with whom can you change the situation? You'd better follow those who escape from the society rather than follow those who escape from the evil persons." He continued his job after saying this. Zi Lu came back and told Confucius all the things. Confucius said disappointedly, "We cannot live with birds and beasts. With whom can we live if we don't live with these people? If the world is peaceful, I will not go on reform with you."

【注释】(1)长沮、桀溺耦而耕:长沮、桀溺,两位古代隐士。真实姓名和身世不详。耦而耕,二人一起干农活。(2)问津:询问渡口。(3)执舆:谓执辔驾车。此时子路问津,孔子代他控制车马。(4)滔滔者:不循河道的洪水,比喻太多的不循正道的坏人。(5)谁以易之:同谁去改变它。以,介词。相当于"与""同"。(6)而:同"尔",即"你"。与其:连词。与下文"岂若"配合表示选择。辟人:避开坏人。士:贤者,好人。(7)辟世:避开乱世。(8)耰(yōu):这里用作动词,谓用耰松土、碎土、平整土地覆盖种子等,也泛指耕种。辍(chuò):中途停止,中断。(9)行:返还,回转。以告:以上文所述的情况报告孔子。(10)怃(wǔ)然:怅惘失意的样子。(11)斯人之徒:此人的同类。

【原文】7 子路从而后,遇丈人[1],以杖荷莜[2]。子路问曰:"子见夫子乎?"丈人曰:"四体不勤[3],五谷不分[4]。孰为夫子?"植其杖而芸[5]。子路拱而立[6]。止子路宿[7],杀鸡为黍而食之,见其二子焉[8]。明日子路行以告。子曰:"隐者也。"使子路反见之。至,则行矣[9]。子路曰:"不仕无义。长幼之节,不可废也,君臣之义如之何其废之?欲洁其身,而乱大伦[10]。君子之仕也,行其义也。道之不行已知之矣[11]。"

【白话译文】

子路跟着孔子赶路落在了后面,遇到一位老人用手杖挑着除草工具。子路问道:“您看见了我的老师吗?”老人说:“四肢不劳动,五谷不辨认,谁是你的老师?”把手杖插在地上,便去除草。子路恭敬地站着。老人挽留子路到他家过夜。他杀鸡、煮米饭给子路吃,还叫他的两个儿子来见子路。第二天子路赶上了孔子,报告了这件事。孔子说:“这是一位隐士。”叫子路转去再看看他。子路到了那里,他却没在家里了。子路说:“不做官是不合理的。长幼间的礼节不可废弃;君臣间的义理为什么要废弃呢?想自身亮洁,却搅乱了大伦常。君子做官是行正义。大道像水流不畅通,早就知道了。”

【英语译文】

Zi Lu lagged behind while heading forward together with Confucius, and then he met an old man who carried grass-wiping tools by a pole. Zi Lu asked, “Have you met my master?” The old man answered, “Who's your master while he never stretches limbs and cannot identify grains?” After erecting the pole in the ground, he went wiping grasses. Zi Lu stood there humbly. The old man kept him in his house that night and cooked chicken and rice for him. Then the old man asked his two sons to meet Zi Lu. The next morning Zi Lu caught up with Confucius and reported it to him . Confucius said, “ He is a hermit. ” Then he sent Zi Lu to visit the old man again. After he reached there Zi Lu found that he was not there. Zi Lu commented, “It's unreasonable for a man not to be an official. Rites among the old and the young can't be rejected and how can rites among monarch and courtiers be rejected? A hermit wants to be innocent himself but violates great ethics. A moral man is spreading righteousness while being an official. We ' ve already known that great Way is blocked just as the stream is blocked. ”

【注释】(1)丈人:古时对老人的尊称。(2)以杖荷莜:杖,手杖,拐杖;泛指棍棒或棒状物。荷,读 hè,肩负,扛。莜,读 diào,古代除田中草用的竹器。(3)四体不勤:四肢不劳动。(4)五谷不分:不能辨认五谷。五谷,五种谷物。说法不一。郑玄注:“五谷麻、黍、稷、麦、豆也。赵岐注:“五谷谓稻、黍、稷、麦、菽也。”王逸注:“稻、稷、麦、豆、麻也。”王冰注:“谓粳米、小豆、麦、大豆、黄黍也。”后以五谷为谷物的总称。(5)芸:除草。(6)拱而立:同“拱立”,指肃立,恭敬地站着。(7)止:挽留,收留。(8)见(xiàn):介绍。(9)行:离家,出门。(10)而:转折连词。可译为

"却"。大伦:朱熹《四书集注》:"人之大伦有五:父子有亲,君臣有义,夫妇有别,长幼有序,朋友有信。(11)不行:本指水流不畅通。这里用水流比喻大道推行。

【原文】8 逸民[1]:伯夷、叔齐、虞仲、夷逸、朱张、柳下惠、少连[2]。子曰:"不降其志,不辱其身,伯夷、叔齐与!"谓"柳下惠、少连降志辱身矣,言中伦[3],行中虑,其斯而已矣。"谓"虞仲、夷逸,隐居放言[4],身中清,废中权。我则异于是,无可无不可[5]。"

【白话译文】

古来被遗落的人有伯夷、叔齐、虞仲、夷逸、朱张、柳下惠、少连。孔子说:"不动摇自己意志,不辱没自己身份,是伯夷、叔齐罢!"又说:"柳下惠、少连降低了自己意志,屈辱了自己身份,可是言语合乎法度,行为合乎思议。那也不过如此罢了。又说:"虞仲、夷逸,逃世隐居,言语大胆,行为廉洁。被废弃,合乎他们的权术。我就和他们不同,没有什么可以,也没有什么不可以。"

【英语译文】

From ancient time, the forgotten persons were Bo Yi, Shu Qi, Yu Zhong, Yi Yi, Zhu Zhang, Liu Xiahui, and Shao Lian. Confucius said, "The men who never changed their will and never insulted their reputation were Bo Yi and Shu Qi." Then he said again, "Liu Xiahui and Shao Lian changed their will and insulted their reputation, however their words were lawful and their actions were wise. Things are like that." Then he said once again, "Yu Zhong and Yi Yi became hermits with bold words and honest actions. It's reasonable for them to be rejected. I' m different from them all. I never persisted on anything at all."

【注释】(1)逸(yì)民:被遗落的人。逸,同"佚",指"遗佚"之义。民,指人,泛指人类。(2)伯夷、叔齐,虞仲,即仲雍与大伯同窜荆蛮者。夷逸、朱张,经传上无记载。柳下惠,见前注。少连,东夷人。(3)中(zhòng):符合。下同。伦,指伦理、纲纪,(4)放言:放纵其言,不受拘束。(5)无可无不可:这里指本来的意义,谓个人出处看时事需要,不固执一己之成见。后来多用于表示对人或事物依违两可没有定见。《红楼梦》五十七回:"薛姨妈是个无可无不可的人倒还易说。"

【原文】9 大师挚适齐[1],亚饭干适楚,三饭缭适蔡,四饭缺适秦[2],鼓方叔入于河[3],播鼗武入于汉[4],击磬襄入于海[5]。

【白话译文】

大师挚去到了齐国,亚饭乐师干去到了楚国,三饭乐师缭去到了蔡国,四饭乐师缺去到了秦国。打鼓的方叔入居于河内,摇小鼓的武入居于汉中,少师阳、敲磬的乐师襄入居于海岛。

【英语译文】

Zhi, leader of musicians in Lu State went to Qi State; Gan, second dining musician went to Chu State; Liao, third dining musician went to Cai Sate; and Que, fourth dining musician went to Qin State. Fang Shu, the drummer lived in the north of the Yellow River; Wu, small drum player lived in Hanzhong; Yang, minor master and Xiang, *qin* player lived on island.

【注释】(1)大师挚(tàishīzhì):大师,鲁国乐官之长。挚,大师之名。(2)亚饭:古代天子、诸侯用饭,都得奏乐,所以乐官有"亚饭""三饭""四饭"的职称。干、缭、缺是"亚饭""三饭""四饭"的任职者的名。(3)鼓:击鼓者。方叔:人名。河:河内。古代指黄河以北的地区,也专指今河南省黄河以北的地区。(4)播:摇。鼗(táo):小鼓。武:摇小鼓的人。汉:汉中。(5)少师:乐官之佐。阳:人名。击磬襄:击磬者叫襄。入于海:进入海岛。

【原文】10 周公谓鲁公曰[1]:"君子不施其亲[2],不使大臣怨乎不以[3]。故旧无大故[4],则不弃也。无求备于一人[5]!"

【白话译文】

周公对鲁公说:"好国君不弃置他的亲族,不使大臣抱怨没被信用,老臣、旧友,只要没犯严重错误,就不要抛弃。对于一个人,不可要求他事事完备。"

【英语译文】

Duke Zhou told Duke Lu, "A good monarch never deserts his relatives and he never makes his ministers complain that they weren't be trusted. Old ministers and friends would never be deserted if they didn't make serious mistakes. Don't demand anyone to be a perfect man."

【注释】(1)周公、鲁公:周公,西周初期政治家。孔子心目中的圣人。姓姬名旦,也称叔旦。文王子武王弟成王叔。辅武王灭商。武王崩,成王幼,周公摄政。继而厘定典章制度,天下臻于大治。后多作圣贤的典范。鲁公,周公之子,鲁国始封之君名伯禽。(2)施(shǐ):"弛",弃置。(3)以:用。(4)故旧:旧交,旧友。大故:指严重的过失或罪恶。(5)求备:谓事事求其完备。义同求全责备。

【原文】11 周有八士:伯达、伯适[1]、仲突、仲忽、叔夜、叔夏、季随、季騧[2]。

【白话译文】

周朝有八位很有教养的人,他们是:伯达、伯适、仲突、仲忽、叔夜、叔夏、季随、季騧。

【英语译文】

There were eight very cultivated men in Zhou Dynasty and they were: Bo Da, Bo Kuo, Zhong Tu, Zhong Hu, Shu Ye, Shu Xia, Ji Sui and Ji Gua.

【注释】(1)适(kuò):人名用字。(2)騧(guā)。这八人事迹不详,无从考查。有人认为是四对双生子。

子张篇第十九(共二十五章)

本篇包括孔子学而不厌、不耻下问、对殷纣王的批评、关于学与仕的关系、君子与小人在有过失时的不同表现等。

【原文】1 子张曰:"士见危致命[1],见得思义[2],祭思敬,丧思哀[3],其可已矣。"

【白话译文】

子张说:"读书人遇到危难时能舍身而赴,遇到好处时能不忘正义,祭祀时能不忘恭敬,守孝时能不忘哀痛,这就可以了。"

【英语译文】

Zi Zhang said, "It's all right for a scholar to face dangers bravely, not to forget righteousness upon receiving something, not to forget being respectful while conducting sacrificial ceremony, and not to forget sadness while mourning his parent."

【注释】(1)士:读书人,知书达礼的人。见危:遇到危险、危难。致命:犹捐躯。(2)见:遇到。下同。得:收受。思:心怀,想到,不忘。下同。(3)丧:指居丧,即守孝。

【原文】2 子张曰:"执德不弘[1],通道不笃[2],焉能为有?焉能为亡?"

【白话译文】

子张说:"保持美德,却狭隘,不够度量。信仰正道,却欠诚实,不专一。这样的人哪里能算有?哪里能算无?

【英语译文】

Zi Zhang said, "If one is moral but narrow-minded, he isn't generous. If one believes right way but lacks honesty he isn't single-minded. How could such kind of person exist? How could such kind of person not exist?"

【注释】(1)执德:犹"秉德",保持美德。不弘:不宽宏,度量不够。(2)通道:信仰正道。不笃:不专一。

【原文】3 子夏之门人问交于子张[1]。子张曰:"子夏云何?"对曰:"子夏说曰:'可者与之,其不可者拒之。'"子张曰:"异乎吾所闻[3];君子尊贤而容众,嘉善而矜不能[4]。我之大贤与[5],于人何所不容?我之不贤与,人将拒我,如之何其拒人也[6]?"

【白话译文】

子夏的学生向子张问怎样交友。子张说:"子夏说了些什么?"答道:"子夏说:'可取的人就同他相交,那不可取的人就拒绝他。'"子张说:"这不同于我所知道的:君子尊敬有才有德的人,也接纳普通人,称赞好人,也同情无能的人。我很有才德吗,对什么人不能接纳呢?我没有才德吗,别人会拒绝我,我为什么拒绝别人呢?"

【英语译文】

Zi Xia's disciple asked Zi Zhang how to make friends. Zi Zhang asked, "What did your master say?" Zi Xia answered, "He said, ' You may make friends with those who are desirable but refuse to do so with those who are undesirable. ' " Zi Zhang said, "This is different from what I' ve known: a moral man respect those men with virtue and ability, and he also accept common people, praise kind men, and sympathize those without ability. Am I a talented man and whomever can't I accept? Am I an untalented man and Why do I refuse others if they would refuse me?"

【注释】(1)交:交友。(2)可者:可取的;合乎要求的。(3)所闻:所听到的,所知道的。(4)嘉善:赞美善人。(4)矜,读 jīn,指怜悯、同情。不能:犹"无能",指没有才能。(5)我之大贤与:之,用在这里(主语和谓语之间),叫结构助词,使句子在形式上成为偏正词组。下同。大贤,谓很有才德。与,语气助词。(6)如之何:怎么,为什么。其:这里用作第一人称代词,代指我。

【原文】4 子夏曰:"虽小道[1],必有可观者焉[2];致远恐泥[3],是以君子不为也[4]。"

【白话译文】

子夏说:"就是小技艺,也一定有可取的,甚至优美的;恐怕它妨碍远大事业,所以君子不为小技艺。"

【英语译文】

Zi Xia sid, "Even little skills are desirable and graceful; but being afraid that they would hinder great cause moral men don't heed little skills."

【注释】(1)小道:礼乐政教以外的学说;技艺。(2)可观者:优美的,可取的。(3)致远:任大事。泥(nì):阻滞,滞留。(4)是以君子不为也:为后省略了宾语代词"之"。

【原文】5 子夏曰:"日知其所亡[1],月无忘其所能[2],可谓好学也已矣。"

【白话译文】

子夏说："每天能知道些自己所不知道的，每月不丢失自己的任何本领，可说是好学的了。"

【英语译文】

Zi Xia said, "It could be studious if someone knows what he doesn't know each day, and he doesn't lose his capability each month."

【注释】(1)其：己称代词，代指自己。所亡(wú)：所未知。亡后省略了"知"字。亡，即无、没有。(2)无忘：不丢失。所能：所能干的事。

【原文】6 子夏曰："博学而笃志[1]，切问而近思[2]，仁在其中矣。"

【白话译文】

子夏说："广泛学习又不改变志向，恳切求教又思考日用伦常，仁德就在这中间了。"

【英语译文】

Zi Xia said, "Humanity and virtue come into being if someone never changes his ambition while learning widely and ponders on daily affairs while consulting others whole-heartedly."

【注释】(1)博学：广泛学习。笃志：专心一志，立志不变。(2)切(qiè)问：恳切求教。近思：就熟知易见者思之。

【原文】7 子夏曰："百工居肆以成其事[1]，君子学以致其道[2]。"

【白话译文】

子夏说："各种工人在工作场所完成他们的工作，君子在学习中获得那个正道。"

【英语译文】

Zi Xia said, "Craftsmen accomplish their jobs on working sites, and moral men obtain the right Way while learning."

【注释】(1)肆:作坊,店铺,市集。(2)致:求取,获得。

【原文】8 子夏曰:"小人之[1]过也必文[2]。

【白话译文】
子夏说:"小人犯过了必定掩饰。"

【英语译文】
Zi Xia said, "A mean man must hide mistakes that he's made."

【注释】(1)之:结构助词。过:动词。犯过,犯错。(2)文:掩饰,粉饰。

【原文】9 子夏曰:"君子有三变:望之俨然[1],及之也温,听其言也厉。"

【白话译文】
子夏说:"君子有三变:隔远点望望他,庄严可畏;走到他身边,温和可亲;听他说话,严厉不苟。"

【英语译文】
Zi Xia said, "A moral man appears differently thrice. He looks awesome in distance; and he looks amiable nearby; and he appears strict while speaking."

【注释】(1)俨然:庄严的样子。

【原文】10 子夏曰:"君子信而后劳其民;未信[1],则以为厉己也[2]。信而后谏;未信,则以为谤己也[3]。"

【白话译文】
子夏说:"君子先守信用,而后可以调用民力;未守信用就调用民力,人民就认为是在虐害他们。君子先守信用,而后可以进谏君上,未守信用就进谏君上,君上就以为是在毁谤自己。"

【英语译文】

Zi Xia said, "A moral man firstly keeps his promise, and then he can make people do things. But if he doesn't keep his promise and make people do things, they think they'rs maltreaed. A moral man firstly keeps his promise, and then he can remonstrate his monarch. But if he doesn't keep his promise but remonstrates his monarch, the monarch thinks himself slandered."

【注释】(1)信:守信用,实践诺言。劳其民:使民劳作,调用民力。(2)厉:虐害,欺压。(3)谤:毁谤。

【原文】11 子夏曰:"大德不踰闲[1],小德出入可也。"

【白话译文】

子夏说:"人在是非大节上不可踰越界限,在作风小节上稍微放松一点是可以的。"

【英语译文】

Zi Xia said, "A moral man shouldn't go beyond boundary of moral principle. And it's alright for him to act on the trivia loosely."

【注释】(1)大德:大节。闲:法度,界限,多指礼义道德规范。(2)出入:谓在要求上稍微宽松一点。

【原文】12 子游曰:"子夏之门人小子[1],当洒扫、应对、进退[2],则可矣,抑末也[3]。本之则无[4],如之何?"子夏闻之曰:"噫!言游过矣!君子之道,孰先传焉[5]?孰后倦焉[6]?譬诸草木,区以别矣[7]。君子之道,焉可诬也[8]?有始有卒者,其惟圣人乎[9]!"

【白话译文】

子游说:"子夏的学生小伙子们,承担洒水、扫地、对答、交往等日常工作,还是可以的。不过这只是末节,探讨他们的根本,却没有,这怎么可以呢?"子夏得知子游的话后说道:"咳!言游搞错了!君子的学问,什么先传授它?什么后着力讲授它？譬如花草树木,是应当分门别类的。君子的学问,怎么可以歪曲呢？有始有终不上岔路的,也许只有圣人了！”

【英语译文】

Zi You said, “The disciples of Zi Xia carry water, wipe the floor, deal with daily affairs. That's alright, however these are trivial things. How could it be that they don't explore these things' causes?” After hearing this, Zi Xia said, “O! Zi You has made a mistake! As for a moral man's learnings, what should be passed on with priority and what should be taught next? For example, plants, grasses, and flowers should be classified. How could learnings of a moral man be twisted? Perhaps only sages could do the same thing from the beginning to the end, with nothing distracting him.”

【注释】(1)门人小子:门人,用在这里谓弟子,学生。小子,本义指男小孩或男性青少年。用为老师对学生的称呼,也用为表示轻蔑的称呼,今用以昵称男性同辈之年轻者或晚辈。(2)当:担任。洒扫:洒水扫地。应对:对答,酬对。进退:前进与后退,引申为日常交往。(3)抑:转折连词,指然而、但是、不过。末:末节,小节。(4)本:探究,推原。本之,谓探究其根本。(5)孰:什么。传:传授。(6)倦:同诲人不倦的“倦”。(7)区以别:以,并列连词,同“而”。区、别是同义词,都有分开、划分的含义。区以别,省略“以”,意义不变。(8)焉可诬:焉,疑问代词,用作状语,指怎么、哪。诬:加以不实之词,歪曲。(9)其:副词,表示推测估计,指也许、大概。

【原文】13 子夏曰:“仕而优则学[1],学而优则仕。”

【白话译文】

子夏说:“做官有余力就学习,学习有余力就做官。”

【英语译文】

Zi Xia said, “If an official is energetic, he will pursue learning. And if a scholar is energetic enough, he will pursue official post.”

【注释】(1)优:朱熹《四书集注》:“优,有余力也。”

【原文】14 子游曰:“丧致乎哀而止[1]。”

【白话译文】
子游说:“守孝尽到哀痛之情就可以了,不要文饰。”

【英语译文】
Zi You said, “It's alright to express the sad feelings while mourning one's parent.”

【注释】(1)丧:特指丧服期满前的“守孝”。致乎哀:义同“致哀”。乎,语气助词,没有实在意义。

【原文】15 子游曰:“吾友张[1]也,为难能也,然而未仁。”

【白话译文】
子游说:“我的朋友子张,是难能可贵的了,然而还未做到仁。”

【英语译文】
Zi You said, “My friend Zi Zhang is praiseworthy for his excellent conduct, however, he's not a man with humanity.”

【注释】(1)张:子张。

【原文】16 曾子曰:“堂堂乎张也[1],难与并为仁矣。”

【白话译文】
曾子说:“高视阔步的子张啊,难以和他一起做到仁啊。”

【英语译文】
Zeng Zi said, “We can not reach the standard of humanity together with Zi Zhang who carries himself proudly.”

【注释】(1)堂堂:形容容貌壮伟。

【原文】17 曾子曰:“吾闻诸夫子[1]:人未有自致者也[2],必也亲丧乎[3]!”

【白话译文】

曾子说:“我听见老师说过:平时人未有自动尽露心情的,说一定有的话,一定是父、母死亡时吧!”

【英语译文】

Zeng Zi said, “I heard the Master had said, ‘Nobody will automatically express his feelings. A person will do so only when his parent dies!’”

【注释】(1)诸:介词。同“于”。(2)自致:谓尽露自己的心情。(3)必也:这里对“未有”而言,相当于“必有的话”。亲丧:父、母死亡。

【原文】18 曾子曰:“吾闻诸夫子:孟庄子之孝也[1],其他可能也;其不改父之臣与父之政,是难能也。”

【白话译文】

曾子说:“我听见老师说过:孟庄子的孝,别的都可能做到,他不改动父亲的旧臣和父亲的政治措施,是难以做到的。”

【英语译文】

Zeng Zi said, “I heard the Master had said, ‘Nobody could be as filial as Meng Zhung Zi who never replaced his father’s courtiers and administrative tactics.’”

【注释】(1)孟庄子:(?—公元前549年),即仲孙速,春秋时鲁国大夫,鲁大夫孟献子之子,以孝著称。

【原文】19 孟氏使阳肤为士师[1],问于曾子。曾子曰:“上失其道,民散久矣。如得其情,则哀矜而勿喜!”

【白话译文】

孟氏使用阳肤为法官。阳肤向曾子请教。曾子说:“在上位的人丧失了治理百姓的正道,百姓早就离散了;心里不服,行为不顺。如果审案得到了真情,就应该同情他们可怜他们,不要沾沾自喜!"

【英语译文】

Meng Shi made Yang Fu a judge. Yang Fu consulted Zeng Zi and the latter said, "Common people have splitted while officials in high rank lose right way to administrate them, who aren't obedient and do things unsmoothly. Don't be pleased with yourself but sympathize them when you got truth while trying a case."

【注释】(1)孟氏:即孟孙氏。阳肤:曾子的弟子,鲁人。士师:古代掌禁令刑狱之官

【原文】20 子贡曰:"纣之不善[1],不如是之甚也[2]。是以君子恶居下流[3],天下之恶皆归焉[4]。"

【白话译文】

子贡说:"商纣的坏,不像现在传说的这么厉害。所以君子畏惧处于下流,一旦处于下流,天下的什么坏名都会沾在身上。"

【英语译文】

Zi Gong said, "King Zhou of Shang Dynasty was not as evil as that was rumored. Therefore, a moral man fears to live in place where evil originates. If so, he'll attract all evils."

【注释】(1)纣:殷商最末之君。周武王讨伐他,他自焚而死。(2)如是:如此,像这么。(3)是以:所以;因此。恶(wù)居:畏惧处于,怕在。下流:比喻众恶所归之处。朱熹《四书集注》:"地形卑下之处,众流之所归。喻人身有污贱之实亦恶名之所聚也。"

【原文】21 子贡曰:"君子之过也,如日月之食[1]焉;过也,人皆见之;更[2]也,人皆仰之。"

【白话译文】

子贡说:"君子的过失,好像日食、月食;犯过的时候,人人都看得见;改正的时候,人人都在仰望。"

【英语译文】

Zi Gong said, "A moral man's mistake is like eclipse. While mistaking, everybody notices him and while correcting, everybody respects him."

【注释】(1)食:同"蚀"。(2)更:变更,更改。

【原文】22 卫公孙朝问于子贡曰[1]:"仲尼焉学[2]?"子贡曰:"文武之道,未坠于地[3],在人。贤者识其大者[4]。不贤者识其小者。莫不有文武之道焉[5]。夫子焉不学?而亦何常师之有[6]?"

【白话译文】

卫国的公孙朝向子贡问道:"孔仲尼的学问是从哪里得来的?"子贡说:"周文王、武王之道,并没有失传,散布在人间。贤人掌握了它的主体大端。次一些的人掌握了它的肢体末节。没有哪里没有文王、武王之道。我的老师何处不学?又为什么要有一定的老师专门传授呢?"

【英语译文】

Gongsun Chao of Wei State asked Zi Gong, "Where did Confucius obtain his learnings?" Zi Gong answered, "The Way of Kings Wen and Wu of Zhou Dynasty was never lost but was spread among people. Men with virtue mastered its essence but common persons mastered its trivial details. There were no places where there was no Way of Kings Wen and Wu. My master learned from every possible man and thing. Why did he need a special instructor to instruct him?"

【注释】(1)公孙朝:卫国大夫。春秋时,除开这个卫国公孙朝,鲁国、楚国和郑国都有一个名叫公孙朝的人;阅读古籍时得注意。(2)焉:疑问代词,作状语。下文焉不学的"焉"与此同。(3)坠于地:坠于地即"坠地"。丧失;失传。(4)识(zhì):记住。(5)焉:语气助词,用在陈述句末,表论断决断或终结的语气。一般去掉不译,指有的,也可译作“呢”“的”。(6)常师:固定的老师。

【原文】23 叔孙武叔[1]语大夫于朝曰:“子贡贤于仲尼。子服景伯以告子贡[2]。子贡曰:“譬之宫墙[3],赐之墙也及肩,窥见室家之好‘夫子之墙也数仞[4],不得其门而入,不见宗庙之美,百官之富[5]。得其门者或寡矣。夫子之云[6],不亦宜乎!”

【白话译文】

叔孙武叔在朝廷里对大夫们说:“子贡比他的老师仲尼强一些。”子服景伯把这话告诉子贡。子贡说:“拿围墙做比喻罢,我家的围墙高齐肩膀,里面房舍的美好情景一览无余,我老师的围墙却有几丈高,找不到大门进去,就看不到他那宗庙的雄伟,房舍的多种多样。能够找着大门的人,或许不多罢。所以,武叔他老人家的话,不也是很自然的吗?”

【英语译文】

Shusun Wushu told courtiers in the court, “Zi Gong is more talented than his master, Confucius.” Zifu Jingbo reported this to Zi Gong and the latter said, “Just set wall as an example. My family's wall is as high as man's shoulders and fine layout inside could be seen completely. On the contrary, my master family's wall is much higher than mine. Failing to find entrance one cannot notice magnificent mouments and various buildings. Perhaps there are a few people who can find the entrance. Therefore, isn't it natural what Wushu said?”

【注释】(1)叔孙武叔:鲁大夫。名州仇。(2)子服景伯:姓子服,名何,字伯,景为谥。春秋末鲁国大夫。(3)宫墙:宫廷的围墙。也泛指房舍及其他建筑的围墙。(4)仞:古代长度单位。七尺为一仞。一说,八尺为一仞。(5)官:房舍。(6)夫子:指叔孙武叔。

【原文】24 叔孙武叔毁仲尼。子贡曰:“无以为也[1]!仲尼不可毁也。他人之贤者,丘陵也,犹可踰也;仲尼,日月也,无得而踰焉[2]。人虽欲自绝[3],其何伤于日月乎?多见其不知量也[4]。”

【白话译文】

叔孙武叔毁谤仲尼。子贡说:“不要这么干吧!仲尼是毁谤不了的。他人的贤能,好比丘陵,还可以翻越过去;仲尼的贤能,好比太阳和月亮,从何处登上,休谈翻越。人们纵然要自行断绝于太阳和月亮,那对太阳和月亮有什么损害呢?只是表示了不知自量罢了。”

【英语译文】

Shusun Wushu slandered Confucius. Zi Gong said, “Don't do that! You cannot slander him. Others' virtue and ability are just like mounds which can be climbed over, however, his virtue and ability are like sun and moon. Where can you ascend? Let alone climbing over. People naturally separate themselves from sun and moon, which does not damage sun and moon at all. They just show that they don't know their limits.”

【注释】(1)以:副词,指此,犹如此、这么。(2)无得:无从,不能。(3)自绝:自行断绝于太阳和月亮。(4)多:副词,指大多、多半、只。见(xiàn):显现,显露,表示。

【原文】25 陈子禽谓子贡曰[1]:“子为恭也,仲尼岂贤于子乎?”子贡曰:“君子一言以为知,一言以为不知,言不可不慎也。夫子之不可及也,犹天之不可阶而升也。夫子之得邦家者[2],所谓立之斯立,道之斯行[3],绥之斯来[4]。”动之斯和。其生也荣,其死也哀,如之何其可及也?”

【白话译文】

陈子禽批评子贡说:“您对仲尼太恭顺了,难道他真比您还强吗?”子贡说:“有地位的人一句话就表现他有知,一句话就表现他无知。说话不可不慎重啊。他老人家的不可赶得上,犹如青天的不可用阶梯爬上去。他老人家的得国而为诸侯,或者得到采邑而为卿大夫,正如我们所说,叫百姓站稳脚跟,他们就站稳脚跟;引导百姓前进,他们就跟上来;安抚百姓,远方的人就来投靠;动员百姓,他们就协力同心。他老人家,生得光荣,死得可惜。怎么能赶得上他呢?”

【英语译文】

Chen Ziqin criticized Zi Gong, "You are too modest towards Confucius. Aren't you more talented than him?" Zi Gong responded, "One word of a moral man shows whether he's knowledgeable or not. While speaking, we should be cautious. That we cannot match him as we cannot climb up heaven by a ladder. Just as we said he, the master as dukes of a state, or as a minister's clan of a feoff, can establish common people, lead common people, and summon common people. He lived honorably and died pitiably. How can I be matched with him?"

【注释】(1)谓:评论,批评。邦家:诸侯,诸侯的领地,叫邦。领地较小的又称国。平常多邦国混称。卿大夫,卿大夫的采邑,叫家。(2)夫子之得邦家者:他老人家的得国而为诸侯,或者得到采邑而为卿大夫。(3)道之斯行:引导百姓前进,他们就跟上来。(4)绥(suí):安,安抚。

尧曰篇第二十(共三章)

该篇主要谈到尧禅让帝位给舜,舜禅让帝位给禹,即所谓三代的善政和孔子关于治理国家事务的基本要求。

【原文】1 尧曰:"咨[1]!尔舜!天之历数在尔躬[2],允执其中[3]。四海有困穷,天禄永终[4]。"舜亦以命禹[5]。曰:"予小子履敢用玄牡[6],敢昭告于皇皇后帝[7]:有罪不敢赦[8]。帝臣不蔽[9],简在帝心[10]。朕躬有罪,无以万方[11];万方有罪,罪在朕躬。"周有大赉[12],善人是富。"虽有周亲[13],不如仁人。百姓有过,在予一人。"谨权量[14],审法度[15],修废官[16],四方之政行焉。兴灭国[17],继绝世[18],举逸民[19],天下之民归心焉[20]。所重:民、食、丧、祭。宽则得众,信则民任焉[21],敏则有功,公则说。

【白话译文】

尧说:"欸!你这位舜啊!上天安排的帝位顺序,这回要落到你的身上啦,老老实实地执行中道吧。如果天下的百姓艰难窘迫,上天给你的禄位就将永远终止。"舜也用这话告诫禹。商汤说:"小人我履冒昧地用黑色公牛做祭品,冒昧地向光明伟大的天帝明明白白直话禀告:有罪的人我不敢擅自去赦免他。您的臣仆的善或恶,我也不隐瞒掩盖,您心里早就知道。我本人如果有罪,不要牵连天下各地;天下各地有罪,都归我来承担。"周朝大行分封赐予,使善良人都富实起来。武王说:"商纣有至亲,不如我有仁人。百姓如果有过失,罪责都在我一人身上。"统一审定度量衡,修复废弃的职官工作,全国的政令通行了。恢复灭亡的国家,承续已断的后代。提拔被遗落的人才,天下的百姓心悦诚服了。在上执政所当重视的:人民、粮食、丧礼、祭祀。宽厚就会得到群众的拥护,诚恳守信就会得到百姓的信任,勤敏办事就会得到成功,公平就会得到百姓的喜悦。

【英语译文】

Sage Yao said, "O! Shun! The post of monarch arranged by the Heaven is now bestowed to you. Just implement the appropriate Way. Your post and salary will be terminated if common people led hard life." Later on Shun warned Yu with the same words. King Tang of Shang Dynasty said, "I venture to use black bull as the sacrifice and I venture to report to the Heaven straightforwardly: I dare not pardon the criminals. I don't hide kindness or evil of your courtiers since you already know them in your heart. If I myself is a criminal, don't extend it to other people; if other people are criminals, I will shoulder them myself." Zhou Dynasty broadly granted titles and territories to its courtiers so humane people became affluent. King Wu said, "King Zhou of Shang Dynasty had intimate relatives but didn't have men with humanity as I do. If common people had any faults, I will shoulder them myself." Systems of weights and measures were rearranged, deserted official posts were reestablished, and administrative orders went smoothly. The wiped-out states were recovered so broken offspring were retracked. The deserted talents were promoted so people all around became obedient. What those in administrative position cared about were people, foods, funeral rituals and sacrificial ceremony. Broad-mindedness leads to people's support; credibility leads to people's trust; diligence leads to fairness; and fairness leads to people's happiness.

【注释】(1)咨(zī):叹词,这里表示招呼,可译作"欸"。(2)历数:古谓帝王代天理民的顺序。(3)允执其中:允,即信实、诚信。中,即中道、无过不及。(4)天禄:天赐的福禄,后常指帝位。(5)命:告诉,告诫。(6)履:汤的名。玄牡:黑色牡牛。商尚黑。(7)昭告:明白地告知。后帝:天帝,上帝。(8)有罪:有罪的人。赦(shè):宽免罪过。(9)蔽:隐瞒掩盖。(10)简在帝心:简,检阅;视察。简在帝心,意谓帝心中明白了解。(11)以:及,连及,牵累。万方:万邦,各方诸侯。引申指天下各地;全国各地。(12)赉(lài):赏赐,赐予。(13)周亲:至亲。(14)谨:严格,严守。权量:权与量,测定物体大小,轻重的器具。(15)审法度:审定统一的长度单位。(16)修废官:修,指治理,整顿。废官,谓有职而无其官或有官而不称其职。(17)兴灭国:恢复灭亡的国家。(18)继绝世:谓封黄帝、尧、舜、夏、商之后。(19)举逸民:谓释箕子之囚,复商容之位。(20)归心:谓诚心归附。(21)信则民任焉:汉石经及一些版本无此五字,后人认为是衍文。

【原文】2 子张问于孔子曰:“何如斯可以从政矣?” 子曰:“尊五美屏四恶[1],斯可以从政矣。”子张曰:“何谓五美?”子曰:“君子惠而不费[2],劳而不怨,欲而不贪,泰而不骄[3],威而不猛。”子张曰:“何谓惠而不费?”子曰:“因民之所利而利之,斯不亦惠而不费乎?择可劳而劳之,又谁怨?欲仁而得仁,又焉贪?君子无众寡,无小大,无敢慢,斯不亦泰而不骄乎?君子正其衣冠,尊其瞻视,俨然人望而畏之,斯不亦威而不猛乎?”子张曰:“何谓四恶?”子曰:“不教而杀谓之虐;不戒视成谓之暴;慢令致期谓之贼,犹之与人也[4],出纳之吝[5],谓之有司[6]。”

【白话译文】

子张向孔子问道:“如何就可以治理政治事务呢?”孔子说:“尊崇五种美德,除掉四种恶劣政风,就可以治理政治事务了。”子张说:“什么叫五种美德?”孔子说::“君子让人民得到实惠又不浪费财物;让人民从事劳役又不生怨;保持自己的欲望却不贪;安宁而不骄傲;威严而不凶猛。”子张说:“怎么叫让人民得到实惠又不浪费财物?”孔子说:“叫人民去做对他们有利的事,这不也是让人民得到实惠又不浪费财物吗?选择可以劳作的时间和场合才让人民从事劳役,又有谁生怨呢?自己想要仁德就得到仁德,还贪求什么呢?无论人多人少,无论势力大小,君子都不敢怠慢他们,这不也是安宁而不骄傲吗?君子衣冠整洁,目不斜视,手脚不乱,让人望而生畏,这不也是威严而不凶猛吗?”子张说:“四种恶劣政风是些什么呢?”孔子说:“不教育就加以杀戮叫作虐;不进行申戒便要成绩,叫作暴;起初懈怠,突然限期叫作贼;同样是把财物给予他人,舍不得出手,叫作小家子气。

【英语译文】

Zi Zhang asked Confucius, “How can we deal with administrative affairs?” Confucius answered, "You can deal with them if you respect five virtues and get rid of four evils." Zi Zhang asked again, "What are five virtues?" Confucius answered, "A moral man benefits common people but doesn't waste materials, makes people labor but doesn't complain anything, desires what's desired but not greedy, keeps calm but not conceited, august but not violent." Zi Zhang asked, "How to benefit common people but not wasting material things?" Confucius said, "Isn't it benefiting common people but not wasting material things when common people are required to do things beneficiary to them? Who will complain anything when they are made to labor at proper time in proper place? What is deserved to own greedily if one can get what he desires? Isn't it calm and not conceited when a moral man deals with people equally whether they have power or not, whether they are strong or weak? Isn't it august but not violent when a moral man dresses neatly with his eyes and limbs in proper places and makes people respect him?" Zi Zhang asked, "What are the four evils in administration?" Confucius said, "It's maltreatment when slaughter happens without education; it's violence when achievement is demanded without precaution; it's cunning when sudden deadline is given while hesitating at first, and it's stingy while giving things to other people without generosity."

【注释】(1)屏(bǐng):摈弃;除掉。(2)费:用财多,靡费,浪费。(3)泰:安宁。(4)犹之:犹言均之,等之。(5)出纳:付出与收入。根据语境上下文这里偏存付出的意思,没有收入的意义了。吝:悭吝,吝啬。(6)有司:官吏。古代设官分职各有所司,故称。因为地位卑下事事都须谨小慎微,管出纳的人最怕出错多付。

【原文】3 孔子曰:"不知命[1],无以为君子也;不知礼,无以立也;不知言[2],无以知人也。"

【白话译文】

孔子说:"不懂命运就不能正确对待利害遭遇,也就没有可能成为君子了;不懂礼,就不知道耳目手足怎么摆放,也就没有可能立足于社会了;不懂分辨人家的言语,也就没有可能认识人了。"

【英语译文】

Confucius said, "A man impossibly becomes a moral man while he doesn't know about fate, incapably facing ups and downs in life. He can not establish himself in society while he doesn't know about rites, incapably placing his organs of five sense, and he cannot tell any person while he doesn't know how to differentiate others' words."

【注释】(1)知命:谓知有命而相信它。否则,见害必避,见利必趋。(2)知言:谓善于分析别人的言语,辨其是非善恶。